Property of Lisa Efthy

THE SEVENTY GREAT INVENTIONS OF THE ANCIENT WORLD

Edited by Brian M. Fagan

with 554 illustrations, 484 in color

THE SEVENTY GREAT INVENTIONS OF THE ANCIENT WORLD

Thames & Hudson

Contents

Chinese cast-bronze three-legged vessel for heating wine

First published in 2004 in hardcover in the United States of America by Thames & Hudson Inc., 500 Fifth Avenue, New York, New York 10110

thamesandhudsonusa.com

Library of Congress Catalog Card Number 2004100250
ISBN 0-500-05130-5

Printed and bound in China by Toppan Printing Co. (Shenzhen) Ltd.

Half-title *Detail of a bronze portable sundial, Byzantine, 5th century* AD

Title page *The Roman aqueduct at Segovia, Spain, end of 1st to early 2nd century* AD

Stone architecture at the Inca site of Machu Picchu, Peru

Technologies

Weaving: a model from the tomb of Meketre, Egypt

Shelter & Subsistence

Transportation

Roman legionaries on a warship: relief from Palestrina, Italy

A Roman road: the Appian Way, Italy

Hunting, Warfare & Sport

Art & Science

A jewelled pectoral from the tomb of Tutankhamun, Egypt

Adorning the Person

Maya musicians depicted in murals from Bonampak, Mexico

Contributors

BRIAN M. FAGAN is Emeritus Professor of Anthropology at the University of California, Santa Barbara, and a foremost authority on world prehistory. Among his many books are *Ancient North America* (4th. ed., 2005) and *People of the Earth* (11th ed., 2003). He also edited *The Seventy Great Mysteries of the Ancient World* (2001). His latest book is *The Long Summer: How Climate Changed Civilization* (2004). **4**, **5**, **28**, **34** (with Barry Raftery), **36**, **46**; *Glue*

ANTHONY F. AVENI is the Russell B. Colgate Professor of Astronomy & Anthropology at Colgate University. He has based much of his research in the Maya area, but has also worked on the ancient astronomy and calendar of the Greeks, Etruscans and the Inca of Peru. Among his most recent books are *Empires of Time: Clocks, Calendars, and Cultures* (2nd ed., 2002), *Ancient Astronomers* (1993) and *The Book of the Year: A Brief History of the Seasonal Holidays* (2004). **57**, **58**

ROGER BLAND is Head of Treasure and Portable Antiquities at the British Museum and was formerly curator of Roman coins in the Department of Coins and Medals. He is the author of *The Cunetio Hoard* (with E. M. Besly; 1983) and has edited five volumes in the series *Coin Hoards from Roman Britain*. **61**

JAMES BRUHN is conducting research on the Roman army at the University of Durham, focusing on ethnicity and interaction between the Roman army and local inhabitants. **47** (with Thomas Hulit)

KARL W. BUTZER is Dickson Centennial Professor of Liberal Arts at the University of Texas, Austin, and editor of the *Journal of Archaeological Science*. He specializes in human-environment relations, is the author of *Archaeology as Human Ecology* (1982), and editor of *The Americas Before and After 1492* (1992). **22**

MICHAEL D. COE is Charles J. MacCurdy Professor of Anthropology, Emeritus, at Yale University. With his late wife Sophie, he is co-author of *The True History of Chocolate* (1996). Among his recent publications are *Reading the Maya Glyphs* (2001), co-authored with Mark Van Stone, and *Angkor and the Khmer Civilization* (2003). **29**

PAUL T. CRADDOCK is a research scientist at the Department of Conservation, Documentation and Science at the British Museum, specializing in all aspects of metals technology from Early Bronze Age copper mines to Bauhaus silver. His publications include: *2,000 Years of Zinc and Brass* (1990), *King Croesus' Gold* (with A. Ramage; 2000) and *Early Metal Mining and Production* (1995). **9**, **10**

DAPHNE DERVEN is the Director of Programs at Stone Barns Center for Food and Agriculture. She specializes in educational programmes about food and culture and research into the origins of food and related technologies. **26**

DAVID DREW is an archaeologist, writer and broadcaster. He has been a major participant in the archaeological and rural development work in Peru of the Cusichaca Trust. He has made many historical and archaeological documentary films, especially for the BBC. He has written articles and books on Andean archaeology and is the author of *The Lost Chronicles of the Maya Kings* (2000). **50**

GARRETT G. FAGAN is Associate Professor of Classics and Ancient Mediterranean Studies and History at the Pennsylvania State University. His research interests include Roman social and cultural history, Latin epigraphy, and ancient politics and warfare. He is the author of *Bathing in Public in the Roman World* (1999). **16**, **18**

LINDA FARRAR is a lecturer in the Continuing Education Department, Warwick University. She specializes in ancient gardens and Graeco-Roman cities. She is the author of *Ancient Roman Gardens* (1998), and contributor to *Pergolas, Arbours and Arches, their History* (2001) and *Encyclopedia of Gardens, History and Design* (2001). **24**

IRVING FINKEL is Assistant Keeper in the Department of the Ancient Near East at the British Museum where he specializes in Sumerian and Babylonian magical, medical and literary texts in cuneiform. He is informally responsible for board games throughout the museum, and has conducted research both on ancient games and the indigenous games of modern India. He is the author of *The Hero King Gilgamesh* (1998) and also writes children's books. **51**

JOANN FLETCHER is an Honorary Visiting Fellow at the University of York and Consultant Egyptologist for Harrogate Museums and Arts. She has worked at various sites in Egypt and the Yemen and her publications include *Oils and Perfumes of Ancient Egypt* (1997) and *Egypt's Sun King: Amenhotep III* (2000). **65**, **66**, **67**, **69**

KAREN POLINGER FOSTER is Lecturer in Near Eastern and Aegean Art at Yale University. She is the author of *Aegean Faience of the Bronze Age* (1979), *Minoan Ceramic Relief* (1982) and *The City of Rainbows: A Tale from Ancient Sumer* (1999). With Robert Laffineur she co-edits *Metron: Measuring the Aegean Bronze Age* (2003). *Zoos & Pets*

IRENE GOOD is a Guggenheim Fellow and Research and Curatorial Associate of the Peabody Museum at Harvard University. Her research interests concern cloth in all its aspects and she is currently focusing on the later Bronze Age period of Western China, Afghanistan and the Indo-Iranian borderlands. She is writing a book entitled *A Social Archaeology of Cloth*. **12**

THOMAS HULIT is conducting research at the University of Durham on the arms and armour of the Middle Eastern Late Bronze Age, particularly the military and socio-economic factors governing their production and use. He also has strong research interests in the materials and manufacturing techniques involved in producing all types of artifacts. **44**, **45**, **47** (with James Bruhn)

ANN HYLAND is the author of many books on the horse in war and endurance riding. She is equestrian consultant to the *Oxford English Dictionary*. Her titles include *Equus: The Horse in the Roman World* (1990), *Training the Roman Cavalry: From Arrian's "Ars Tactica"* (1993), *The Medieval Warhorse* (1994), *The Warhorse 1250–1600* (1998), *The Horse in the Middle Ages* (1999), *The Horse in the Ancient World* (2003), plus many practical horsemanship titles. **33**, **48**

RALPH JACKSON is Curator of the Romano-British Collections at the British Museum. He specializes in Roman metalwork and in the archaeology of ancient medicine, and his publications include *Doctors and Diseases in the Roman Empire* (1988). **64**

GEOFFREY P. KILLEN is a specialist in ancient furniture and woodworking. He is a leading furniture historian and his publications include *Egyptian Woodworking and Furniture* (1994), *Ancient Egyptian Furniture*, Vol. I (2nd ed., 2002) and Vol. II (1994). He regularly lectures and gives demonstrations of ancient woodworking processes and techniques in Britain and America. **15**

PATRICK E. McGOVERN is a Senior Research Scientist in the Museum Applied Science Center for Archaeology (MASCA) at the University of Pennsylvania, where he also serves as Adjunct Associate Professor of Anthropology. Among his publications his most recent is *Ancient Wine: The Search for the Origins of Viniculture* (2003). He has pioneered the emerging field of biomolecular archaeology over the past two decades. **27**

SEÁN McGRAIL was Chief Archaeologist at the National Maritime Museum, Greenwich, London; and then Professor of Maritime Archaeology at the University of Oxford. He is now Visiting Professor at the Centre for Maritime Archaeology, University of Southampton. His latest book is *Boats of the World* (2004). **37**, **38**, **39**, **40**, **41**

J. P. MALLORY of the School of Archaeology and Palaeoecology at the Queen's University, Belfast, specializes in the early prehistory of the Indo-European-speaking peoples. He is author of *In Search of the Indo-Europeans* (1989) and co-author of both *The Tarim Mummies* (2000) and the *Encyclopedia of Indo-European Culture* (1997). **32**

WILLIAM H. MANNING is Emeritus Professor of Archaeology at Cardiff University, specializing in Roman archaeology with a particular interest in the Roman imperial army and Roman technology, tools and equipment. He is the author of *The Catalogue of Romano-British Iron Tools, Fittings and Weapons in the British Museum* (1985), *Report on the Excavations at Usk*, vols 1–7 (1981–95), and *Roman Wales* (2001). **19**

CHRIS MEIKLEJOHN is Professor of Anthropology at the University of Winnipeg. His research focus is in bioarchaeology, with ongoing long-term projects on human skeletal material from the Mesolithic and Neolithic of Denmark, Portugal and Iran. He is author and co-author of many articles concerned with the nature of the agricultural transition and the place of skeletal data in the interpretation of the event. **31**

STEVEN MITHEN is Professor of Early Prehistory at the University of Reading. His research interests include the evolution of the human mind, prehistoric hunter-gatherers and the use of computer simulation in archaeology. His current field project is based in Wadi Faynan, Jordan. His publications include *The Prehistory of the Mind* (1996) and *After the Ice* (2003). **1, 2, 3, 6, 20, 52**

DOMINIC MONTSERRAT is a Fellow of the Institute of Archaeology, University College London, and of the Royal Asiatic Society. He has a particular research interest in the cultural appropriation of the ancient world, on which he has written extensively. Among his books are *Sex and Society in Graeco-Roman Egypt* (1996), *Akhenaten: History, Fantasy and Ancient Egypt* (2000) and the exhibition catalogue *Ancient Egypt: Digging for Dreams* (2001). **70**

PAUL NICHOLSON is Senior Lecturer in Archaeology at Cardiff University. He is the author of *Egyptian Faience and Glass* (1993), co-author of the *British Museum Dictionary of Ancient Egypt* (1995) and co-editor of *Ancient Egyptian Materials and Technology* (2001). He has excavated in Egypt since 1983. **11**

COLIN O'CONNOR is Emeritus Professor of Civil Engineering at the University of Queensland and has written four books: *Design of Bridge Superstructures* (1971), *Spanning Two Centuries: Historic Bridges of Australia* (1985), *Roman Bridges* (1993) and *Bridge Loads* (with P. Shaw; 2000). He is currently completing a major history of stone bridges. In 2003 he was awarded the inaugural John Monash medal of the Institution of Engineers, Australia, for his work on engineering heritage. **35**

JACK OGDEN is a specialist in the materials and technology of jewelry, and director of Osmiridium Ltd, a precious metal consultancy company. His publications include *Jewellery of the Ancient World* (1982) and *Interpreting the Past: Ancient Jewellery*

(1992). He was the founder of the Society of Jewellery Historians and has lectured widely in Europe and the USA. **68**

JOHN PETER OLESON is Distinguished Professor in the Department of Greek and Roman Studies at the University of Victoria. He has excavated numerous sites on land and underwater around the Mediterranean, and has published extensively in the areas of Etruscan tomb architecture, ancient hydraulic technology, maritime archaeology and the Roman Near East. Among his publications are *Greek and Roman Mechanical Water-Lifting Devices* (1984), *Greek and Roman Technology, A Sourcebook* (1999) and *Deep-Water Shipwrecks of Skerki Bank: The 1997 Survey* (2004). **17, 23; Sounding Weights**

BARRY RAFTERY is an internationally renowned authority on Iron Age Ireland. He is Head of the Department of Archaeology and Professor of Celtic Archaeology at University College, Dublin. He has conducted extensive excavations on prehistoric trackways in Ireland and his publications include *Pagan Celtic Ireland* (1994). **34** (with Brian Fagan)

BORIS RANKOV is Senior Lecturer in Ancient History at Royal Holloway, University of London. He was rowing master on the reconstructed trireme *Olympias*, is joint author with John Morrison and John Coates of the second edition of *The Athenian Trireme* (2000), and is Chairman of the Trireme Trust. He is currently director, together with David Blackman and Jari Pakkanen, of a major research project funded by the Leverhulme Trust on Ship Sheds of the Ancient Mediterranean. **49**

CHARLOTTE ROBERTS is a Reader in Archaeology at the University of Durham. Her research focuses on palaeopathology, especially the evolution and palaeoepidemiology of infectious diseases. Her recent publications include *Health and Disease in Britain: Prehistory to the Present Day* (2003), 'The bioarchaeology of tuberculosis: a global perspective on a reemerging disease' (2003), and *The Past and Present of Leprosy* (2002). A Fellow of the Society of Antiquaries, she is also the Vice President of the Paleopathology Association. **63**

ANDREW ROBINSON is the author of *The Story of Writing: Alphabets, Hieroglyphs and Pictograms* (1995), *Lost Languages: The Enigma of the World's Undeciphered Scripts* (2002) and *The Man Who Deciphered Linear B: The Story of Michael Ventris* (2002). He is Literary Editor of *The Times Higher Education Supplement*. **54, 55, 56**

ELEANOR ROBSON is a Lecturer in the Department of History and Philosophy of Science, University of Cambridge, where she specializes in the intellectual history of ancient Iraq. She is the author of *Mesopotamian Mathematics, 2100–1600 BC* (1999) and co-author of *The Literature of Ancient Sumer* (2004). **60, 62**

PETER ROWLEY-CONWY is a Reader in environmental archaeology in the Department of Archaeology, University of Durham. His research interests include hunters, fishers and gatherers,

the origins of agriculture, and early farmers. He has conducted research in many parts of Europe, as well as in Egypt and various parts of Asia, and is also working on the early history of the discipline of archaeology. **21, 25, 42, 43**

RICHARD RUDGLEY is the author of a number of books including *The Alchemy of Culture: Intoxicants in Society* (1993) and *The Encyclopaedia of Psychoactive Substances* (1998). He has also written and presented a number of documentaries on historical and archaeological matters for British television. **30**

BILL SILLAR is a Lecturer at the Institute of Archaeology, University of London and Associate Fellow of the Institute of Latin American Studies. His research interests cover the archaeology and ethnography of the Andes, ceramics, material culture and technology. His publications include *Shaping Culture: Making Pots and Constructing Households. An Ethnoarchaeological Study of Pottery Production, Trade and Use in the Andes* (2000). **8**

KATE SPENCE is an Affiliated Lecturer in the Faculty of Oriental Studies, University of Cambridge. She has excavated in Egypt since 1988 and specialized in the architecture of ancient Egypt. **13, 14**

RICHARD TALBERT is Kenan Professor of History and Classics at the University of North Carolina, Chapel Hill, and closely involved with its Ancient World Mapping Center (www.unc.edu/awmc). His research interests span Roman administration, mapmaking and worldview. His publications (some co-authored) include *The Senate of Imperial Rome* (1984), *Barrington Atlas of the Greek and Roman World* (2000), *The Romans from Village to Empire* (2004) and *Space in the Roman World: its Perception and Presentation* (2004). **59**

WILLEKE WENDRICH is Associate Professor of Egyptian Archaeology at the University of California, Los Angeles, and author of *Who is Afraid of Basketry: A Guide to Basketry Analysis for Archaeologists and Ethnographers* (1991) and *The World According to Basketry: An Ethnoarchaeological Interpretation of Basketry Production in Egypt* (1999). She co-directed an archaeological project in Berenike and is currently excavating in the Faiyum (Egypt). Her main interests are landscape archaeology, craft specialization and apprenticeship. **7**

T. G. WILFONG is Associate Professor of Egyptology in the Department of Near Eastern Studies, University of Michigan, and Associate Curator for Graeco-Roman Egypt at the Kelsey Museum of Archaeology. He has written a number of articles and books, including *Women of Jeme: Lives in a Coptic town in Late Antique Egypt* (2002), and has curated several exhibitions, including 'Music in Roman Egypt' (1999) at the Kelsey Museum of Archaeology. He is currently working on a study of music-related artifacts from the University of Michigan's 1924–35 excavation of the Roman period Egyptian town of Karanis. **53**

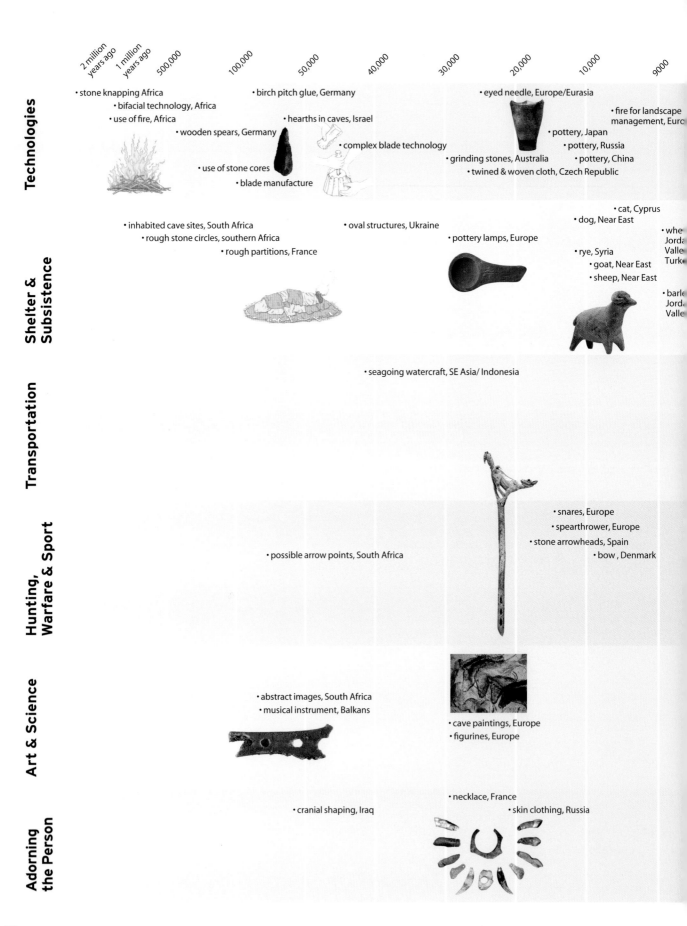

Technologies

2 million years ago · 1 million years ago · 500,000 · 100,000 · 50,000 · 40,000 · 30,000 · 20,000 · 10,000 · 9000

• stone knapping Africa
• bifacial technology, Africa
• use of fire, Africa
• wooden spears, Germany
• use of stone cores
• blade manufacture
• birch pitch glue, Germany
• hearths in caves, Israel
• complex blade technology
• eyed needle, Europe/Eurasia
• fire for landscape management, Euro
• pottery, Japan
• pottery, Russia
• grinding stones, Australia
• pottery, China
• twined & woven cloth, Czech Republic

Shelter & Subsistence

• inhabited cave sites, South Africa
• rough stone circles, southern Africa
• rough partitions, France
• oval structures, Ukraine
• pottery lamps, Europe
• cat, Cyprus
• dog, Near East
• whe Jorda Valle Turk
• rye, Syria
• goat, Near East
• sheep, Near East
• barle Jorda Valle

Transportation

• seagoing watercraft, SE Asia/ Indonesia

Hunting, Warfare & Sport

• possible arrow points, South Africa
• snares, Europe
• spearthrower, Europe
• stone arrowheads, Spain
• bow , Denmark

Art & Science

• abstract images, South Africa
• musical instrument, Balkans
• cave paintings, Europe
• figurines, Europe

Adorning the Person

• cranial shaping, Iraq
• necklace, France
• skin clothing, Russia

10

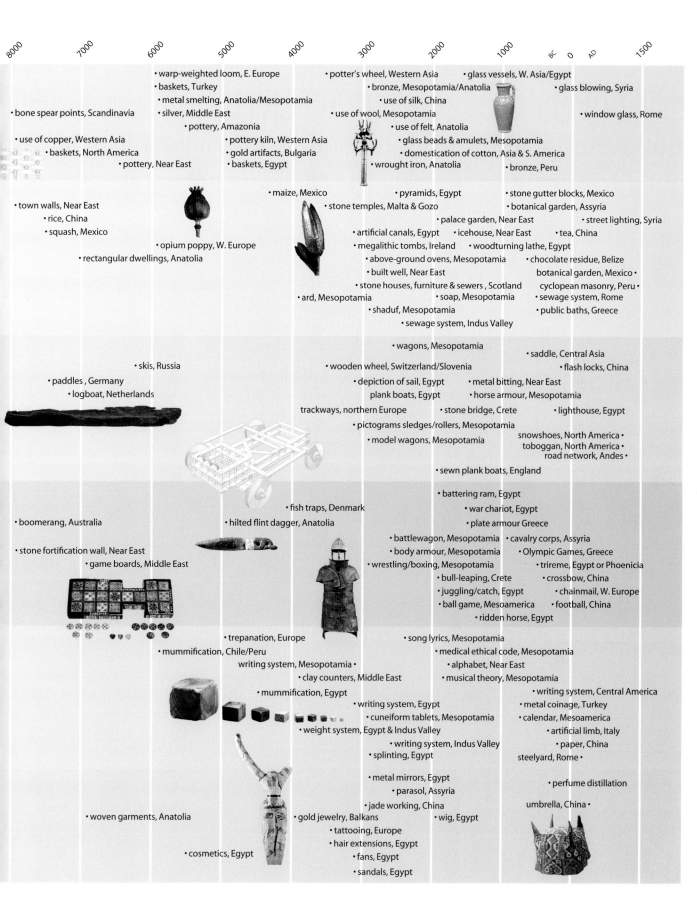

Introduction

We are *Homo sapiens sapiens*, the 'wise person', capable of fluent speech, of forethought and reasoned argument. For more than 50,000 years – the exact date is disputed – we have possessed cognitive abilities far superior to any other animal. We have a restless curiosity and are brilliant opportunists and innovators, rarely content with the status quo.

Not that all these qualities are unique just to anatomically modern humans. At least two-and-a-half million years ago, our archaic predecessors survived successfully using the simplest of stone and wood technology, which they slowly refined with a series of inventions – among them the fire-hardening of pointed wooden spears, the knapping of razor-sharp stone flakes and the taming of fire. But the pace of innovation quickened with the appearance of modern humans. The history of the past 50 millennia is paved with remarkable inventions, some of them as fundamental as metallurgy, others inconspicuous yet of staggering importance. The humble needle is one such innovation, for it made tailored arctic clothing possible.

Inventions hold a particular fascination for all of us, partly because of our modern-day preoccupation with technologies of every kind. To watch a modern-day stone worker, or lithic technologist as they call themselves, fabricating a replica of a fine projectile point is to return to times when people made stone tools as effortlessly as they now change the oil in their cars.

The first human invention? It was at least 2.5 million years ago that our early ancestors living on the African savannah began to make crude stone tools. Stone technology then developed over the millennia, and by the Solutrean period of western Europe, c. 20,000–15,000 BC, beautiful flint artifacts such as these points from Le Placard, in France, were being produced.

Ability and invention go together. Early hominids were no fools and knew how to survive in a hostile world. The Neanderthal armed only with a stone-tipped spear lived in landscapes teeming with predators. Killing a large animal like a bison required consummate stalking expertise as well as great bravery. The spear-wielding hunter literally had to jump on the back of the animal.

The skills and experience behind the inventions are as important as the technologies themselves. True inventors have special creative abilities that are still little understood. In ancient times, one was careful observation – realizing, for example, the potential of a firebrand lit from a tree ignited by a lightning strike and using it to scare off predators. Another would have been seizing on chance – a lump of copper ore accidentally melting in a hearth perhaps led to a potter, familiar with firing clay, trying to melt another lump. A third would have been quiet and patient experimentation, as must have been the case with making fine furniture. Then there was need – a pressing necessity for more grain (cultivation), deep waters to be crossed (canoes), spacing babies (contraception), and so on. We look back at the past from a distance too remote to identify individual inventors, but we marvel at their restless creativity and ingenuity.

Here we examine a wide range of inventions from what we call the 'ancient world', a term that defies precise definition. A century ago, we would have equated it with the ancient Mediterranean

world, with Egypt, Greece, the Near East, Mesopotamia and Rome. Today, the 'ancient world' covers every continent and everything from African hominids to early maize farmers in Mexico and Chinese royal burials. Our stage is the world, so we content ourselves with the broadest of definitions. Our 'ancient world' covers all periods of human history and all parts of the world: up to AD 500 and the fall of Rome in the Old World, and

The earliest known examples of representational art date from around 30,000 years ago, but whether this is due to accidents of survival or represents a true turning point in human development is still much debated. This Upper Palaeolithic antler carving of a bison licking itself dates to around 11,000 BC and is from La Madeleine rockshelter, France.

The wheel seems to have been invented in the 4th millennium BC, and the earliest wheeled vehicles are probably from Mesopotamia. At first wheels were solid, either cut from a single block or made from three pieces of wood fixed together. This model of a two-wheeled cart drawn by oxen is from Mohenjo-daro in modern Pakistan, and dates to the mid-3rd millennium BC.

Right *A Neolithic painted ceramic vessel from Egypt, dating from c. 4000 BC, depicting a boat with masts, sails and crew.*

Below *The large wheel of a chariot in a pit burial for a nobleman of the Western Zhou dynasty (c. 1050–771 BC), near Xi'an, China. In Bronze Age China, the war chariot was the pre-eminent symbol of power.*

AD 1520, the date of the siege of the Aztec capital, Tenochtitlán, in the Americas.

From the dazzling array of inventions made in ancient times this book tells the story of 70, chosen from a potential list of hundreds. No one will agree with all our choices, but they are spread widely enough in time and space to reflect the diversity of innovations that have changed human history in many ways. They include inventions unimagined as being significant a century ago – to mention just a few: stone grinders, basketry, furniture, drugs and camel saddles. Few people perhaps know that

a new design of load-carrying camel saddle opened the Sahara Desert to long-distance trade, or that the Chinese invented the wheelbarrow.

Survival of the evidence

Our knowledge of the remarkable inventions of the past comes from a very fragmentary record, where, mostly, organic remains such as wooden spears or textiles do not survive the centuries and millennia. Imagine the problems in studying modern industrial society on the basis of two spark plugs, a china plate, a carving knife and a handful of glass beads – which is basically what archaeologists do. This makes the search for inventions particularly difficult, unless they are marked by a characteristic artifact such as, for example, a triangular stone point used by a Neanderthal spearman or a distinctive pit dug to store ice by a Chinese emperor.

As American archaeologist Kent Flannery once remarked, it is fruitless to search for the first maize cob, or the very first example of any technological invention. All we can hope to identify is the approximate date at which major innovations occurred, or chart the changes in human toolkits triggered by such advances as the use of copper metallurgy or glass-making. Fortunately for science, many inven-

Left *Assyrian reliefs provide us with some of the most detailed and accurate depictions of horses and their equipment from the ancient world. This detail, from Nineveh (7th century BC), shows two horses with elaborate bridles and saddle cloths, accompanied by an archer.*

Below *A warrior protected by body armour, possibly of leather, and a plumed helmet stands poised, wielding his spear; terracotta figurine from Jalisco, west Mexico.*

tions have left sufficient archaeological traces to give some indication of when they appeared and to allow us to track their trajectory through time.

A journey through human innovation

The Seventy Great Inventions of the Ancient World is divided into six parts. We begin with 'Technologies', with stone and fire, wood and bone – the basic raw materials used by humans to craft a broad range of artifacts for foraging, agriculture and animal husbandry. These four technologies encompass most of ancient times and remained in use into the 20th century. We examine the evidence for early basketry and clay vessels, which came into widespread use after the beginnings of farming after 10,000 BC. With agriculture came textiles and weaving, and then metal technologies, first used for ornaments and ceremonial artifacts, later for utilitarian tools and weapons.

'Shelter & Subsistence' explores the ingenious ways in which people have devised housing, from simple brush shelters to stone architecture. With more permanent dwellings came an elaboration of furnishings and carpentry, attempts at more efficient heating and lighting, and the first plumbing and drainage systems, all inventions that are still

Right *The plough was probably the single most important agricultural invention. It was in use in China by the Han dynasty (206 BC – AD 220), as depicted on this brick, and perhaps as early as 500 BC.*

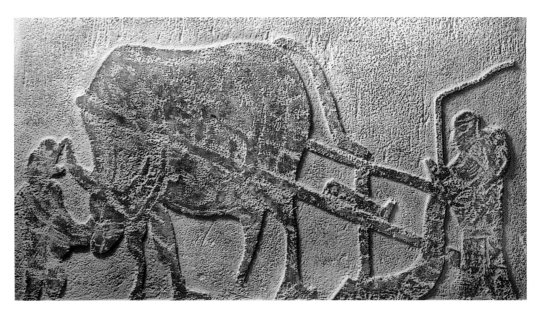

Below right *A triumph of metalworking skill, this gold cup from Vapheio in Greece (15th century BC) vividly depicts a man hunting and capturing a wild bull.*

Below *Athletes competing in a foot race, depicted on a vase that was itself awarded as a prize to the victor in the Panathenaic Games in Athens (560–555 BC).*

the subject of human ingenuity in the present. We describe the invention of agriculture and irrigation, and the passion for gardening that dates back to the beginnings of civilization. Cooking is as early as fire, but achieved the highest levels of elaboration with urban civilization. There has always also been a demand for refreshing beverages, food preservation and stimulants.

'Transportation' begins with skis, wheels and carts and surveys the inventions needed to make effective use of the camel and the horse. We travel along ancient roads and go to sea in canoes and the earliest ships under paddle and sail. 'Hunting, Warfare & Sport' shows how inventions for the chase and battle were inseparable. For tens of thousands of years, ancient hunters used the simplest of nets, traps and spears against animals of all sizes. The spearthrower, boomerang and bow and arrow extended range and improved accuracy. Spears and bows soon became weapons of war, as did metal daggers and swords. With the advent of standing armies, weaponry expanded to include siege engines and crossbows, and people protected themselves with armour. Increasingly well-planned fortifications defended city, garrison and town. Chariots and cavalry revolutionized war. So did galleys and warships when armies took to the water. We also explore the close link between war and competitive sports such as the Olympic Games, and the contests of the mind that took place in the smaller arena of the board.

'Art & Science' covers the eclectic realm of the earliest artistic traditions, of music and painting. We describe the controversies surrounding the beginnings of writing and the human fascination with the passage of time and the movements of the heavenly bodies. Early science was also concerned with numbers and counting, with weights, measures, and medicine, even surgery and mummification.

Finally, 'Adorning the Person' looks at the ways in which people have used body art and tattoos to identify themselves, establish kin ties or make themselves attractive. From body art, it is but a short step to clothing and jewelry, to cosmetics and perfumes, used in the art of seduction and displaying sexual prowess, epitomized by the ingenuity lavished on contraceptives and aphrodisiacs.

These articles are authoritative and dispassionate, thanks to the expertise of the distinguished contributors. They provide a balanced perspective on inventions large and small, important and sometimes trivial. Where possible, they identify some of the controversies surrounding them, readily admitting when definitive answers cannot be provided. There is an unusual and complete scientific honesty in these pages.

BRIAN FAGAN

A Nazca pottery vessel from Peru (c. AD 400), in the form of a woman with body decoration. Tattooing may have had a protective or therapeutic role, serving for instance as a permanent amulet during pregnancy and childbirth. Several pre-Columbian cultures also used stylized designs on the torso, limbs and face as a mark of high status.

Humans have used nets for fishing for tens of thousands of years. One found in Russia measures some 30 m (100 ft) in length and dates to around 10,000 years ago, but as they are made from organic material even earlier examples may not have survived. In this Assyrian relief from Sennacherib's Southwest Palace at Nineveh (c. 700–692 BC), Iraq, a man uses both a net and a line to catch fish.

17

Technologies

Some of the basic technologies that have served humanity for millennia were developed in the earliest times. The first toolkits were made from stone and wood, and stone tools are the most enduring and best known of all human implements. They evolved slowly over millions of years, from the simple choppers and flakes of the first toolmakers to the refined blade tools made by modern humans from about 50,000 years ago.

Archaeologists have unravelled the secrets of stone technology by analyzing both tools and the byproducts of manufacturing them, and through experiments. We know little of wooden artifacts, which survive only rarely, such as the spears found at Schöningen, northern Germany, dating to 400,000 years ago. Our remote forebears tamed fire and used it to harden such spear points, as well as for protection and warmth, and to fire brush as a way of encouraging new plant growth to attract game. The firestick has rightly been described as the most potent of all human artifacts.

Later archaic humans invented more elaborate stone technologies. The fabrication of standardized blades some 50 millennia ago produced an explosion of more specialized stone tools, among them burins. Such graving tools allowed people to groove antler and bone, unleashing the potential of a new technology to make fine spear points, harpoons and such inconspicuous devices as the eyed needle. Around 25,000 years ago, Eurasians were wearing tailored, layered clothing, which enabled them to hunt in subzero temperatures in winter. By the end of the Ice Age, around 12,000 years ago, many groups were using smaller-scale stone technology, which played an important role in the development of the bow and arrow, a dramatically more efficient hunting weapon.

Flint and bone weapons, over 11,000 years old, from Montana, in North America. Beautifully crafted using some of the oldest human technology, such tools could be used for a multitude of functions and were extremely practical.

Plant foods assumed increased significance at the end of the Ice Age. The technology of plant gathering and processing was always simple, often consisting of little more than a milling stone and a grinder. Technology became more elaborate as humans created tougher working edges for axes, an essential part of toolkits in a more forested world. The ground stone axe and adze allowed people to fell large trees, to fashion house posts and beams, to hollow dugout canoes. These improved living standards, fenced pastures and allowed people to travel and make fish traps.

Hunter-gatherers are limited in their mobility by their ability to carry food back to camp, whether parts of a butchered animal or freshly harvested grain or nuts. For thousands of years, people used skin cloaks, which doubled as clothing. Like Australian Aborigines or African San of today, they also had simple bark containers. Basketry developed originally out of basic skills with plant fibres, but soon reached a high level of refinement in a world where small seeds and nuts were staples and had to be carried and stored. The clay pot relied on a simple firing technology familiar to anyone who sat by a camp-fire, and, while less portable than baskets, had the advantage of being fire-resistant and durable. Metallurgy developed seamlessly from pottery, for the temperatures needed to melt copper ore are relatively low. Native copper can also be hammered, as was commonplace in the North American Midwest. Copper, gold and silver had important roles in early societies as ornamental metals, made into pendants, bracelets and other symbols of rank and social standing. Bronze, then later iron, became utilitarian technologies, used for implements of tillage and weapons of war.

Prestige and innovation went hand-in-hand, especially when the end-product was a scarce or elaborate artifact, whose use or display was restricted to a privileged few. Such was the case with glass and fine textiles, both of which distinguished their owner as a person of rank. Many inventions resulted not from economic necessity, but from our constant search for the exotic, for objects and technologies that set one person apart from the rest.

The earliest known major find of gold artifacts in the world comes from the late Neolithic cemetery at Varna, in Bulgaria, dating to the 5th millennium BC. Graves in the cemetery also contained pottery, flint tools, jewelry and axe heads, representing several of the early technologies.

Stone Tools

*The situation in which these [stone] weapons were found may tempt
us to a very remote period indeed; even beyond that of the present world.*

JOHN FRERE, 1799

I f we were to measure the importance of an invention in terms of its duration at the cutting edge of human technology, stone tools would win hands down. It was at least 3 million years ago that one of our early human ancestors living on the African savannah first used a piece of rough, unmodified stone for some task, perhaps to crack open a nut or break a bone apart to gain access to the edible marrow inside.

Although later joined by wood, bone and antler as raw materials for early prehistoric tool making, stone remained pre-eminent until the invention of metalworking, a mere 7000 years ago. In fact, 3 million years of stone tool technology may be a vast underestimate. Some chimpanzee groups today use stone hammers and anvils to crack nuts; although these groups may have invented such technology in the relatively recent past, their capacity to do this suggests the 6-million-year-old common ancestor of chimpanzees and modern humans may also have used stone artifacts.

An accidental discovery

It is likely that the first stone tools were discovered, rather than invented. An unmodified nodule of stone can be a very effective tool, providing either a hammer, a sharp edge for cutting or a missile for throwing. Not surprisingly, therefore, in the earliest known archaeological sites of East Africa stones are often found that are unmodified but have been transported from their source. Archaeologists call such tools 'manuports', and it was perhaps from using these that our early ancestors first learnt how to manufacture stone tools.

When a stone nodule is used as a hammer it often breaks in half, or flakes become detached. These flakes can provide sharp edges and would have been useful for cutting apart animal carcasses – a key task for the hominids living on the African savannahs of 2.5 million years ago. And it was a task

that had to be done as quickly as possible owing to the dangers from prowling hyenas and lions. It may therefore not have been long (in an evolutionary sense) before hominids started knocking rocks together with the deliberate intention of producing sharp flakes to use in butchery. That knocking, or 'knapping' as archaeologists call it, made the difference between a simple discovery and the invention of a stone tool.

We know that hominids were knapping stone by at least 2.5 million years ago because scatters of flaked quartz have been found in sediments in the Omo and Kada Gona regions of Ethiopia. Differentiating between stone that has been deliberately flaked and that which has naturally fractured is often very difficult, and it isn't until after 2 million years ago that archaeologists can identify a distinct technology. This is known as the 'Oldowan culture', found in East and South Africa between 2 and 1.5 million years ago.

It was first described by Mary Leakey from her excavations in Olduvai Gorge in Tanzania. The

Olduvai Gorge, in Tanzania, the area where evidence for the earliest distinct technology of deliberately flaked tools was found, and hence named the 'Oldowan culture'.

Above *Examples of Oldowan choppers, nodules from which flakes have been removed, as shown in the diagram. The flakes themselves then might be used as they were, or further worked to produce scrapers.*

Right *A fine Acheulian handaxe, from St Acheul, France, and a diagram of the technique used to produce such tools. These handaxes are bifacial – that is, worked on both sides – and their makers had a clear idea of what the final shape should be, so that they were more standardized in form and technique than tools of the Oldowan industry.*

question – Oldowan tools do not appear to have been effective hunting weapons, although a carefully thrown chopper or unworked nodule might have brought down small game.

Although microscopic identification of cut marks on bones confirms that Oldowan tools were used for butchery, they could also have been employed for many other tasks – cutting grass stems, sharpening sticks, removing bark, cracking nuts and pounding insects. It seems most likely that soon after 2 million years ago, our ancestors had become dependent upon using stone for their survival.

Developing technology

New and more complex ways of working stone were slow to appear. By 1.4 million years ago hominids had begun to remove flakes from both sides of a stone nodule in an alternate fashion. This is known as 'bifacial' technology to distinguish it from the 'unifacial' Oldowan choppers. It allowed

most characteristic artifact is the 'chopper', a nodule of basalt or chert from which one or more flakes have been removed. Many of the detached flakes were probably used just as they were, but some were further chipped around their edges – a technique known as retouching – to make 'scrapers', the chipping being intended either to shape or simply blunt the edge, and hence prevent it from cutting into the user's hand.

Oldowan tools are often found clustered in large numbers (several thousand flakes) and intermixed with fragmented bones from animals such as antelopes and zebras at what must have been repeatedly used butchery sites. Whether the animals had been hunted and killed or merely scavenged from carnivore kills is a much debated

hominids to create artifacts that archaeologists call 'handaxes', which are pointed and pear shaped, and 'cleavers', which have a flat edge, like a wide chisel. Another key difference between such bifaces and Oldowan tools is that they had a deliberately imposed form – the hominids clearly had an idea of what they wanted their tools to look like before they began removing flakes. Many bifaces are highly symmetrical, far more than seems necessary for maximizing their utility alone.

By 500,000 years ago hammers made from antler and bone were being used to remove 'thinning' flakes from bifaces, which helped to produce tools which have a considerable aesthetic appeal to the modern eye. By this date our ancestors had dispersed from Africa into Asia and Europe and were using a wide range of stone types. The most important was flint – this has such a fine crystalline structure it fractures in very predictable ways and provides especially sharp edges. Whenever flint was available, it was the favoured raw material.

New methods of working stone gradually appeared, although the rate of innovation by our ancestors such as *Homo ergaster*, *Homo heidelbergensis* and *Homo neanderthalensis* still seems remarkably slow by modern standards. In addition to the bifacial methods, the Neanderthals who lived in Europe and Western Asia from *c*. 250,000 to 30,000 years ago used a technique that archaeologists call the 'Levallois' method. This involved the removal of flakes to shape a nodule (the core) so that it had a convex surface; a striking platform was then prepared and with one blow a large flake of a predetermined size and shape was removed. The core was often prepared again for the removal of a second, and then perhaps a third or fourth flake; in some cases the flakes were pointed in shape and with no further modification were hafted on to wooden shafts to make spears.

The Levallois method was also used by *Homo sapiens* – modern humans – which had evolved in Africa some time before 130,000 years ago. By 50,000 years ago they began to favour other types of stone tool manufacture. One of these involved the preparation of cores so that many long, thin flakes – known as blades – could be detached, which formed the 'blanks' for making scraping

The Levallois technique of the Middle Palaeolithic involved the careful preparation of a core, such as the one seen left, so that flakes of a predetermined form and size could be struck off.

tools, burins (with a chisel-like edge), and arrowheads (p. 28). Some blanks were shaped by 'pressure flaking' – forcing a point of antler or bone against the edge of a flake so that a tiny chip was removed – which enabled intricate shapes to be produced, such as effective barbed and tanged arrowheads.

But the technique that became most widespread, especially after the end of the last Ice Age, was 'microlithic' technology. This involved the careful breakage of blades into small pieces which were then chipped into specific shapes and used as components in a wide variety of tools, notably as points and barbs for arrows, and as blades for knives and sickles. Microlithic technology appears to have been independently invented in all continents and provided the most efficient and effective use of stone ever known.

KEY DATES

unmodified stone tools	3 million years ago
stone knapping	2.5 million years ago
bifacial technology	1.4 million years ago
Levallois technique	250,000 years ago
blade manufacture	100,000 years ago
microliths	20,000 years ago

Fire

I am warm, I have seen the fire.
Isaiah 44: 16

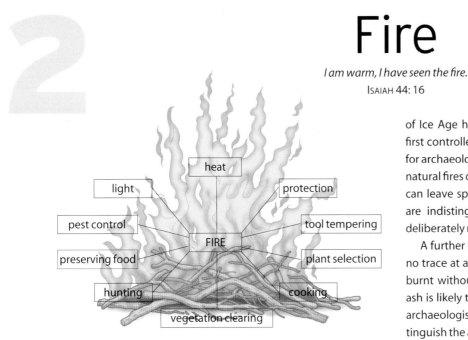

While fire itself may not be a human invention, its controlled use was certainly a critically important innovation in human evolution. Whether our ancestors lived by hunting and gathering or by farming, fire provided heat, light, protection and a means to alter their surrounding environment by burning off vegetation for either clearance or pest control.

As such, fire has long been an immensely valuable tool, as evident from hearths at the campsites of Ice Age hunter-gatherers. But quite when the first controlled use of fire began has been difficult for archaeologists to ascertain. The problem is that natural fires occur in many types of woodlands and can leave spreads of charcoal and burnt soil that are indistinguishable from the remains of fires deliberately made by people.

A further difficulty is that camp-fires may leave no trace at all, especially if wood has simply been burnt without any stone surround; the scatter of ash is likely to be blown away leaving nothing for archaeologists to find. And we may also wish to distinguish the act of capturing and using fire that has naturally occurred from that of deliberately creating it, such as by chipping stones to make a spark or vigorously rubbing wooden sticks together.

Experimental studies have shown that if a camp-fire was repeatedly made on the same spot two types of distinctive archaeological traces may survive. First, the soil beneath may become oxidized to depths of up to 15 cm (6 in); natural fires are unlikely to oxidize soil deeper than 1 or 2 cm (0.4–0.8 in). Second, the magnetic properties of the soil below the fire may become affected, displaying quite different magnetic orientation from sites where there has either been no burning at all or only relatively light natural fires, such as burning tree stumps.

The archaeological evidence

These two indicators – oxidization and magnetism – along with the distinctive basin-shaped profile of multiply used fireplaces, have identified the earliest known camp-fire in the world. This is at the site called FxJj20 at the locality of Koobi Fora, Kenya, dating to 1.6 million years ago. One patch of heavily oxidized soil was identified as the remnants of a camp-fire that had been kept burning for at least four or five days. Several thousand stone artifacts and fragments of bone were found close to this feature. Few, if any, of these showed signs

of having been burnt and so the fire does not appear to have been used for roasting meat or heat-treating stone before knapping.

The probable function of the FxJj20 fireplace was to provide some warmth and light and to deter predators. Hyenas, lions and other carnivores would have been both competitors for carcasses and potential predators. The fire would have been made by an early species of *Homo*, probably *Homo ergaster*, that lived by hunting, gathering and scavenging on the African savannah. But whether it was being intentionally created or simply taken and conserved from natural fires is unclear.

Other than the FxJj20 example, fireplaces are very rare in the archaeological record of pre-modern humans. One probable example comes from the site of Beeches Pit in Norfolk and dates to 500,000 years ago. Again, this is no more than an area of heavily burnt soil that seems to have been too intense and localized to be due to natural causes. It would seem most unlikely, however, that early hominids such as the Neanderthals could have lived in Ice Age Europe without making use of fire. Their cave sites often contain thick layers of ash which appears to have been spread from fireplaces to warm the ground on which they slept. At other sites, for instance Kebara Cave, Israel, the excavation of deep deposits has revealed many small hearths repeatedly built at the same location. But deliberately built stone hearths are practically unknown.

It is not until after around 10,000 BC that we find clear evidence for the controlled use of fire to alter landscapes. Many recent hunter-gatherer groups, such as the Australian Aborigines and Native Americans, have used fire to burn off vegetation and encourage the growth of new shoots to attract game. Mesolithic communities in northern Europe appear to have done the same thing. The best-studied example is Star Carr in Yorkshire, dating from 9500 BC. Detailed studies of charcoal fragments from lake sediments have shown that people repeatedly came and burnt off the reeds. Although this may have been primarily to increase visibility across the lake, it would have had the effect of encouraging the growth of plants and flushing out small game and wild fowl for hunting.

Above *Reconstruction showing a group of* Homo erectus *in a basic rock shelter using fires for different purposes.*

KEY DATES

earliest camp-fire	1.6 million years ago, Kenya
discrete hearths within caves	60,000 years ago, Israel
use of fire for landscape management	9500 BC, Europe

Left *An accumulation of hearths repeatedly built at the same location by Neanderthals, around 60,000 years ago, excavated within the cave deposits of Kebara, Israel.*

Wooden Tools

Just occasionally, an archaeological discovery leaves one speechless.
ROBERT DENNELL, ON THE SCHÖNINGEN SPEARS, 1997

Modern chimpanzees use wooden tools for several different functions: this one is foraging for insects. Since chimpanzees can make and use such tools, it seems likely that our earliest human ancestors would also have had this capacity.

Archaeology is often a desperately frustrating discipline because so much evidence from the earliest periods of human existence has not survived. At least, we assume that it hasn't – we can never be entirely sure. Wooden tools are a prime example of this. The earliest known piece of shaped wood is no more than 400,000 years old. But by that time human ancestors were making sophisticated stone tools, had dispersed from Africa into Europe and Asia, had a stature comparable with modern humans, walked efficiently on two legs and had brains at least two-thirds the size of ours. It is entirely reasonable to assume that they had already been making and using wooden artifacts for many thousands, if not millions, of years – but none have survived.

Chimpanzees use wooden tools for several different tasks: to wave and throw during threat displays, for collecting ants and termites, and as anvils for hammering nuts. Termite sticks are modified by removing the leaves from twigs and biting the ends to create a tool of the right size. As chimpanzees can make and use wooden tools, such abilities are also most likely to have been within the capacity of our early human ancestors, perhaps as far back as 6 million years ago – the time of the common ancestor between humans and chimpanzees. Those ancestors would have faced many of the same problems that chimpanzees have solved with their wooden tools – how to extract insects from their nests or water from a hollow tree trunk. The likelihood that our early ancestors used wooden implements is further enhanced by experimental studies with replica Oldowan stone tools. These are effective at shaving wood, and those made soon after 2 million years ago may have been used for making wooden spears.

Rare survivals

Wooden spears are indeed the earliest type of wooden tools that have been discovered. In 1995 three were excavated at Schöningen, Germany, dating to 400,000 years ago. Made from spruce, they were designed like modern javelins, with their maximum weight and thickness at the front, and long, tapering tails. They were found with many horse bones

Right A rare survival: the tip of one of the Lower Palaeolithic hunting spears found at Schöningen, Germany. Made from spruce and measuring about 2 m (6.5 ft) long, they were shaped like a modern javelin.

KEY DATES

spears	400,000 years ago, Germany
worked wood	750,000–240,000 years ago, Israel
pointed sticks	over 125,000 years ago, England & Germany

Mesolithic sites in Denmark and Sweden, dating to between 7500 and 4500 BC, have provided a particularly rich array of wooden tools. Remnants of a wicker cage have been found at the site of Ageröd V, which was manufactured by weaving together branches of cherry and alder with pine roots – a work of art, natural science and practical need twisted and knotted into one. In the same period, willow bark was braided and tied to make fishing nets, and pine bark turned into floats. Canoes were hollowed from trunks of lime and paddled with heart-shaped blades carved from ash. Hazel rods were used to make fences to divert fish into traps (p. 173), and birch bark was folded and sewn into bags for carrying flint blades. Elm boughs were shaped into bows.

All these wooden tools tell of an intimacy with the natural world that is lost today and illustrate the handiwork of people who loved their craft.

Left *The excavation of the wooden spears at Schöningen was led by Hartmut Thieme. The spears were found lying among stone implements and animal bones, including those from more than 10 horses, leading the excavator to suggest that the spears were used for hunting rather than simply for driving predators away from carcasses.*

and are assumed to have been used to hunt these and other large mammals. Along with the spears, a stick pointed at both ends and three worked branches of silver fir were also found. Grooves had been cut into the branches and they may once have held stone flakes – making them the earliest known composite tools.

Before the discovery of the Schöningen spears, two other pointed sticks were known from Europe – one from Clacton (England) and one from Lehringen (Germany) – both more than 125,000 years old. Another particularly early piece of worked wood has come from the site of Gesher Benot Ya'aqov in the Jordan Valley. This is a piece of charred willow, 25 cm (10 in) long. Its surface is flat and is said to have been polished and cut at an angle to the wood's grain – most unlikely for a natural fracture. The date of this wooden plank – if indeed that is what it is – remains unclear, but is thought to be between 750,000 and 240,000 years ago.

Root & branch

Although these archaeological traces are scant, it seems likely that throughout human evolution our ancestors were inventive about using wood to make a variety of tools. But we only begin to see substantial evidence for both imaginative and technical abilities at woodworking after the end of the last Ice Age when artifacts survive in water-logged deposits. Such deposits inhibit decay, preserving wood and revealing how it had been used, in all its forms – branches, bark, roots – to make an immense variety of implements.

Left *A large fragment of a wicker cage from Ageröd V, Sweden, dating to between 7500 and 4500 BC. It was made of cherry and alder branches woven together with pine roots, demonstrating how familiar Mesolithic people were with various kinds of wood and their different properties.*

GLUE

Adhesives are as early as humanity, occurring naturally in the form of pine pitch oozing from a sapling or sticky sap from a tree trunk. Stone Age hunters made extensive use of vegetable substances of all kinds, especially wood pitch, to mount spear points and other artifacts. Birch pitch was recently discovered in Germany dating to 80,000 years ago, which is thought to have been used to secure stone blades in wooden shafts. And Stone Age farmers soon discovered hide glue, widely used by Egyptian carpenters, made by extracting gelatin from ox skins. Hide glues were ideal for furniture and were used to fabricate pharaoh Tutankhamun's throne. They are still widely used by cabinet makers and are the glue of choice in antique restoration to this day. The Egyptians and Romans also made use of fish glue, extracted by heating fish skin or bones in water and then applied with a brush. The purest isinglass, a form of gelatin, comes from sturgeon. Fish skin glue was much used in medieval times in the process of gilding illuminated manuscripts. Synthetic adhesives have now replaced most animal and vegetable glues.

Composite Tools, Blades & Chisels

Whatever the ultimate inspiration or the intermediate cause, it was by their hands that the early Europeans dragged themselves out of the primeval mire of savagery, struggled up the long and undulating slopes of barbarism and ultimately attained to some kind of civilization.

GRAHAME CLARK, 1952

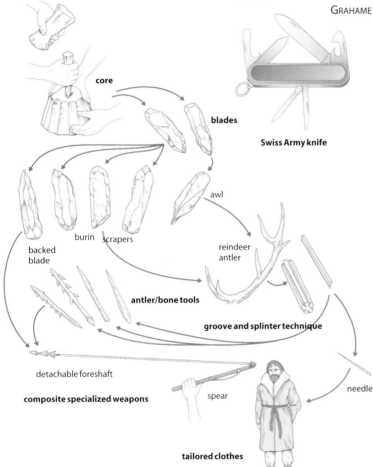

core

blades

Swiss Army knife

awl

burin scrapers

backed blade

reindeer antler

burin

antler/bone tools

groove and splinter technique

detachable foreshaft

composite specialized weapons

spear

needle

tailored clothes

Above *The 'Swiss Army Knife effect' of blade technology, which allowed late Ice Age people to fashion specialized tools from standardized blanks and then to make antler and bone artifacts.*

Right *These small Mousterian flakes from Le Moustier, France, were made by Neanderthals.*

tively standardized flakes. These flakes were thin enough to be mounted at the end of spear staves – sinew or fibre bindings lashed the point to the shaft. With their lethally sharp points and edges, these spears were capable of penetrating thick hide and inflicting serious wounds.

Such weapons achieved a high degree of refinement in European and African societies during the late Ice Age, after 12,000 years ago. But even before this, by 50,000 years ago, Neanderthal hunters in western Europe were already pursuing large and formidable prey including bison, wild ox, and mammoth with composite weapons.

The 'Swiss Army knife effect'

Most experts now agree that anatomically modern humans – ourselves – first developed in tropical Africa some time before 130,000 years ago. Small

Archaeologists call them composite tools – artifacts with more than one part. Around 250,000 years ago, stoneworkers made a major advance in stone technology: instead of relying on flakes removed opportunistically from irregular cobbles, they first shaped the stone into carefully prepared cores, designed to produce either a single, large thin flake, or a series of rela-

Homo sapiens populations had moved out of Africa into south-western Asia by 100,000 years ago, but they still used the simple composite tools of earlier times. Around 45,000 years ago, modern humans reached their full cognitive potential, the ability to reason, plan and innovate just like ourselves. Almost at once, we witness the development of more sophisticated stone technologies that unlocked the full potential not only of tools made of stone, but of antler, bone, ivory, leather and wood – to mention but a few raw materials. For the first time in history, we find the 'Swiss Army knife effect'.

The familiar Swiss Army knife consists of a knife chassis with powerful hinges festooned with a varied array of attachments – everything from blades and bottle-openers to scissors, saws and tweezers. Each of these attachments depends on the chassis, but together they form an astoundingly versatile tool. Late Ice Age Europeans developed their own form of Swiss Army knife toolkit by using blade technology. The Cro-Magnons made blade tools with a punch: they used carefully selected, fine-grained stone such as flint or chert, shaped it into cylindrical cores, then struck off as many standard-sized, parallel-sided blades as they could.

Blade technology produced thin, beautifully regular end-products, which could be mounted as razor-sharp points on a spear, or easily shaped into a knife with a blunted back that could safely be held in the hand. A few deft blows would notch a blade to make a spokeshave or sharpen a tougher edge for a woodworking tool or simple saw. The ends or sides could be blunted to make a wide variety of scrapers for processing hides. Point the ends of a blade and you have an awl for boring holes in leather or wood. Most important of all, the stone worker could fashion chisel-like burins by carefully directing strokes at the ends to make engravers – tools for grooving deep into

KEY DATES

stone cores	250,000 years ago
'Swiss Army knife effect'	45,000 years ago

fresh antler, or for levering long splinters from mammoth tusks.

Think Swiss Army knife: the blade core was the chassis, the hinge for dozens of different, relatively standardized tools. Stoneworkers could carry cores of fine stone with them on their daily round, a stock of raw material that was always to hand. In a few seconds, a skilled stoneworker could punch off a blade to fashion a knife, a scraper or a chisel, just as the modern-day knife owner opens an attachment for the task at hand.

Blade technology started a revolution in human development. For the first time, humans had a versatile and easily manufactured toolkit that opened up the full potential of antler, bone and other materials (p. 30) to make highly effective, much more specialized artifacts of all kinds.

Left *A burin blade from Le Placard, France, dating from the Upper Palaeolithic. Such blades opened up the possibilities of materials including antler and ivory to produce a new range of tools.*

Below *Clovis points from North America, found in a cache. Smaller points could be mounted on a detachable foreshaft and then a wooden spear shaft to create highly effective hunting weapons.*

Bone & Antler Tools

Carving bone required integrated thought about the characteristics of both stone and plant material. The elaboration in the range of scraping and engraving tools used for such tasks as cleaning hides and carving bone required thought about the nature of animal products during the process of tool manufacture.

Steven Mithen, 1996

A perforated antler fragment, perhaps used as a thong straightener. Such objects were called 'batons de commandement' or sceptres by early French prehistorians who were unsure of their function. This example, from La Madeleine rockshelter, France, dating to around 11,000 BC, is engraved with four horses on this side, three on the reverse.

Humans used bone and wood for all manner of tasks from the earliest times, but only rarely do finished artifacts survive. Bone is preserved more frequently than wood, to the extent that we can be fairly certain archaic humans did not manufacture formal bone tools. If they did make them, they were casual, spur-of-the-moment artifacts, created by flaking bone with a sharp stone blade.

Antler and bone technology was a product of modern humans, especially in the northern latitudes of Europe and Eurasia, where it often substituted for wood in treeless environments. Such materials came into use as a direct result of the Swiss Army knife-like blade technology of the European Cro-Magnons (p. 28). The chisel-ended burin allowed humans to cut deep grooves through the outer surface of fresh reindeer and elk antler. They

This spearthrower weight, from Enlène Cave, France, dating to around 11,000 BC, is carved in the form of two ibexes (mountain goats) embracing, playing or fighting. Antler was skilfully carved by humans at this time into objects of practical use but also of great aesthetic beauty.

eyed needle	25,000 years ago
bone spear points	8000 BC, Scandinavia
multi-part tools	1000 BC, Bering Strait

would then bore into the spongy interior with a stone awl, thread a thong through the hole and lever out a long splinter. Such blanks could be used to shape all kinds of hunting weapons, among them spear points, single- and double-barbed harpoons, especially effective against sea mammals, and finely serrated fish spears, or leisters.

The Cro-Magnons and their Eurasian neighbours developed remarkably sophisticated antler and bone technology. Their more specialized artifacts included spearthrowers (p. 175) with finely carved animals, strange implements called batons, possibly used to straighten sinew and also sometimes decorated with carvings of animals, as well as snow knives. The new technology lent itself to both carving and engraving, for which the Cro-Magnons and Siberians were famous.

Specialized antler and bone technologies were a product, very largely, of northern environments in later times. Fully grown deer antler is an excellent material for making barbed or simple spear points and was widely used by bone workers in both the Old and New Worlds. In addition, animal limb bones were ground and scraped into tools, then hardened in the fire before polishing with beeswax. In about 8000 BC, the Maglemosian hunter-gatherers of Scandinavia developed an elaborate range of bone spear points, many of them used as fish spears.

Antler and bone technology reached its apogee with the Punuk, Old Bering Sea and Norton peoples of the Bering Strait after 1000 BC. These people crafted elaborate, multi-part weapons for hunting seals, walruses and whales. Many artifacts are works of art in their own right and had both ceremonial and functional roles in society. Judging from burials of the time, expertise at making bone tools was a sign of social status, and included the manufacture of bone and ivory masks.

The techniques for making antler and bone tools were basically simple and were adopted from

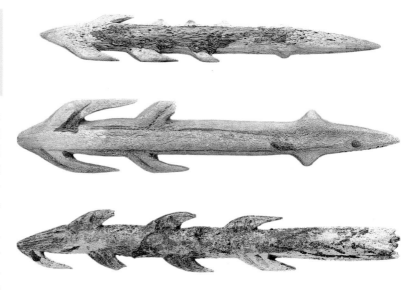

woodworking. They involved rubbing and grinding bone, as well as polishing it against coarse-grained stone, then finishing the surface with beeswax. Once the burin had opened up the potential of antler and bone, humans added lethal and highly practical weapons to the human armoury.

Reindeer antler harpoons with barbs, from Grotte de la Vache, France, c. 11,000 BC. Harpoons were highly effective weapons because they penetrated the prey's hide and stayed in place, causing internal bleeding and trauma.

NEEDLES & SEWING

About 25,000 years ago, Cro-Magnon people living in the harsh late Ice Age climate of Europe and Eurasia invented an inconspicuous but revolutionary artifact – the eyed needle, such as these from Le Placard, France. Again, the 'Swiss Army knife effect' came into play, for a sharp flint knife was required to shape a fine sliver of bone or ivory and a fine awl was needed to bore the hole. The needle was one of the most important inventions in human history, for it made tailoring possible – the fitting of layers of garments to an individual's body. It also allowed a tailor to meld hides, furs and other materials with different protective qualities into such garments as a hooded anorak or a sealskin boot with rabbit fur lining.

Layered clothing allows fast adjustment to rapidly changing temperatures; important today, this was vital in the harsh climates of the late Ice Age. Closely fitting, layered clothing allowed men and women to fish, hunt and work outside, and to add and shed garments as temperatures changed or when sweating during hard work. The needle was the nearly invisible invention that allowed late Ice Age people to live year-round on Europe and Eurasia's vast tundras, and eventually to settle extreme northeast Siberia and move into the Americas, some 15,000 years ago.

Grinders, Polishers & Polished Axes

My life is one demd horrid grind.
MR MANTALINI IN *NICHOLAS NICKLEBY*, CHARLES DICKENS, 1839

The great majority of stone artifacts that archaeologists discover were created by their makers chipping at nodules to remove flakes (p. 21). These are just one class of stone tool, however; other types were made by grinding and polishing the raw material. In many cases the smooth surfaces came about simply from the use of slabs and nodules of stone for grinding coarse materials, notably dry seeds, cereal grain and minerals.

Such artifacts become particularly prevalent on sites dating from the end of the last Ice Age, after around 12,000 years ago, a time when there were many types of wild plants to collect or people had begun to cultivate cereals. But the earliest examples reach back to the height of the Ice Age at 20,000 years ago, and perhaps beyond.

The earliest evidence

Some of the oldest known grinding stones come from Cuddie Springs in New South Wales, Australia. This water-hole site is the only locality in Australia where human artifacts have been found associated with the bones of now-extinct large animals, known as megafauna. Recent excavations recovered 33 grinding stone fragments from a trench 150 cm (59 in) deep, with layers dating between the present day and more than 30,000 years ago.

A grindstone rim fragment from Cuddie Springs, Australia, made from sandstone and possibly up to 30,000 years old. These artifacts were found in association with the bones of large animals that are now extinct.

Many of the fragments came from layers which contained bones from butchered animals. Microscopic remains of plant tissues and a distinctive polish on the stone confirmed that they had been used for grinding seeds.

Although these fragments may not be impressive to look at, they are extremely important for understanding prehistoric lifestyles. Recent Aborigines have been dependent on grinding stones to survive in the desert regions of Australia; before the Cuddie Springs finds the oldest known grinding stones were only 5000 years old. The new discoveries suggest that people may have been able to occupy the Australian deserts throughout the particularly arid period of the last Ice Age.

Notably early grinding stones have also come from Africa, especially from the site of Wadi Kubbaniya in the Nile Valley. The people who occupied this site 20,000 years ago collected a large array of plant foods and caught catfish when they spawned soon after the annual Nile floods. Excavations have revealed numerous grinding stones and identified the sandstone cliff from where slabs were taken and flaked into a suitable shape. Further late Ice Age examples have come from Rose Cottage Cave in South Africa. Residues survived on the surface of these grinding stones, indicating that some had been used for plants that contained starch and others for grinding minerals, probably to make pigments for painting cave walls and bodies.

Perhaps the largest array of grinding stones, and the most impressive, comes from the Natufian and early farming communities of Western Asia, around 12,500 BC (p. 91). They are found in a great variety of shapes and sizes, including massive mortars, large shallow grinding slabs and stones with 'cup-holes'. It seems likely that each was used for a particular

grinding stones	30,000 years ago, Australia
ground stone vessels	12,500 BC, Western Asia
polished stone axes	Neolithic & Bronze Age Britain

Left *Natufian limestone pestles and mortar from Hayonim terrace. It seems likely that different stones and mortars were used for processing different plants. Some were carefully smoothed and shaped, requiring an investment of time and labour, and may have conferred status on their owners.*

plant – cereal grain, acorns, pistachios – but exact identifications have so far proved elusive. Many of these implements had been deliberately shaped and smoothed before use; doing so required a considerable investment of time and effort and hence it is likely that they were regarded as being of some value. Some were very finely made and may have conferred status on their owners.

Polished axes

Prehistoric stone axes were also deliberately smoothed and polished by both hunter-gatherers and early farmers. Most hunter-gatherers simply chipped axes from nodules of stone and left the surfaces rough. The process of grinding and polishing to create a smooth appearance was very laborious and seems to have occurred only when required for special purposes. For instance, removal of the ridges left from chipping makes a stone axe far more efficient for felling trees. Polishing also creates very attractive implements and it is evident that these were keenly traded over long distances.

One of the best records of such movement comes from Neolithic and Bronze Age Britain, where petrological studies have been able to iden-

tify the quarries from which axes originated. Some are found several hundred kilometres from their source, often placed with human burials. They were clearly highly valued objects that were more likely to have been ostentatiously displayed than actually used for felling trees.

Below *A cache of basalt ground stone artifacts from the Natufian site of Wadi Hammeh 27, Jordan, as discovered. The group includes a pestle still in a mortar, a second mortar and two grinding stones.*

Baskets & Basketry

The baskets began to walk, and they entered the water after having eaten many Indians.
They are the cayman alligators – you've only got to look at their skins to see that.

DE CIVRIEUX, CITED BY GUSS, 1989

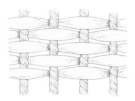

Weaving: strands are rigid, or fixed in a loom, and interlaced with crossing strands.

Below *A Roman relief from Neumagen, Germany, 2nd century AD: the lady of the house sits on a wicker chair while her hair is styled.*

Gathering and storing foodstuffs are not uniquely human activities – ants and squirrels are just two creatures that do the same. The use of containers for such foodstuffs is, however, a human invention, and a very early one, which enables the transport and storage of bulk goods and fluids. The earliest containers would have been made of various perishable materials, none of which have survived the ages. Hence the term 'Stone Age' is applied to a period when people must have also made extensive use of a range of organic materials.

Before the invention of pyrotechnology, the techniques of controlling fire by which humanity produced pottery and metalwork, natural objects such as eggs, shells and gourds were used as containers. And with relatively minimal effort, animal materials such as skins and bladders were also transformed into containers. Other plant materials, such as leaves, bark and twigs, could be folded and intertwined to hold goods. And from very early periods in human prehistory incredibly fine basketwork was produced that could hold fluids such as milk and water.

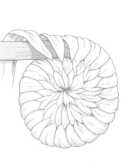

Perishable organic materials survive only in exceptional circumstances of preservation, such as permafrost, waterlogged situations or extremely dry conditions, as found in caves, tombs or desert sites, and our knowledge of ancient basketry is based on finds from such locations. The earliest surviving evidence of basketry is Neolithic and comes from several areas of the world – from North America (Hinds Cave, *c.* 7500 BC), to Turkey (Çatalhöyük, *c.* 6000 BC) and Egypt (Faiyum A, *c.* 5000 BC). For Asian basketry, we have to rely mostly on the study of present-day and historic examples.

Techniques & materials

Basketry is made from lengths of leaves or twigs that are often allowed to retain their original form. The basic techniques are very similar all over the world – variations lie in the raw materials used, and the shape, decoration and function of the finished basket. Technological differences are mostly noticeable in details such as the insertion of new lengths of material and the start and finishing of the work. But using this limited range of techniques, basketmakers created an enormous variety in the pattern, spacing and rigidity of the strands.

Techniques used changed through time also. In ancient Egypt, for instance, plaited basketry was not produced until the Graeco-Roman period, while twining, coiling and weaving were widespread techniques, found from the earliest periods of Egyptian civilization and still used today.

Northern European basketry was usually made of more rigid materials – willow rods, pine roots, hazel skeins and dogwood were among the preferred materials. We have very few examples of Roman period baskets, but depictions on reliefs show beautiful examples of wicker chairs. Rushes and sedges were used to produce mats. Southern European basketry was made mostly of less sturdy materials, such as halfa grass and rushes, using the twining technique.

Most basketry remains from Mesopotamia have been found in the form of impressions in the soil or on the bases of pots. Coiling was the most widespread technique, but remains of plaited mats occur side by side with coiled baskets from the Neolithic period onwards.

Above left *A large reed basket from the tomb of Tutankhamun, in Egypt, 14th century BC, still containing dried fruit.*

Above *Coiling is a technique in which a rod or bundle of material (the 'foundation') is fixed in a coil, with a strand that wraps around it and holds it in place.*

Left *An openwork basket from Roman Egypt.*

Below *Plaiting or weaving in three orientations is used widely for lattice work.*

African basketry was generally made of flexible materials, such as palm leaf and grasses. There are many surviving examples from ancient Egypt – the pharaoh Tutankhamun had more than 120 coiled baskets, most of them filled with dried fruits, to take with him to the afterlife.

The preferred material in Asia was bamboo, and modern examples of basketry from Indonesia, the Philippines, China, Vietnam and Japan show that a trained basketmaker can create true works of art out of finely cut strips of bamboo. Plaiting was the most frequently employed technique. Apart from bamboo, other widely used materials were grasses, rotan (a climbing palm species) and pandan.

Neolithic as well as historical native North American basketry employed sotal, yucca, agave, tree roots and grasses. The earliest examples from the Americas show as wide a variety in techniques and materials as more recent basketry. The colourful decorative patterns produced mostly in coiled, but also in plaited, Native American baskets of the last few centuries are stunning. South American baskets were made of vine, palm leaves, grasses and wood splints, mostly created using plaiting or twining techniques. Plaited trays were decorated with bi-coloured, intricate geometrical patterns that often contain a world of meaning.

Function & meaning

Basketry of all forms was used for a wide variety of purposes. From studying ethnographic examples around the world, it soon becomes apparent that the function of a particular basket is often very specific. Thus, for instance, a bread basket could not possibly be employed for storing dried dates. Basketry can even be used to contain fluids and to cook in (by throwing heated stones in the liquid-filled basket). Still today, very finely coiled basketry is used when milking camels in the Sahara and for cooking fluids in some traditional Native American rituals.

Basketry was produced not only as functional, often disposable, packaging material, but also as finely crafted heirlooms. From a finely plaited ring, made of one leaf of shining golden straw, to a complete house on the steppes of Mongolia, the versatility of this invention is almost beyond imagination.

In many areas of the world basketry had meaning and metaphors interlaced in its fabric or its decoration. Categories such as male and female, age and social status, contact with the gods and spirits, requests for protection, health, wealth and happiness were an intrinsic part of this seemingly modest material.

KEY DATES

earliest evidence for basketry	North America, *c.* 7500 BC
	Turkey, *c.* 6000 BC
	Egypt, *c.* 5000 BC

Below right *An early 18th-century lidded rivercane Cherokee basket, from the southwestern United States. Such baskets are made from strips of cane, which are dyed and plaited to create the patterns.*

Below *Plaiting is a technique in which a number of strands, which have not been fixed, are made into a fabric by interlacing them with crossing strands.*

Pottery

Pot-making is perhaps the earliest conscious utilization by man of a chemical change....
The essence of the potter's craft is that she can mould a piece of clay into any shape
she desires and then give that shape permanence by 'firing'.

V. GORDON CHILDE, 1956

Pottery in one form or another has become a ubiquitous part of our material culture. Many people live in houses built with bricks and tiles, and most civilizations have relied on ceramic cooking pots, serving bowls, storage vessels or religious figurines. But the origins of pottery must be explained from the viewpoint of the hunter-gatherers and early agriculturalists who first pioneered the shaping and firing of clay. The multiple locations and diverse contexts in which pottery was first developed suggest that there was no single cause for these independent inventions. The identification of the earliest pottery, combined with disputes over dating, leads to vibrant debate and constant revisions to our knowledge.

Pottery technology

Pottery-making combines all four of the basic elements identified by the Greeks (Earth, Water, Fire and Air), using raw materials that are widely available. Clays used in making pottery consist of fine-grained, flat, plate-like crystals, which glide over each other when wet, making the material easily malleable. The earliest pottery was primarily shaped by pinching, coiling, slab-building or moulding. Potters alter the properties of the natural clay by adding tempers (such as sand, shell or grass) to reduce some of the plasticity, promote drying and reduce shrinkage. During firing the clay's mineral structure is permanently destroyed, causing the crystals to melt at the edges and fuse together.

In speculations about who might have been responsible for making the earliest pottery, it has been argued that women's role as foragers, cooks and managers of the home-base may mean that they were in the best position to bring together the necessary techniques of digging, grinding and mixing the clay paste, as well as forming, decorating and firing the first pots.

Multiple origins

The introduction of pottery has long been regarded as one of the landmarks in the development of human culture. V. Gordon Childe, in 1936, considered pottery making, together with the domestication of plants and animals, as integral components of the 'Neolithic Revolution'. Later, however, he acknowledged the unexpected results of Kathleen Kenyon's excavations in Jericho, where she demonstrated that a period of settled agriculture had existed prior to the adoption of pottery. But Childe died before the discovery that the Jomon pottery of Japan had been used by Palaeolithic hunters, gatherers and fishermen.

Although recent archaeological work has demonstrated that pottery was invented in a number of different circumstances and that there is no consistent relationship between the origins of pottery, the development of agriculture and living

Above *The head of an animal from Dolní Věstonice, Czech Republic. Thousands of fragments of small ceramic figures of animals and a few humans were excavated from this campsite of mammoth hunters, dating to c. 22,400 BC.*

Below *Knowledge of the malleable qualities of clay was well developed by the Upper Palaeolithic, as shown by these bison, 63 and 61 cm long, at Tuc d'Audoubert cave, France. The clay was shaped using fingers and a spatula-like tool (15,000-10,000 BC).*

For 10,000 years Jomon pottery was produced by foragers, fishers and hunters with no evidence for agriculture. By Early Jomon (4500 BC), the pottery is normally made with flat bases, and the beakers and deep jars are decorated with modelled appliqué clay and cord impressions ('jomon' means cord marked) to create textured designs which become more and more flamboyant over time. This vessel is from the Late Jomon period, 2nd millennium BC.

River, 13,000–11,000 BC, Transbaikal, 9000 BC), China (Yangzi River, 11,000 BC; Yellow River valley 8800 BC; and more controversially Wannian, 12,000 BC) and North Africa (Southern Sahara, 7500 BC), all of which were hunter-gatherer societies when they began to make pottery.

In contrast to this, it is now also widely recognized that throughout most of Western Asia, including Mesopotamia, the Levant and Anatolia, people were farming before they began using pottery. For instance, in the area of the Zagros Mountains people did not start to make pottery until 6300 BC, some 2000 years after adopting wheat and barley agriculture, domestic cattle and sheep, and living in settled villages. Furthermore, the comparatively late development of pottery in this region seems to be a local invention. The 'slab construction' used to make the pottery may have drawn on the prior use of daub, mud brick and plaster (which required chalk or lime to be burnt at temperatures in excess of 800°C/1472°F) for houses, as well as the use of sun-baked clay storage containers. After its invention, pottery was rapidly adopted throughout Western Asia for the storage, cooking and serving of agricultural produce.

in settled, rather than nomadic, communities, these three activities become interdependent in the continuing development of most societies.

The earliest date for pottery anywhere in the world has been claimed for the 46 sherds, probably from a single vessel, excavated at Odai Yamomoto, in the north of Honshu, the main island of Japan. Of these sherds, 30 had carbonized material on the surface, possibly indicating its use as a cooking pot; this carbon was dated to 14,000 BC. There are also several cave sites, such as Fukui, Sempukuji, Kamikuroiwa, with Incipient Period Jomon pottery securely dated to 10,500 BC.

Both the dating and the association with hunter-gatherers for this early Jomon pottery were at first controversial, and many archaeologists rejected them, but there are now similar dates for the first pottery in the far east of Russia (lower Amur

The earliest pottery in the Americas has been identified at Taperinha and Pedra Pintada in Amazonia, Brazil (5500 BC), where small, low-fired bowls are found in shell mounds created by foragers using the river's resources. It is not clear whether the occurrence of pottery in other parts of the Americas was caused by the spread of knowledge from Amazonia, or if its development in northern Colombia (4500 BC), coastal Ecuador (3200 BC), coastal Peru (2460 BC), Panama (2140 BC) and southern Mesoamerica (1805 BC) were independent inventions.

Ancient potters in South America developed a very wide range of natural oxides which they applied as fine slips and then burnished in order to achieve a smooth polished surface. For instance the Nazca of Peru used at least 15 different pigments applying up to 11 different colours on a single vessel. This vessel (AD 1–700) was probably a drum that would have had a skin stretched over the mouth (on which it is resting in this photograph).

Major differences in style, form and the social context of vessel use clearly show, however, that the technology was modified and developed for the needs of local people. For instance, in Mexico, the coarse, plain Purron-Espiridión pottery of the central highlands is contemporaneous (1600 BC) with the highly decorated fine bowls and jars of Barra pottery from coastal Chiapas. It has been argued that the latter drew on techniques for decorating gourds to adorn pottery used within competitive feasting or ritual display, whereas the more functional highland pottery was deliberately undecorated to down-play any social differences within a largely egalitarian society.

Functions of early pottery

In many cases, as noted, evidence for pottery production appears prior to that for agriculture, but the question remains, why was it developed? Most examples of 'pre-Neolithic' pottery societies were located on the banks of major rivers or seashores, where the varied environments provided a wide range of rich resources for hunters, gatherers and fishers. American archaeologist Brian Hayden has argued that pottery was initially a 'prestige technology' used by affluent foragers to display foods in feasting or rituals, showing off the wealth, or generosity, of the provider.

Surprisingly little of the earliest pottery is blackened by the sooty deposits and carbonized material which usually characterize the repeated use of a cooking pot on an open fire, or the very large pots that we associate with long-term storage. Bowls for presenting and serving are much more common forms, as well as jars that may have been used for cooking shellfish, possibly by placing hot stones inside the vessel.

It seems likely that some of the first examples of pottery, such as the vessels found in the cave sites of earliest Jomon, in Japan, were employed at seasonal camps of mobile foragers. But the production and use of multiple fragile containers is not conducive to a mobile lifestyle, and pottery production and use may have been one of the major factors which both encouraged and enabled the Jomon, and others, to develop fully sedentary communities.

A Chinese Neolithic painted bowl, used as a coffin cover; Yangshao culture, from Banpo, c. 5000–4000 BC. The bowl was placed over a jar containing the burial of a child, a method that was used by several societies in China at this period.

Developing traditions

In the longer term, cooking pots played a fundamental role in altering human diet, transforming many plants that would otherwise be toxic or unpalatable into basic foodstuffs (p. 113). As people became more aware of the diverse properties of ceramic materials, pottery was used for an increasing range of functions, and differences in forms and decoration could express social differences and religious concepts. Increasing sophistication and craft specialization also led to pottery's role as an object of exchange or as a container for tradable commodities. Furthermore, ceramic technology played a role in the development of other technological advances, such as providing crucibles for metalworking (pp. 41 and 46).

Kilns – semi-permanent structures allowing heat from burning fuel to be more efficiently channelled to the pottery vessels – are known from at least 5000 BC in Mesopotamia and the Near East. They make it possible to achieve both greater control over temperature and a more consistent atmosphere surrounding the pots, facilitating the production of painted and glazed pottery. A glaze is produced when the surface of the pottery

KEY DATES

earliest pottery	14,000 BC, Japan
	5500 BC, Brazil
kiln	5000 BC, Mesopotamia & Near East
potter's wheel	3500 BC, Mesopotamia & Near East

Above *Most early pottery was fired in open firings, where pots are surrounded by the fuel. This can mean that much of the heat is lost, but skilful arrangement of the pottery and fuel can achieve temperatures up to 900°C. The low protective wall that formed a wind break round this firing in Raqchi, Peru, has been removed, but the ash from animal dung and grass fuel rests on top of a layer of bowls which protected the larger, more vulnerable, jars.*

Far right *Skilled control of kiln firing is best illustrated by the precise conditions needed to achieve Attic red-figure ware pottery produced in Athens 530–330 BC. This wine vessel, depicting the sphinx who guarded the dead, was one of a group of pots found in a grave near Capua, Italy.*

Right *Detail of a wall-painting in the tomb of Baqt, at Beni Hasan, Egypt, c. 1970 BC. The scene begins with potters preparing the clay by treading it; they then shape vessels on turntables and finally fire them in kilns.*

becomes fully vitrified, a process assisted by the presence of a flux such as lead oxide which lowers the temperature at which vitrification occurs. Although faience was produced in Egypt and Mesopotamia from the 5th millennium BC, alkaline glazed pottery (using plant ash) was developed at the same time as glass (1500 BC) in Mesopotamia (p. 49); lead glaze was developed more or less simultaneously over a thousand years later (c. 100 BC) in China, the Mediterranean and Egypt.

The potter's wheel, common in Mesopotamia and the Near East from about 3500 BC and introduced to Egypt and the Aegean c. 2400 BC, provides a centrifugal force against which the potter can squeeze and lift the very moist clay, allowing the skilled potter to make many more pots per hour. Potters forming their vessels on the wheel usually prefer fine plastic pastes, a coarse fabric being both irritating to the potter's hands and less responsive to the forming technique. On the other hand, finer fabrics tend to be less tolerant of sudden changes in firing temperature and benefit from the steadier, controlled firing that a kiln can offer, explaining the frequent (but not universal) co-occurrence of wheel-forming and kiln-firing.

In China continuing experimentation with kiln technology and ceramic pastes achieved very high-temperature firings, leading to the development of porcelain. New World potters did not use the wheel, and, although they developed a range of kiln-like structures, production focused on relatively low-fired earthenware pottery with a greater emphasis on creating complex sculptural forms and elaborate decoration using oxides.

Copper, Bronze, Gold & Silver

In truth, in all works of agriculture, as in other arts, implements are used which are made of metals …
for this reason metals are of the greatest necessity for man.

GEORGIUS AGRICOLA, 1556

The exploitation of metals had a profound effect on human society. Metals also represent an important stage in humanity's technical development as the first truly synthetic materials. Pyrotechnology had come of age and inorganic chemistry had begun.

As an invention, metals, like pottery, pose a problem that has long been debated – was metallurgy invented in a limited number of places, in the Middle East for the Old World, and in the central Andes for the Americas, or did metallurgy emerge independently in a large number of places when human social evolution had reached the required sophistication? Joseph Needham, the historian of Chinese science and technology, addressed this question and concluded that simple technologies are likely to have been invented again and again, but that complex ones probably spread out from a limited number of centres.

So, in the case of metals, copper and lead smelting are relatively simple and may well have been invented in many places (see below), but the more complex iron smelting is likely to have been invented just once (see p. 46). With the simpler technologies, perhaps small items of metalwork from the existing metal-producing centres could have been traded or gifted over large distances, inspiring the local invention of metallurgy in those areas fortunate enough to possess the necessary native metals and ores.

Copper

The hunter-gatherers of the Palaeolithic period seem to have had no use for metal. The first metal, copper, occurs naturally in a metallic form, and was used in very limited quantities from about the 8th millennium BC by Neolithic communities in the Middle East. It is found, along with exotic and interesting semiprecious stones, fashioned into beads or pendants. It seems that the copper was valued for its aesthetic qualities – the time when metal could challenge stone as the material for tools and weapons lay millennia hence. Around the 6th millennium BC, possibly in Anatolia or northern Mesopotamia, the first metals were smelted, that is the metal ores, usually oxides or carbonates, were heated in a reducing atmosphere with charcoal to produce the molten metal.

Native copper becomes very brittle when worked unless heated to red heat (annealing). If this heating is taken up to about 1100°C (2012°F) the metal melts. Once this was discovered it would soon have been realized that here was a way to turn tiny fragments of unusable copper into a single ingot, by strongly heating them in a pottery crucible, covered with charcoal to stop them oxidizing until they melted. Native copper occurs in parent copper mineral deposits, and it would also have been noted that if the green minerals

A complex copper casting, perhaps a sceptre or staff, found in the so-called Cave of the Treasure, at Nahal Mishmar, Israel, and dating to the 4th millennium BC.

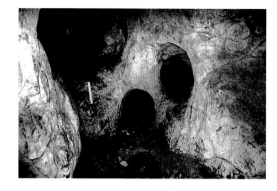

A small mining gallery at Kestel, southern Anatolia. This is the world's earliest tin mine, worked in the 3rd millennium BC.

Below left A Greek red-figure vase, known as the 'Foundry Cup', 5th century BC, showing metalworkers making bronze statues.

Below right Reconstruction of a furnace and bronze-casting pit, in this case for making statues, Classical Greece.

were included there was more copper in the crucible at the end. Finally, some genius left the native copper out altogether and just heated the copper minerals with charcoal to produce metal. Fragments of the crucibles used for this process have been found in the Middle East and the Balkans through the 6th and 5th millennia BC. By the 5th millennium BC, copper smelting is attested in Central Europe, and in the British Isles by the mid-3rd millennium BC. Copper smelting is currently believed to have begun around the 4th millennium BC in China, and in the Andes of central South America by about the end of the 2nd millennium BC.

It would have been noted that the molten copper retained the shape of the bottom of the crucible in which it had set. It followed that if the molten metal was poured into a shaped hollow in dry ground or a suitably carved stone it would set into a useful shape. Casting had been invented.

Bronze

Copper is actually quite difficult to cast and is a rather soft metal. A much better material could be obtained by mixing two metals to make an alloy. The most familiar alloy of antiquity is bronze, the alloy of copper with about 10 per cent of tin, although amounts vary greatly between 5 and 15 per cent. Bronze appears in the Old World in Mesopotamia and Anatolia around the beginning of the 3rd millennium BC. The one problem is that tin is a relatively rare metal. Recently, archaeologists have found remains of early production at Kestel in the Taurus Mountains of southern Anatolia, and the mine seems to have been worked through the 3rd millennium BC, but no later.

Almost certainly bronze was discovered independently each time copper metallurgy began in an area that had tin ores. Thus, in the British Isles there is a short period of copper artifacts in the mid-3rd millennium BC and then around 2200 BC tin bronze takes over in Britain and in western Europe generally. Almost certainly the tin deposits in the southwest of Britain had been discovered. Similar changeovers happened in northern China and in Southeast Asia around 2000 BC.

Molten bronze is much more fluid than copper, has a lower melting temperature and sets more slowly, and so is a better casting metal. Bronze is also much harder and stronger than copper, and thus is a better material for tools and weapons. At long last the supremacy of stone was challenged – the Bronze Age had arrived.

In the Americas bronze usage begins around 1000 BC in the area of present-day Peru, utilizing the tin sources of the Andes. Bronze-working spread slowly and only reached Mesoamerica in the mid-1st millennium AD, once again utilizing local copper and tin sources. In the Americas a range of small tools and ornaments were made, but it would be fair to say that there never was a Bronze Age comparable to the Old World.

Many parts of the Old World, notably the Middle East and India, do not have good tin sources and so there was an incentive to discover an alternative. This was brass, the alloy of copper and zinc. The problem here is that at the temperature required to smelt zinc it is a highly reactive gas. Thus metallic zinc was not isolated until much more recently. Instead brass was made directly by reacting oxidized zinc ore and charcoal with molten copper in a sealed crucible. This process seems to have been discovered somewhere between Greece and north India in the last centuries BC. Brass was soon being extensively used by the Romans.

KEY DATES

copper	8th millennium BC, Middle East
copper smelting	6th millennium BC, Anatolia or northern Mesopotamia
bronze (Old World)	3rd millennium BC, Mesopotamia & Anatolia
bronze (Americas)	1000 BC, Peru
brass	last centuries BC, Greece/north India
gold (Old World)	5000 BC, Bulgaria
gold (Americas)	2nd millennium BC
silver	5th millennium BC, Middle East

Gold

Gold appears relatively late in the archaeological record in the Old World. The first gold artifacts, dating to about 5000 BC, are from a Neolithic cemetery at Varna, Bulgaria. Almost always found as a metal (rather than an ore), gold typically contains between 5 and 30 per cent of silver. Initially it was used without refining, possibly with the addition of some copper. The introduction of coinage towards

A composite bronze vessel, a zun-pan, *found at Leigudun, with elaborate decoration, demonstrating the great skill of Chinese bronzeworkers at an early period, around the first half of the 5th century BC.*

the end of the 7th century BC in Lydia, western Anatolia, changed this (p. 250). Coins were pieces of precious metal of guaranteed weight and purity and so it was essential that those producing coins could control their composition and refine the gold to separate out the silver. This was done by taking gold dust or thin foils and gently heating them in a pot with common salt, a process known as parting. The chlorine and ferric chloride vapours so generated removed the silver from the gold as volatile silver chloride, leaving behind pure gold. Gold refining spread with the expansion of the use of coinage. Parting methods underwent little change until the post-medieval period in Europe and even later in other parts of the world.

In South America metallurgy began during the 2nd millennium BC and the working of precious metals was always important. South American peoples did not refine their gold, but they could control the composition, producing a metal known as tumbaga. Copper was first added to the natural gold-silver alloy and the artifact was made by hammering or casting. Next, the surface was treated with astringent chemicals to oxidize the copper, which was removed with strong brine or organic

acids made from fruit juices. The surface could then be burnished to give the appearance of pure gold.

Silver

Silver was used in the Middle East on a small scale from the 5th millennium BC. Native silver must have been used, or silver ores that were so rich that they could be smelted directly. However, most silver occurs as trace amounts in other metals, especially lead. The discovery of silver in lead ores, and the methods to release it, around 1000 BC, form the first attempts at the extraction of small amounts of one material from another. In the process, known as cupellation, the silver-bearing lead was heated to about 1100°C (2012°F) in a strong blast of air. This oxidized the lead to lead oxide – which either blew away, poisoning everyone around, or formed a molten mass of litharge. The silver would not oxidize but remained as a metal, 'floating like oil on water' as Pliny described in his *Natural History* in the 1st century AD. After the discovery of the cupellation process, silver became much more common and was used for prestige tableware, and formed the backbone of coinage systems everywhere.

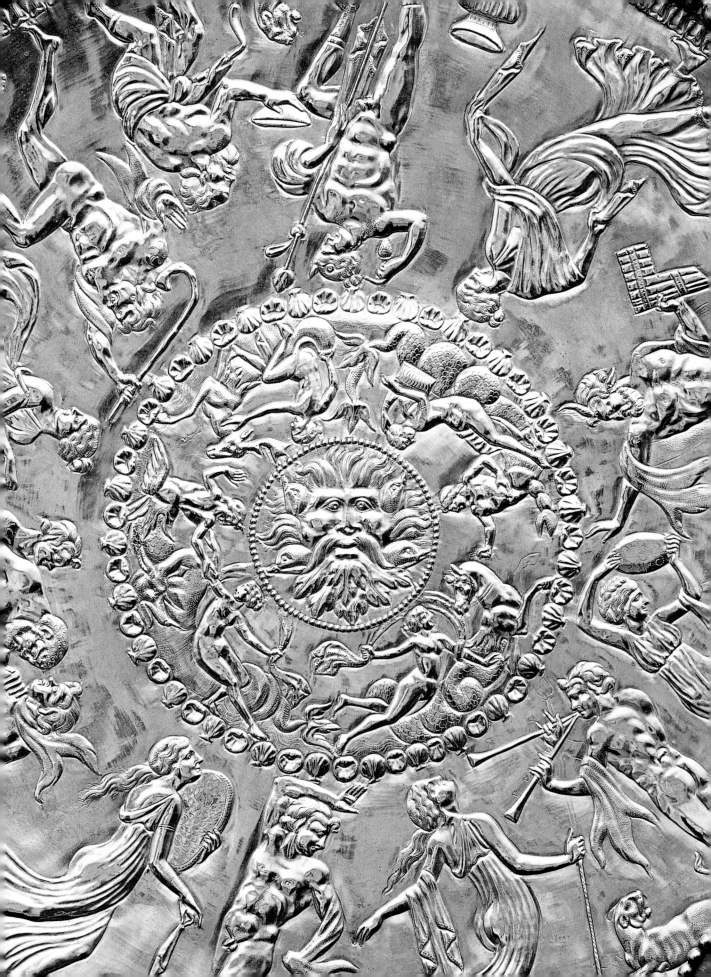

Iron & Steel

*As when a smith dips a great axe or adze into cold water amid loud hissing to temper it –
for therefrom comes the strength of steel – even so did his eye hiss around the stake of olive wood.*
HOMER, THE BLINDING OF POLYPHEMUS, 8TH CENTURY BC

Right *King Tutankhamun's dagger, found in his tomb in the Valley of the Kings, Egypt, dating to the 14th century BC. The hilt is of gold, the pommel of crystal, but the blade is most precious – it is of iron.*

Below *A Scythian helmet consisting of iron plates, 5th century BC, from Kurhan 2, near Novofedorivka, Ukraine.*

Ferrous metallurgy quite probably was a single invention that spread out around the world from the Hittite regions of northeastern Anatolia, where the ancient Greeks claimed iron had originated. It is possible that iron was invented independently in China. In the Americas iron was never smelted before the arrival of Europeans, but the Inuit of the far northeast, around Baffin Island, battered tiny amounts of iron from some huge iron meteorites that had landed there. An even smaller amount was obtained from the telluric, or native, iron deposits found on Disko Island off Greenland, apparently the only use of true native iron anywhere on earth.

Iron ores are very common, yet iron was the last metal of antiquity to be smelted because it has a relatively high melting point (1530°C/2786°F), which means that it was smelted as a solid.

And until quite sophisticated slag-forming processes had evolved, it was not possible to smelt it at all. The product was a solid lump, known in English as the *bloom*, containing bits of ore, fuel and slag which had to be squeezed out by hammering at white heat to create wrought iron. This technology probably evolved in the late 3rd millennium BC, but for many centuries iron remained a precious, almost mystical material, associated with meteoric iron, the 'metal from heaven'.

Tutankhamun had a single dagger with a blade of smelted iron set in a gold hilt as one of the treasures in his inner coffin when he was buried around 1322 BC. There is also a famous letter from the Hittite ruler Hattusilis III to an Assyrian king, apologizing for his inability to supply iron at present, but hoping the king will accept the accompanying present of a single blade. So in 1250 BC, a single iron blade from the one available source of iron was an appropriate placatory gift to another monarch; but just a few centuries later iron-making stretched from Switzerland to China, and a royal storehouse of the 8th century BC at Khorsabad in Mesopotamia contained thousands of iron ingots and weapons, together weighing many tons.

Steel

The probable reason behind this explosive growth was the invention of steel, the alloy of iron with about 0.2 to 0.5 per cent of carbon. Iron objects would have been packed in charcoal dust and heated strongly for many hours, or even days, so that some of the carbon diffused into the iron. If this steel was heated to redness and then plunged into water, a much harder and stronger steel resulted. Homer refers to the quenching of steel in the horrible but graphic simile of the blinding of the Cyclops Polyphemus by Odysseus, who plunged a burning brand into his single eye, which sizzled like hot steel entering water. Examples of heat-treated steel are known from the beginning of the 1st millennium BC.

Iron and steel were a formidable combination that brought about many changes in society, both direct and indirect. No longer were communities dependent on supplies of copper and tin, often brought in from long distances and presumably at great expense. Most could now produce and fashion their own iron, and it was superior to any metal that had gone before. The overall effect was a great increase in metal usage, although not many new types of artifact. Over most of the Old World iron and steel were shaped by hammering – as iron could not be melted it could not be cast. Even so, major items were produced, as exemplified by the Delhi Pillar made in the 3rd century AD.

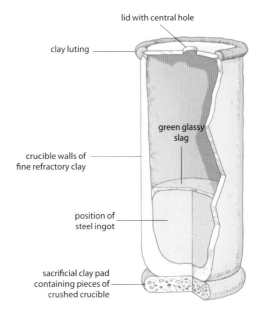

lid with central hole

clay luting

green glassy slag

crucible walls of fine refractory clay

position of steel ingot

sacrificial clay pad containing pieces of crushed crucible

Above *Cutaway drawing of a crucible used to produce crucible steel, excavated from early Islamic levels at Merv, 9th–10th centuries AD.*

Crucible steel

Steel made from bloomery iron had two serious problems: the iron contained slag inclusions which acted as centres of weakness; and it was also impossible to get a uniform carbon content through the iron. The obvious solution was to melt the steel, but the equally obvious problem was how to attain temperatures in excess of 1400°C (2552°F).

It seems these problems were solved by the late 1st millennium BC in the north India–Central Asia region. Finds of steel from the Hellenistic city of Taxila in the north of present-day Pakistan, include several that are free of inclusions and have a uniformly distributed carbon content that must originate in crucible steel.

Further evidence was provided by the Alexandrian alchemist, Zosimus who wrote in the 3rd

Left *A detail of the Delhi Pillar, India, weighing over 6 tonnes, forged in the 3rd century AD from many pieces of wrought iron.*

century AD that Indians made steel by placing soft (that is wrought) iron in a crucible with leaves and bark, sealing it and heating it very strongly. The product was a molten steel out of which marvellous swords could be wrought. Artifacts of crucible steel of all periods were always forged, never cast.

Crucible steel was widely used throughout the Middle East, Central Asia and India, but curiously, Europe seems to have been ignorant of the process until the 18th century, and China developed its own extraordinary and precocious iron industry.

China and early cast iron

Iron production began in China around the 9th century BC. It may have been introduced from the West, but equally it could have been an independent invention. Almost from the beginning, the Chinese produced liquid iron, known now as cast iron and made by what today is called the blast furnace process. To produce cast iron, the furnace conditions are made hotter and more reducing by adding a higher proportion of charcoal. In this process some of the carbon begins to dissolve in the iron, which reduces the melting point down to about 1200°C (2192°F) and gives a carbon content of 4.3 per cent. This white cast iron is extremely

hard and brittle, difficult to cast and impossible to work in any manner.

The great achievement of the Chinese was to make the iron more tractable. They did this by prolonged controlled heating of the castings to produce a range of cast irons, including grey cast iron, which is still probably the most widely used metal, and even malleable cast iron. Alternatively they burnt out the carbon altogether to produce wrought iron.

The blast furnace process was much more efficient and this enabled the Chinese to produce iron artifacts on a prodigious scale. By the Han period, 2000 years ago, China incontestably led the world in iron technology and production. By the 5th century AD there is evidence that coal and coke were beginning to be used to smelt iron – the world's first Industrial Revolution had begun.

Diagram showing stack moulds for the multiple casting of iron components for chariots. The individual moulds (a and b, exterior and interior) were linked by the central pouring channel (c), enabling dozens of identical components to be cast simultaneously (d). Mass production was in full swing in China over 2000 years ago.

a   b   c   d

Glass

There is a story that once a ship belonging to some traders in natural soda [nitrum] put ashore here [near the River Belus] and that they scattered along the shore to prepare a meal. Since, however, no stones for supporting their cauldrons were forthcoming, they rested them on lumps of soda from their cargo. When these became heated and were completely mingled with the sand on the beach a strange liquid flowed in streams; and this, it is said, was the origin of glass.

PLINY THE ELDER, 1ST CENTURY AD

Glass is a remarkable, and anomalous, material. It is a super-cooled liquid usually made by heating silica, soda (= alkali) and lime together. Products made from glass are normally created while the material is in its heated state. Perhaps most significantly, it is possible to make glass transparent – for the first time in human history it was possible to see what was inside a container without opening the lid. In later times this property allowed scientific observations to be made in a manner unthinkable without this incredible material.

The origin of glass is somewhat obscure, but long predates the account given by Pliny the Elder (quoted above) in the 1st century AD. Glazed stones such as quartz and steatite were known in the Near East from at least as early as the 5th millennium BC, and so-called 'Egyptian faience' (a material made by glazing ground quartz) from around the same time. Despite this, it took several thousand years before the idea of utilizing the glaze without the stone or ground quartz 'core' was taken up. Indeed, the earliest glass objects we know of should probably not be considered as glass, in that they were not deliberately produced as such, but were accidents of faience manufacture.

Making glass

We do not know what prompted the making of the first deliberate glass – perhaps it was the realization that drips of faience glaze were translucent, or even transparent, and that small objects could be made from the glaze alone without the need to produce a core. Whatever the reason, this development seems to have taken place in Mesopotamia (Iraq and northern Syria) around 2500 BC, and the objects produced are small beads and amulets such as might have been produced accidentally earlier on. However, as Veronica Tatton-Brown and Carol Andrews have noted, 'few glass items of any kind are known from anywhere until the first vessels were made in Western Asia sometime before 1500 BC.' From this time onwards glass develops quite rapidly, spreading to Egypt and then to the eastern Mediterranean. Glass does not appear in China until the end of the Zhou period, when it is known in tombs dating to the 4th and 3rd centuries BC.

Most of what we know of the *making* of glass from its constituents, and of the early *working* of the resultant material, comes from Egypt, notably from the site of Amarna (mid-14th century BC). Here glass seems to have been

Above *This blue glass vessel is one of the earliest datable glass vessels from Egypt, coming from the reign of Thutmose III, 15th century BC. At this period glass-blowing had not been invented and so the jug was produced using the core-forming technique (see diagram overleaf).*

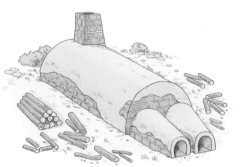

Left *Reconstruction of a 6th–7th century AD glass furnace at Bet Eli'ezer, Israel. Glass is first melted in the large tank which measures c. 2 x 4 m (6.6 x 13 ft), and is then broken up into manageable pieces once it has cooled and solidified.*

formed from its raw materials, possibly in a single-stage operation, to produce circular, slightly tapering ingots such as those known from the Uluburun shipwreck found off the Turkish coast.

It is possible that, as in the medieval and later world, glass might also have been made in a two-stage process: the raw materials would first be heated together at a relatively low temperature (800–900°C/1472–1652°F), in a process known as fritting, to allow the gases produced by the reaction to escape; then, on cooling, the sugary material produced (frit) would be ground and melted again at higher temperatures of around 1100°C (2012°F).

Glass vessels

The earliest glass vessels from Western Asia, Egypt and the eastern Mediterranean were made by a process known as core-forming (see diagram). A core of mud, straw and dung or other friable materials was first formed around a rod and made to the shape of the interior of the desired vessel. This was dried, perhaps lightly fired, and then coated with glass. There is debate as to how the glass was added – it may have been achieved by heating lumps of raw glass and pressing the heated core against them so that they stuck, or the core may

have been dipped into the molten glass batch which was then wound around it. The glass-covered core would then be rolled smooth on a flat surface, known as a marver, and shaped to give the form of the outside of the vessel. Rods of different colours could be softened and applied to the body and then marvered in; by pulling the coloured threads with a tool they could be made into chevron or swag shapes. The vessel stand was then shaped using pincers, and the rim might be added using a coloured rod. Handles were also added separately.

The finished vessel, still with its core inside, would now be set aside to cool very slowly in a process known as annealing. In later times we know that this was done in a chamber of the main melting furnace. Here the piece might cool over several days, during which time the stresses developed in the glass would be released, leaving it in a useable state. This annealing process is necessary for glass whether or not it is core-formed. The core would then be removed by breaking it up a little at a time. It is not usually possible to remove all the core, and an impression of its texture is left on the inside of the vessel, making it appear more opaque than would otherwise be the case.

Vessels might also be made by taking rods or canes of glass, slicing them thinly and arranging the slices in a mould of the required vessel shape. This could then be heated so that the edges of the slices softened and melted together. In this way multi-coloured glass could be made; this is strictly known as mosaic glass, but is often called 'mille-fiori' following its development in the Italian Renaissance. It is also possible to cast glass as a solid shape in a mould, or even to work an object from cast blanks. The glass headrests found in the tomb of the Egyptian pharaoh Tutankhamun may have been made by casting the basic form and then carefully polishing and grinding to produce the finished shape.

Glass-blowing

The greatest single invention following that of glass itself is glass-blowing. Sometime in the 1st century BC, probably on the Syrian coast, it was realized that rather than simply collecting glass on a

Above *Stages in the making of an Egyptian core-formed vessel.*

Right *A gold-band lidded box of the 1st century AD, probably found in Italy. Bands of different colours – dark blue, green, purple, white plus gold foil – were cast and formed into the wavy pattern.*

Left *A bowl of mosaic glass, or 'millefiori', created using a mould. This is a typical product of a workshop in the eastern Mediterranean of the 2nd century BC.*

Below *The Portland Vase: this late 1st-century BC or early 1st-century AD vessel is made of deep blue glass that has been blown and then 'cased' in a layer of white glass. Next, the two layers were blown together as a single object to achieve the final shape, the handles added and the vessel annealed. The white layer was laboriously cut away to give the cameo effect. It is a striking example of the accomplished work already being undertaken a short time after the invention of glass-blowing.*

rod to pull into vessel handles or to make canes, it would be possible to use a hollow rod to blow air into the glass, thus dispensing with the core. By rolling the hot glass bubble on the marver stone and using tongs and other implements, the bubble could be shaped into the desired vessel. This technique rapidly spread across the Roman world, but took some five centuries to reach China. Elsewhere it rapidly became the norm for glass production well into the 19th century AD.

A refinement on glass-blowing is mould-blowing. In this technique the bubble of glass is blown into a mould made of several pieces which has any desired decoration carved into it. In this way vessels which included complicated scenes or inscriptions in relief could be produced. Handles or other appendages could be added by applying softened glass from the batch, just as before. Mould-blowing is known by the late 1st century AD and with mechanized refinements is still in use today.

Window glass

Window glass is another Roman invention, known in Italy from the 1st century AD. The glass itself is of the same basic composition as for vessels, but unlike some vessel glass it was less commonly decolourized and so retains a green or

A two-handled cup signed by the Roman glassmaker Ennion. This piece, made in the mid-1st century AD, is an example of mould-blown glass. The decoration was produced in the mould as part of the body, and the vessel then had handles added and was annealed. Once annealed, the 'lid-moile' – the top of the glass bubble where it attached to the blowing iron – was removed to leave the vessel in the form seen here.

bluish-green tinge. Window glass can be produced by pouring a pool of glass, pressing it into a flat disc and then stretching it with tongs to make a rectangular shape from which panes can be cut (after it has annealed).

This was the main technique in use between the 1st and 3rd centuries AD and produces a translucent glass which is shiny on one side and matt on the other. Alternatively, a cylinder of glass can be blown which is then cut longitudinally and unrolled to produce a flat sheet of glass. The glass so produced can then be cut into smaller panes as required. This method is known from the 3rd century AD onwards; the glass produced has two shiny surfaces and is transparent.

More rarely window glass was made by the 'crown glass' process, whereby a bubble of glass is blown and a rod, known as a pontil, is attached on the opposite side of the bubble to the blowing iron, and the iron itself is then removed. The now open-ended bubble is revolved rapidly until centrifugal force causes it to 'flash' open, creating a circular disc from which the window panes can later be cut. The crown, or 'bull's eye', is the point at which the pontil was attached. This technique is known from late Roman and, more especially, Byzantine times.

Cylinder blown glass panes made in a modern reconstruction experiment: the one on the right is not yet flattened out.

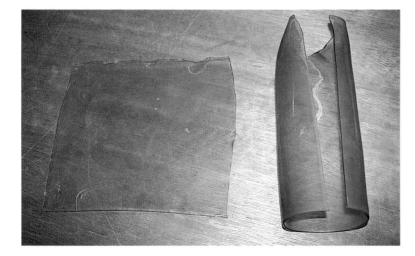

KEY DATES

glazed stone	5th millennium BC, Near East
glass beads & amulets	c. 2500 BC, Mesopotamia
glass vessels	c. 1500 BC, Western Asia & Egypt
glass-blowing	1st century BC, Syria
window glass	1st century AD, Rome

Textiles & Weaving

The brother spoke to his younger sister. The Sun god Utu, spoke to Inanna, saying,
'Young Lady, the flax in its fullness is lovely. … A piece of linen , big or small,
is always needed. Inanna, I will bring it to you.'
THE COURTSHIP OF INANNA AND DUMUZI, *c.* 2000 BC

Perhaps one of the more humble but still revolutionary steps in human development was the invention of a mechanized process to create a web of thread, or cloth, namely the loom. The advent of the loom, even in its simplest form, allowed the transformation of fibres and threads into a whole new class of durable, flexible, wearable materials, capable of bearing symbolic, social and aesthetic information.

The invention of the loom is ancient, and it has gone through repeated modifications and variations, culminating in the Jacquard loom capable of automatically producing complex compound weaves such as brocade. The invention of the fly-shuttle led to the Industrial Revolution, and the punchcards of the drawloom spawned the binary logic of the computer age. But none of these later ingenious inventions would have been devised were it not for the simple prior invention of spinning fibre into thread.

Spun thread

True draft-spinning is the twisting together of shorter fibres to create longer, stronger threads. This is done by hand and can be done more swiftly by using a spindle, which can retain spin longer if it holds a weight, or spindle whorl, to increase torsion. Spindle whorls are ubiquitous finds in

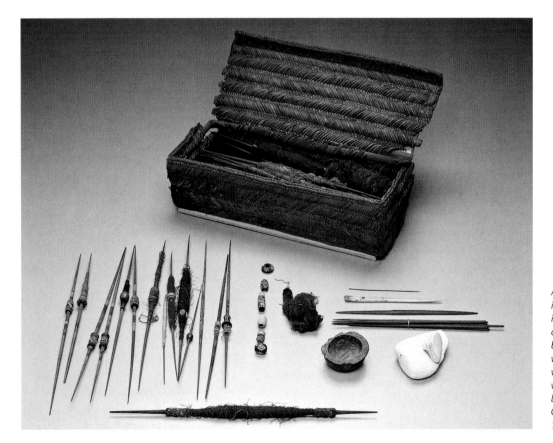

A weaver's workbasket with implements, reputedly found in a woman's grave. The contents include spindles, bobbins, some with cotton wound round and others with camelid fibre, and wooden spindle whorls. Late Intermediate Period, Chancay, Peru, AD 1000–1416.

archaeological sites. The qualities of the fibre (or fibres) used in making thread – length, direction of natural twist, scales or other surface features – each contribute to how the thread will 'draw'. These principal factors, together with fibre count and amount of twist in spinning, determine how the thread behaves. Thus the nature of the fibre used is very important in cloth.

The earliest fibre used in spinning came from plants, most probably the easily accessible soft downy seed hairs from plants such as cotton, thistle and milkweed. Current research points to South and possibly Southwest Asia as areas with the earliest domesticated cotton, *c.* 2500 BC. About the same time on the northern coast of Peru and Ecuador, New World varieties of cotton were domesticated and used in textiles, while highland dwellers began to work with camelid fibre.

Another type of fibre is bast, which consists of bundles of fibre cells from the stems of woody weeds such as hemp (*Cannabis* sp.) or nettle (*Urtica* spp.), and domesticated plants such as flax (*Linum usitatissimum*). Flax was the staple fibre in Predynastic Egypt. In Sumer and Babylon the wonderful

qualities of wool were discovered at about the same time that writing began, *c.* 3400 BC. Further east, cocoons from various wild silkworms began to be used for making thread – the earliest evidence for silk use is from Liangzu Neolithic in southern China, *c.* 2700 BC.

Methods of producing fabrics from looping and knotting thread can be traced back deep into prehistory. Another method of producing non-woven fabric involves displacing parallel threads on a fixed frame, called 'sprang'; a technique known in both the Old and New Worlds.

Felt

Fabric can also be produced from non-spun fibres, namely felt. This is made of matted or compressed animal fibres, which become permanently interlocked through mechanical means, using friction, heat and moisture. This process is sometimes encouraged by the addition of whey, which helps the scales on the fibres distend. Felt is very strong, withstands repeated wetting and drying, and is an extremely good insulator of heat. Clearly it developed only after the first exploitation of woolly

fleece and goat hair. And it was not found in the pre-Columbian New World, as camelid fibres do not have the same felting qualities as goat hair and sheep's wool. Felt is mentioned in Mesopotamian economic and legal texts, from Ur III (*c.* 2100 BC) to the Old Babylonian period. But the earliest archae-ological evidence is found in central Anatolia at Beycesultan, *c.* 2600 BC.

The loom

Although there are depictions of looms in ceramics and artwork as early as 5000 BC in Badarian Egypt, it is certain that looms were known before this. Recent evidence from Çayönü in Turkey shows that around 10,000 BC textiles were being 'twined', that is, weft threads were twisted around warps in much the same way as in basketry, but instead of being

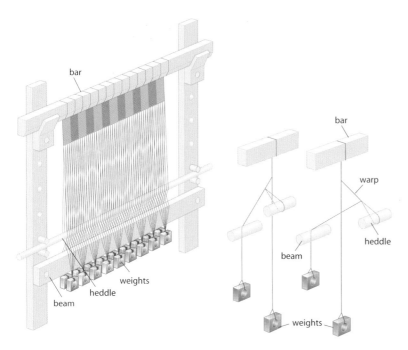

Above *Diagram of a simple loom. The warp threads hang from a bar and are separated by the movable heddle.*

Below *Weavers at work on a horizontal loom: model from the tomb of Meketre, c. 1985 BC, Egypt.*

Above right *A scene from an Attic Greek lekythos, c. 540 BC, showing a warp-weighted vertical loom.*

worked in a circular form, they were bound on to a frame, on a flat plane, with flexible warp threads. Even more spectacular evidence has come from Upper Palaeolithic sites on the eastern European Plain, such as Dolní Věstonice in the Czech Republic. Textile impressions in clay indicate both twined and plainwoven cloth were in use *c.* 27,000–22,000 BC.

This early evidence raises important questions in the field of textile history: what is the difference between a 'woven' textile and a 'twined' textile? And what constitutes mechanized weaving? Most specialists would define a textile as 'a web of inter-laced threads produced on a loom'. A woven textile can be distinguished from a twined textile by a close examination of its structure.

Weaving makes use of two systems of strands of material, most commonly in the form of thread. One system of strands is known as the warp and is parallel to the weaver; the opposing one is known as the weft (also 'woof' in older usage), which is per-pendicular to both warp and weaver. This is one set of binary components in weaving. Another is found in the binding, or interlacing, of wefts into warp in the simplest form of weaving, known as 'plainweave' or 'tabby'. This is where the loom comes in. By separating warp threads into odd and even sections, one section can be lifted at a time, and the weft thread passed through. The opposite section of warp can then be lifted, allowing the weft to pass through once more, and the action is repeated. Weaving thus takes place through the placement of wefts within the space, or 'shed', made by lifting specific warps at any given time.

Other types of weave work either on warp variations, such as paired warps, or weft variations, such as supplemental weft 'floats' which carry a design in the sequence of warp threads over which they pass; or there can be a variation of both. Some of the most complex weaves were done on relatively simple looms, with pattern rods in place to aid in picking out warp threads at any given pass of a weft, but still requiring hand-picked placement for the weave to be executed. During weaving any thread is either lifted or at rest – another binary system.

Loom types

Through time, the rudimentary looms of the ancient world gave way to new and more complex types, from the simple horizontal ground loom of Western Asia, the backstrap loom of Southeast Asia and the vertical frame loom of northern Eurasia, known also in New Kingdom Egypt. From each of these forms of loom came ingenious approaches to creating multiple shed formations (draft) in a mechanized fashion.

In the New World, a very different development took place. While looms stayed quite simple astonishing weave structures were created, which in some cases continue to defy reconstruction. In North America a vertical weaving frame was used, and in Mesoamerica and South America both the vertical frame and the backstrap loom were used. Nowhere has weaving developed to such a high art as in the Andean region of South America, where textiles of complex weave are known even from the earliest times.

KEY DATES

textile impressions	*c.* 27,000–22,000 BC, Czech Republic
twined textiles	*c.* 10,000 BC, Turkey
warp-weighted loom	*c.* 6000 BC, E. Europe
use of wool	*c.* 3500 BC, Mesopotamia
use of silk	*c.* 2700 BC, China
use of felt	*c.* 2600 BC, Anatolia
domesticated cotton	*c.* 2500 BC, South/SW Asia
	c. 2500 BC, Peru/Ecuador
treadle loom	AD 25–220, China

One of the most profound technological changes took place with the advent of the heddle. This device allows the lifting of designated warp threads into a shed. The more heddles there are in a given loom, the more complex a weave can be mechanized. Although it is not clear where or when this device was invented, what appear to be heddle bars are depicted on the very early Badarian bowl from Egypt mentioned above. Another important development was the treadle loom, which is, according to current knowledge, a Chinese invention, dating to around the Eastern Han period. By shifting the mechanization movement to the feet, a weaver is freed up to work with both hands much more efficiently.

Of the vertical loom type, one is especially interesting as it alone leaves behind traces that can be recovered archaeologically: the warp-weighted loom. This loom, first evidenced *c.* 6000 BC in eastern Europe, spread as far north as Norway and as far south as the Mediterranean; as far west as Spain and as far east as Syria. In what may simply be a case of independent invention, a tantalizingly similar type of loom exists among the native peoples of the Northwest Coast of America.

Cloth and its related processes of manufacture are integral aspects of social life as well as material culture in all human societies. Current archaeological research has begun to attend to these humble crafts of fibre procurement, spinning and weaving, as more sophisticated analytical techniques are being used to tease out information from the archaeological record.

simple looping

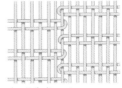

dovetailed tapestry

interlocked plaiting

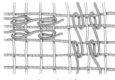

stemstitch embroidery

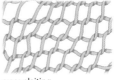

cross plaiting

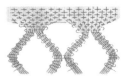

openwork tapestry

plainweave with weft float variation

Diagrams of different types of weave.

Left *Pottery figurine of a Maya noblewoman weaver seated at a backstrap loom, Jaina, AD 600–900.*

Shelter & Subsistence

Grass shelters, caves and rockshelters, thatched mud huts, stone mansions and imposing palaces: people have always lavished ingenuity on their shelter. For millions of years, humans lived on the move and their houses were often transitory, a simple brush shelter set up against the prevailing wind or a convenient rocky overhang or cave, the opening closed off with grass or hides. With agriculture and more intensive foraging came permanent settlement – the sedentary village and durable houses, occupied for several generations. Here food and artifacts were stored, meals were prepared, and people gave birth and died, sometimes being buried under the floor.

Houses were always built of the most convenient materials and with designs best adapted to the local environment. The late Ice Age hunters of the Ukraine fashioned winter dwellings scooped out of the soil and roofed with hides or sod supported on a frame of mammoth bones. Fired and unfired mud brick served well in the semi-arid environments of southwestern Asia, where thick walls provided good insulation. Ancient European farmers lived in temperate lands where timber and thatching grass abounded, allowing them to build substantial houses, often large enough for extended families.

The dynamic changed with stone, first used on any scale to fashion the great megalithic tombs of Stone Age Europe, followed by the pyramids of Egypt. Building in stone implies even greater permanence, and stone buildings became a mark of prestige, residences of gods and goddesses, and of the mighty. Only with the later empires did stone architecture become commonplace in towns and

The spectacular Inca site of Machu Picchu, Peru, perhaps a country palace of the Inca king, with well-built stone houses constructed on the terraces of the mountain top.

cities. And as it became more common, so innovations like the arch and the vault came into use.

With permanent housing came other inventions, especially furniture – chairs and beds, chests and tables – which required much higher woodworking skills involving such artifacts as the lathe, drills and specialized carving tools. A basic hearth was no longer sufficient for household comfort. The Romans experimented with hypocausts and simple forms of central heating, as well as with plumbing and water supplies, and also lighting. Sanitation became an important consideration when people began living in greater numbers in close juxtaposition, as did the technology of bathing. With crowding came a need for security, to protect precious grain and valuable possessions, even for the safety of one's family.

Housing and subsistence went together. The development of agriculture more than 10,000 years ago was not so much a dramatic invention as a logical extension of ancient foraging practices. By deliberately planting wild grasses more food supplies could be ensured. At first farmers used the simple artifacts of their predecessors. As the new economies spread rapidly, implements of tillage were developed, culminating in the scratch plough, a more effective way of turning over the soil.

Water was always a concern. Irrigation developed from simple beginnings in Egypt and Mesopotamia into massive, centralized waterworks controlled by a powerful bureaucracy. The swamp gardens of ancient Central America and the valley irrigation schemes of northern China and the Peruvian desert were also under close control. Irrigation required the movement of water, the development of pumps and watermills, which went hand in hand with such innovations as the rotary quern for grinding grain. And perhaps the greatest delight of all cultivation, the garden, came into fashion in early towns and cities, epitomized by the legendary Hanging Gardens of Babylon.

The domestication of animals was another great advance. There were the working animals – cattle, goats, pigs, and sheep – but also the pets and exotic animals kept in private parks and zoos for the delectation of monarchs. Some pets, like the Egyptian cat, achieved a divine status.

Some of humanity's more pleasurable inventions enhanced domestic life, with innovations in cooking and cuisine, and the consumption of grain surpluses as fermented beverages, important to fulfilling social obligations of hospitality. Food preservation was a problem in a world without refrigeration, although the Romans and Chinese emperors came up with ingenious solutions such as ice huts and deep pits, while Aztec nobles could buy mountain ice in city markets. Finally, we explore the world of exotic drinks, of tea and chocolate, and of the drugs and narcotics that played an important role in ancient religious life.

A magnificent Roman villa and its garden depicted in a fresco from the House of Marcus Lucretius Fronto, Pompeii, Italy. In their villas and towns, the Romans perfected techniques of water supply, sanitation, plumbing and heating.

Houses

Some in the group began to make coverings of leaves, others to dig caves in the mountains.
Many imitated the nest building of swallows and created places of mud and
twigs where they might take cover.

Vitruvius, 1st century AD

Dwellings in their most basic form provide shelter from adverse environmental conditions. In practice, houses are often far more complex and can play an important role in defining and structuring relationships within both the household and broader communities. Their form and material are influenced by locally available materials and environmental conditions, as well as by the lifestyle of the inhabitants.

Attempting to isolate the archaeological origins of the house is a frustrating and controversial exercise. Early evidence is difficult to locate, interpret and date, while the fact that a number of animals, birds and insects also build structures of various kinds could be said to remove 'building' from the category of great human inventions. We know that early hominids, like other animals, sought out natural shelters such as caves: evidence for possible inhabitation by australopithecines has been found at sites such as Swartkrans Cave in South Africa (1.8–1 million years ago), although the interpretation of bone deposition remains controversial.

In some later cases, the inhabitants made further modifications to their environment. In the cave at Lazaret in southern France evidence dated to around 130,000 years ago suggests that the inhabitants were already using rough stone walls and timber to build partitions and awnings.

The earliest evidence

Although caves provided shelter against the elements and some protection against predators, proximity to water was actually the most important consideration when siting a camp, and most early hominids seem to have lived in open-air settlements. At sites close to rivers, streams or lakes, humans built temporary shelters from whatever materials were locally available; the vast majority of which will have left no traces archaeologically.

Our earliest evidence may date as far back as the era of *Homo erectus* (*c.* 1.7–0.7 million years ago), perhaps contemporary with the domestication of fire (p. 24). Rough oval or circular rings and crescents of stones or pebbles found at sites in southern Africa are thought to have surrounded temporary structures, probably consisting of bones or poles covered with skins, although the precise form of these 'tents' and even whether they had roofs is debated. More secure evidence comes from much later sites, such as a camp at Molodova I in the Ukraine (*c.* 44,000 years ago) where evidence for 11 oval structures has been discovered, along with a larger structure of mammoth bone.

Plan and reconstruction of a Palaeolithic dwelling at Molodova, Ukraine, a tent structure covered with skins. Mammoth bones were probably used to weigh down the hides. Inside were a number of hearths.

Above *Reconstruction of a dwelling made from mammoth bones excavated at Mezhirich in the Ukraine, dating to around 15,000 years ago.*

Below *An artist's reconstruction of a house at Çatalhöyük, Turkey, dating to c. 7000 BC. Entry was through a hole in the roof by means of the ladder.*

Building materials

A potentially more productive approach to studying housing is to examine the way in which different building traditions developed. These can be shown to be closely linked to the materials available at any given site and also to the specific environmental conditions from which the inhabitants were seeking shelter. In some cases, locally available materials and environmental conditions changed little between ancient times and the early modern age, and interesting parallels can sometimes be drawn between archaeological remains and vernacular building traditions that still survive today.

Evidence for early framed structures, in the form of post-holes, is found in many parts of the world where wood was readily available. Wooden frames were tied together with rope made from plant fibres or with leather straps, and could be thatched with plant materials or covered with matting, cloth, bark or animal skins. The coverings of these structures were often quite portable and they were thus particularly suitable for temporary habitations; material for the frames could be obtained at the new site.

The Plains Indian tipi was constructed from straight poles lashed at the top and covered with animal hides: such structures are still in occasional use today. Traditional Chumash Indian houses in North America were hemispherical and were constructed from a frame of bent willow poles thatched with bull-rushes or a similar material; an opening was left at the top of the structure which could be closed if it rained.

Where wood was unavailable, fieldstone, mud, turf and blocks of snow and ice could all serve as building materials. Such materials are heavy and are therefore usually used only in permanent dwellings. In Europe and Central Asia a tradition of building huts out of mammoth bones flourished between 25,000 and 12,000 years ago. At Mezhirich in the Ukraine a number of such huts have been excavated, dating to c. 15,000 years ago. Mandibles and other bones were arranged over a frame of tusks and the whole may have been covered with mammoth hides. One of the huts has been calculated to have used bones from over 95 animals, although it is not thought that the mammoths were killed specifically for building material. At Kostenki, mammoth bones were cut and used as sockets for timber posts which would otherwise have rotted in the damp ground. In the 19th century the Inuit and Chukchi built structures of whale bone, using primarily the jaws and ribs and covering these frames with hides.

At Jericho in Palestine the earliest evidence for occupation dates to before 9000 BC, and it is possible to trace developments in local house construction. The earliest houses were built of clay lumps, probably with an additional timber frame. These were replaced by mud-brick dwellings, at first circular and later rectangular, some with several chambers. Çatalhöyük in Anatolia was a large and flourishing town perhaps as early as 7000 BC, consisting of numerous complex rectangular dwellings built contiguously. Access to these houses was through openings in the roofs, and streets were therefore surplus to requirements.

Environmental conditions

While the form of a dwelling is partly dictated by construction materials, the local environmental conditions are also an important influence. In arid (hot dry) climates solid masonry or mud tend to be the preferred building materials as these are poor conductors of heat; thick walls slow the rate at which the heat absorbed from the sun is transferred to the interior of the house. Flat roofs are common as rainfall is not a significant problem. Where possible, interior spaces have high ceilings with small openings set high in the walls to encourage air-movement, and openings face towards any prevailing cool wind. Houses with these features are found today throughout North Africa and are well attested archaeologically at sites such as Amarna in Egypt (c. 1350 BC).

Underground dwellings and rock-cut houses such as the extraordinary dwellings cut into tufa pinnacles in Cappadocia are also found in these climates: the mass of surrounding earth reduces daily temperature fluctuation below ground and conditions remain cool in high summer. Over 40 million people are still thought to live in cave-houses and subterranean dwellings in China alone.

In tropical (hot wet) conditions, lightweight permeable structures are often found, which promote maximum air movement. Pitched roofs are common as these encourage water to run off, and dwellings are often raised on poles to keep inhabited areas clear of standing water. Dwellings with such characteristics are found in many tropical environments, such as equatorial Africa and parts of Southeast Asia and Central and South America. Archaeological evidence of timber structures is rarely preserved in such climates, but ancient Egyptian wall reliefs of around 1500 BC record dwellings of this type observed on trading missions to East Africa.

In cold climates houses are often structured around a hearth and may be oriented towards the sun or away from any prevailing cold wind. Roofs

A view of the site of Deir el-Medina, at Thebes, Egypt, the village where the workers who built the royal tombs of the Valley of the Kings lived. The modest houses, built of rough stone and mud brick are quite standard in layout, with an entrance, living area and kitchen. Stairs led up to a flat roof where many of the daily household activities would have taken place.

Right *East African houses on stilts, possibly thatched structures on a timber frame, depicted in an ancient Egyptian wall relief from the Temple of Hatshepsut at Deir el-Bahri, c. 1500 BC.*

Below *The atrium of the House of Amandio at Pompeii. Beneath the opening in the roof is the* impluvium, *which collected rainwater. A shrine to the household gods was often found in this area.*

tend to be pitched to throw off persistent and heavy rain, while in areas with high snowfall roofs are steeply pitched: snow is heavy and can crush a lightweight roof if it is allowed to pile up.

Long processes of trial and error also led to the development of building forms and construc-tion methods suitable to withstand the natural disasters to which a region was prone. Solid construction stands up better to wind than light-weight framed structures. Raising a house on stilts can provide some protection against flooding and mud-slides, and also venomous reptiles and

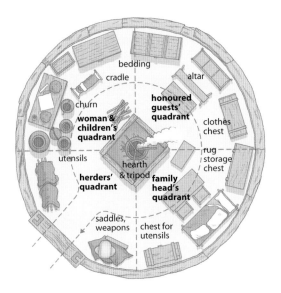

KEY DATES

cave sites	before 1 million years ago, South Africa
stone circles	before 0.7 million years ago, southern Africa
rough partitions	before 130,000 years ago, France
structures	before 44,000 years ago, Ukraine
clay houses	before 9000 BC, Palestine
rectangular dwellings	before 7000 BC, Anatolia

Left *The spatial organization of a modern Mongol yurt, showing the complexity sometimes found even in single-room dwellings.*

Below *Chinese model of a manor house (with and without roof). Early Western Han, 2nd century BC, from Yuzhuang. This is a fortified house, with outer wall, gates and tower, all reproduced in great detail.*

insects and other predators. Solid masonry proves stronger in resisting earthquakes than framed structures.

Houses as social structures

Although houses at their most basic are little more than protection against the environment, in practice there is scope for great complexity and differentiation of form, scale and decoration within many building traditions. Houses also play an essential role in structuring social interaction. Even within single-room dwellings such as Mongolian yurts the space may be notionally or physically subdivided. In multi-chambered dwellings, such as those at Amarna in Egypt or at Roman Pompeii in Italy, particular rooms, as well as having different practical functions, may be associated with different individuals or groups within the household or may provide different environmental conditions.

Ethnographic studies, such as of the Batammaliba in West Africa, frequently reveal complex and layered symbolic associations and rituals in the context of the dwelling, as well as a clear role in physically structuring and expressing the relationships between different members of a household. When houses are gathered into settlements, a range of associations and hierarchies within the larger group may also be expressed architecturally through scale, complexity of form or decoration, and proximity.

Stone Architecture

… a monument of eternity and everlastingness, of fine sandstone worked with gold throughout.

FROM AN INSCRIPTION OF AMENHOTEP III, KING OF EGYPT, 14TH CENTURY BC

Although rough fieldstones were used in construction in many parts of the world from early periods, the term 'stone architecture' usually refers to buildings or structures of worked stone. Traditions of stone architecture developed where good-quality stone was locally available, although occasionally blocks of stone were transported great distances. In Egypt blocks weighing up to 1000 tonnes were transported hundreds of kilometres for building projects, largely by boat; in Roman times imperial porphyry was exported from Egypt to Rome. The bluestone monoliths used to build Stonehenge were almost certainly quarried in southwest Wales, some 240 km (150 miles) away, and even the larger sarsens were transported a distance of 30 km (18 miles).

Foundations of stone

The most impressive early evidence for stone architecture is found in the Near East and Europe. The town walls of Jericho were constructed of stone as early as 8000 BC. In France, the Grand Menhir Brisé in Brittany is a stone monolith which, when complete, weighed around 280 tonnes. It is thought to have been worked, transported 12 km (7.5 miles) and erected around 4500 BC. Stone was used for many

A megalithic stone temple at Ggantija, on the island of Gozo, built between 3600 and 2500 BC. Some of the blocks, weighing up to 20 tonnes, are carefully worked and jointed.

kinds of buildings: the extraordinary megalithic tomb at Newgrange in Ireland dates to around 3100 BC; monumental stone temples on Malta and Gozo date to between 3600 and 2500 BC; and houses at Skara Brae in Orkney (3100–2500 BC) were also stone built (p. 71).

Pyramids & temples of Egypt

It was in Egypt that stone architecture took off. Despite earlier examples of stone construction elsewhere, the scale of the Egyptian monuments and the continuity of the building tradition are unrivalled. The Step Pyramid complex of Djoser at Saqqara, built c. 2630 BC, has long been considered the first example of truly monumental stone architecture, although an enigmatic but monumental stone enclosure nearby, called the Gisr el-Mudir, is now known to be a little earlier. The roots of architectural stoneworking in Egypt, although modest, can be traced right back into the prehistoric period at the site of Nabta Playa, where a small stone circle and evidence of stone carving have been found, possibly dating from as early as 5000 BC.

By the time the Step Pyramid was built, Egyptian craftsmen were already highly skilled at making stone artifacts, in particular vessels, often cut from very hard stone. Worked stone elements are also found in the tombs of the earliest Egyptian kings at Abydos of around 3000 BC.

The Step Pyramid complex displays many signs of craftsmen attempting to get to grips with a new material. The limestone blocks are fairly small but, for the first time, they were dressed into precise rectangular forms and carefully fitted with minimal joints. The designs of the buildings and architectural elements were based on structures built from other materials – niched mud-brick walls and post-and-matting structures – with all the details carefully rendered in stone. The architect was unsure of the structural properties of stone as a material: columns were left engaged to small

Above *The Step Pyramid of King Djoser at Saqqara, Egypt, c. 2630 BC. In the foreground are shrines built in the form of reed and matting structures.*

Below *The valley temple of King Khafre, Giza, Egypt, c. 2500 BC. The pink granite monoliths were quarried in Aswan and transported over 700 km (435 miles) to Giza. The temple was originally roofed with granite slabs.*

buttress walls and many of the 'buildings' have solid rubble cores; interior spaces are often little more than narrow corridors.

Over the next few generations, stone architecture developed rapidly in Egypt. In subsequent pyramids, such as those at Giza (*c.* 2500 BC) much larger blocks of limestone were used, giving greater stability and allowing taller pyramids to be built. Ramps were used for dragging blocks into position, although many of the construction techniques used are still poorly understood. The temples attached to these pyramids were also impressive examples of stoneworking. Vast pink granite monoliths were quarried in Aswan, transported to Giza, and polished and erected as pillars while, in later pyramid temples, monolithic pink-granite columns were carved with plant capitals. Black basalt was also used to contrast with the white limestone and pink granite, the colours chosen for symbolic as well as decorative qualities.

It is only really in the temples of the later periods (*c.* 1500 BC onwards) that larger and more complex covered spaces were constructed. Probably the most famous is the hypostyle hall of Sety I and Ramesses II in the temple at Karnak, with its massive columns and raised central 'nave' lit by clerestory windows. Rock-cut temples are also found, such as that of Ramesses II at Abu Simbel (*c.* 1280 BC).

The proximity of the desert plateau to the Nile Valley for much of its length ensured that prominent outcrops of workable stone were usually within a few miles of any major building site. Stone had two further characteristics in which the Egyptians were interested: it would last eternally, ensuring a visible presence on earth, and it could be carved with fine detail and elaborate relief (as long as the quality was good). Blocks were held in position by gravity as it was only later that strong mortars were discovered.

Only simple tools were used: limestone and other soft stones are thought to have been quarried using stone picks before about 1500 BC; the blocks were dressed with copper-bronze chisels and copper-bronze saws were used to create close-fitting joints. Stone tools were used to pound trenches around blocks of granite and to work and polish hard stone, although evidence suggests

Above *Cyclopean masonry at Sacsawaman, the temple-fortress overlooking Cuzco, the former Inca capital in Peru, c. AD 1500. The megalithic stones were finely worked and fitted together perfectly.*

that the Egyptians could cut hard stone using copper tools in conjunction with quartz sand.

Other stone traditions

Egyptian stone architecture is unique in terms of the scale and number of monuments, the quality of the stonework and the longevity of the tradition. However, stone architecture developed independently in many parts of the world. Impressive structures occur in situations where there was sufficient technical knowledge to quarry and work the stone (suggesting craft specialization), a large workforce and the desire to expend valuable resources creating monumental architecture.

In the Americas, the Incas used cyclopean masonry to great effect at sites such as Sacsawaman (*c.* AD 1500). Aztec architecture at Tenochtitlán (*c.* AD 1400) features a range of stone pyramids and shrines, while Maya monuments such as the Tomb

KEY DATES

town walls	before 8000 BC, Near East
stone temples	before 3500 BC, Malta & Gozo
megalithic tombs	before 3100 BC, Ireland
stone houses	before 3000 BC, Scotland
pyramids	*c.* 2630 BC, Egypt
cyclopean masonry	*c.* AD 1500 Peru

Opposite *The interior of the vast hypostyle hall at Karnak, Egypt, c. 1300 BC. The roof was spanned with single great slabs of stone. Columns had to be spaced quite closely because before the invention of the true arch, the distance that could be spanned by slabs was limited.*

The Parthenon at Athens, Greece, 447–438 BC, is an outstanding achievement of stone architecture and still influential today.

Right *The Sassanian Arch of Ctesiphon, Iraq, built c. AD 550, is a self-supporting arch of fired brick which spans 25 m (82 ft).*

of Pakal, Palenque, are earlier still (*c.* AD 675). In Europe, some of the most important developments in stone architecture took place in Greece, and monuments such as the Parthenon at Athens (447–438 BC) remain influential today. The design of Greek stone architecture is thought initially to have been influenced by the forms of wooden buildings, with columns, low pitched roofs and protruding beams. The skill of Greek stone masons is legendary: vertical and horizontal surfaces are actually slightly curved to compensate for visual distortion and the pediments and friezes were adorned with elaborate sculptures.

ARCHES, VAULTS & DOMES

A true arch is a curved structure spanning an opening; it is built of carefully fitted stones or other material and is capable of supporting its own weight and the weight of any structure above it. A vault is an extruded or continuous arch, usually covering a rectangular space. A dome is a rounded vault usually covering a circular or square space. The technique of corbelling – in which courses of blocks are laid so that each slightly overhangs the course below until a space is bridged – was often used to cover spaces in early stone architecture, although not considered as a true vault or dome. Examples are found in the Grand Gallery of the Great Pyramid at Giza (c. 2550 BC) and in 'beehive' tombs such as Maes Howe on Orkney (*c.* 2700 BC) or the Treasury of Atreus at Mycenae (*c.* 1350 BC).

Early stone architecture, such as that of Egypt and Greece, was roofed by spanning gaps with thick slabs of stone or timber. Neither stone nor timber is strong enough to bridge large gaps and, as a result, only narrow doorways and windows could be built and covered halls were packed with closely spaced columns to support the beams. Arches allowed wider openings to be spanned, while vaults and domes could be used to create large covered spaces unencumbered by columns. Although true arches and vaults are occasionally found in earlier architecture, it was only during the Roman period that these building forms were fully developed, aided by the discovery of strong mortars for binding and the availability of wood for building formwork. Arches were widely used in constructing bridges and stretches of aqueducts such as the Pont du Gard in southern France, while vaults and domes are found in monuments in Rome of the 1st century AD, such as the Colosseum and the Pantheon.

Furniture

Then I lopped the leafy crown of the olive,
clean-cutting the stump bare from roots up,
planing it round with a bronze smoothing-adze ...
Working from there I built my bed, start to finish,
I gave it ivory inlays, gold and silver fittings,
wove the straps across it, oxhide gleaming red.
HOMER, 8TH CENTURY BC

Once people had acquired the necessary skills and specialized tools to be able to work natural materials accurately, furniture could be made, initially to provide comfort and storage and then as a means of displaying an individual's status. At first furniture was made from materials that were readily available to the local community, but with the development of trade the movement of a variety of raw materials gave rise to the manufacture of more elaborate and decorative pieces.

Neolithic furniture

Some of the earliest evidence of furniture used within a domestic environment can be found at the Neolithic village of Skara Brae, on the Orkney Islands, off the north coast of Scotland (3100–2500 BC). As wood was, and is, a scarce resource on Orkney, the inhabitants built their furniture, like their homes, from stone. Items of a personal or symbolic nature were displayed in a type of 'dresser' constructed from slabs of stone, while the walls of the houses are recessed with cupboards

The Neolithic homes at Skara Brae, Orkney, would have provided their inhabitants with a comfortable existence. However, there would have been little privacy and it is possible that a screen may have been strung across the two taller stones of each bed thus partitioning them from the room. In front of the 'dresser' and facing the rectangular kerbed hearth was placed an imposing stone seat. The floor box, to the right of the dresser, is believed to have stored live fishing bait.

Howard Carter discovered an impressive collection of furniture in the tomb of Tutankhamun (14th century BC), including the first example of a Z-type folding bed frame, which used an ingenious system of metal hinges.

lined with stone. Each of the houses contained two stone box beds, which would have been fitted with mattresses of bracken or heather and covers of animal skin. Sunk into the floor of one house was a box-shaped cavity which was made watertight with a clay lining and may have been used to store fishing bait.

Furniture of the pharaohs

Ancient Egyptian homes would have been sparsely furnished, particularly those of the poor. Wooden furniture was reserved for people with a privileged position, while ivory was exclusively used in the manufacture or embellishment of royal furniture. Most homes would have contained little more than stools, tables, boxes, stands and screens made from reed stems bound together with rush. A small platform built from mud brick served as a bed by night and a bench to sit on during the day.

During the Predynastic period (5500–3100 BC), crude attempts were made to construct bed frames using the branches of trees bound together and covered with a matting of plant fibre and twigs. It is not until the beginning of the Dynastic period and the introduction of copper woodworking tools that wooden furniture began to be constructed in one of the three recognized constructional forms: stool, frame and carcass. This shows that carpenters were familiar with the working properties of wood and were able to form simple cut joints. At first they were limited by the poor quality of indigenous wood, but by the 4th dynasty, in the mid-3rd millennium BC, imported timber from forests within modern Syria and Lebanon allowed carpenters to design and manufacture marvellous pieces of furniture.

The furniture of Queen Hetepheres (c. 2600 BC), discovered in her tomb at Giza, illustrates these improvements. The queen was buried with a complete set of personal furniture, including a carrying chair, bed frame and a portable bed canopy. Attached to the end of her sloping bed frame was a footboard, while at the top was placed a gilded headrest – Egyptians did not use pillows but laid their heads on a wooden or stone stand. Within each open arm panel space of the queen's gilded armchair was a spray of three tied papyrus flowers, the heraldic plant of Lower Egypt, confirming her status as a royal wife.

Throughout the Dynastic period, bed frames and chairs were supported on legs carved to resemble animal legs. During the Early Dynastic period, a bovine form was favoured for low bed frames and stools. Chairs designed during the Middle Kingdom (2080–1940 BC), show that carpenters had now a clear understanding of measurement, proportionality and anthropometric design. Chairs have angled backrests of full height and the seat height was raised using slender and taller gazelle-shaped legs.

Royal furniture was richly embellished with religious and state symbols inlaid in precious metals, exotic woods, ivory and brightly coloured semiprecious stones. A remarkable collection of furniture, including an elaborate golden throne, was discovered in the New Kingdom tomb of the pharaoh Tutankhamun (1332–1322 BC), at Thebes.

Egyptians also used a range of different types of stool. The lattice stool was braced with angled struts of timber incorporating the technique of triangulation to increase rigidity. Artisans sat on three-legged stools, while folding stools were made from two interlocking frames pivoted together with a pair of bronze rivets. The middle classes used animal-leg and round-leg stools with double cove seats on which a cushion was placed.

Furniture in the Near East

Furniture manufactured in Assyria and Anatolia developed quite separate design characteristics, largely on account of the cultural diversity which had evolved in these individual city-states. We have evidence from Assyrian excavations that metal fittings began to be attached to furniture. For instance, in the palace of Ashurnasirpal II (c. 883–859 BC) at Nimrud, a wall-relief depicts the king seated on an elaborate backless throne. The quality and detail of the carving indicates the use of cast metal furniture fittings.

The ornate furniture placed in the Phrygian tumulus burials at Gordion, in Turkey, which date to the 8th century BC and the time of Midas, show that here people used three-legged banqueting tables. A mixed fermented beverage was served to them from bronze cauldrons mounted on wooden serving stands, the front panels of which were elaborately inlaid with intricate geometric patterns.

Queen Hetepheres' tomb at Giza was excavated by the American Egyptologist, George Reisner. He found that the wooden parts of the furniture had decayed to a fine powder. However, from the positions of the remaining inlay and gold sheaths which covered the furniture it proved possible to reconstruct the bed canopy, carrying chair, bed frame, an armchair, curtain box, headrest and a small bracelet box.

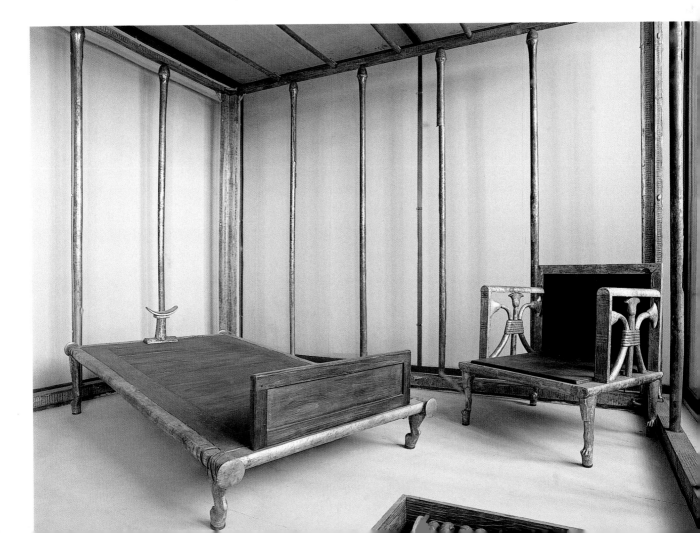

Greek & Roman furniture

Evidence of Greek furniture is found only in vase painting and sculpture as no wooden furniture has survived. The earliest examples show strong Egyptian influence, but by the 5th century BC a new style of furniture developed that is recognizably Classical in form.

The Greeks used a number of different types of stool, couch, table, box and chair. When dining from a table they preferred to lie on a couch, known as a *kline*. They also used the *kline* as a bed, and illustrations show that it was larger and higher than an Egyptian bed. Diners could prop themselves on a pillow placed against the headboard. A new type of chair, the *klismos*, was widely in use by 450 BC. This had curved legs and a rounded top rail, which gave

comfort and support to the curvature of the back and provided a relaxed and natural seating posture.

Technical advances in woodworking gave a large proportion of Roman society access to simple furniture. The invention of the woodworking plane and improvements in iron tool technology encouraged the development of a thriving furniture industry.

The Romans were also great innovators, modifying Egyptian and Greek designs. The magistrates' stool, the *sella curulis*, is recognized as the symbol from which justice was administered across the Roman empire. Carpenters introduced panelled cupboards with shelves and doors that were used either to store scrolls or display a variety of personal effects. Furniture was also cast in bronze and the tops of tables were made from sheets of polished marble.

Chinese furniture

Evidence reveals that the earliest Chinese were a mat-level culture who ate from low tables and slept on simple covered bed frames. A raised wooden platform was later introduced to elevate the individual, but the seating posture, cross-legged or kneeling, remained unchanged until the influence of Buddhism saw the introduction of the chair.

Furniture was often lacquered and inlaid with mother-of-pearl or painted with traditional Chinese motifs. Polished hardwood forms of fine quality are also attested that show a thorough understanding of line and form.

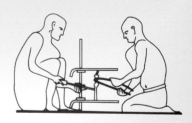

Furniture in the Americas

The stool was used throughout the New World as a badge of office, becoming central to the rituals preformed by each culture. The *duho*, a type of ceremonial stool used by caciques (chiefs), nobles, and shamans of the Taíno culture of the Caribbean has been linked to the hallucinogenic powers of spiritual communication. Examples were carved from wood or stone, some having sweeping high backs rendered in human, animal or hideous anthropomorphic forms. Others are found with elaborately incised designs or occasionally inlaid with shell, gold and bone.

From simple beginnings furniture developed steadily throughout ancient times utilizing new materials, techniques and inventions to create objects of function and form that were used to provide comfort and create a sense of cultural identity.

Opposite above *Assyrian relief showing King Ashurbanipal and his queen seated at a banquet, c. 645 BC. The details of the furniture suggest that the fittings were cast in bronze or another metal, perhaps gold.*

Opposite below *Roman couches and footstools, as seen here in a reconstruction of the Villa P. Fannius Synistor at Boscoreale, are often highly ornate. The framework and legs might be intricately carved from bone and then inlaid with tinted glass. Often both ends of the couch were raised and it had a mattress and pillows.*

Below left *The* klismos *was probably the most perfectly proportioned chair in the ancient world. Its influence is seen over 2000 years later in both French and English Neoclassical chair design. Using illustrations from vases and sculpture, T. H. Robsjohn-Gibbings reconstructed the elegance of the* klismos.

THE WOODTURNING LATHE

The precise date for the invention of the woodturning lathe has been the subject of much debate between historians and technologists. Many scholars hold the view, as reported by Pliny, that the lathe was a Greek invention attributed to Theodorus of Samos in the 5th century BC. The first pictorial evidence of wood turning using a simple reciprocating lathe is found in a carved wall relief in the Ptolemaic tomb of Petosiris at Tuna el-Gebel in Egypt (**above**), dating to the reign of Philip Arrhidaeus (323–317 BC).

Confirmation that the Phrygians practised wood turning has been shown by contiguous long chisel marks on the surface of wooden plates preserved in a burial mound at Gordion, Turkey, which dates to the 8th century BC, the time of King Midas. However, evidence for even earlier possible use comes from Egypt. A small number of round stool legs with clear pivot holes under their feet and deep, square-shouldered grooves around their circumference – suggesting that at some stage during their manufacture they were turned against a stationary chisel – have been radiocarbon dated to between 1630 and 1420 BC.

Lighting & Heating

It strikes me as amazing that practically no task can be completed without fire.

PLINY THE ELDER, 1ST CENTURY AD

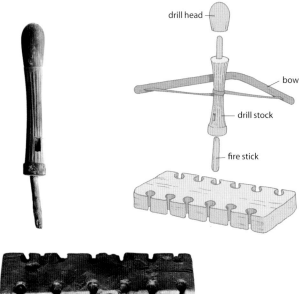

drill head

bow

drill stock

fire stick

Above *The wooden bow fire-drill found in the tomb of Tutankhamun, Egypt, 14th century BC, and a diagram to show how it would have been used. The drill holes were lined with resin to promote friction.*

Right *A Palaeolithic lamp carved from stone found in the cave at Lascaux in France. The artists who created the astonishing cave paintings of Stone Age Europe would have worked by the light of such lamps– though many would have been simpler – or torches.*

Opposite *A remarkably elegant Chinese lamp in the shape of a young woman; gilt bronze, late 2nd century BC. The sleeve of the woman's robe acts as the chimney for the lamp.*

In Greek myth, the secret of fire – 'a teacher in every skill and a means to mighty ends', according to Aeschylus (*Prometheus Bound*, 109–10) – was jealously guarded by the gods until Prometheus stole it and thereby initiated the technological advancement of mortals. The two uses of fire discussed here – heating and lighting – fully justify the Greek perception of its centrality to human progress.

Earliest developments

The use and control of fire by humans stretches back to our earliest ancestors (p. 24), who eventually developed fire-making by wood (or bone) friction. A fine example of a bow fire-drill was found among the artifacts in Tutankhamun's tomb (14th century BC), and a fire-drill was also used to rekindle the sacred fire in the temple of Vesta at Rome, if the perpetual

flame went out – an event the Romans feared as an omen of disaster.

For fuel, the ancients burnt predominantly wood. By the Bronze Age various types of plant matter (including charcoal and pitch) were also used, as well as oil, fat and coal, though the last only in Roman Britain and China. The different classes of fuel were recognized to have peculiar properties that made them suitable for specialized tasks. For instance, the Mesopotamians held that charcoal made from a particular kind of poplar tree was best for glass furnaces, and the Greek writer Theophrastus (*Inquiry into Plants*, 5.9) noted the various properties of woods and their relative usefulness for the production of fire. Such a body of lore had evidently accumulated over centuries of experience and experiment.

Initially, open camp-fires would have served as sources of both heat and light. Firebrands could be taken from the fire as torches if it was necessary to venture far from its light, but the formal separation of the two functions had to await the invention of candles and lamps.

Ancient lamps & lighting

The torch is the most basic form of lighting and was used extensively in the ancient world down to quite recent times. Wick-burning lamps are attested from as early as the late Palaeolithic period (*c.* 30,000–10,000 years ago). The artists who painted the cave walls of Europe would have worked by the light of lamps or torches. The essential elements of such lamps are a reservoir of fuel (usually olive oil, but fat or animal

oils could also be used) and a wick (often a reed, plant fibres or hair). In Classical times, salt might be added to the olive oil to prevent it overheating and so extend the lamp's luminosity.

Since hundreds of thousands of examples survive from the ancient world, the differences in the form of the lamp can be traced over time, and from culture to culture. Bivalve seashells were used at first, having a natural shape conducive to the required function – a shallow bowl with ridges to accommodate the wick at the rim. Indeed, when the Mesopotamians later made lamps out of pottery or metal, they would often fashion them in the shape of seashells.

Artificially made lamps can be simple carved bowls of stone with a projecting end; others are plain pottery saucers with a pinched side for the wick; yet others are more elaborate – shaped and decorated, and equipped with multiple wicks. Closing off the fuel reservoir allowed greater control over the rate of combustion, and thus of illumination. Attempts to manipulate the wick automatically were less successful. Experiment has shown that an ancient 4-oz castor-oil lamp can provide light for over 18 hours.

By the Roman period, pottery lamps were mass-produced and traded all over the empire. Lamps were usually set in niches in the walls of buildings, placed on stands or hung on chains from the ceiling. To generate even more light, the Romans developed the candelabrum, a stand that could accommodate many lamps. For outdoor use lanterns were available – essentially protective casings for the standard lamp. The candle was a relatively late development, appearing in the Bronze Age. In ancient times it was made by the dip-and-draw process – the candle is built up around the wick through successive immersions in tallow (from animal fat) or beeswax. Candles, too, could be bunched on to candelabra to illuminate a room.

Despite the availability of all these lighting methods, public lighting was all but unknown in most ancient communities, so that going out after dark required taking your own light with you. People of substance would be accompanied by torch-bearing servants who, in the absence of a police force, would also serve as bodyguards. Some public buildings might be illuminated at night, perhaps for special occasions, but there was nothing like regular street lighting until AD 350, when Antioch in Syria became the first city in the world to boast public illumination. In contrast, the first lighthouse had appeared much earlier as an aid to navigation (p. 169), in the form of the Pharos at Alexandria.

Above *A Roman lamp, from the House of Fabius Rufus, Pompeii, 1st century AD. This is an unusually large and elaborately decorated example of the typical Roman lamp, found all over the empire in many different variations on the basic form.*

Right *A brazier from the House of the Menander, Pompeii, 1st century AD. The internal iron container still held ashes from its use as a heater.*

Heating systems

The centrality of the hearth to many ancient dwellings (from caves to villas) is clear not only from physical remains but also by the personification of the hearth as a deity, such as Hestia in Greece or Vesta in Rome. Fixed hearths, such as the circular one in the throne room of the Mycenaean palace at Pylos, Greece (*c.* 1300–1200 BC), eventually gave way to moveable braziers, fuelled by charcoal. Water- and wine-heating stoves are also well attested for the Roman period.

The most sophisticated heating system of the ancient world, however, was developed by the Greeks and perfected by the Romans. It is commonly called the 'hypocaust', from the Greek *hypocausis*, 'burning below'. A primitive form of the hypocaust consisted of simple subterranean tunnels which channelled hot gases from a furnace underneath parts of rooms where heating was required and then out through chimneys in the walls and roof.

Under the Romans this simple 'annular' system gave way to a more complex device. In its developed form, the Roman hypocaust had multiple elements. First, the entire floor area of a room, not just a section of it, was raised on pillars (*pilae*), giving rise to the Latin name for the system, *suspensura* ('the suspension'). Next, the walls were rendered hollow by the use of specially designed box tiles. It is possible, though disputed, that special tiles in the roof may have served the same purpose, but too few Roman roofs survive intact to verify this. In this way, hot gases from a furnace could, in theory, wholly envelop a room.

The degree of heat could be regulated by making more (or fewer) of the walls into radiating surfaces. In bath buildings, a boiler was placed over the hypocaust's fire in the furnace room, so that the same flames heated both water and space simultaneously. Gases from the fire were drawn into the hollows under the floor and vented via the box tiles and chimneys, while pipes connected the boiler with the heated pools. Examples of the hypocaust are found not only in baths, however, but in the living quarters of the affluent and the barracks of military officers stationed in chilly northern climes.

Below *A schematic diagram of a Roman hypocaust and an actual example from the Stabian Baths at Pompeii.*

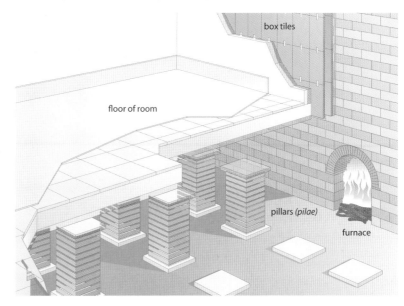

box tiles

floor of room

pillars (*pilae*)

furnace

Water Supplies & Plumbing

With such numerous and indispensable structures carrying the water from so many sources, compare, if you please, the idle pyramids, or the famous but useless buildings of the Greeks.

FRONTINUS, ON THE AQUEDUCTS OF ROME, 1ST CENTURY AD

Above *The stepped tunnel at Mycenae, Greece, built of corbelled masonry to ensure secure access to a spring, and dating to 1250 BC.*

Below *A Greek black-figure vase-painting of women fetching water from a spring-house, 510 BC. This method of supplying water for the home would have been a daily task for many people, usually women, in the ancient world.*

Water supplies are critical to human survival, since individuals require at least 8 litres (2 gallons) of water per day for drinking, cooking and washing. Even in hyper-arid parts of the world, small groups of people have consistently found sufficient water to support themselves, a few domestic animals and modest agricultural activity. In urban environments the necessity of arranging a water supply was complicated by high demand, the pollution or exhaustion of local water sources, the need for complex water transport and storage systems, and the disposal of waste water. Engineering and administrative solutions were found to these problems, and by the 2nd century AD, the public water system of the enormous city of Rome provided approximately 1000 litres (264 gallons) of water per person daily.

Finding water

In most situations, the main requirements were first finding a water supply, then providing access to it, and also arranging for its transport, storage and disposal. The people of ancient Egypt and Mesopotamia had a natural water supply at hand in the great rivers that flowed through their arid lands. They also built canals for irrigation and transport. The Yangzi and Yellow (Huang Ho) rivers played a similar role in China, while the tropical areas of Mesoamerica enjoyed a multiplicity of smaller water sources. Along the north coast of the Mediterranean, rainfall is usually more abundant and streams and lakes also constituted a common source of water.

Springs are frequent in limestone landscapes throughout the world, and every ancient culture preferred spring water for its purity, clarity and coolness. Roman authors such as Galen, Vitruvius and Pliny the Elder discuss the methods for determining the health-giving qualities of a particular spring. The flow of such springs could also be enhanced, as at Corinth, by cutting into the water-bearing stratum. Even a submarine spring on the sea floor near the Syrian island of Aradus was exploited by lowering a lead funnel over it on a long leather pipe.

Where springs did not exist, an aquifer could be tapped with a well, which might be lined with planks, stone blocks or even pre-fabricated ceramic cylinders. Vitruvius and other Greek and Roman authors describe signs in the topography, soil, surface water and vegetation that indicate the presence of an accessible aquifer. If conditions required it, wells were excavated as deep as 100 m (328 ft).

Access to water

Pools of water attract human and animal traffic, and unimproved springs soon become muddy and polluted. All ancient authors concerned with water supply emphasize the need to keep springs and wells free of reeds, vegetation and mud. At Byblos (in modern Lebanon) even before 3000 BC a small pool was dug to receive spring water and keep the area around it dry, and over time stone walls, paving and steps were provided. Bronze Age cities such as Megiddo and Mycenae arranged access to subterranean spring-fed pools by means of

A reconstruction of the Nymphaeum of Herodes Atticus, at Olympia, Greece, a fine example of the sometimes elaborate public spring-houses that were built in many cities across the Classical world.

stepped, corbel-vaulted tunnels. Jerusalem had a complex system to ensure continued access to the water supply if the city was under siege. In the Bronze and Iron Ages, people around the Mediterranean built proper spring-houses to collect water, protect it from the sun and pollution, and provide convenient access to the flow.

Public spring-houses appeared in all the Greek and Roman cities, sometimes with monumental facades several storeys tall combining rich architectural decoration with sculpture, jets of water and a large pool. A variety of devices for lifting water in quantity for more convenient use were developed in Mesopotamia and Egypt, and by the Greeks and Romans (p. 101).

Transport of water

In ancient societies women were usually responsible for the local transport of small quantities of water from a spring or cistern to the home, either in jars or in leather bags slung on donkey or camel. The transport of water in large quantities or over long distances required gravity-flow water conduits. Channels cut in the earth were in use by the Neolithic period and were the basis of the subsequent irrigation systems of Southwest Asia, China and Mesoamerica (p. 97).

Cut-stone gutter blocks, providing a more permanent, leak-proof channel for relatively small streams of water, came into use by the 2nd millennium BC, as did terracotta pipes. Early examples are seen at Ur in Mesopotamia, Mari in Syria and Knossos on Crete. Stone gutter blocks distributed spring water around the Olmec centre of San Lorenzo (c. 1000 BC) and tapped a river-fed reservoir at Teotihuacan (c. AD 300).

Clay pipelines were very popular throughout the ancient world because they were inexpensive to manufacture, relatively easy to lay and provided a clean water supply with the added convenience and security of a subterranean course. The municipal water-supply systems of Classical Athens and Hellenistic Pergamon were created using such pipes. Even in early imperial Rome, where lead pipes had become common, Vitruvius notes that terracotta pipelines were preferable for the purity of their water and the simplicity of repair. In China, bamboo pipes were an effective alternative.

A Roman bronze stopcock from Pompeii, 1st century AD. A valve regulated the flow of water in the pipe to which it was attached.

The fountain in the House of the Fontana Grande at Pompeii, covered in multicoloured mosaics; water cascaded down the steps at the back to fill the tank.

Lead pipe systems were common in Roman public baths, in combination with large bronze water heaters. The pipes were made by rolling a lead sheet in one of several standard widths around a mandrel to shape it, then soldering the longitudinal V-joint or folded joint. Pipes were overlapped end to end and soldered, and the flow regulated by means of bronze stopcocks. In some cases bronze valves allowed the mixing of hot and cold water to adjust the temperature of the output.

Although most households in a Roman city fetched water from street corner fountains, permission could be obtained through licensing or bribery to lay a pressurized lead pipeline from a nearby public cistern or water main. Numerous domestic piping systems have survived at Pompeii and Herculaneum. Lead pipes were not a significant health hazard, since most municipal systems in the Mediterranean world supplied very hard water that

quickly left a calcium carbonate deposit, insulating the water from the lead.

The main drawbacks of conduits of more than local scope were the time and effort required for construction, the need for constant maintenance and their vulnerability to accidental or intentional damage. In consequence, regional pipelines and aqueducts were rare in the pre-Roman Mediterranean world, where small states did not have the resources to build and protect them. Exceptions were 8th-century BC Jerusalem and the cities of the Assyrian empire, the contemporary qanats of Persia, and the ceramic pipe system of Hellenistic Pergamon. A remarkable water supply system was built about 690 BC by Sennacherib to carry water from the cliffs at Bavian to Nineveh, including a stone aqueduct at Jerwan that was 280 m (920 ft) long, carrying a 12-m (39-ft) wide channel, 1.6 m (5.25 ft) deep, over five corbelled arches.

Qanats were gently sloping subterranean tunnels that tapped the aquifer at the foot of a mountain range. The course of the channel and the proper water level were found by sinking access shafts in a line, 30 to 50 m (98 to 164 ft) apart. From the bottom of these shafts the channel could be excavated and levelled; they also facilitated maintenance. The subterranean water course could extend from a few kilometres up to 20 or 30 km (12.4–19 miles) to a settlement, depending on the depth of the source and surface topography.

The peace, high urban populations and prosperity of the Roman and Byzantine empires allowed the construction of hundreds of aqueduct systems varying in length from a few kilometres to the 242-km (150-mile) long Vise system serving Constantinople. The largest cities required many separate systems. By the 3rd century AD, 11 aqueducts totalling 502 km (312 miles) in length brought roughly 1,000,000 cu. m (35,315,000 cu. ft) of water to the city of Rome every day.

For nearly every aqueduct system most of the conduit was subterranean, consisting of concrete and masonry channels. The channel was elevated on an arcade only at low valley crossings or in order to preserve height (and thus water pressure) close to the target city. One of the longest arcades carried the Aqua Claudia along the last 10.5 km (6.5 miles) of its course to the city of Rome. While pressurized pipelines could be laid out at any slope, Roman gravity-flow aqueducts typically had a gradient of no more than 1 per cent to avoid damage from the larger flow within. Gradients range, however, from a minimum of 0.03 per cent at Nîmes in southern France to 2.8 per cent at Carthage.

Bridges, such as the spectacular Pont du Gard near Nîmes, were built to carry aqueducts over valleys up to 50 m (164 ft) deep. Beyond that depth the flow was conducted down the hill under pressure in large lead pipes and up the other side to the continuation of the gravity flow channel.

Water storage

Unless very deep, urban wells were subject to pollution from percolation of the contents of adjacent cesspools into the aquifer. In such circumstances water collected in cisterns is cleaner. Most urban homes in the ancient Mediterranean world were supplied with cisterns fed by rain-water running-off from the roof and courtyard. On the small arid islands of the Aegean, such as Delos, public and domestic run-off cisterns were critical, since rainfall

KEY DATES

built well	3000 BC, Near East
tunnels	Bronze Age, Levant & Mycenaean Greece
stone gutter blocks & terracotta pipes	2nd millennium BC, Near East, Crete
stone gutter blocks	c. 1000 BC, Mexico
aqueducts	312 BC, Rome
lead pipes	1st century AD, Rome

was nearly the only water source. In large cities such as Rome or Constantinople, enormous open or roofed reservoirs were constructed to assure a reserve supply of water in the event of siege, interruption of the aqueduct supply or daily surges in demand. At the Maya centre of Uxmal and at the great city of Teotihuacan, public reservoirs and household cisterns were a response to the annual dry season and the porous karstic landscape.

Given the universal human need for water, it is not surprising that effective rural and urban water systems developed early in the Bronze Age and continued to evolve through the 1st millennium AD.

The Roman Pont du Gard near Nîmes, southern France – this spectacular bridge was built to carry an aqueduct across a deep valley, thus maintaining the slight but vital gradient necessary for gravity-flow water supply.

Bathing & Sanitation

*What is bathing when you think about it? Oil, sweat, filth,
greasy water, everything loathsome*

MARCUS AURELIUS, 2ND CENTURY AD

The Great Bath at Mohenjo-daro, in modern Pakistan. This unique feat of hydraulic engineering, which may have been ritual in function, dates to the mid-3rd millennium BC. Built of brick it measures 12 x 7 m (39 x 23 ft) and was emptied via a large drain. The city itself was equipped with complex sewer systems and almost every house had a bathing compartment.

Concern for hygiene in the ancient world must be carefully differentiated from modern concepts of sanitation. Without knowledge of microbes, 'cleanliness' to the ancients primarily meant the removal of visible dirt. The limited governmental apparatus of ancient states could not accommodate the drawing up, let alone the implementation of hygiene policies of the sort familiar since Victorian times – there were no Assyrian, Greek or Roman Public Health Acts.

That is not to say that pragmatic concerns for some aspects of public hygiene did not manifest themselves in antiquity. Vitruvius recommended against founding towns on or near marshes (*On Architecture*, 1.4) and advised that latrines should be located so as to channel ordure away from public spaces. But such purely practical measures need not reflect a generalized concern for public health as we understand it. The mere presence of aqueducts, fountains, drains, sewers, public baths or even latrines need say little about how 'hygienic' ancient cities were. Much depends on how these facilities were used, and that would depend on what was deemed 'cleanliness'. That many private toilets in Pompeii are located in or near the kitchen serves as a reminder that we must avoid grafting modern assumptions on to ancient conditions.

Drains & sewers

The removal of refuse only became a pressing problem when people adopted a settled lifestyle (nomads or hunter-gatherer bands can just move away from their mess). As a result, drainage systems – properly defined as serving to remove excess water – and sewers – for waste removal – only make an appearance in the Neolithic period at sites such as Skara Brae, on the Orkney Islands, Scotland (c. 3100–2500 BC). Here, in each of six houses, subterranean ducts lead from small rooms which apparently served as latrines, joining into a single channel to remove refuse. Sophisticated sewer systems are also found at larger urban sites such as Mohenjo-daro (c. 2500 BC) in the Indus Valley. Channel junctions at this site have access steps to permit periodic unclogging and cleaning.

Not everyone saw the need for a communal sewage system, however. No sign of drainage has been found at the otherwise sophisticated settlement at Çatalhöyük (c. 7000 BC) in Turkey, where manual removal of refuse or individual cesspits must have been considered sufficient. Rudimen-

tary or open sewers sufficed for some as – surprisingly – appears to have been the case in Classical Athens, the city of the Parthenon. Although water-supply was taken care of (p. 81), the 5th-century BC drainage system was limited to a single large duct in the marketplace; the rest of the city, it seems, was left to its own devices. Against this background, allusions in a play by Aristophanes (*Wasps* 256–59) to stepping in 'mud' on the Athenian street become somewhat more concerning than they might initially appear.

The main element in Rome's sewage and drainage system was the Cloaca Maxima or Great Sewer, which emptied into the River Tiber. Initial construction probably dates to the 5th century BC. By the 1st century BC, it was so large that Marcus Agrippa is said to have sailed through it.

The Romans built multi-seater public latrines from at least the 2nd century BC and later lavished great care and expense on them, sometimes embellishing them with sculpture, frescoes and mosaics. These public latrines are at Ostia, near Rome.

Opposite *Reconstruction of the Baths of Caracalla, Rome, built in the early 3rd century AD. By this time, public baths had been an integral feature of Roman towns for at least four centuries. The largest baths in Rome, such as this one, had a vast bathing block set in a garden precinct with lecture halls, art galleries and sports tracks.*

Below *The cold room of the Forum Baths at Pompeii. Bathers passed through a sequence of rooms at different temperatures, ending in a cold plunge.*

The Etruscans appear to have had extensive drainage and sewage systems, with stone-covered channels under the streets, if sites like Marzabotto (*c.* 500 BC) are an accurate guide. The Romans were outstanding hydraulic engineers and took concern for sewage removal to new heights in the ancient world. The imperial city was equipped with a system so extensive that Pliny the Elder (*Natural History*, 36.104) considered it the single most remarkable feature of an otherwise wholly remarkable place: Rome, he says, could be described as a city suspended in the air above its sewers.

The core element of Rome's sewage system was the Great Sewer, the *Cloaca Maxima*, traditionally assigned to the kings of the 6th century BC. Investigation of the surviving remains, however,

suggests a date in the following century for initial construction, although it may have remained uncovered until the 2nd century BC, at least in part. By 33 BC, the vaulted duct was so capacious that Marcus Agrippa, right-hand man to the emperor Augustus, is said to have taken a sailing trip through it.

Sophisticated drainage and sewage systems are a regular feature of Roman cities all around the empire, as is the latrine. Investigations at Pompeii have revealed private latrines in virtually all the city's houses and apartments, those on upper floors connected to subterranean sewers or cesspits by pipes embedded in the walls. Public toilets, too, are a peculiarly Roman phenomenon, but they did not prevent people defecating in public places, as the injunctions against the public 'crapper' (*cacator*) inscribed on some street-front properties at Pompeii make distressingly clear.

Public baths & bathing

The option of bathing naturally in the sea, lakes, streams or rivers was always open to ancient people. Domestic bathtubs are attested in Bronze Age Knossos on Crete, but it was not until the Classical and Hellenistic periods in Greece that public baths emerged. The typical Greek public baths, like the one at Gela in Sicily, featured individual tubs arranged around the inside wall of a room. Sitting in their separate hip-baths, Greek bathers performed their ablutions collectively with the other bathers in the room. Sometimes steam-rooms could be included in these simple facilities.

The Romans, however, raised public bathing to an art form. Like the Greeks, the Romans bathed collectively but in communal pools. Combining the hypocaust heating method (p. 79) with complex hydraulic supply and drainage systems, bathing was elaborated into a complex procedure involving passage through gradations of heated

space and water, intense sweating and a cold plunge. Rooms for exercise, massage and simple relaxation were added until, by the 1st century AD, Roman public baths had evolved from relatively unassuming facilities into vast leisure complexes built by emperors for the populace and covering large areas. That only about 18 per cent of the area of these imperial baths (mostly in Rome) were devoted to bathing activities tells us that by this era bathing had become far more than the act of getting clean – baths were places to meet friends, drink, gossip and watch the world go by. In short, they were essential nodes of community contact.

Roman baths were not necessarily models of splendour and cleanliness, however. The combination of heat and humidity, and the everyday wear-and-tear of intense usage, meant that many operated in a run-down condition. Even in well-maintained establishments, water quality may not have been the best, especially in the heated pools. It is unclear how often the water was changed, and the communal use of pools becomes problematic when we read of oiled or unguent-caked bathers using them. Even more worrying are references to ill bathers going to the baths alongside healthy ones, since bathing was considered medically remedial. We have no way to judge the baths' role in actively spreading disease, but there is enough evidence to question their sanitary operation.

SOAP

Ancient Mesopotamian recipes for soap made from animal fat and alkali are known from *c*. 2000 BC, but they appear to have been primarily medicinal rather than cosmetic. The same is true of Egyptian soap-like unguents. The Greeks preferred to scrape dirt from oiled skin with an instrument called a *strigil* (**right**), a habit they passed on to the Romans. Pliny reports (*Natural History* 28.191) that *sapo*, made from animal fat and ash, was imported from the Gauls, who used it to dye their hair red. By the 2nd century AD the doctor Galen was promoting the use of soap for cleaning. It fell out of use in the Dark Ages, however, and did not reappear in Europe until the Middle Ages.

Security

[Penelope] climbed the high stair up to her room and with sturdy hand grasped the fine bronze key with its easy curve and ivory handle.... The Queen came to that distant room and set foot on the oaken threshold.... At once she undid the thong from the hook, put in the key and with sure aim shot back the bolts.

HOMER, 8TH CENTURY BC

Right *An early but important stage in the development of security was the invention of doors which turned on pivots in threshold and lintel. This stone door is in the late Roman fort at Azraq, Jordan.*

Below *Houses could be made more secure by windows barred with iron grilles, set high up out of reach of intruders, as in this example from Herculaneum, southern Italy, 1st century AD.*

The desire for personal security is a fundamental human characteristic. Armies and city walls might provide security from major threats, but the individual remained responsible for safeguarding themselves and their possessions from theft. Attempts to do so took many forms, culminating in the Roman period in the development of increasingly sophisticated forms of locks.

Early developments

For most societies in the Near East and Egypt, security took the form of high walls, barred doors and guards. Doors which turned on pivots set into the threshold and lintel were developed at an early date, long before the true hinge, which only entered general use in the Iron Age. Both devices allowed doors to be opened and closed, a major step in the development of basic security. This was complemented by the use of a bar which could be slotted into bolt holes in the door frame or adjacent wall to prevent the door being opened.

An additional element of security was often provided by sealing either a storeroom or individual containers with a seal impression in clay or wax. This provides no real physical barrier, but made any breach of security immediately visible; fear of detection may have served as a deterrent. Such seals and their impressions, usually in clay and preserved when accidentally burnt, are common discoveries on sites in the Near East and eastern Mediterranean. The clay seals on the blocked doorway of Tutankhamun's tomb in the Valley of the Kings, Egypt, are a rarer survival. In the Greek and Roman periods such seals often took the form of finely engraved intaglios usually set in finger rings, used to seal letters and other documents.

The development of the lock

Personal security in the home has been achieved by trying to make entry more difficult for intruders. This is clearly seen in the houses of Pompeii and Herculaneum, with their high walls, small windows set high up and protected with strong iron grilles, and tall doors reinforced with bands and studs of metal which were kept closed with strong bars internally. Such bars were highly effective, but they had the great disadvantage that they could only be opened from the inside; this was not a problem when the doors were guarded but was when the house had to be left unoccupied. The first, and simplest, solution was to have a slit in the door through which a curved rod (a latch-lifter) could be passed. Its tip engaged in a hole in the bolt; by sliding, or lifting it if it was pivoted, the bolt could be opened. It was in use in China at much the same time as in Greece, and has remained popular in many parts of the world to the present day.

Although such simple latches continued to be used throughout antiquity, opening them cannot have been unduly difficult for anyone with a latch-lifter and sufficient time. To remedy this, additional security was often provided by placing wooden pegs, or tumblers, above the bolt which dropped into holes in it when it was closed. To free the bolt and open the door these tumblers were lifted with a simple key which had prongs at its end, called a lift-key. This was inserted through a hole in the door and the prongs engaged in holes in the pegs which allowed them to be lifted. The bolt could then be slid open by a cord passing through a small hole in the door. Such locks are known in the Greek and Roman world and China well before the end of the 1st millennium BC.

Tumbler locks

The latch and simple tumbler lock appear to have been the commonest, and possibly the only, forms, until the Roman period: latch-lifters and lift-keys are frequent finds on Roman sites, the surviving ones usually made of iron. The majority of these simple devices would in fact have been made of wood, but more elaborate locks with metal bolts and keys, in which the key both raised the tumblers and slid the bolt, appear throughout the Roman

The clay seal impression sealing the blocked doorway of the tomb of Tutankhamun in the Valley of the Kings, Egypt.

world late in the 1st millennium BC, probably as a result of the increased availability of iron.

The tumblers of such locks dropped into the bolt by the force of gravity, but this was only practical when the lock could not be turned upside-down. A major development was an iron spring which pushed the tumblers into the holes in the bolt and held them there, allowing locks to be used on such things as boxes and chests which were movable. Greater security was then provided by arranging the tumblers in a pattern which could only be freed from the bolt with a key with a bit which replicated the pattern of the tumblers. Such slide-keys were pushed into the bolt from below to lift the tumblers and then slide the bolt and open the lock. The key-hole has a characteristic inverted L-shape.

Roman keys (left to right): barb-spring padlock key; tumbler lock lift-key; tumbler lock slide key; rotary lock key; key handle; rotary key on finger ring; bronze key handle.

Lever locks

The most advanced form of Roman lock was the lever lock, which, in a slightly modified form, is still in use today; it was probably the most elaborate and widely used mechanical device in the ancient world. It had a single, pivoted tumbler held down by a spring. A series of fixed wards prevented the wrong key from turning in the lock, and the key,

which had slots in its bit to allow it to pass through the wards, was rotated to lift the tumbler and then slide the bolt.

Padlocks

Lever locks were often used as padlocks, but the commonest form of padlock worked on a different, simpler principle. In this, the bolt had flat springs welded or riveted to its tip behind which they splayed out to give the appearance of barbs. When the bolt was pushed through the bolt-hole in the lock case these springs were first compressed and then, when the bolt was in the case, sprang out to prevent it being removed. It was released with a key which slid over the springs and compressed them thus allowing the bolt to be withdrawn.

In various forms, such locks are still in use throughout Asia, and it was the normal form of lock used in China from early in the 1st millennium AD until relatively recent times.

Right and above *Reconstruction and diagram to show the mechanism of a tumbler lock. Top: locked; centre: the key is inserted to lift the tumblers and free the bolt; bottom: the key slides the bolt to open the lock.*

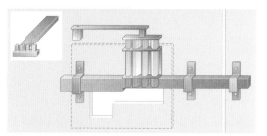

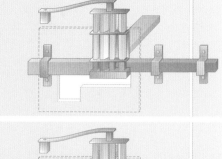

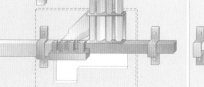

Far right *Diagram of the mechanism of a Roman lever lock from Caerleon, Gwent.*

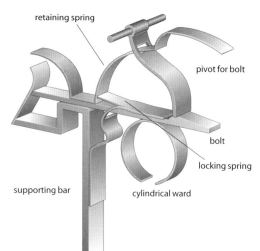

retaining spring

pivot for bolt

bolt

locking spring

supporting bar

cylindrical ward

Cereal Agriculture

*Ten thousand years ago, at the edge of the spring-fed oasis at Jericho,
the world changed forever.*
BRUCE SMITH, 1995

20

After at least 3 million years of living by hunting and gathering, humans independently 'invented' agriculture in several different regions of the world – Western Asia, China, Mexico, South America and New Guinea – during the first few thousand years after the Ice Age came to an end around 10,000 BC. In tropical latitudes, roots and vegetables were the first domesticates, but elsewhere wild grasses – cereals – were domesticated.

The domestication of wild cereals to produce the types of wheat, barley, rye, rice and millet that we know today is a biological process, involving genetic change to enhance the food value of the plant. But the adoption of agriculture also required people to change their settlement patterns, social organization and technology.

From hunter-gatherers to farmers

We know more about the development of cereal agriculture in Western Asia than any other region of the world. Although popularly referred to as one element of the 'Neolithic Revolution', it was in fact a gradual process and was closely associated with environmental changes at the end of the Ice Age. Even when that was at its height at 20,000 BC, hunter-gatherers in the Jordan Valley gathered plant foods, including wild wheat and barley – as is evident from the site of Ohalo II. Hunter-gatherers would have been aware of the life-cycle of plants and the 'invention' of agriculture seems unlikely to have arisen from any new-found knowledge.

Nor did cereal agriculture arise to relieve the hardships of a hunter-gatherer lifestyle: studies of Australian Aborigines and the San of South Africa reveal that they work far fewer hours a day than subsistence farmers. So the development of cereal farming seems to have been a gradual process related to the desire of people to live in large groups in sedentary communities. This required

the intensive cultivation of wild foods which unintentionally led to the domestication of cereals.

The first sedentary communities of Western Asia arose around 12,500 BC. Increased rainfall and temperature had made wild plants and animals abundant, enabling people to create villages of small, circular dwellings. These are known as Natufian communities. Excavations at sites such as 'Ain Mallaha in Israel reveal a great number of mortars and grinding stones (p. 32), used for processing not only cereals but also acorns, pistachios and almonds. Stands of wild wheat and barley were probably protected and cultivated by eliminating pests and weeds and sowing additional seed.

Such cultivation may have started the biological change to the domesticated strains. People perhaps unconsciously preferentially collected

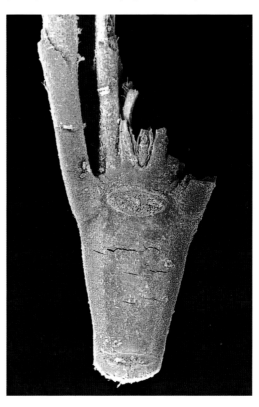

A fragment of a barley spikelet from Netiv Hagdud, Jordan Valley. It is by such analysis at the microscopic level that archaeologists can ascertain whether cereals were wild or domesticated. At Netiv Hagdud, much of the barley found at the site was still in its wild form.

seed from those few plants – genetic mutants – which had seed-heads that did not automatically 'shatter' when the grain was ripe. By saving and sowing some of the seed from such plants, this characteristic became more widespread and eventually dominated the crop, which was now unable to re-seed itself. Plants with the largest grains and which ripened simultaneously were also selected. The result was strains of cereal which provided abundant harvests but were unable to survive without human intervention – they were domesticated. Daniel Zohary, a plant geneticist from the Hebrew University, Jerusalem, described them as plants that have to 'wait for the harvester'.

Microscopic examination of plant fragments found in excavations can ascertain whether they belonged to wild or domestic cereals. The earliest known specimens of the latter are of rye and come from the site of Abu Hureyra in Syria, dating to 11,000 BC. The first traces of domestic wheat and barley are not known for another 2000 years, from Jericho and Tell Aswan in the Jordan Valley.

These villages were first occupied just after the end of the Ice Age and are referred to as 'Pre-Pottery Neolithic A' (PPNA), the key period of transition to cereal agriculture. Some plant remains, for example at Netiv Hagdud, a site contemporary with Jericho and no more than 50 km (31 miles) away, show that much of the barley cultivated remained in its wild form. It seems people sowed the seed of wheat and barley in the rich alluvial valley soils and the plants thrived, allowing people to live all year round on the stored surplus

Detail of a wall painting from the tomb of Menna, Egypt, dating from the early 14th century BC. Here two surveyors are measuring the wheat crop before it is harvested.

from their harvest. Consequently, by 8000 BC villages such as Jericho, which began as a cluster of small, circular dwellings, had become sprawling towns with substantial rectangular buildings inhabited by specialized craftsmen and traders.

Although the earliest known domesticated wheat grains come from the Jordan Valley, genetic evidence suggests that the plants may have originated further north. A study comparing the genetics of modern wheat and surviving wild plants in the Near East found that the closest match was in the Karacadag Hills in southeastern Turkey. Nearby, a remarkable early Neolithic site has recently been discovered – a hilltop religious sanctuary known as Göbekli Tepe. It seems that large numbers of hunter-gatherers regularly congregated here and cut massive pillars of stone, erected them in enclosures and carved them with depictions of wild boar, foxes and snakes. It was perhaps the need to feed such gatherings by intensively cultivating the wild wheat around the site that drove the process of domestication. People returning to their settlements in the Jordan Valley may have taken the seed, planted it in the valleys and transformed themselves into farmers.

The domestication of rice

Archaeologists know far less about the invention of rice farming, even though rice feeds more people today than any other single foodstuff and hence its domestication was unquestionably one of the most important events of human history. Having searched for the origin of rice agriculture in Southeast Asia, archaeologists have now located it in the Yangzi Valley of southern China.

The earliest specimens of domesticated rice grains come from the settlement of Pengtoushan, dating to around 7500 BC. This seems to have been a village not dissimilar to early Jericho, where hunter-gatherers had settled down to a sedentary lifestyle with a reliance on annual harvests of rice. But quite when rice cultivation began remains unclear. Phytoliths – minute deposits of silica that form within plant cells – from rice plants found in Diaotonghuan Cave suggest that by 12,000 BC the inhabitants of the Yangzi Valley were gathering large quantities of wild rice. This may have caused the same type of biological change that transformed the wheat and barley of Western Asia.

Whereas grinding stones (p. 32) were essential equipment accompanying the increasing reliance on cereals in Western Asia, in China pottery vessels appear to have been crucial. These were being made by 10,000 BC – some millennia earlier than in the west (p. 37) – and were most likely used to boil rice. Chaff from harvested rice plants was used as a temper for the clay and it was only by finding fragments of charred stems and grains within pottery sherds at Pengtoushan that the significance of rice was identified.

New World plant domestication

There were two early centres for plant domestication in the Americas – Central Mexico and the Andes. Although the types of plants in each were different – maize, beans and squash in one, and quinua (from the chenopod group of plants, often known as goosefoot) in the other – the process of domestication in both was undertaken by people who were still living entirely mobile lifestyles.

Maize evolved from a wild grass called teosinte that still grows in remote areas of Mexico. The type growing on the slopes of the Balsas River Valley in Central Mexico is especially similar – in biochemical terms – to modern maize. It may therefore have been within that valley that prehistoric plant gatherers began to cultivate the teosinte intensively – repeatedly selecting those plants with the largest grains for both food and seed for new plants.

Wild beans, on the other hand, grow throughout Central America. A cluster around the modern city of Guadalajara has been identified as the ancestor of the common domesticated bean (*Phaseolus vulgaris*) that comes in many different forms, including red, pinto and kidney. All have one key difference from their wild ancestor – if the harvester does not come, the beans cannot spread their seed. And as with plants elsewhere, the transition to domesticated beans came about as people repeatedly chose – either intentionally or by accident – pods which had less tendency to split apart.

The wild ancestor of squash has not yet been located. There are certainly many wild varieties still growing throughout Mexico, all of which have

small, green fruits. It seems likely that one of these will be identified as the specific progenitor of the domesticated varieties with larger, orange fruits.

For all three Mexican plants, the archaeological evidence for the date and process of domestication remains rather patchy. Remains from the cave of Guilá Naquitz in the Oaxaca Valley have the earliest radiocarbon dates, suggesting that squash had undergone biological change to a domestic strain by 7500 BC, and teosinte had evolved into maize by 4200 BC. Recent evidence from the genetics of modern maize, however, suggests that domestication had occurred by 7000 BC.

Quinua is one of two plants that dominated the early prehistoric food-producing economies of the high-altitude basin and valleys of the Andes, the other being the potato. It became a key crop of the Incas and is still grown by subsistence farmers today for its high protein content. As with domesticated wheat, the domesticated quinua cannot drop its seed naturally, nor can it delay germination, which results in the simultaneous ripening of all plants within a crop.

The earliest quinua known is from Panaulauca Cave in the Junin Basin of Peru. The seeds, dating to 5000 BC, had thin 'testas', or seed coats, comparable to those of domesticated quinua, indicating a reduced ability to delay germination. At this time the occupants of Panaulauca Cave were keeping herds of camelids –

Above *Planting rice in a paddy field – a scene from a Han tomb in southwest China. The domestication of rice was one of the most significant events in human history.*

Below *A silver maize cob from Peru, 15th century AD. Maize was an essential foodstuff in the Americas and was imbued with religious symbolism.*

llamas and/or alpacas – which had evolved from wild ancestors after several millennia of hunting.

Camelids eat the wild varieties of quinua, but cannot digest the seeds, which pass through the animals' gut undamaged and are deposited with a quantity of natural fertilizer, often far from where the plants had originally grown. If the early herders had begun to corral their herds at night, stands of chenopods would have flourished within their organic soils. By simply relocating the corrals, and using the fences to protect the thriving new stands from grazing, a substantial food source could have easily arisen close to a settlement. It would then have been a small step for cultivation – weeding, watering, transporting – to have begun the subtle, unintentional genetic alterations, transforming the wild chenopods into domesticated quinua.

Another plant was domesticated in the Andes, but unlike quinua this one was to play a major role in global history after it was taken to Europe in the 16th century – the potato. There are several variants of wild and cultivated potatoes in South

KEY DATES

domesticated rye	11,000 BC, Syria
domesticated barley	9000 BC, Jordan Valley
domesticated wheat	9000 BC, Jordan Valley, SE Turkey
domesticated rice	7500 BC, China
domesticated squash	7500 BC, Mexico
domesticated potato	6th millennium BC, Andes
domesticated maize	4200 BC, Mexico

America today and the Lake Titicaca basin is the centre of genetic variability – a sign that this is where the first domesticated variants arose.

No archaeological traces of early cultivation have yet been found within the basin and surrounding river valleys. But almost all excavation so far has taken place in the highland caves which are unlikely to provide a complete picture. If open settlements are discovered and investigated, the domestication of the potato may be found to have arisen as part of a joint package with the llama, alpaca and quinua.

GRANARIES

Cereal agriculture had social and economic consequences beyond simply supplying a greater amount of food than could be acquired from wild plants alone. Produce had to be stored – both to provide seed grain for future sowing and as food for the lean winter season. Storage required granaries to be constructed and arrangements to be made for the distribution of the stored foodstuff. Issues of ownership arose, as did a means for some individuals to acquire political power by controlling access to the grain.

That such issues arose at the dawn of cereal agriculture is evident from the recent excavations at the site of Jerf el-Ahmar, once beside the Euphrates in Syria and now drowned by the waters of a new dam. The site dates to soon after 10,000 BC, making it contemporary with the earliest village at Jericho, and it has similar circular dwellings. In the midst of these a large, subterranean building has been interpreted as a food-storage facility for the community (**right**). Direct evidence – in the form of surviving grain – was absent as it had evidently been cleaned out when the settlement was abandoned. Before this, however, a human head was placed within the building and a decapitated body splayed out on the floor. Such depositions suggest that the storage and distribution of grain was far more than a routine, economic activity – it was one intimately related to the religious beliefs and ritual practices of the community.

Early prehistoric granaries may have also been found at the village of Beidha in southern Jordan, dating to c. 8000 BC. Four stone-built chambers in the centre of the village were probably used for storing grain. They were located directly opposite a particularly impressive building within the village, suggesting that its occupant had been able to control access to the stores. These were also empty when excavated, but in the Faiyum region of Egypt, 67 'grain silos' were discovered some 1 km (0.6 miles) from the earliest farming settlement in the region, Kom K, and dating to c. 5000 BC. The silos here contained large quantities of wheat and barley. Quite why the Faiyum silos were so far from the settlement remains unclear; perhaps it was to ensure that they were kept secret from visitors to Kom K.

From Digging-Sticks to Ploughs

No man, having put his hand to the plough, and looking back, is fit for the kingdom of God.
LUKE 9:62

The digging-stick is probably the archetypal human tool – a universal general-purpose implement used by hunter-gatherers and farmers alike. Its lineal descendant is the plough, which made possible new levels of productivity. Precisely as its name suggests, the digging-stick is a stick used for digging. It may have been among the first artifacts used by early hominids; most recent hunter-gatherer societies used it, and for a variety of purposes. In Australia it was ubiquitous, employed for digging for roots, witchetty grubs, animals in burrows and water. It was easily made and transportable over long distances.

The digging-stick was probably the first agricultural tool. Early cultivation involved small areas, and the digging-stick was all the technology required. Hoes and spades are in many ways simply variants, and they allowed intensive agricultural regimes to be developed. In Mexico before European contact, cultivation involved the construction of *chinampas*, gardens reclaimed from swamp lands. The Aztecs and their predecessors had no ploughs – they had no traction animals to draw them – this major, productive agricultural system was based on the digging-stick.

The plough

The plough – an implement to cut continuous furrows, drawn along by animals – is an Old World implement that appears some time after the start of agriculture. It is often assumed that before the plough, agriculture involved shifting cultivation – the use of temporary plots, the fertility of which declined after a couple of seasons, necessitating moving on and clearing a new plot. Digging-sticks would have been used in such systems. As in Mexico, however, small-scale, continuous garden

cultivation is a viable alternative. Detailed studies of the weeds found in the earliest cereal samples from central Europe show that this was the type of agriculture practised.

Why, then, develop the plough? The answer is that it enabled overall production to be increased by allowing a larger area to be cultivated, though

A digging stick in use in cultivation in New Guinea today. Probably the archetypal human tool, it may have been one of the first artifacts employed by humanity.

A drawing from the 'Labours of the Months – Agriculture through the Year: December', by Guamán Poma, 1599. December was the month for planting potatoes and oca, an edible tuber, with the aid of a foot plough. Like the Aztecs of Mexico, the Incas had no ploughs as they had no traction animals.

KEY DATES

ard	by 4th millennium BC, Mesopotamia
ard marks	3500 BC, England & Scandinavia
mouldboard	possibly 500 BC, China

Above *An ancient Greek farmer driving an oxen pulling a simple plough; the Nikosthenes Cup, 6th century BC.*

Below right *The marks left by an ancient farmer using an ard, preserved in the ground below a Neolithic burial mound at Steneng, Denmark.*

Below *An Etruscan bronze model showing a ploughman with two yoked oxen; from Arezzo, Italy, c. 430–400 BC.*

production per hectare probably remained the same. Human populations could thus increase.

The earliest plough type was the ard, or scratch plough. This simply scored a groove in the surface of the field and did not turn the soil. It is essentially a hooked digging-stick towed by two oxen, perhaps made from a single piece of wood, so the share wears out rapidly. Some more complex ards have replaceable shares. The ard does imply a high level of commitment to agriculture. The oxen are vital, but take a long time to train and must be fed even when they are not working. Fields are also a long term investment.

It is not known when or where the ard first appeared. Ards were made of wood until the invention of iron led to metal shares, and so survive only rarely. The oldest evidence is from 4th-millennium BC Mesopotamia – in the form of pictograms, rather than actual examples. Since these writing systems only evolved at this time, ards might have been present earlier. In Europe, waterlogged conditions have preserved some wooden ards from about 2000 BC onwards, but remarkable evidence reveals that they were in use earlier. Burial mounds were sometimes built on cultivated fields, and the soil beneath

them has been found to retain ard furrows. Those at South Street in southern England date to about 3500 BC. Such survivals reveal that arding was carried out criss-cross, in two directions. Ard marks dating from the mid-3rd millennium BC have been found in northern India, but the ard may well have been used much earlier.

Ploughs for heavier soils evolved later. The mouldboard is a curved surface placed alongside the share, in order to turn the soil over. This both kills weeds and brings up nutrients from below the reach of an ard, increasing productivity. The date of this development is uncertain. It was present in Europe by the 1st millennium AD, but was certainly in use in China by the Han dynasty (206 BC – AD 220), and perhaps as early as 500 BC.

Plough agriculture was the economic mainstay of most Old World civilizations, though not those of the New World. It was probably the single most important agricultural invention, and without it the course of Old World history would have been very different.

Irrigation

*[The Nile] soaks both the fallow and the seed land … for as long as the farmers wish.
Since the water comes with a gentle current, the river is readily diverted from their
fields by small earthen dams and then, by cutting these, the river is again
let in upon the land when needed.*

DIODORUS SICULUS, 1ST CENTURY BC

The idea of irrigation is simple and has probably been used in most climates since people first began to plant crops. Water from a hand-held container, or a rill cut from a flowing stream, increases the likelihood that seeds will germinate and that transplanted seedlings or plant cuttings will survive. In an environment with some dry weeks or months during the growing season, supplementary water will produce better results, perhaps even saving the harvest during a drought year. But it was a big step to expand agriculture from a humid or semi-arid environment, with enough rain to produce a harvest in most years, to drylands, where rainfall usually is inadequate.

Fertile floodplains

Most of the early urban civilizations in Western and East Asia and coastal Peru were situated in arid environments, and not by accident. The common factors are: seasonal floods from mountain streams or rivers that drain distant mountains; an annual residue of fresh and fertile silt on small or large floodplains; and a warm growing season that provides the necessary energy for rapid plant growth. The result was a much higher productivity that could support larger populations than rainfed agriculture on non-floodplain land with average soils that lose their nutrient levels with constant cropping.

Egypt, Mesopotamia and the Indus Lowlands represent large, seasonally flooded plains where fresh sediment rejuvenates the soil regularly, as it does in the middle Niger Basin and the Great Plain of China. It was the combination of floodplains and irrigation that made possible the agriculture to support complex, urban civilizations – with their population centres, craft specialization and trade networks.

How does one develop a technology sufficiently dependable to harness an adequate water supply that allows cities to grow? To envisage this, the achievements of the industrial era must be put aside – dams, concrete-lined canals, miles of heavy-gauge piping and fuel-powered pumping stations. Major floodplains were irrigated for five millennia without such means, by adapting the enormous annual pulses of water and energy that swept natural floodplains.

At first there were no 'great inventions'. People worked *with* their particular river, trying to optimize the degree of inundation, so that the retained soil moisture would suffice to bring crops to maturity. They sowed on the wet mud as the floods receded, and they might hand-water their vegetable gardens or orchards, but the first devices to facilitate mechanical lifting of water came after millennia of incremental change. And there was only one crop of staple grains per year, unlike the

Remains of the Marib dam, in Yemen, which developed over many centuries between 700 BC and AD 580. It was designed to collect and store the rare but torrential rainfall of southern Arabia to provide irrigation for a large area that would otherwise be arid. It was last breached by an exceptional flood and never rebuilt.

two or three crops that we associate with modern, perennial irrigation.

The initial stages of natural irrigation on the Nile floodplain, during the 6th and 5th millennia BC, can be reconstructed on the basis of ethnographic models from the Sahel region of Africa. The Senegal, middle Niger and Chari-Logone rivers have floodplains inundated in late summer as a result of monsoonal rains upstream. No effort is made to control influx or outflow of water from these free-draining alluvial basins, yet such 'recessional agriculture' is highly productive and requires little labour.

During the low-water season, the Nile River flows in a deep channel. As the increasingly muddy waters rise to flood stage, they spill out over the floodplain, depositing sandy muds near the banks, which build up into natural levees. These are 0.5–2.5 m (1.5–8 ft) higher than the undulating basins of the floodplain. Once the levees have formed, only unusually high floods flow over them, and so they provide reasonably safe sites to build settlements. The basins flood for four to six weeks, as the water spills through breaks or low points in the levees; and when the flood recedes, the remaining water drains back into the main river channel, leaving behind a fresh increment of fertile silt and mud.

Low floods might not fill all the basins or soak them long enough, and an obvious remedy was to admit more water – deliberately breaching a levee, and later holding back the water by blocking low exit points. Another step is to subdivide natural basins by building mud walls as cross-

Egyptian stone mace-head showing the 'Scorpion King' symbolically cutting a new irrigation canal with a large hoe. The man at the right holds a wicker basket to receive the earth and the wavy lines at the base represent water. From the end of the Predynastic period, c. 3100 BC.

dykes, and artificially raising levees. The next progression is to dig canals to channel water to particular fields, to estate orchards or to more distant parts of a basin.

Artificial irrigation

In Egypt this transition from natural to artificial irrigation took place during the 4th millennium BC, judging by a carved mace-head of 3100 BC that shows a ceremonial opening of canals to feed a grid of fields. But during Old and Middle Kingdom times, water still had to be lifted by hand or in buckets suspended from a shoulder yoke. The shaduf was introduced from Western Asia by 1350 BC, and the animal-driven chain-of-pots or saqiya is verified after 300 BC (see also p. 103). Only the latter could irrigate summer staples, such as sorghum, on a large scale.

In Egypt, the subdivision of the Nile floodplain into basins meant that irrigation was operated on a local scale, outside the control of central government. That was not so in Mesopotamia, where the floods, derived from mountain melt-waters, crested during the late spring. Since wheat is prone to blight in hot weather, planting began in autumn, but flood irrigation could only be applied

late in the growing season, with a June harvest (compared to March in Egypt). The Tigris channel is too deep to allow extensive irrigation, while the Euphrates floods are violent, carry less fertile sediment and rapidly silt up canals, requiring heavy-duty maintenance. Flood basins are therefore poorly developed and the plain is liable to salt

An Egyptian wall painting showing a shaduf being used to water an opulent garden; from the tomb of Ipui, Deir el-Medina, 19th dynasty, c. 1240 BC.

FROM THE SHADUF TO ARCHIMEDES' SCREW

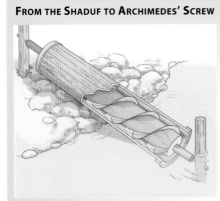

The shaduf or sweep is an ungainly instrument, consisting of a long pole, anchored in a notched post or tied to a crossbeam; one end is weighted down by a pack of mud, while from the other hangs a long rope with a pot at the end. The pot is dipped into the water, then raised and swung round, balanced by the counter-weight, and its contents are emptied into a small ditch.

This pole-and-bucket lever reduced the effort of lifting water pots, but it could raise water no more than 1.5 m (5 ft) – though a string of three or four shadufs might operate along a riverbank. It was a slow and inefficient process, capable of watering only a garden plot or filling a small tank.

The shaduf is first documented in Mesopotamia on an Akkadian cylinder seal (c. 2370–2200 BC), and appears in Egypt in art of the Amarna period (c. 1346–1334 BC). During Classical times it diffused around the Mediterranean Sea to Iberia, and later to northwestern Europe and China, eventually finding its way to the Spanish New World.

Much more efficient was the animal-driven chain-of-pots with two large interlocked wooden wheels, one vertical, the other horizontal, the saqiya. Water could now be lifted 3.5–7.5 m (11.5–25 ft) to operate continuously and water 8 to 10 ha (20 to 25 acres) in a day. Presumed to have been invented in the Persian empire by 500 BC, it

has also been attributed to Hellenistic Egypt in the early 3rd century BC. The saqiya spread throughout the Arab empire, and became a major irrigation device in Latin America, capable of raising water from very deep wells.

The noted mathematician Archimedes of Syracuse (287–212 BC) was famed for his inventions, including war-machines. One novel device of his – Archimedes' Screw – was designed to pump water out of a ship: a cylinder enclosing a helix was turned to raise the water (diagram **left**). A similar device, called a tambur, is still used in Arab countries for small-scale irrigation and short lifts, but the iron Archimedes screw was uneconomical to produce until the industrial era.

Another great invention of Western Asia that provided a water supply and aided irrigation was the qanat (p. 82), an underground canal dug by means of a chain of wells, bringing water from mountain areas down to oases, where it emerged at the surface.

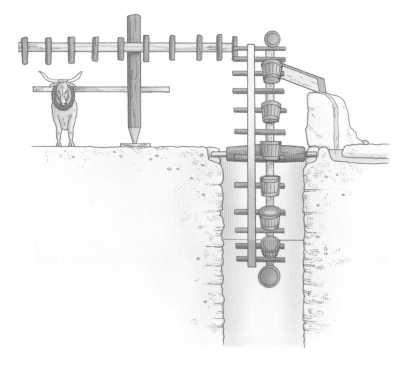

*The saqiya is an animal-driven device, with one vertical and one horizontal wheel (**above**). The Roman tomb painting from Alexandria (**below**), 2nd century AD, shows one powered by oxen.*

accumulation and terminates in marshes. Natural irrigation was not attractive, and by 4000 BC settlements began to grow on long canals tapping the water of the Euphrates and distributing it through an increasingly fine mesh of radial canals. During the 3rd millennium BC, urban centres were concen-

trated along the lower end of such canal systems, away from destructive floods on the banks of the Euphrates. Radial canal systems were also created on the Diyala and Karun floodplains east of the Tigris.

The progression of artificial irrigation was therefore greatly accelerated in Mesopotamia, and its management more complex, requiring co-operation between rival city-states, while the extended nature of the web of long canals made it vulnerable to the rise and fall of dynasties. In some periods, large parts of the canal network were abandoned and returned to desert; later the canals re-expanded, sometimes in new locations, perhaps reflecting shifts of the main river or local salinization. Experimentation with a new form of irrigation began about 600 BC, creating artificial basins that could be flooded with irrigation water, analogous to those of the Nile floodplain; but this system was abandoned after the Arab conquest in AD 636.

Another of the great achievements of Mesopotamian irrigation was the construction of a 275-km (172-mile) long canal, leading from the Tigris River, perhaps during the 5th century AD. But by the 11th century, most of the Mesopotamian irrigation network had been abandoned, and remained so until after 1918. By that time, its Egyptian counterpart, which had never collapsed, had already moved into the industrial era.

The early irrigation systems of the Indus plains and the Great Plain of China remain to be studied systematically. But the Indus floods come in mid-summer and are sufficiently destructive to cause river shifts, favouring periodic abandonment as in Mesopotamia. In the case of Peru, smaller rivers were brought under partial control, mainly during the 1st millennium AD, but a single long canal was never operationalized.

Handmills, Watermills & Pumps

Rest your mill-turning hands, women! … Demeter has reassigned to the water nymphs the chore you once performed. They leap against the wheel's rim, turning the axle and cogs that make the heavy pair of millstones spin …

ANTIPATER OF THESSALONICA, 1ST CENTURY BC OR AD

The many species of food grasses yield grains that for millennia have provided a significant portion of human nutritional needs. However, the hard, often husked seeds must be processed before consumption, usually by pounding, grinding or soaking. From the Upper Palaeolithic period, rounded rubbing stones (p. 32) were used to crush and grind grain foods on a flat bedding stone . With the appearance of domesticated grain crops in the Neolithic (p. 91), more efficient, specially shaped querns developed. A broad, flat-sided stone was pushed backwards and forwards against a sloping, saddle-shaped surface, grinding the seeds. In Mesoamerica this grinding table, still called by its Aztec name *metate*, was used to process soft kernels of maize for making tortillas. Hard, porous volcanic stones such as basalt were particularly effective.

The design of querns evolved to facilitate the flow of seeds and increase output. The 'push mill', used throughout the eastern Mediterranean until 150 BC, involved a large rectangular rubbing stone with a hopper that fed grain through a slot to the surface of the bedding stone. The upper stone was moved by pushing and pulling on a long handle.

Rotary mills

Dramatic improvements in milling came with the switch to rotary action in the Mediterranean world between 500 and 200 BC, possibly spreading from Spain eastwards. Rotary action allowed both more convenient and efficient working as well as the application of animal and water power. The rotary quern consisted of a circular bedding stone with central pivot that carried a runner stone with a short vertical handle set into its outer edge. The operator turned the upper stone with one hand while feeding grain into a hole or small hopper around the pivot (rynd) with the other. The flour trickled out the edges. The spacing between the stones could be adjusted by means of the rynd, to allow production of fine or coarse flour.

By 200 BC mules were put to work turning large rotary mills with an hourglass-shaped upper stone,

Left *A simple rotary quern – grain was fed through the central hole with one hand while the upper stone was turned with the other. Although simple, the invention of the rotary quern was a great step forward in milling.*

Below *A metate and* mano *(the grinding tool), from Los Moquitia, Honduras, Classic–Postclassic period. Although this particular example is ceremonial, plainer versions were essential tools in Mesoamerican homes, used to grind cooked maize kernels into a dough.*

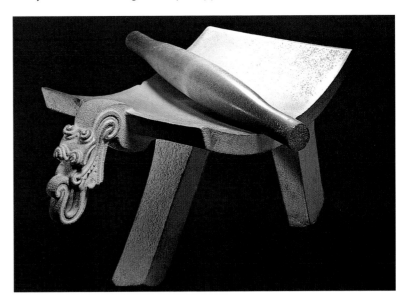

A Roman relief from a sarcophagus of the 2nd century AD, showing a mule-driven Pompeian hourglass-shaped mill.

the top part of which was a grain hopper. Milling establishments usually also baked bread, and the partial mechanization of the task of grinding grain led to people in cities around the Mediterranean buying bread rather than making it at home.

Watermills

The application of water power to milling was a major advance. Comments in ancient Greek and Latin technical authors suggest that this innovation occurred at Alexandria in Egypt in the mid-3rd century BC. The earliest archaeological evidence dates only to the 1st century AD. The typical Graeco-Roman watermill, sometimes called the 'Vitruvian mill' after the Roman architect who described it, had an upright paddle wheel with a large, wooden angle-gear drive that transformed the horizontal rotation of the paddle wheel axle to the vertical rotation of the spindle driving the upper millstone.

The earliest literary and archaeological evidence shows paddle wheels driven by water flowing either beneath the paddle wheel (undershot) or over it (overshot). The more efficient breastshot arrange-

ment, in which water hits the back side of the wheel, may be several centuries later. There is as yet no proof for the existence before the 7th century AD of the simple 'Norse' or 'Greek' mill, in which a horizontal paddle wheel is attached directly to the foot of the axle driving the millstone.

Watermills spread rapidly through the Roman empire, and by the 2nd or 3rd century AD industrial-scale milling installations were associated with

A Han dynasty bronze model of a peasant working a millstone. The millstone, set in a square box, would be turned by the man pushing and pulling on the pole.

aqueducts, as at Barbegal in Provence, where 16 wheels were housed in one building. While it is difficult to estimate the output of a Roman watermill, the smallest probably produced 10 times as much flour as a push mill, and the labour was more or less free. Aside from the ship's sail, the watermill represents the only mechanical application of an inanimate energy source in the ancient world.

Mechanical water-lifting devices

All societies have to lift water for drinking, watering animals, irrigation, drainage, washing and numerous industrial applications. Mechanically complex water-lifting devices were invented at Alexandria in Egypt in the 3rd century BC: the water-screw, compartmented wheel, bucket-chain and force pump. Prior to this, the inhabitants of the Mediterranean world and Mesopotamia relied on the shaduf (p. 99), the pulley and bucket system, and the *cerd*, a large, self-emptying water sack lifted over a pulley by draft animals. All these ancient devices were so appropriate to their social and physical environment that they remain in use today.

The wheel with compartmented body, used for irrigation and drainage, had water-tight, wedge-shaped compartments radiating outwards from a heavy axle. As the wheel turned, water entered the compartments through openings around the rim, then poured out at a higher level through openings near the axle. Such wheels could be turned by men treading on the rim or by animals through an angle gear called the saqiya. In this gearing system, the animals walk in a circle, turning a vertical shaft supporting a large, horizontal cog wheel. This wheel meshes at right angles with a vertical gear wheel mounted on and turning the axle of the compartmented water-lifting wheel. The saqiya gear transmits power in a direction opposite to the geared Vitruvian watermill, but the principle is the same and the design of the watermill probably was based on the saqiya-driven compartmented wheel.

To lift water higher, a spoked wheel was fitted with a hollow rim divided into numerous separate compartments. As the wheel turned, water entered each compartment through an opening in the forward end, then poured out of the same opening as the compartment passed over the top of the

Artist's reconstruction of the run of Roman watermills at Barbegal, Provence, with 16 wheels harnessed into one run.

Below *This working reconstruction of a Roman device for raising water using manpower was based on evidence of two actual water-wheels found in London, dating from between AD 63 and 108. This sophisticated device would have been capable of delivering large amounts of water.*

wheel. These wheels could be turned by someone treading on the circumference, by a saqiya gear system, or even – since less torque was needed – by paddles fixed to its rim. Because of their high lift, such wheels were often used to lift water to elevated cisterns feeding pressurized pipe systems serving urban baths. In the Late Roman period the compartments were replaced with ceramic pots.

Pumps

While the compartmented wheel is an anonymous invention, the names of the inventors of the water-screw and force pump have survived. In the mid-3rd century BC, Archimedes developed the water-screw (p. 99). At about the same time in Alexandria, Ctesibius invented the piston pump. This so-called Ctesibian device involved a pair of pistons working reciprocally in two parallel, upright bronze cylinders. As one piston was lifted, it drew water into the cylinder through a flap valve in its base; at the same time, the other piston descended and drove the water in the second cylinder through

These norias, large wooden water-wheels – the largest is around 20 m (66 ft) in diameter – lift water from the River Orontes at Hama in Syria. Water enters the boxes as the wheel turns and is then poured out at the top of the towers, from where it is channelled to fields and to the town. The wooden paddles help drive the wheels. First developed in the Byzantine period, the oldest surviving example dates from 1473.

KEY DATES

rotary mill	after 500 BC, Spain
watermill	mid-3rd century BC, Egypt
complex water-lifting	3rd century BC, Egypt
force-pump	3rd century BC, Egypt

a flap valve into a vertical pipe. Continuous working of the two piston rods by means of a pivoting handle forced a stream of water out the pipe into a reservoir or moveable nozzle. The alternate name *sipho* mimicked the hissing sound of spouting water, a unique form of delivery that fostered use of the force pump as a fire extinguisher.

Unlike the suction pump, not invented until the 15th century, the force pump had to be placed in the water it lifted. During the Roman imperial period, local craftsmen in the European provinces reproduced the sophisticated design inexpensively by boring cylinders and connecting tubes in blocks of wood, which were then mounted at the bottom of wells to provide drinking water.

Two pumping devices used an endless loop of containers, allowing very high lifts or the lifting of water from deep, narrow spaces such as wells. The bucket-chain, driven by a saqiya gear or over the axle of a tread wheel, had a pair of rope or chain loops carrying a series of metal, wooden or ceramic containers. As the upper axle on which the loops were suspended turned, the containers dipped into the water, emptying their contents into a catch trough as they passed over the axle at the top.

The chain-pump was used for draining ships' bilges. Small wooden disks with a central hole were strung on a rope loop at frequent intervals and held in place by knots. One side of the loop hung free, while the other passed through a wooden pipe, the lower end of which was mounted in the bilge sump. A windlass drew the rope upwards through the pipe, and as each disk entered the pipe it pushed water up the pipe ahead of it.

Mechanical water-lifting devices were both ubiquitous and important throughout the Mediterranean world and the Near East from the Hellenistic period onwards. They made a significant contribution to agricultural productivity, sea trade, craft production, public hygiene and urban amenities.

Gardens

I made gardens and parks and planted all kinds of fruit in them.
I made reservoirs to water groves of flowering trees.
KING SOLOMON, ECCLESIASTES, 2: 4–6

A vignette from the Book of the Dead of the Egyptian scribe Nakht (c. 1350–1300 BC). He is shown standing with his wife in their garden, which includes a rectangular pool surrounded by trees; more trees, including a palm, are behind them.

Many cultures have a concept that includes a tree of life, or a garden with abundant fruit (such as the biblical Garden of Eden). An ancient Sumerian myth of the 4th to 3rd millennium BC tells how Shukallituda discovered that by planting a shade-giving tree, other plants were able to grow below in its protection, hinting at the initial impetus in gardening.

The earliest 'gardens' are in Mesopotamia and Egypt, areas which are largely arid, and so they relied on a network of irrigation channels and water-lifting devices (pp. 80, 97 and 101) to bring water from their great river systems to fields and gardens. Gardens developed from a need to provide a special enclosed area where the gardener could give constant care to more tender and thirsty plants such as vegetables and fruit trees. From these enclosed gardens came the desire to include one in courtyard spaces within palaces. By the beginning of the 2nd millennium BC, palm trees gave shade in the palace gardens at Mari (in modern Syria).

Egyptian gardens

Egyptian tomb inscriptions of the 4th Dynasty (*c.* 2575–2540 BC) show that high-ranking officials already had gardens. Tomb reliefs sometimes depict small garden plots, and by the 18th dynasty (1539–1292 BC) frescoes bring such gardens colourfully to life. A rectangular enclosure had at its centre a rectangular pool surrounded by rows of plants and trees. Temples were provided with a

Relief from the North Palace of Ashurbanipal at Nineveh, in modern Iraq, c. 645 BC, showing a palace garden watered by irrigation channels.

sacred precinct where special plants (often scented ones) could be grown to provide offerings to the gods. Some pharaohs planted a grove of trees to grace the grand forecourt of their mortuary temple and tomb. The first to do this was the 4th dynasty ruler Snofru.

Hatshepsut, the 18th dynasty female ruler, had special incense trees shipped from the land of Punt to beautify her own mortuary temple and tomb. Her stepson Thutmose III led military expeditions into Canaan and Syria, bringing back as part of his booty many new trees and flowers; the plants were depicted in carvings in a chapel at Karnak known as the Botanical Garden. These new additions gave gardeners a greater range of plants and aided the diffusion of plant species. Plants were grown and studied for medicinal properties and the Egyptians and Assyrians both compiled pharmacopoeia.

Assyrian & Babylonian gardens

In the 11th century BC the Assyrian king Tiglath-pileser I created a botanical garden from species collected during his military expeditions, and later kings such as Sennacherib (c. 704–681 BC) created pleasure gardens at Nineveh. Relief carvings depict Sennacherib's garden – of which he was immensely proud – consisting of a landscaped park, terraced on a hillside. Texts reveal that he also created a game park.

In Babylon, Nebuchadnezzar (605–562 BC) is credited with the construction of one of the Seven Wonders of the ancient world, the Hanging Gardens. Here, terraces were artificially built up using mud bricks, and the luxuriant vegetation spilling over the terraces made a great impression in such a low-lying area. Gardens were becoming sophisticated in design, but were still the prerogative of the ruling class; their subjects aspired to own a produce-type garden.

Ancient Persian gardens

The Persians, who later conquered the lands of Mesopotamia, continued the practice of creating park-like gardens, both for hunting and for pleasure, such as those of Cyrus the Great at Pasargadae in the mid-6th century BC. Following Alexander's defeat of the Persian empire, the Greeks were greatly impressed with these pleasure gardens and carried on the tradition. They kept the Persian name for them, which in translation became

Garden plants in a Roman fresco from Pompeii (Casa del Bracciale d'Oro). The rose was the most favoured of all (its earliest occurrence in European art is in a Bronze Age fresco from Knossos). The Romans hunted for new species, especially of roses, and commenced the great diffusion of plant species in the West.

paradeisoi, and this in turn was later translated into Latin (then English) to become paradise.

Greek groves & gardens

Greek gardens were primarily for growing produce; there were, however, communal areas such as groves around sacred places and temples. Groves outside cities were often areas where citizens would gather to exercise, stroll and debate; some, such as the Academy in Athens, became the haunt of philosophers. Theophrastus, head of the Lyceum philosophical school (*c.* 371–287 BC) wrote a botanical thesis (*Inquiry into Plants*) and when he died he left his private garden to the citizens. Another philosopher, Epicurus (341–270 BC), was said to have had the first garden within the city. After the conquest of the east by Alexander, ideas were introduced from Persia and Egypt.

Roman gardens

Simple gardens have been discovered at the early Roman colony of Cosa, north of Rome (4th–3rd centuries BC), and at Pompeii. Importantly, these were within the city, and generally at the back of the house. What is so different in Italy and the West is that the middle-class owned gardens, as well as aristocrats and rulers. Following Rome's conquest of Greece, and later Asia Minor, Romans were increasingly influenced by eastern opulence. The idea of Greek colonnades and Persian paradise were transferred to luxurious homes in the capital.

By the 2nd century BC it was becoming fashionable to have a peristyle garden within the home. These gardens were situated in an internal open court (a source of light for surrounding rooms) and the space often became very decorative. Altars and shrines were placed in gardens, and statuary was introduced, originally looted from Greek sites, but later on copies and adaptations were produced by Roman workshops for a mass market.

After the construction of aqueducts (p. 82), water was piped to villas and houses in cities, so water features could be installed. Pools and fountains graced many gardens, as well as *nymphaea* (shrines of a water nymph) and topiary. *Pergulae* (pergolas) came into use to provide shady promenades, while arbours and benches allowed rest in

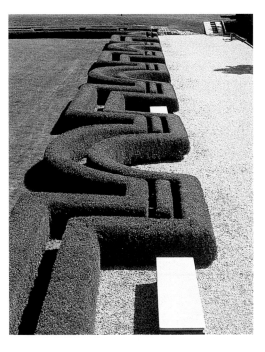

Left *Box topiary hedge at Fishbourne Roman Palace planted in the original bedding trenches found by archaeologists. Pliny the Elder records that Gaius Matius invented the art of topiary during the reign of Augustus (the craft was named after the* topiarius, *a landscape gardener).*

Below *A luxurious Roman house, the Casa di Loreius Tiburtinus at Pompeii, with a terraced garden fitted with an alfresco dining area (at the rear) and pool, under a vine-covered pergola.*

pleasant surroundings. Alfresco dining also became popular. Ornamental plants were sought for gardens, and new species were introduced. Manuals giving agricultural and horticultural (the Latin for garden is *hortus*) advice were written, and techniques were improved.

Gardens of ancient China & Japan

The Shang dynasty (*c.* 1600–1100 BC) was known to have enclosed hunting parks (*you*), which included a raised platform for ritual purposes. The Zhou (1100–221 BC) stocked these with rare plants as well as animals. Under the Qin (221–207 BC) the *you* was transformed into a park (*yuan*) with artificial ponds, and began to take a garden-like form. These parks became a symbol of imperial power.

The Han emperors (206 BC–AD 220) enhanced their *yuan* with plants and birds from all over their empire. They also sought to recreate a mystical landscape associated with immortality: hence the concept of 'Three Mountains of the Immortals' in a lakeside setting. This idea of a mythic rock garden was reproduced throughout the empire in private gardens by using scaled-down versions of famous mountains. In the 3rd century AD, private gardens became a refuge of peace in a troubled time. Later gardens were influenced by ideals of nature, as reflected in landscape painting and poetry.

Murals in the Tepantitla compound at Teotihuacan, Mexico, c. AD 400–500, possibly depict a paradisiacal garden, with water, flowering trees and plants, and animals. Behind the central figure in this detail, interpreted as the Great Goddess of the site, rises a huge morning glory plant. Other plants depicted in this mural have been identified as having medicinal properties.

KEY DATES

palace garden	2000 BC, Syria
temple grove	*c.* 2613 BC, Egypt
botanical garden	*c.* 1000 BC, Assyria
game parks	7th century BC, Assyria
paradeisoi gardens	*c.* 545 BC, Persia
garden parks	*c.* 220 BC, China
peristyle garden	2nd century BC, Rome
topiary	*c.* 27 BC–AD 14, Rome
botanical garden	AD 1440–69, Aztec

Japanese gardens were influenced by Chinese examples, but as Japan is such a mountainous country they were smaller in scale. Ancient chronicles of the 5th century AD mention fishponds and winding streams, and by AD 612 we hear that a landscape gardener was employed by empress Suiko. Her southern garden had a Chinese-style bridge, lake and rock sculptures forming a landscape in miniature.

Gardens in the Americas

Horticulture developed independently in the New World. Evidence of intensive plant breeding and cultivation in Aztec produce gardens has been found on raised fields (*chinampas*) in swampy areas. Spanish conquistadores, such as Bernal Diaz, record seeing wonderful Aztec gardens, filled with herbs, flowers and sweet-smelling trees, and ponds and streams of water. Such pleasure gardens were confined to aristocratic circles; vegetables and fruit were grown by lower classes.

Sources describe park-like gardens at Tezcoinco, where Nezahualcoyotl, the 15th-century ruler of Texcoco, created a grove of majestic trees around a sacred hill. The gardens had pools, fountains and carved historic emblems on the rocks. The Aztec emperor Motecuzoma I (AD 1440–69) was known to enjoy hunting game in special parks encircled by water; but he was also responsible for founding the renowned botanical gardens of Huastepec – he ordered people to gather plants from coastal tropical regions for inclusion in his gardens. Spanish officials were sent to study them and to introduce worthy new species to Europe.

The Domestication of Animals

Domestic animals have been vital parts of most agricultural economies. Meat is only one useful product: humans also use bones, teeth, horn, antler, skin, sinew, marrow and intestines from dead animals, and blood, milk, manure, eggs, fibres and working and transport potential from live ones.

What is a domestic animal? This question is more difficult to answer than many people might think. We must distinguish *domestication* from *taming*. Individuals of many species can be tamed, but they differ from wild individuals only in their behaviour. Probably the best definition of domestication is the separation of a group of animals from the wild gene pool. The reproduction of this group is under human control, so humans may (by deliberate selection or not) bring about physical changes.

No definition is perfect, and this one does throw up some anomalies. For example, it would define goldfish in a garden pond as domestic, while tame pigs that wander into the undergrowth and breed with wild boar would be wild – but it is probably as good as we can get. For archaeologists, the key point is that the physical changes arising from separation from the wild gene pool may allow us to recognize the process in the past, though only after the animals have been domestic for long enough for the changes to occur.

Man's first friends

The earliest recognizably domestic animal by this criterion is the dog. Animals small enough to be distinguished from wolves, their wild ancestor, are found on the settlements of hunter-gatherers in

A drawing in ink on a limestone flake depicting a dog of the pointer type, from Western Thebes, Egypt, c. 1305–1080 BC. The dog is particularly well observed by the artist, and was probably used in hunting.

northwest Europe dating to the early postglacial, around 11,000 years ago. Even earlier domestication may have occurred in the Near East. These animals must have been domesticated to assist in hunting and it is not clear why hunters did not domesticate them much earlier. Individual wolves may have been tamed for this purpose, but they would be indistinguishable archaeologically from wild ones. Perhaps as forests began to cover Europe and humans needed to track wounded animals, a dog's sense of smell became more important.

Other carnivores were also domesticated, but not until after the start of farming. Grain stores attracted mice, providing a niche for domestic cats. The earliest domestic cats are currently from Early Neolithic Cyprus. They are recognizable not because of any biological change, but because Cyprus had no native wild cats; the animals can only have got there through human transport.

Herd animals

Domestic herd animals form part of most agricultural systems. Yet animals that are now universal mostly originated in limited areas of the globe. The Near Eastern agricultural system, based on wheat and barley, included domestic sheep, goats, cattle and pigs, and these were dispersed to other systems in the Far East (based on rice), Africa (sorghum and millet) and subsequently the Americas (maize). Recent work has shown that the pig

was independently domesticated in China before the arrival of the Near Eastern farming system, and cattle may also have been domesticated in India. The only other agricultural system to domesticate large herd mammals was in Peru, which contributed llamas and alpacas. Some systems domesticated no large mammals; Mexico's largest domesticate was the turkey.

The first domesticated herd mammal is currently thought to be the goat. The signs may be a shift towards the killing of younger animals around 10,000 years ago. This remains controversial because changes in hunting methods might also result in different kill patterns – but, as noted, physical changes would take some time to occur. Goats and sheep show these changes earliest, and these species were rapidly exported by farmers from their original areas in the Near East across much of the Old World. Once sheep and goats occur outside the restricted areas in which they lived wild, we can be sure they were domestic.

Domestic pigs are less easy to identify in this way because the wild form was so much more widespread. Some argue that the pigs of early European farmers were 'semi-domestic' descendants of local wild stock, allowed to roam. Recent work, however, shows that there are true domestic pigs, smaller than the wild ones. This would not be the case unless they were indeed under close control and not able to breed with the wild populations.

Neolithic pottery figurines from China, depicting a pig, a sheep and a cockerel, c. 2400–2000 BC. It has recently been shown that the pig was independently domesticated in China.

A fragment of a painting from the tomb of Nebamun, at Dra Abu el-Naga, Egypt, c. 1390 BC. The cattle are being driven past Nebamun for inspection, with scribes ready to record the numbers. In many early societies cattle were indicators of wealth and status.

Secondary products

The stimulus to domesticate herd mammals must have been a desire to maintain the supply of products from the *dead* animal. An increasing human population may have put pressure on wild stocks, leading to protection, ownership and domestication – although the details remain obscure. Once domestic, however, many other products were available from the *live* animal. Some believe that these so-called secondary products began to be exploited at around 3500 BC, and many may have been. Dairy products (milk, cheese, yoghurt etc.) may yet turn out to be earlier.

The impact of transport and traction was huge – in addition to being ridden, a horse may pull a cart full of food or trade goods, a plough, or a war chariot. Botai in Kazakhstan (dated to 4000 BC) is one site where the earliest domestic horses have so far been found, which has produced hundreds of thousands of horse bones. Most come from hunted animals, but since this weight of meat and bone had to be brought back to the settlement in the first place, something must have carried it. This, and artifactual evidence for harnessing, suggest that some horses were domestic – used mainly to hunt and transport their dead wild relatives.

Domestic animals gave farmers manure to fertilize their fields, transport to move their produce around, dairy products to supplement their crops – and a meat bank if the crops were inadequate. Chaff

Below left Cattle and sheep being led to a banquet on the Standard of Ur (c. 2600–2400 BC). As well as exploiting animals for their meat, humans also used live animals for their 'secondary products', including wool and milk, as depicted in a milking scene (below right), from a temple at Al-Ubaid (c. 2550–2400 BC).

domesticated dog	12,000 years ago, Near East
domesticated cat	c. 9000 years ago, Cyprus
domesticated goat	10,000 years ago, Near East
domesticated sheep	10,000 years ago, Near East
domesticated horse	4000 BC, Central Asia

and straw, inedible by humans, could act as food or bedding for the animals. In a sense, farmers with crops and animals have domesticated an ecosystem, not a series of separate economic attributes: the combination was greater than the sum of parts. Once this had occurred, the history of farmers and early empires, particularly in the Old World, was heavily dependent on its domestic livestock.

Left *A llama herder drives his animals in pairs on a vessel of the Lima Culture, AD 200–600, from Peru.*

Below *Leashed monkeys brought to the Assyrian court, shown in a relief dating to the 9th century BC.*

ZOOS & PETS

The world's first zoos were established at the royal courts of ancient Egypt and Mesopotamia. Though little archaeological evidence survives, numerous images and texts document the menagerie animals and shed light on their cultural significance. Zoos enhanced royal prestige, demonstrated far-flung imperial dominion and inspired the earliest natural history studies. There were opportunities for the public to marvel at the animals as they passed en route to the zoos, but there was probably limited access once they were installed.

Notable Egyptian representations of zoo creatures include the Syrian bears brought to the pharaoh Sahure (c. 2450 BC); the baboons shipped to the female ruler Hatshepsut (mid-15th century BC); and the prodigious rhinoceros exhibited by Ramesses II (13th century BC). Thutmose III (15th century BC) boasted of his menagerie's remarkable birds that laid eggs daily, apparently domestic fowl from India, the first to be seen in Egypt.

Mesopotamian royalty also maintained menagerie collections from the 3rd millennium on. The Assyrian kings of the 9th to 7th centuries BC took particular interest in

obtaining unusual animals from their ever-expanding empire. Images abound of apes, monkeys, elephants, Bactrian camels and other exotic fauna intended for the menageries of Nimrud and Nineveh. Among the many innovative wonders at the Assyrian king Sennacherib's 'Palace Without Rival', built round 700 BC at Nineveh, were the first zoo exhibits to replicate the native habitats of the creatures displayed. According to his inscriptions, the uncaged animals flourished and 'produced young in great numbers', still a sign today of a successful zoo programme.

The keeping of household pets surely developed at the same time as the domestication of animals. From historical periods in the ancient Near East, we have pictorial and textual records of pets, especially dogs and cats. Many of them were given names such as 'Blackie' and 'Brave One'. Certain pets, such as the favourite cat of the Egyptian crown prince Thutmose in the 14th century BC, received elaborate burials and grave-goods. In addition, pets figure in much ancient Near Eastern literature in roles ranging from the heroic to the humorous.

Wild animals, including monkeys, baboons, bears, lions and gazelles, were occasionally

tamed. Reliefs and wall-paintings depict them performing various tasks for their owners, or cavorting mischievously in otherwise staid settings. Mesopotamian records refer to aspects of their care, for instance training bears and making leashes for lions.

Cooking

He has discovered the art of making fire, by which hard and stringy roots can be rendered digestible and poisonous roots or herbs innocuous. This discovery of fire, probably the greatest ever made by man excepting language, dates from before the dawn of history.
CHARLES DARWIN, 1871

Cooking has been described as a cultural act and one of the attributes that distinguishes us from all other species; many theories exist about its origins. Most archaeologists agree that cooking began about 500,000 years ago, although some believe that 300,000 years ago is more accurate. A few scientists support the very controversial theory that early hominids were cooking in Africa 1.76–1.5 million years ago.

Survival and food supply are intertwined; extending the range of foodstuffs would have had important benefits for our ancestors. Meat and many plant foods can be eaten raw, but cooking can render them non-toxic, edible, palatable and more digestible, thereby increasing their energy value. The near universal adoption of cooking can perhaps be attributed to the change it creates in flavour and texture, leading to increased experimentation with different foods. No one agrees whether early cooking was utilized more for tubers, plant foods or meat.

Early evidence

All over the world, the connection between fire and food was made again and again. The basic cooking techniques are global and limited only by technology. In keeping with a nomadic lifestyle and limited technology, the early kitchen had no specific equipment. Rocks, sticks, skins, baskets, even a carcass or organs, were all used as equipment and vessels for cooking. Archaeological evidence for early cooking is found in the form of hearths and burnt bone, soil and rock. A range of sites, dating from about 500,000–300,000 years ago, have hearths which indicate that food may have been roasted there. One such is at Zhoukoudian, China – though the findings there are much disputed; at the site of Terra Amata, France, dwellings contained hearths; and a fireplace was excavated at Menez-Dregan, also in France.

As we move forwards in time, the evidence for cooking becomes more substantial and less controversial. Vanguard Cave in Gibraltar has hearths which have been dated at 100,000–86,000 years ago. At another cave site in the Dordogne region of France, excavated by the University of Bordeaux and designated Grotte XVI, hearths have been dated at 66,000–54,000 years ago, with evidence

Left *Greek terracotta model of a man grilling food directly over hot coals – this is one of the fundamental methods of cooking.*

A bronze tripod, with a pair of lifting hooks and a ladle; Warring States Period, c. 433 BC, found in a tomb at Leigudun, China. When discovered, the cauldron still contained ox bones and soot was visible on its base, showing that it had been used for cooking, possibly in the funerary feast.

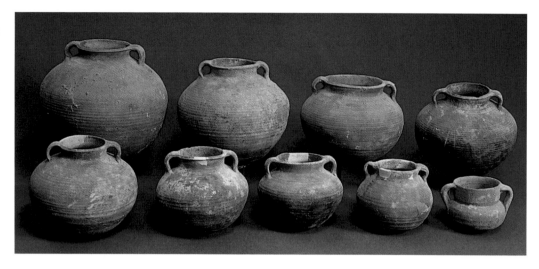

A range of ceramic cooking vessels of different sizes from Dan, Israel, 10th–8th centuries BC. The advent of ceramic vessels changed cooking completely – the food could be cooked by direct heat and in larger quantities.

which could indicate the smoking of meat and fish. This cave was inhabited by Neanderthals. Hearths at Abric Romani, near Barcelona, in Spain, date to 53,000 years ago. Clear evidence for cooking is present by 34,000–28,000 years ago at, for example, Zagreb Vindija cave in Croatia. While most of these early kitchens are in caves, there is also some evidence for cooking taking place inside temporary, tent-like dwellings.

Methods & materials

There are five fundamentals to cooking. Direct heat using flames or coals roasts or grills, and is arguably the foundation method of cookery. The second fundamental method utilizes indirect or wet heat.

A traditional tabun oven, still in use to bake bread in the Near East.

Sometimes called steaming, it can employ leaves, seaweed, moss or clay to protect the food while it cooks. The third primary method of cooking is immersion in a liquid, allowing boiling, or simmering. Baking, or dry heat roasting, is the fourth primary cooking method. The final way to cook is through frying, either by immersion in hot oil or using a smaller amount of oil to quick fry, or sauté.

In some areas, food supplies and the pantry were expanded and stabilized through the domestication of plants and animals (pp. 91 and 109). Ceramic containers and/or the extended pantry led to major advances in both cooking methods and the quantities that could be prepared.

Cooking changed dramatically with the advent of ceramic containers. The earliest pottery known, Jomon pottery of Japan, has been dated to 14,000 BC by carbonized material on the surface, possibly indicating its use in cooking (p. 38). And in the Zagros Mountains region pottery appears around 6300 BC. Containing liquids in a pottery vessel would allow cooking with direct heat, rather than the passive hot rock system. The ability to cook by immersion would result in food preparations ranging from fermented beverages (p. 116) to soup. Ceramic vessels also created the opportunity for cooking larger quantities.

Ovens were generally underground pits lined with clay and heated by a direct fire. Like preheating one of today's ovens, baking would have used the heat absorbed by the interior clay lining. In Mesopotamia, the people of the city of Ur were using above-ground ovens over 5000 years ago. Larger ovens would allow both the production of quantities of baked goods and create bakers, perhaps the first specialized cooks.

The next big advance occurred when metal began to be used in cooking. Early metal pots were much more durable, and far better at conducting heat, than the fragile, heavy and short-lived pottery containers. Examples from 2000–771 BC have been found at Dayangzhou in Jiangxi, China. Clay vessels were used as the models for early bronze vessels and specialized forms appear, such as meat cooking vessels. In some parts of the world, particularly the Americas, native peoples acquired metal cooking vessels only after European contact, by trade.

Even in areas with limited fuel, metal containers allowed the final significant type of cooking. Frying uses oil at a very high heat, which can only be achieved by sustained heat concentrated within a metal container. This method cooks food quickly and therefore allows fuel conservation. Open fire hearths gave way to more contained cooking fires with metal pots and more specialized equipment. In many parts of the world, fire became increasingly contained, and fireplaces, footed fire hearths and chimneys evolved, as did the production of a wide variety of metal vessels, iron grates, spits and other tools.

KEY DATES

cooking hearths	500,000–300,000 years ago, China?, Europe
	100,000–86,000 years ago, Gibraltar
	34,000–28,000 years ago, Croatia
ceramic cooking vessels	14,000 BC, Japan
above-ground ovens	5000 years ago, Mesopotamia
metal cooking vessels	2000–771 BC, China

Below *Two women baking bread: the dough is mixed in the tall jars and then put into small clay pots for baking. The painting is from the tomb of Antefoqer at Thebes, in Egypt, c. 1950 BC.*

Bottom *Bronze cooking vessels in a kitchen in the House of the Vetii at Pompeii. The use of metal vessels was another big step forward in cooking, being more durable and better at conducting heat than pottery.*

27

Fermented Beverages

There is no department of man's life on which more labour is spent, as if nature had not given us the most healthy of beverages to drink, water …

PLINY THE ELDER, 1ST CENTURY AD

Right *The oldest wine jar in the world: a 7400-year-old 'vintage' from Hajji Firuz Tepe, Iran, which contained an organic residue.*

Below *A jar that contained a Neolithic mixed fermented beverage of honey, rice and fruit (probably grape or hawthorn tree fruit), according to molecular investigation; from Jiahu in Henan province, China, 7th millennium BC.*

Fermented beverages are one of the greatest discoveries made by humans around the world. Probably first accomplished during the Palaeolithic period, beverage-making had become a well-organized craft by Neolithic times (*c.* 8500–4000 BC in Asia). Except for the peoples of cold polar climates, where sugar sources are non-existent, humans have shown a remarkable propensity to find ways to ferment various natural crops and products – honey, grapes and other fruits, chocolate, cereals including barley, wheat, maize, millet and sorghum, and exotic plant exudations from agave, yucca, taro, cactus, palm tree resin, to mention only a few.

The conversion of simple sugars to alcohol will occur in nature under the right conditions. Many fruits, including grape, fig, apple and berries, harbour the 'wine-beer-bread yeast', *Saccharomyces cerevisiae*, on their skins. Once a sugar-rich juice has been exuded from the fruit, these micro-organisms naturally begin multiplying by feeding on the monosaccharides of the juice – within a day or two in warmer climates. Yeast of the same species also exist in honey, by far the richest natural source of simple sugars (60–80 per cent by weight); when diluted to one-fifth honey and four-fifths water, the yeast begin fermenting the honey to mead.

A natural propensity

A propensity for sugar and alcohol is found throughout the animal world, from flies to birds to elephants, which readily gravitate to ripe, fermenting fruit and honey. It is not difficult to imagine Palaeolithic humans being drawn to sweet, brightly coloured fruit, and gathering it up in containers made of wood, stone, leather or fibres. Under the accumulated weight of the fruit above, fermenting juices would collect at the bottom of the vessel. This 'wine' would have been quickly appreciated and created again if possible. Lacking the knowledge or the means to preserve the beverage, however, it could only be made at harvest-time, and had to be drunk quickly.

Intentional fermentation

As an intentional human activity, the Neolithic period was the first time that all the necessary pieces fell into place for the momentous innovation of fermented beverage-making. Permanent settlements led to specialized production, increasing demand and trade. The invention of pottery meant that the beverages could be stored in stoppered, durable jars.

Based on an expanding knowledge of their anti-microbial properties, herbs and tree resins were added to the beverages to prevent them from turning to vinegar or, minimally, to cover up bad odours and tastes. Chemical analyses of ancient Mediterranean and Middle Eastern wines in particular have shown that tree resins were used for thousands of years, a practice that persisted only in Greece in the form of retsina.

Most importantly, Neolithic humans began domesticating plants, especially cereals, fruit trees and vines, thus guaranteeing larger, more predictable yields and products with other desirable characteristics (e.g. higher sugar). Bee-keeping might well have begun in this period as well, although definitive evidence is lacking.

In trial and error fashion, the ancient beverage-maker must have realized that by adding grapes or another fruit high in natural yeast to whatever sweet substances were locally available, fermentation was easier and quicker. On opposite ends of the Asian landmass – in Neolithic villages of upland Mesopotamia, the Caucasus and Turkey in the West and in communities in the Yellow and Yangzi river basins in the East – archaeological, botanical and chemical data have shown that a fermented beverage was first made by combining honey, fruit and cereal. Whether the innovations occurred independently is not known, but the advantages of adding a fermenting fruit juice or diluted honey was apparently appreciated in both areas.

The problem in fermenting cereal sugars is that they are not associated with naturally occurring yeast and thus cannot be directly fermented. Moreover, grains are largely comprised of starches (polysaccharides) that are not digested by the yeast. Ancient humans eventually learned how to break down the complex sugars of cereals into simpler ones by malting barley in the Near East and by saccharifying rice and other grains using moulds in China. To start the fermentation process, the beverage-makers had two choices: either wait for some air-borne, adventitious yeast to colonize the brew (as is still the case with Belgian lambic beers and Chinese rice wines), or, more pre-

dictably, to introduce *S. cerevisiae* directly by adding fermenting fruit or honey.

By using a yeast 'starter', as is implied in the earliest beer recipe dedicated to the ancient Mesopotamian beer-goddess Ninkasi, a more predictable end-product was assured. Having established a colony of *S. cerevisiae*, it could be collected and transferred from one batch to the next. By 'automatic selection' (humans isolating yeast strains based on their observations), the wine yeast evolved into the beer and bread yeasts.

Another advantage of *S. cerevisiae* is that once an alcoholic content of 5 per cent by volume is reached, detrimental micro-organisms, which can cause undesirable flavours and aromas and even disease, are killed off, while the yeast survives and continues fermenting available sugars to produce a drink with more than twice this amount of alcohol. Gradually, in the non-hygienic, experimental settings of Neolithic beverage-making, this yeast came to predominate.

Fermented beverages became increasingly more specialized. Single-product drinks, such as grape wine, barley beer, rice wine and honey mead, eventually displaced mixed beverages. Although the more specialized beverages were sometimes held up as marks of civilization – or barbarity, depending on one's vantage point – the knowledge and expertise

Above *A Mesopotamian banquet scene, the forerunner of the ancient Greek symposium, as depicted on an impression of a lapis lazuli cylinder seal from Queen Pu-abi's tomb in the Royal Cemetery at Ur, c. 2600–2400 BC. A male and female imbibe barley beer through drinking tubes from a wide-mouthed jar, as dignitaries below raise their cups, probably containing wine, which is served from a spouted jar.*

Above *'Phrygian grog', a mixed fermented beverage of grape wine, barley beer and honey mead, was served with this bronze lion-headed situla, or bucket, recovered from the 'Midas Tumulus' at Gordion, and dated to c. 700 BC, Turkey.*

Chamber 10 of Tomb U-j at Abydos, Egypt, filled with wine jars. The tomb belonged to a king and dates to around 3150 BC, when the Egyptians imported wine from the Levant.

KEY DATES

intentional fermentation	Neolithic, Mesopotamia & China
oldest wine jar	7400 years ago, Iran
wine-making industry	c. 3000 BC, Egypt

mented beverages made from cereals – rice and millet wines in China, barley and wheat beers in northern Europe, and maize beer (chicha) in the New World – played similar roles in society and religion, marking major life events (birth, puberty, marriage, military victory, worship and death).

Once a fermented beverage had assumed a major role and established an economic foothold in one region, it could spread and encompass cultures elsewhere. Initially, a new beverage is introduced to elite members of a society through trade and ceremonial exchange. The prestige attached to the beverage and the vessels used to serve and drink it, which were often made of luxury materials, facilitated the transference. After its acceptance, the next logical step was to begin local production, thus assuring a more steady supply, at a lower cost and tailored to local tastes.

A prime example of this process is the establishment of a royal wine-making industry in the Nile Delta around 3000 BC. The earliest kings of Egypt imported their wines from the southern Levant. By transplanting the domesticated Eurasian grape vine to Egypt, where the wild grape had never grown, and drawing upon Levantine wine-making skills, the pharaohs created an enterprise that lasted thousands of years and was of far-reaching significance. Larger-scale production meant that wine could be integrated into society at large. Egypt's network of trade and political connections led to the further extension of the 'Near Eastern wine culture' in time and space, a process that continues up to the present in the New World.

The other important fermented beverages of the world followed similar courses from elite emulation to local production to mass acceptance, as illustrated by Chinese rice wine being adopted by the Japanese elite some 7000 years after its invention and by the progressive, millennia-long march of chicha and chocolate (p. 120) in the Americas.

that went into making any fermented beverage was considerable.

Power & prestige

Universally, humans were primed by their genetics and environments to discover how to make fermented beverages. Almost without exception, these beverages assumed prime roles in the social customs, religions, cuisines, pharmacopoeias and economies of cultures everywhere, as is still evident today. The Judaeo-Christian tradition is focused on wine, as a symbol of sacrifice and life itself, as might have been expected for cultures originating in upland regions where the Eurasian grape vine thrives. In lowland regions or where natural sources of sugar were less plentiful, fer-

Vintage scene from the tomb of Nakht, Thebes, Egypt, c. 1400 BC. While two pickers gather in the harvest, five other men, holding on to ropes, tread the grapes. The red must is collected and fermented in amphoras, which are stoppered and labelled.

Food Preservation

If garum [fish sauce] has contracted a bad odour, place a vessel upside down and fumigate it with laurel and cypress and before ventilating it pour the garum in the vessel.

APICIUS, A RECIPE FOR FIXING SPOILED FISH SAUCE, 1ST CENTURY AD

28

S now, ice, smoke and wind were the basic food preservation processes of antiquity. We know that late Ice Age people made use of permafrost to store food – 14,000 years ago, late Ice Age hunters at Mezhirich in the Ukraine buried mammoth flesh and other foods in deep pits dug into the frozen tundra. Zimri-Lin, ruler of Mari in southeastern Syria, constructed an icehouse near the Euphrates in 1700 BC.

Icehouse technology was well established in China as early as the 7th century BC. At Yongcheng in Shensi Province, a shallow pit with sluice gates served as a refrigerator, the surplus water draining into a nearby river. Zhou emperors of the 4th and 3rd centuries BC maintained as many as 94 servants charged with chilling both royal wine and the royal corpse when deceased. The first emperor of China, Shihuangdi, used an icehouse of huge ceramic rings sunk 13.7 m (45 ft) into the ground. Ancient Americans also prized ice. The great market of the Aztec capital, Tenochtitlán, stocked ice brought by runners from nearby peaks.

Drying meat in the sun and wind was a common technique. Ancient Plains Indians in North America used the wind to dry much of the meat from game drives, then pounded it with fat to make pemmican.

KEY DATES

permafrost storage	14,000 years ago, Ukraine
icehouse	1700 BC, Syria
icehouse	7th century BC, China

Drying and smoking also goes back well into the late Ice Age. Egyptian reliefs show fish butterflied and laid out to dry in the sun and fowl hung to dry. Salting was a well established preservation technology in Roman times. The Romans used rock and sea salt, and also evaporated sea water in earthenware vessels or on salt flats such as those at the mouth of the River Tiber near Rome.

Below left *Two men prepare birds by plucking and cleaning them and hanging them to dry, in a scene from the tomb of Nakht, Thebes, Egypt, c. 1400 BC.*

Below *The Romans preserved and transported vast quantities of various foodstuffs, including olives and garum – a very popular fish sauce – in terracotta amphorae, as seen here in the House of the Citarist at Pompeii.*

ICE CREAM

Ice cream originated as frozen or semi-frozen desserts and drinks made by pouring mixtures of fruit or berry juices, sugar and water over snow, packed into cups and clay vessels. Alexander the Great is said to have been especially fond of snow and ice mixed with honey and nectar in the 4th century BC. The Chinese were probably the first to develop a concoction of ice and milk that vaguely resembled the familiar sherbet of today as early as the 7th century BC. Roman emperors like Nero were ardent consumers of iced fruits and juices. Their ice came from nearby mountains and was stored in insulated pits. By the 16th century, the sherbet-like concoctions had developed into a form of 'cream ice'.

Chocolate & Tea

Oh, divine chocolate!
They grind thee kneeling,
Beat thee with hands praying,
And drink thee with eyes to heaven.
MARCO ANTONIO ORELLANA, 18TH CENTURY

Right *Cacao pods and beans: the beans have to go through a complex process, including fermentation, winnowing and grinding, before the highly prized chocolate flavour is achieved.*

Below *An Aztec stone sculpture of a man, possibly a merchant, holding a cacao pod, c. AD 1200–1521. The cacao tree did not grow in the Aztec heartland, so the beans had to be imported.*

Among the world's three great, non-alcoholic recreational beverages – tea, coffee and chocolate – chocolate has the most venerable history, since it has been in use for at least 26 centuries. It is produced from the seeds of the cacao plant (*Theobroma cacao*), a spindly undergrowth tree of the Central and South American tropical forests.

The essential steps in the manufacture of chocolate are basically the same everywhere: 1) harvesting the large seed pods; 2) spreading the cacao beans to allow fermentation to take place, at which point the pulp surrounding the seeds is converted to alcohol and runs off; 3) cleaning and then roasting the beans; 4) winnowing the beans to remove the useless shell; and 5) grinding the beans, often with the addition of heat. Until fermentation, winnowing and grinding have taken place, the full chocolate flavour of this highly complex substance (it has over 500 chemical constituents) is not achieved.

The real mysteries are how the complicated chocolate process was first discovered, and when and where this took place. We cannot answer the first question, but circumstantial evidence, partly linguistic, points to the Olmec civilization of the Mexican Gulf Coast, which flourished from about 1500 to 400 BC. From the Olmecs it seems to have spread to their cultural heirs, the Pre-classic Maya of southeastern Mexico and Central America. There is firm evidence for the Maya use of chocolate as early as 600 BC: chemical analysis of a residue within a spouted jar from a site in Belize showed the presence of theobromine, an alkaloid stimulant specific to chocolate.

During the kingdoms of the Classic Maya civilization (AD 250–900), there is abundant

archaeological and pictorial evidence for the widespread use of the chocolate drink among the elite class – the rulers, their courts and their followers. Once the beans had been ground on *metates* (quernstones), the resulting chocolate paste – what modern manufacturers call 'cocoa liquor' – was mixed with water and sometimes with flavourings such as vanilla and chilli pepper. To produce the much-desired foam, which was taken with a spoon, the chocolate-maker would pour the drink at a height from one cylindrical vessel into another. The drink itself would be quaffed from gourd cups.

The context within which the drink was taken seems to have been highly ceremonial: diplomatic gatherings, the receiving of tribute, elite marriage negotiations and the like. The beautifully decorated pottery containers were themselves desirable objects of exchange, and bore ritual texts describing the drink, and naming the ceramic artist and his patron (the owner of the vessel).

When the Aztecs first arrived in central Mexico from a homeland in the northwest, around AD 1300, they came as semi-barbarians, but soon absorbed

A palace scene on a Classic Maya vase (AD 250–900): in the centre a ruler seated on a throne gestures over a cup of foaming chocolate.

much high culture from the earlier civilizations there. One of these new elements was chocolate, but because the cacao tree requires a frost-free environment, they had to import the beans from the Mesoamerican lowlands. When the Spaniards invaded the Aztec empire in 1519, they found the drink in widespread use among royalty and nobility, and among merchants and warriors, but forbidden to commoners.

Both among the Aztecs and the Maya of Yucatan, the Spaniards also found that cacao beans themselves had a high monetary value, and were used as small change and to pay members of the bureaucracy. Initially, the conquistadores were repelled by the drink, but once they had made it more palatable to European tastes by adding cane sugar (an Old World domesticate), and serving the drink hot instead of at room temperature, they became confirmed 'chocoholics'.

By the end of the 16th century, the chocolate drink had passed to the Spanish court, and from them eventually to all Europe. Until the French Revolution in the late 18th century and its aftermath, it generally remained a prerogative of the aristocracy and high-ranking churchmen in the Catholic countries of Europe. However, in 1828 the Dutch confectioner Coenraad Van Houten patented a process to remove the fat or 'cocoa

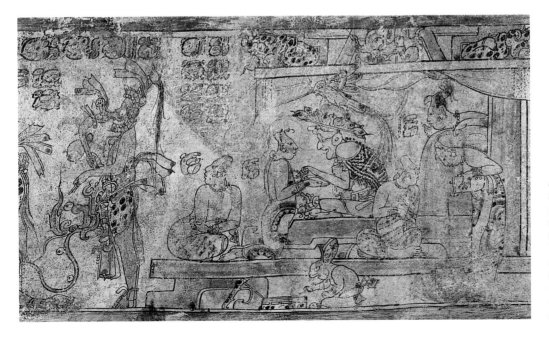

At the right of this palace scene on the Princeton Vase (Classic Maya, 8th century AD) a woman pours chocolate from one vessel to another. This is the earliest known depiction of the process used to produce the foam which was the favoured form in which chocolate was consumed.

Above *A cacao tree appears centre right of this Maya vase, with two men harvesting the pods. On the left cacao seeds are being roasted over a fire, and in the centre a man is probably grinding them on a metate.*

Right *The Maya glyph for cacao.*

Opposite below *A fine parcel-gilt silver tea basket; Tang dynasty, 9th century AD, from the Famen monastery, Fufeng. The tea ceremony first developed during the Tang dynasty and was taken from China to Japan, probably by Buddhist monks.*

butter' from the chocolate paste; the resulting powder could be moulded into solid chocolate bars, or used as coatings, or mixed with water and imbibed as 'cocoa' – a very weak relative of the traditional beverage. In the hands of manufacturers like the Cadburys and the Frys in England, chocolate and cocoa powder soon became a highly lucrative business. The invention of milk chocolate by the Swiss was one more step in converting what had been an aristocratic drink into a solid food of the masses.

Tea

Tea is an infusion from the leaves and buds of a species of camellia, *Camellia sinensis*, a native of China. The plant may be 'plucked' or harvested at five years, and may continue to produce for the next 25. Chemically, it is far simpler than chocolate; its stimulating effect is due to caffeine, but it also contains a large amount of tannic acid.

The origins of tea drinking are obscure and more mythological than historical in nature. According to one, undoubtedly apocryphal, story, the virtues of tea were discovered about five millennia ago by a Chinese emperor when some leaves from a nearby wild tea bush fell into a pot of boiling water. More reliable historical sources make it seem likely that the origin of tea is to be found in Sichuan Province in southwestern China, certainly by the Han dynasty (206 BC–AD 220). From there, tea drinking gradually spread to the rest of China, arriving much later in the north, during the Tang dynasty (AD 618–907).

The Tang dynasty was a time of innovation and eclecticism, with many foreign influences. Tea and the drink brewed from it took several forms: the dried leaves could be sold in their natural state or as cakes or powders, and could be flavoured with various substances such as ginger and tangerine peel. Today's tea purists would be horrified, but Tang tea addicts could even take their drink with *kaymak*, a kind of clotted cream. It was in Tang China that the tea ceremony was first developed, being introduced from there to Japan, probably by Buddhist monks.

KEY DATES

chocolate manufacture	? 1500–400 BC, Mexico
earliest chocolate residue	600 BC, Belize
tea	206 BC–AD 220, SW China

There are five kinds of Chinese tea:

- Green tea, which is the unfermented, dried leaf. The very finest teas are green, especially the Dragon Well variety, favoured by the imperial court.
- Black tea (classified by the Chinese as 'red'), fermented before baking. This is the tea preferred by Western tea drinkers after the custom and the substance had spread to Europe.
- Wulong tea, which is only partially fermented.
- Compressed or brick tea, produced for export to non-Chinese minorities and other peoples of Inner Asia, such as Mongolia and Tibet (where it can even be used in soup), and to Russia.
- Scented tea, flavoured with flowers such as jasmine, gardenias and magnolias.

From China, tea cultivation spread to Japan, Java, India and Sri Lanka. Tea drinking did not become established in Europe until the early 17th century, being imported by the Dutch East India

Company. And because of its initially high price, it was not until the 18th century that tea began to rival and even outstrip chocolate and coffee in popularity.

Coffee, the third and latest of our non-alcoholic recreational drinks to be invented, first appears in Arabic sources of the 10th century AD and thus lies outside the purview of this essay.

Above *Tea picking on a plantation in Sri Lanka. The tea plant is native to China and was taken from there to other parts of the world. The origins of tea drinking are surrounded by myth, but it probably began in southwest China during the Han dynasty.*

CHEWING GUM

The chewing of various natural gums and latexes for recreational and hygienic purposes has been practised in many cultures over the ages. Among the Aztecs, for example, bitumen from natural seepages along the Gulf Coast was chewed by girls and women to make their breath sweet (or so we are told) and to clean the teeth. They, and the Maya of Central America, probably also chewed the cured latex or *chicle* from the sapodilla (*Manilkara zapote*), a tall tree of the tropical rain forest.

The story of modern chewing gum begins in the 1860s in Staten Island, New York, where a young photographer named Thomas Adams was looking for a cheap substitute for the *Hevea brasiliensis* that was used to make rubber. By an odd fluke of history, the exiled ruler of Mexico, Antonio López de Santa Anna – conqueror of the Alamo – was also a resident in Adams' boarding house, and introduced him to *chicle* from his native land. While Adams failed to make rubber from the latex, he found that it made a pleasant chew, and began to retail unflavoured gum in a local drugstore. It was an instant success.

The next step was to add flavourings, which could only be carried out by blending them with sugar and (later) corn syrup. Sold now in specially wrapped, flat sticks, by the end of the century chewing gum had conquered the American public, vended by confectionery giants like the American Chicle Company and the Wrigley Company.

Drugs & Narcotics

On a framework of tree sticks, meeting at the top, they stretch pieces of woollen cloth. Inside this tent they put a dish with hot stones on it. They then take some hemp seed, creep into the tent, and throw the seed on the hot stones. At once it begins to smoke, giving off a vapour unsurpassed by any vapour bath one could find in Greece. The Scythians enjoy it so much they howl with pleasure.

HERODOTUS, 5TH CENTURY BC

An ivory pipe, possibly for smoking opium, from Kition, Cyprus, c. 1220–1190 BC; it was found with the vessel opposite below.

Right *A large Late Minoan pottery figurine of a goddess adorned with poppy heads, Gazi, Crete, 13th century BC. The poppy heads appear to have been slashed as they are today to extract and collect the opium.*

Below *A Late Bronze Age Cypriot pottery vessel in the shape of a poppy capsule, found in Egypt.*

Mind-altering drugs are often perceived as being a modern innovation, but psychoactive chemicals like LSD and heroin are merely the tail-end of the story of the human interaction with drugs that stretches back to remote prehistory. Many plants with psychoactive properties have been used in history not just for their mind-altering effects but also as medicines and poisons.

While people have probably always taken drugs for hedonistic reasons, their use in prehistoric and ancient times was usually connected with the realm of the sacred. Psychoactive plants allow the user to enter altered states of consciousness, which were perceived as ways into the realm of gods, spirits and ancestors. The

visions they caused were considered to be of great value for spiritual and sometimes physical well-being. Typically their use was surrounded by ceremony and ritual. Shamans and priests prepared the plants, often in secret, and decided who could take them and when.

Our knowledge of prehistoric and ancient drug use relies, in the absence of written reports, on three types of evidence. First, botanical remains directly associated with burials and other archaeological sites. Second, artifacts which either contain the residues of psychoactive species or were clearly used for drug-taking (such as pipes). And third, artistic motifs depicting mind-altering plants.

Opium cults in Eurasia

The opium poppy was first domesticated by Neolithic farmers somewhere in the region of the western Mediterranean, perhaps as early as the 6th millennium BC. Although the seeds may have been used in cooking, its narcotic properties were probably made use of both in medicine and in ceremonies, and it was associated with funerary rites from the Stone Age onwards. A number of Neolithic burials dating from around 4200 BC discovered in a cave at Albuñol, close to the coast of Granada in Spain, were found to contain numerous opium poppy capsules.

Alongside these medical uses the ceremonial role of the narcotic poppy continued. Among the artifacts found at the site of Kition in Cyprus are two decorated ivory objects dating from *c.* 1220–1190 BC – one was a cylindrical vase that has been identified as a vessel used for smoking opium and the other an opium pipe. A terracotta figurine of a goddess whose head is adorned with poppy heads was found at the Late Minoan site of Gazi in Crete, dating from the 13th century BC. Mycenaean signet rings from around the same period also depict a goddess holding what are probably opium poppies, and this association is echoed later by Classical Greek images of Persephone.

During the same era as these Mediterranean opium cults were flourishing, the ritual use of the poppy was also an important part of the religious life of peoples far away in Central Asia. In the deserts of Turkmenistan, Russian researchers have identified the remains of opium, cannabis and ephedra (a plant with amphetamine-like properties), and artifacts associated with their use, at a number of ancient temples and fortified buildings. Shrines within these complexes were used to prepare the drugs and the scale of the operation has led the excavators to suggest that the priests were dispensing ritual intoxicants to the population of the entire region.

Left *On this gold ring from Mycenae, Greece, dating from the 15th century BC, the seated figure on the left, possibly a goddess, is holding three poppy capsules.*

By the Bronze Age there appears to have been a thriving international opium trade. Imported poppy-shaped pots of Cypriot origin have been found in abundance in Egypt. They date from the New Kingdom period 18th Dynasty (*c.* 1539–1292 BC) and most were found at Amarna, the short-lived city built by the pharaoh Akhenaten. Ancient Egyptian medical writings describe the use of opium for a number of complaints, and later Greek and Roman medicine likewise found it an indispensable substance because of its unparalleled powers of pain relief.

Cannabis in ancient cultures

On the vast steppe lands of Asia the most important drug plant was cannabis. Sought after for its extremely strong fibre, the hemp plant was fundamental to cordage technology from prehistory onwards, but its trance-inducing and hallucinogenic properties were also highly prized.

As the prehistoric Kurgan cultures of the steppes migrated westwards they brought their cannabis cult with them. In Romania, a Kurgan burial of the later part of the 3rd millennium BC was found to contain a curious pottery artifact known

Left *A cylindrical vessel made of ivory from Kition, Cyprus, c. 1220–1190 BC, possibly connected with the smoking of opium and found with the pipe opposite above.*

Left *Statue of the Aztec god Xochipilli, decorated with motifs of psychoactive plants.*

Right *Drawing of the vessels and tent frame found in a burial at Pazyryk, corresponding to the description of ceremonies involving cannabis described by Herodotus.*

to archaeologists as a 'pipe-cup'. Analysis of the object revealed that it contained charred cannabis seeds. Another contemporary 'pipe-cup' from the north Caucasian Early Bronze Age also had residues indicative of cannabis smoking.

The ritual use of cannabis continued on the steppes into the Iron Age. Finds unearthed during the excavation of a number of Scythian burial mounds at Pazyryk in southern Siberia included two copper vessels, both with charred cannabis seeds in them, alongside a tent frame made up of a number of metal rods. These finds, dating from around 400 BC, echo in a remarkable fashion an account given by the 5th-century BC Greek historian Herodotus of the ceremonies of the Scythians at the other end of the steppes, in the Black Sea region (see quote at the head of this article).

As a result of the influence of the steppe cultures, cannabis spread slowly but surely across the continent of Europe, probably displacing indigenous opium cults in many instances. According to Greek sources, the Thracian shamans used cannabis in order to enter trances, and the discovery of the drug associated with the Hallstatt D wagon-burial at Hochdorf, dating to 500 BC, suggests it also had a ceremonial significance in Iron Age Germany. Sporadic finds of cannabis in later eras show that it continued to be used down to Viking times, but by that stage alcohol had all but replaced it and it had lost the important role that it once played in many societies.

Sacred hallucinogens in the Americas

The Aztecs used a considerable number of different psychoactive plants and the consumption of these drugs was controlled by priestly elites and shamans. One of their gods, Xochipilli, 'Prince of Flowers', literally embodies the ecstasies induced by the sacred hallucinogens and other drugs of the Aztecs – the mushroom, the morning glory and tobacco – as a 16th-century statue of him adorned with motifs depicting them shows. Among the most important of these ritual drugs were species of hallucinogenic mushrooms which they called *teonanacatl*, meaning 'flesh of the gods'. This epithet makes it abundantly clear that they perceived it as a sacrament.

Cacti containing the hallucinogenic alkaloid mescaline have been in use for thousands of years in both North and South America. The peyote cactus grows in the desert regions of Texas and Mexico, and prehistoric art found in rock shelters there, dating from between 4000 and 3000 years ago, not only depicts the cactus itself but also deer antlers which are still closely connected symbolically with peyote by the Huichol Indians of today. This points to the remarkable tenacity of the elements of the peyote cult.

Similarly, shamanic use of the San Pedro cactus is culturally ingrained in the Andean region, where numerous artifacts attest to its prominence over a period of nearly 3500 years. A temple carving at Chavín de Huantar in highland Peru, dating from around 1300 BC, shows a mythological figure holding the cactus.

An ornate pottery vessel belonging to the same Chavín culture depicts the shamanic animal par excellence – the jaguar – emerging from a cluster of San Pedro. The cult lives on today among shamans of the Andes who, although they profess Christianity, cling tenaciously to the spiritual and healing properties they believe the cactus to contain.

It can be seen from this brief survey that the Old World use of narcotic, hallucinogenic and other drugs was both deeply embedded in many cultures in prehistoric and ancient Eurasia and intimately bound up with their ceremonial and religious life.

KEY DATES

domesticated opium poppy	6th millennium BC, western Mediterranean
cannabis 'pipe-cup'	3rd millennium BC, Central Asia
peyote cactus imagery	4000/3000 years ago, Texas & Mexico
San Pedro cactus imagery	1300 BC, Peru
opium-smoking vessel	*c.*1220–1190 BC, Cyprus

In the New World it can also be seen that the shamanic and priestly use of psychoactive drugs was both prevalent and ancient. In some ways this is even clearer in the Americas, where the widespread use of alcohol occurred far later, thus providing us with a wealth of historical and ethnographic information which demonstrates the striking continuity in practices from the prehistoric period to the present day.

A carved relief from Chavín de Huantar, Peru, depicting a strange, mythological character holding a San Pedro cactus. The use of this cactus, which has hallucinogenic properties, was perhaps connected with shamanic rituals.

Transportation

People have always moved around on foot in search of game or plant foods, to find new hunting territories and simply to visit relatives. Many groups defined their home bases in terms of the distance that they could walk away from them and return in one day. The amount they could transport was limited to the loads they could carry on their backs and still travel a reasonable distance. For this reason, toolkits were light and portable and people tended to butcher their game where they killed it.

The first innovations came in snowy terrain, where people needed to travel and hunt in the depths of winter. They invented snowshoes, sleds for towing loads, with runners that skimmed along the ground, skis and then skates. These were specialized adaptations, but the wheel, cart and watercraft, products of early civilization, released humanity from the back-breaking tyranny of carrying loads themselves – a major limitation for the Maya and Aztec civilizations, who had no draught animals and did not develop wheeled transport.

The domestication of the horse revolutionized travel and communications, as well as warfare, but the wheeled cart required smooth, dry terrain for its most effective use. Winding tracks had always joined village to village, village to town, many of them wide enough for sleds. But wheeled vehicles easily became bogged down in mud and required bridges of stone or wood, or at least fords, to cross streams and rivers. The simple track became wider, more elaborate, culminating in the Roman road, which passed arrow straight from point to point across the landscape.

The Romans designed and built their roads to move legions rapidly from one part of the empire to the other, as an artifact of control. So did the Inca of the Andes, whose roads zigzag across some of

A terracotta model of a cart drawn by a bullock, dating from the Han dynasty in China. The invention of the wheeled cart meant much larger loads could be carried greater distances.

the most arduous landscape on earth. Their road system was so effective that a message could pass from Lima on the coast to Cuzco in the highlands quicker by runner than by horse. In dry country the camel was an even more effective means of transportation than the horse, traversing roadless tracts and operating for days in deserts. However, camels only came into their own with the development of different saddle designs that enabled warriors to fight from them, and the carrying of heavy loads.

Logs and simple rafts of tree trunks ferried people across rivers, lakes and short stretches of water long before the invention of the dugout canoe, probably soon after the Ice Age, or perhaps even earlier. The dugout is the most long-lived of all watercraft, and is still in use today in places. Such canoes reached considerable size in areas such as the Pacific Northwest coast of North America, where huge cedars abounded. With ingenuity and opportunism, people living near water developed simple planked canoes or skin boats, which developed eventually into much larger ocean-going craft. Egyptians and Mesopotamians built the first large vessels for river use. They invented the sail

A Roman relief from a marble sarcophagus showing sailing ships in stormy seas.

and developed refined forms of the oar and the rudder to propel and steer boats of all sizes.

Ancient seafaring was a hazardous venture in a world with no reliable weather forecasts and only limited sailing ability. The Pacific Islanders developed a consummate expertise at open water sailing in outrigger canoes, with the navigation skills to match. A wise skipper kept his eyes glued to the horizon and carried plenty of stone anchors for use in emergencies. Navigation was a matter of local knowledge, combined with an intimate understanding of winds and currents, handed down from one generation to the next.

At night, the captain navigated by the stars. Most ocean travel was from headland to headland, harbour to harbour, with only short passages out of sight of land until the discovery of the monsoon winds of the Indian Ocean at about the time of Christ. These allowed sailing ships to voyage to India and back on the wings of the monsoon in the course of a year. The Romans relied so heavily on large merchant ships that they developed lighthouses to allow ships to pass along the coast at night or see ports like Alexandria from far offshore.

Skis, Snowshoes, Toboggans & Skates

In the winter when the swamps and muskegs and barrens harden in the cold, and the lakes congeal into ice, and the ground is covered by a mantle of snow, then the Wendigo, the cannibal frost-fiend, holds sway, and he skims swiftly over the surface of the snow on his fleet snowshoes carrying cold and terror wherever he goes.
EDWARD DE THOMAS DRUMMOND, 1916

These inventions have both shared attributes and clear differences. All provide transportation in the northern hemisphere winter. However, while skis, snowshoes and skates are placed on the human foot and are designed to aid movement, either on snow (skis and snowshoes) or ice (skates), the toboggan is drawn behind an individual or animal to carry people or goods. They also have different origins: skis appear to be clearly Old World, while snowshoes are largely New World. There is some suggestion that both derive from something closest in form to the toboggan, though where this took place is not clear.

In addition, these inventions are primarily made from perishable materials. Skis and toboggans are mostly wood; snowshoes have an outer wood frame and cord latticework. Archaeological preservation is therefore rare. For all but skates the earliest record shows them fully developed. No records predate the Holocene (the past 10,000 years), though northern hemisphere environments suggest Ice Age antecedents. Availability of wood is critical, the exception being the skate, which is almost too recent for consideration here.

Skis

Skis are present in Eurasian ethnographic sources from northern Scandinavia to the Ainu of Japan, but are absent from the New World record. Of the four inventions considered here, the archaeological record is clearest for skis, though finds are largely European. The archaeologist Grahame Clark documented over 20 Scandinavian boreal forest sites where skis had been found, from southern Norway to central Finland. The finds date from around 10,000 years ago to the Iron Age, but more precise archaeological breakdown is problematic.

Early work by K. B. Wiklund recognized two classes of skis. The 'southern' style has the foot held on top between raised side pieces, while the 'arctic' or 'northern' style has the foot secured to the runner by hide loops. The former is short and broad, adapted for loose, heavy snow, with a classic Stone Age example coming from Riihimäki in southern Finland. The latter – longer, narrower and more suited to hard-packed snow – is found ethnographically across northern Eurasia. A classic example, from Kalvträsk in northern Sweden, has been dated to *c.* 3000 BC. Rock carvings of skiers are also known from Norway, Sweden and Russian Karelia, with Norwegian examples dated to the 2nd or 3rd millennium BC.

Most Scandinavian finds appear to be roughly dated to the later Stone Age. Recent findings, however, extend the dates back to the Boreal period, the north European chronological stage defined by pine and hazel forest, and usually dated as ending *c.* 5500 BC. Remains of skis uncovered in

*Two rock engravings depicting people skiing: one (**left**), from Karelia, dating from the late Stone Age, shows skiers hunting animals; the other (**right**) is from Norway and dates from the Iron Age.*

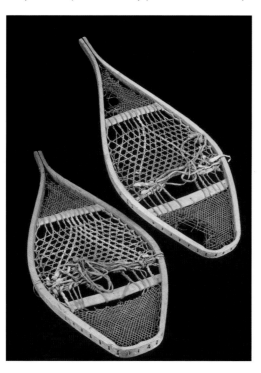

the early 1960s at Vis I in northwestern Russia date to the late 7th or 6th millennia BC. These have the classic shape, with upturned 'prow', and some are decorated. The excavator compared them with other Boreal age, but otherwise undated, finds at Heinola in Finland and Nizhneye Veretye in Karelia. At least one of the decorations at Vis is interpreted as the head of an elk (moose), a common iconographic image in this part of northern Europe, with classic finds coming from Oleni Ostrov in Karelia.

Compared to more recent examples, early skis are relatively short and broad, with lengths of 1.5 to 1.7 m (5 to 5.6 ft) and breadths of 15 to 20 cm (6 to 8 in). By the Iron Age, skis differ in size between left and right. The former is longer, from 3 to 3.5 m (10 to 11.5 ft), and is a sliding ski. The shorter right ski, from 1 to 2 m (3 to 6 ft) in length, is a 'kick' ski which provides momentum. Only one pole was used. Differences in type of wood are recorded and longer skis were usually made of pine or spruce in Scandinavia. Skis of this type are recorded in Norway and Karelia into the 19th century.

Snowshoes

In North America snowshoes take the place of skis. They are ubiquitous in early post-contact descriptions in North America and, like the toboggan (below), can be taken to be a pre-Columbian invention. Also like the toboggan the distribution is subarctic boreal forest rather than true arctic; neither are commonly found in use by Inuit groups. Snowshoes are also known ethnographically in northeastern Siberia, among groups like the Chuckchi and Yakut, but not further west.

The outer frame is flexible and resilient, made of a wood such as ash. The inner lattice or lacing is from hide – deer, moose or caribou, depending on location. They are worn with a soft, high ankle moccasin, usually of hide. As neither the wood frame nor inner structure are preserved in the normal archaeological record we know effectively nothing of the real antiquity of this device.

There is considerable variation in snowshoe form, based on a mixture of cultural and practical factors. The basic form is almost circular with maximum efficacy in deep, soft snow. Sometimes called 'bearpaw' snowshoes, these are associated with Algonkian-speaking groups of northeastern and north-central North America; the 'swallowtail' form is also known from the northeastern area. Other forms exist including the narrower, much longer and sometimes pointed forms associated with Athapaskan groups of the northwest. These are more efficient for fast moving, including running.

It has been suggested that, like the ski, the snowshoe derives from a flat board strapped to the foot. However, its alteration to the snowshoe does not appear to have gone through a true ski-like stage, suggesting an independent origin from a possible but unknown circumpolar precursor.

Snowshoes of the Athapaskan type, used by Algonkin Indians in Quebec. This pair is quite broad in order to cope with soft deep snow.

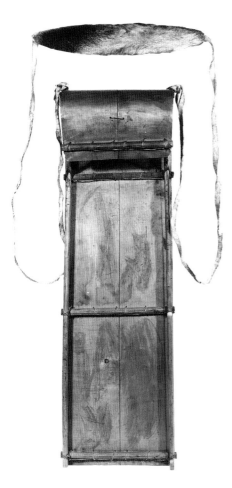

skis	late 7th or 6th millennium BC, Russia
snowshoes	pre-Columbian, North America
toboggan	pre-Columbian, North America
skates	9th century AD, Sweden

Left *A toboggan made by Huron Indians in Quebec during the early 1900s. A tumpline-type dragging cord is attached at the front.*

areas, such as the Northwest Coast, after contact. There appears to be no evidence of the toboggan in Europe that cannot be explained as an introduction from North America after contact, *c.* AD 1500.

Skates

Skates are used for personal transport on ice, a very specific development. A north European origin seems clear, with no obvious other sources. The true skate appeared very recently, though an origin based on adaptation of sled runners while possible is largely undocumented.

A true skate, with bone runners, appears to be first documented in 9th-century AD Sweden. Skates with wooden runners and iron facing appear in the 14th century, with fully iron runners found by the 17th century. A possible late Roman precursor is seen in Roman sandals found in the City of London in association with bone sled runners. This suggests a shift in use of runners from something pulled to a personal means of transport.

A dog-drawn toboggan of traditional Cree type in a photograph taken in the 1920s or 1930s by the Revd R.T. Chapin, in the area of the Island Lake and Sandy Lake First Nations communities in Manitoba, Canada.

Toboggans

Of the inventions considered here, the toboggan differs in being pulled, possibly by a person on skis or snowshoes, or by a dog or dogs, rather than being a buoyancy device for an individual on snow or ice. The English name is derived from the Anishinabe (Algonkian) 'nobûgidaban', a clear indicator of a North American origin.

The classic toboggan consists of flat boards, usually hardwood, lashed together by cleats at right angles. The front is curved, using heat or steam, to provide a smooth riding edge, as in skis. The presence of the toboggan at contact in North America indicates a pre-Columbian origin, though there is no surviving archaeological evidence. Ethnographically it is subarctic rather than arctic and appears to be generally found among northern Athapaskan- and Algonkian-speaking groups. Evidence suggests it spread from this base into other

Wheels & Carts

The wheel was the crowning achievement of prehistoric carpentry; it is the precondition of modern machinery, and applied to transport it converted the sledge into a cart or wagon – the direct ancestor of the locomotive and the automobile.

V. Gordon Childe, 1936

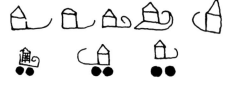

Pictograms of sledges and early wheeled vehicles from Uruk, Iraq, 4th millennium BC. These form some of our earliest evidence for the invention of the wheel.

Notwithstanding generations of cartoonists who have delighted in portraying enterprising cavemen carving massive stone wheels, the invention of the wheel is set much later, to the 4th millennium BC, when Eurasia was abandoning its stone-based technologies for one dependent on bronze. The precise location of this invention remains uncertain. We can say only that the wheel was apparently invented at least twice in human history – earliest in an indeterminate area between Mesopotamia in the south and the Danube in the north, and, independently and much more recently, in Mesoamerica, by *c.* 200 BC–AD 200. The evidence for the earliest wheeled vehicles in the Old World comes in three forms: depictions of vehicles; clay models of wagons or their wheels; and the remains of actual vehicles.

From sledges to wagons

What little archaeological evidence exists, coupled with evolutionary speculation, suggests that the antecedent of the wagon may have been the sledge, a low flat platform, often set on narrow runners that minimized friction and allowed heavy loads to be dragged along. The sledge obviously served on snow (p. 131) but could also be employed on flat ground, and it provides a likely method by which workers hauled large stones such as those erected at Stonehenge. Experimental archaeology suggests that the use of a sledge more then doubles the ability of a work team to pull a heavy block.

Friction could be further reduced by placing two or more timber logs as rollers underneath the sledge. Forward motion would then depend on continually replacing the rollers as the sledge was pulled. Where the weights being conveyed were not excessively heavy, this permitted the next major conceptual leap. Rather than constantly replacing the rollers beneath the sledge, they might be 'trapped' underneath if they were held in

A war wagon from the Standard of Ur, mid-3rd millennium BC, clearly showing details of the construction of the solid wheels.

position between pegs. This would result in effect in an axle-cum-wheel unit – the earliest wagon. The two rollers could themselves be modified into lighter supports – axles plus wheels.

Deposits dating to *c*. 3200–3100 BC from the city of Uruk in southern Mesopotamia have yielded pictograms of both sledges and what appear to be sledge bodies set atop either rollers or four wheels. The evidence for vehicles becomes far more abundant in the Early Dynastic period (3000–2300 BC) in the same region, which yields not only artistic representations but also models.

The archaeological evidence

The most spectacular evidence comes in the form of remains of actual wagons recovered from cemeteries at Kish and the royal burials at Ur, dating to *c*. 2600–2400 BC. From these we learn that the earliest wagons were narrow, permitting one or two occupants in tandem. Although a rotating axle may have been earlier (and certainly simpler), already by the Early Dynastic period there is evidence for a fixed axle that allows the far more efficient use of freely rotating wheels. The vehicles were drawn by either cattle, particularly when carrying a heavy load, or by some form of equid (asses or onagers). Horse-traction would not really be effective until the invention of the spoked wheel and chariot (p. 196). The Mesopotamian evidence suggests that the vehicles were used in combat as mobile battle-platforms and also in ceremonies, including at funerals as hearses for royalty.

Consensus favours Mesopotamia as the source of our earliest vehicles and sees the spread of the wagon as one component in the diffusion of an entire 'traction complex' that also includes the plough yoked to one or more oxen. But the empirical evidence is no earlier in Mesopotamia than for vehicles across eastern Europe. For example, a Neolithic site in Poland (Bronocice), dating to 3450–3100 BC, has yielded a ceramic vase that depicts what are generally interpreted as five four-wheeled vehicles (each has a fifth wheel shown in the middle) attached to a V-shaped yoke.

Clay models of unequivocally four-wheeled vehicles found in Hungary date to around 3600–2800 BC. From about the same period (*c*. 3400–3000 BC) we have the actual remains of wooden wheels from Switzerland and Slovenia. Some of the most impressive evidence derives from the region north of the Caucasus. Of the 500 burials of the Novotitorovka culture, dating to the period *c*. 3500–3000 BC, 90 have yielded the actual remains of wagons, while neighbouring cultures across the steppe lands have also produced a considerable range of vehicle remains.

Wherever vehicles were invented earliest, they seem to have diffused rapidly across this central area. The fact that we find similar terms for the wheel or wagon among the various language families across this region, e.g. Sumerian *girgir*, Hebrew *galgal*, Georgian *gorgal* and Proto-Indo-European *k^wel-k^wel-*, may suggest the rapid expansion of both the technology and the vocabulary of the wheel. From this central region, wagons diffused to India by the 3rd millennium and as far east as the Central Asian frontiers of China by *c*. 1000 BC, by which time the wagon had already been outstripped by the chariot which was introduced to China by *c*. 1200 BC (Mandarin *gulu* and Cantonese *gukluk* 'wheel' might also be related to the other Eurasian words).

Wheel technology

The earliest vehicles more often take the form of four-wheeled wagons than two-wheeled carts, although this might be a product of their social

Above *A single piece wooden wheel with integral nave, mid-3rd millennium BC, from De Eese, Netherlands.*

Left *A wooden wheel found recently in Ljubljana marshes, Slovenia, dating to 5100 to 5350 years ago. Made from two panels, it is 70 cm (27.5 in) in radius and 5 cm (2 in) thick. The axle hole is square, showing that the wheel and axle rotated together.*

Above *Remains of a wagon at Trialeti, Georgia, dating from the 2nd millennium BC. The large wheels of tripartite disc construction are 1.15 m (3.8 ft) in diameter.*

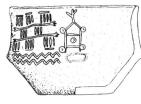

Above *Wheeled vehicles on a Neolithic pot from Bronocice, Poland, and a pottery vessel in the form of a wagon, early 3rd millennium BC, from Szigetszentmárton, Hungary.*

Opposite above *A wheeled toy deer or dog, Remojadas, Veracruz, Classic Period. The wheel was invented independently in Mesoamerica, though only, it seems, for such toys – there is no evidence for actual wagons.*

mortises and tenons to make a tripartite wheel. The resulting vehicle would weigh in the order of 670–700 kg (1477–1543 lb) and with a pair of oxen pulling would move at about 3.2 km (2 miles) per hour. The spoked-wheel became widespread around the beginning of the last millennium BC.

The social implications of the invention or introduction of vehicles in a society are complex. Functional applications such as portage of goods, firewood and families are obvious, and they would stimulate attendant technologies of carpentry and road building, as well as magnifying existing exchange systems. But the ownership and use of the vehicles is far from understood. There is ethnographic evidence to suggest that when vehicles have been introduced to non-vehicle societies, they may become communal property and require constant decision-making concerning their use.

What is striking is the abundant evidence from both Mesopotamia and Europe for the wagon as a funerary vehicle, and despite the considerable effort required in manufacture, during the late 4th and early 3rd millennia BC they appear to have been ritually consumed on a large scale. Possibly their religious purpose outweighed any functional constraints to maintain them; alternatively, they may have had such short use-lives that their ritual 'wastage' in burial may not have appeared so costly.

context – wagons were the preferred status vehicle for burial. The wheels are either single block disc wheels or tripartite wheels. While a thin slice of a round tree-trunk might appear the most natural technique for fashioning a wheel, this was impractical (at least to Early Bronze Age societies without access to large metal saws) and would yield an entirely unstable wheel that would be liable to fracture. The single block wheels recovered from excavations indicate that the tree was cut longitudinally and planks were wedged out and then carved into a circular shape. Where trees of suitable girth were not available, another and very popular technique was to take three pieces of wood and fasten them together with

A reconstruction of one of the wagons found in a burial of the Novotitorovka culture, north of the Caucasus, c. 3500–3000 BC. Remains of wagons have been found in 90 of the 500 burials known.

New World wheels

The evidence for the wheel in the New World is much more recent and problematic. It is confined to models from El Salvador and across Mexico that date from the end of the Pre-Classic period, *c.* 200 BC– AD 200, and continue up until the Spanish conquest. The models are not actually of vehicles but rather the means of locomotion for toy animals such as dogs, deer and even alligators. At the base of their legs two wooden axles supplied the support for clay disc wheels. There is no evidence for actual toy wagons nor is there any suggestion that such objects existed in Mesoamerica. Obviously, then, an appeal to an evolution from sledge to rollers and ultimately wheels is hardly convincing and the conceptual leap involved here might merely be from some form of rotary motion to small-wheeled toys.

It is frequently claimed that the failure of the New World to develop wheeled vehicles was due to the absence of any suitable draught animals. This explanation may not entirely suffice as human-drawn wheelbarrows in China are capable of carrying up to six passengers and the terrain of a number of regions in Mexico could easily have accommodated some form of wheeled vehicle. But in China the transition to human-drawn vehicles was preceded by the light spoke-wheel and horse traction. Without this experience it is perhaps unlikely that Mesoamerica could have made the conceptual leap to lightweight vehicles and human draught.

KEY DATES

pictograms sledges/rollers	*c.* 3200–3100 BC, Mesopotamia
oldest wheels	*c.* 3500–3000 BC, Switzerland & Slovenia
model wagons	*c.* 3600–2800 BC, Hungary
wagons	*c.* 2600–2500 BC, Mesopotamia
wheeled models	*c.* 200 BC–AD 200, El Salvador/Mexico

WHEELBARROWS

Although the origin of wheeled vehicles and chariots may be placed in Europe and Western Asia, it was the Chinese who not only invented the wheelbarrow, but also constantly experimented with its form to create a huge variety of types. Chinese tradition attributes its invention to Zhuge Liang, a 3rd-century AD general and inventor (wizard) who is credited with the 'wooden ox' and the 'gliding horse'. A 5th-century commentary suggests that a man could carry the same burden over 6 m (20 ft) with the 'wooden ox' in the time an unaided man might cover only 1.8 m (6 ft). A later commentary suggests that the 'wooden ox' had its shafts in the front and was pulled, possibly indicating the evolutionary development of the wheelbarrow. The chariot, known in China since *c.* 1200 BC, could be modified into a hand-pulled cart (not unlike a rickshaw) and then modified into a single-wheeled vehicle that was initially pulled and then, with the shafts relocated to the rear, pushed (the 'gliding horse').

Both literary and archaeological testimony, however, suggest that the wheelbarrow preceded Zhuge Liang by at least several centuries, though it would not appear in Europe until more than a thousand years later when it was used for hauling stone for the building of castles and cathedrals about AD 1200.

Many different wheelbarrow types were designed in China over the centuries, the illustration (**above**) is from a brick of the Eastern Han period, AD 25–220. The traditional one comprises a large central wheel, the upper part protected by a housing. The wheel was placed under the centre of the vehicle which permitted heavy loads to be pushed with the weight positioned above the axle and not, as is normally the case of the European wheelbarrow, between the front-positioned wheel and the arms of the person pushing. Chinese wheelbarrows are often mentioned in the context of warfare for carrying supplies over poor roads or along narrow trackways or mountain passes (a year's food supply for a man could be carried in a single barrow, i.e. about 152 kg or 3 cwt). They might also be propped up about a camp at night to provide an instant line of fortification.

Wheelbarrows could also be used to convey passengers. Indeed, the earliest literary references are to the 'pulley barrow' of the 2nd century AD where a wheelbarrow is employed to carry about a single living relative, or, occasionally, their corpse. Today, wheelbarrows in China are capable of carrying up to six passengers.

The Chinese also engaged in several improvements in wheelbarrow traction. Literary evidence indicates that they could be pulled with the help of an ox or horse. But surely the most extraordinary improvement, appearing at least by the 16th century, was the addition of 1.5- or 1.8-m (5- or 6-ft) high sails where the terrain and prevailing winds permitted.

Horses & Horse Equipment

A horse! A horse! My kingdom for a horse.
SHAKESPEARE, KING RICHARD III, IV 7, 1591/2

The Equidae evolved over 50 to 60 million years from dog-sized *Eohippus* in North America. They migrated across what is now the Bering Strait into Siberia and spread throughout Asia, Africa and Europe. Around 10,000 BC they became extinct in North America and were only reintroduced with the arrival of Europeans in the late 15th century. The horse, *Equus caballus*, helped shape man's military exploits, although *Equus asinus* (donkey) and *Equus hemionus* (onager) also played their part. The wild horse had three ancestors, *Equus ferus stenonis, Equus ferus gmelini* (tarpan), both now extinct, and *Equus ferus przewalski*, of which the last wild specimen was sighted in Mongolia in 1969. This strain is now bred in zoos and is being reintroduced into the wild.

Gold comb depicting a scene of combat between three warriors, one of whom is mounted. It was found in a Scythian tomb at Solokha in the Ukraine, though it may have been made by a Greek goldsmith; 4th century BC.

Domestication & development

Research into mitochondrial DNA by scientists shows that horses were domesticated in several different places. Current evidence indicates that *first* domestication was on the Eurasian Steppe around 4000 BC. There, late Neolithic, Eneolithic and early Bronze Age sites, such as Dereivka, Ukraine, and Botai in Kazakhstan, have equid remains, though none offer conclusive proof of domestication. It is probable, however, that herd drives for meat were, for practical purposes, conducted from horseback. Unfortunately the Steppe offers no literary or pictorial evidence, but the Near East does.

Stud records from Girsu and Diyala, in modern Iraq, dating to *c.* 2300 BC, include onagers, donkeys,

mules and a few horses. Though scarce in Meso-potamia, records from the Ur III period (*c.* 2100 BC) show horse numbers rising. Sumerian proverbs of this period, used as school exercises, refer to horseriding. The horse, after it had thrown its rider, says 'If my burden is always to be this, I shall become weak'. In the first half of the 2nd millennium BC there are scattered literary and visual records of horses being ridden.

A caballine map can be sketched using military documents from Egypt, Syria, Mitanni, Hattusas, Assyria, Urartu and Persia. Many of these places continued to produce quality horses throughout antiquity, and some still did so up until modern times. Syria, for instance, was very important. Following Egyptian victory at the Battle of Megiddo in *c.* 1458 BC, 2041 mares, 191 foals and 6 stallions went to Egypt with Thutmose III (*c.* 1479–1425 BC). The mares were scheduled for breeding. Seleucus Nicator (305–281 BC) had a huge royal stud at Apamea, on the River Orontes. Syria continued as a source of good horses in Roman, Crusader, Mamluk and Ottoman times.

The area known as Turan, which included Turkmenistan, Uzbekistan, Bactria, Kazakhstan and Ferghana, produced a sizeable, quality horse by 1000 BC. Alexander the Great (336–323 BC) obtained military mounts from Bactria; China's Han emperor Wudi (141–87 BC) got his superior mounts from Ferghana. Today Turan still produces good stock collectively known as Turkoman horses.

Greek and Roman literature shows continuity of Median, Persian, Armenian, Cappadocian and Syrian breeding; there are also references to other sources in Thessaly, Thrace and Sicily, eventually including Gallic and Germanic stock. Repeated incursions into settled lands by nomadic mounted peoples, from the Scythians, *c.* 700 BC, to the Avars of the 6th century AD, allowed a greater diversity in the equine mix, most significantly when Philip of Macedon (359–336 BC) purchased (according to Justinus) 20,000 'noble mares' from the Scythians. Xenophon in the 4th century BC and Pelagonius in the 4th century AD describe good equine characteristics. With few exceptions the ideal Greek and Roman horse's conformation accords well with modern precepts.

Detail of horses from a relief showing a procession of tribute bearers at Persepolis in ancient Persia, 5th century BC. The artist has taken great care over the depiction of the bridle, bit and reins.

Antiquity's horses are often stated to be pony-sized, that is 14.2 hands high (hh) and under (with 4 in, or just over 10 cm, to the hand). This is an incomplete picture. To be useful, warstock needed decent height and body mass and enough examples exist to show that larger horses were by no means rare. The horse excavated at the fortress at Buhen, Sudan, dating to *c.* 1675 BC, was 14.3–15 hh; an Achaemenid skeleton was 16 hh; Steppe burials have yielded horses that were 14.3–15 hh, and similar heights were not uncommon in the Roman period. Assyrian documents note 'large' and 'mighty' horses from Egypt, Cappadocia and Iran. However, a sturdy 14–14.2 hh animal is perfectly able to carry a fully accoutred man.

Control mechanisms

Control mechanisms were adapted from those used on bovines, with a ring through the nasal cartilage. This acted much as a modern twitch, the painful restraint releasing endorphins in the brain, rendering the animal controllable. Early evidence from Steppe cultures points to control via a snaffle

Right *The Newstead snaffle in action on Katchina: note how the curb strap and noseband produce a hard squeezing pressure when the rider's hand is raised well above the withers, as would happen when a trooper used his shield to cover his upper body and thighs.*

Below *Greek cup by Euphronios showing a mounted horseman, c. 510 BC.*

bit of rope or hide, but only the antler tine cheek-pieces have survived. The earliest certain metal bitting dates to the 15th century BC and comes from the Near East, but the possibility does exist for a 17th-century BC model.

All early bits were snaffles which exert *direct* control via the lips, bars of the mouth, tongue and palate. They came in a huge range – straight bar, jointed, and ones with disc cheekpieces with internal prickers which punctured the soft external mouth tissue if the horse resisted lateral pressure. Internally the canons (mouthpiece) also varied: some had sharp metal twists, others a square, sharp-edged section. They could incorporate metal burrs, sharp rotating discs or pointed

Right *Bronze bit from Luristan (western Iran), 10th century BC. As well as being decorative, the cheekpieces exerted considerable lateral pressure on the soft external mouth tissue of the horse.*

'keys'. Those with a U-shaped port could pinch the tongue and pressure the palate.

Muzzles prevented aggressive horses, usually stallions, from biting each other or their handlers. They also kept the horse's mouth shut so that bit action was not negated. Early muzzles were basket-weave nosebands. Later ones enclosed the whole nose and were open work to facilitate respiration. Metal *psalia* (hackamores) used with bits kept the horse's mouth shut. They are noted in the Assyrian era, but were more common in Parthian and Roman times.

Curb bitting did not arrive until late antiquity. Curb action, which can be extremely severe, is via the rein attached to the shank below the mouth. The *indirect* rein was used: a curb chain, or more usually in ancient curbs a solid bar, held the jaw in a vice and indirectly pressured the poll.

Harness, saddles & stirrups

Chariot horses (p. 196) were yoked like oxen, an inefficient method for horses, especially when driven to capacity at speed. Muscle and nerve damage in neck and shoulder would have occurred, resulting in frequent lameness. An ameliorating feature was the yoke saddle in front of the withers which assisted in traction. The terret, a ring on the yoke through which the reins passed, prevented the reins trailing and allowed increased pressure on the bit without extra force being applied.

Assyrian carvings show horses with saddle cloths. Xenophon described his 'cloth', which gave the rider a secure seat, prevented galling the horse and protected its belly. Far more than a cloth, this was surely a treeless saddle. In the Pazyryk, Altai, burials of the 5th to 3rd centuries BC saddles were found made of two rigidly stuffed cushions, each with a front and rear bow arch, on a felt backing. Wooden spacers between the cushions prevented the structure splaying and protected the withers and spine. Saddles appear on Scythian artifacts of the 4th century BC.

The Chinese used saddles with front and rear retentive moulding in the Qin dynasty (221–207 BC). Parthian and Roman cavalry saddles had front and rear horns. Diocletian's *Edict on Prices* of AD 301 included saddle costs: pad saddles ranged from

KEY DATES

metal bitting	15th century BC, Near East
horse armour	15th century BC, Mesopotamia
saddle	5th–3rd century BC, Central Asia
stirrup loops	2nd century BC, India

100 to 250 *denarii*; military saddles at 500 *denarii* reflected sturdier construction.

Stirrups had a long heritage before they became standard equipment. Stirrup loops first appear on carvings of the 2nd century BC at Sanchi, India; China was using stirrups by AD 302. During the 5th century they had been developing among the nomads of Siberia and the Altai, but it was the Juan Juan (the Avars) who brought them into the Byzantine sphere in the 6th century. They then spread into the Persian and Arab worlds.

Horse armour

Armour for chariot and cavalry horses evolved over the centuries. Tablets dating to the 15th century BC from Nuzi (modern Kirkuk, Iraq) describe layered body armour for chariot horses, consisting of hair sheathed in leather and the whole overlaid with metal scales. The horses' head, poll and neck were similarly protected. Egyptian and Assyrian reliefs show horses with armoured body housings. The Achaemenids of Persia armoured both their chariot and cavalry horses, and Xenophon outlined the panoply of Persian cavalry and listed the requirements for the Greek heavy cavalry. The horse wore a chamfron (head armour) and breastplate; thigh pieces protected the rider and parts of the horse and were incorporated into his 'cloth' saddle. A sarcophagus from Daskyleion in Phrygia shows this thigh armour.

The Seleucids, Parthians, Armenians, Sarmatians and some Romans also protected their horses. In the reign of Hadrian (AD 117–138) Arrian described the horse armour of cataphracts (armoured cavalry), consisting of chamfron and scale housings. At Dura Europos in Syria two almost complete housings were found dating to the 3rd century AD. In the later Roman empire nine units of heavily armoured *clibanarii* were attested in the *Notitia Dignitatum*. Oriental armies armoured their horses down to the 19th century AD. In the West the *clibanarii* and *cataphractarii* re-emerged as the duo of armoured knight and destrier (war-horse) in the high medieval era.

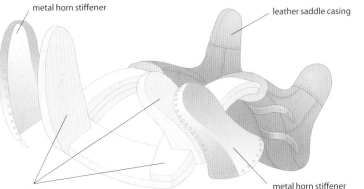

metal horn stiffener

leather saddle casing

wooden frame

metal horn stiffener

Top *The large-horned Roman saddle field tested on an Arabian stallion, Nizzolan. The horns facilitated good rider retention.*

Above *Drawing of a four-horned Roman saddle.*

Left *Reconstructed Roman horse chamfron, based on the example found at Vindolanda, northern England, late 1st or early 2nd century AD.*

Tracks & Roads

For my part, I travel not to go anywhere, but to go.
I travel for travel's sake. The great affair is to move.
ROBERT LOUIS STEVENSON, 1878

It is probable that throughout prehistory there was far greater population movement than is often assumed. The arteries of prehistoric travel are in general difficult to identify in the archaeological record, for movements along rivers, through forests and across dry land are rarely traceable today. In areas of peatland, however, from at least the 4th millennium BC, trackways were built, generally of wood, and these have survived in the waterlogged conditions, often in states of pristine preservation.

A reconstructed section of the Sweet Track, in southern England. This has been dated by tree-ring analysis to 3807 BC, making it the earliest known so far. The crossed timber posts supported the plank trackway, raising it above the surface of the marsh.

Though known elsewhere, the greatest concentrations of wetland tracks occur in northern Germany and the adjoining eastern Netherlands, in southwestern England and the Irish midlands. They exhibit great variety, both in size and in methods of construction. Local conditions were obviously important but clearly it was the intended purpose of individual trackways that was critical. The earliest known is the so-called Sweet Track in southern England, which is precisely dated by tree-ring analysis to 3807 BC. As well as being the oldest, it is also unique, consisting of a stretch of longitudinal planks 1800 m (5906 ft) long, skilfully raised on crossed timbers above the wet bog surface.

Commonest, however, were the many simple tracks consisting of bundles of branches placed longitudinally on the bog surface. Extended roundwoods, split planks and panels of woven hurdles were also used from the 3rd millennium BC onwards. There were other variations, but all were relatively simple tracks likely to have been of no more than immediately local importance.

Tracks which were larger and of greater technical sophistication were already being built in the later 4th millennium BC. These consisted of horizontal timbers, sometimes roundwoods, sometimes planks, frequently laid on a substructure of longitudinal stems. In Germany and the Netherlands associated wheels and other items confirm that such substantial tracks were primarily for use by vehicles. The purpose of trackways of comparable size from Britain and Ireland, dated to the 3rd and 2nd millennia BC, is, however, unclear, as the wheel is unknown here before the 1st millennium BC.

As the steering mechanism of vehicles improved, narrower trackways were built. Furthermore, the substitution of oxen by horses, with the subsequent increase in speed, meant that more attention was paid to ensuring a level surface.

Technically, the finest of the tracks were constructed in the 8th century BC in the Oldenburg area of Germany. These were made of carefully hewn and skilfully laid oak planks, secured in place by long narrow runners on their upper and lower surfaces which ran through stout, perforated uprights. Such impressive tracks were probably the work of specialist road-builders and the discovery of planks identified as coming from a single oak in tracks no less than 38 km (24 miles) distant from one another, is a striking indication of large-scale, highly organized road construction.

Later on, in the Iron Age, massive tracks of transversely placed oak planks, up to 4 m (13 ft) in width, while perhaps less technically accomplished, are also impressive. They are mainly found in northern Germany, but a single, massive example comes from far to the west, in a bog at Corlea in Ireland. All these structures are astonishingly similar to one another in size and construction. Most striking, however, is the evidence of tree-ring dating, which indicates that the Irish and the three largest German examples are of remarkably similar date, all having been built within a few decades of one another in the second half of the 2nd century BC.

All unquestionably built for wheeled transport, these are roads in the truest sense and must clearly be seen as the surviving elements of wider regional networks of communication. This has been plausibly argued for one of the German tracks which was probably part of a system of routes linked to the transportation of iron ores. These massive constructions clearly reflect the combined efforts of significant population groupings, organized and motivated by strong centralized leadership. The possibility that the Irish example reflects links with north Germany is intriguing but remains a matter for discussion.

Roads

Roads, as we have seen, developed in response to the invention of wheeled vehicles, and, in particular, to the use of the horse to pull them. A level surface was needed, well drained, as firm as possible, and easily navigated at speed. Such roads took much effort to construct, for unlike a track they could not twist and turn through narrow villages,

across river shallows, and through thick forests. They involved considerable modification of the landscape and large numbers of people to construct them.

The earliest roads traversed Mesopotamia over 5000 years ago, linking the cities of Sumer with the Mediterranean coast and the highlands. Along them travelled heavily laden caravans of asses. The roads themselves have now vanished, but have been located using satellite imagery which reveals patterns of stunted vegetation across the landscape. Many of these, like the routes across the Sinai Desert from Egypt, were caravan roads, never

Above *The Corlea ancient trackway, conserved in a museum. This trackway in Ireland is very similar in both construction technique and date – the second half of the 2nd century BC – to several examples in Germany. They were built to carry wheeled vehicles.*

Below *Corona satellite imagery revealing the network of routes radiating from Tell Brak in Syria.*

Above *A Roman road at Ostia. The Romans built a vast road network which enabled them to control and administer their empire.*

Below *The Silk Route, a web of tracks, roads and caravan trails, was one of the great trade routes of the ancient world, linking East and West.*

Bottom *The ruins of the Tang dynasty city at Gaochang, Xinjiang, in China, one of the settlements built along the Silk Route.*

maintained, but in use for many centuries. Knowledge of them passed from one generation of caravan families to the next.

There were all kinds of roads, most built to enhance communication – in the case of the Mycenaeans by chariot or cart. Local roads linked quarries with cities in Archaic Greece, while fine processional ways led to the oracle at Delphi and formed the Athenian Sacred Way. Other roads were as much statements of political power and of the reach of the state as purely functional means of connecting two points. One example is the Royal Road of the Achaemenid empire that linked Susa, Sardis and Persepolis, which was 2500 km (1550 miles) long. The road may not have been continuous, but it did have rest houses.

Road construction required large numbers of workers, whether conscripted, paid or enslaved. Such deployments did not occur on any scale until the Romans transformed the face of their empire with a huge road system. The first portion of the Appian Way running south from Rome was completed in 312 BC, its technology probably a copy of earlier Etruscan practices. By the 1st century BC, Roman planners were developing a vast road network, complete with milestones, that linked far-flung communities with Rome.

The early emperors made road building a massive undertaking, extending highways to the outer limits of the empire and covering around 85,000 km (53,000 miles). The emperor Claudius celebrated his return from a successful campaign in Britain in AD 43 by completing a road across the Alps into Gaul. Roman roads proceeded in arrow-straight stretches across the landscape, providing an effective way for an emperor to move his legions over long distances in short periods of time.

Many Roman roads are still preserved in the courses of modern routes. This is a testimony to their planning and to their sound construction, which followed a broadly standardized practice, adopted from methods used by the Etruscans, Egyptians and others. The builders typically dug two trenches about 12 m (40 ft) apart, using the soil to build up a well-drained core for the roadway, the *agger*, about 0.9 m (3 ft) thick. Although precise construction methods varied from area to area, many roads had several layers: a *statumen*, of packed stones for drainage up to 0.6 m (2 ft) thick, followed by 22 cm (9 in) of concrete – the *rudus*. A further 30 cm (12 in) of concreted gravel and sand formed the *medium*, topped by the *summum dorsum*, comprising gravel, packed stone or, sometimes, stone slabs. The roadway was bounded by curb stones. Dimensions varied considerably. The famous Appian Way was about 11 m (33 ft) across, with a central two-lane roadway of 4.5 m (15 ft). Lanes for one-way traffic lay on either side.

Just as in the West, Chinese roads developed from ancient trade routes and a need for improved communications to exert control over an expanding empire. Emperor Qin Shihuangdi built the first extensive road network in the late 3rd century BC. China later became one terminus of the Great Silk Route, a web of tracks, roads and caravan trails that linked East and West as early as the time of Christ.

Andean lords in South America were also well aware of the need for efficient roads to link their growing states. By AD 1200, Chimu rulers had insti-

tuted an annual *mi'ta* tax of labour for the state, whereby every able-bodied adult had to labour on public works such as highways for a specified period of time. The Inca conquered the Chimu in the 1460s, by which time they were already building their own intricate road system, complete with rest houses, that linked the highlands and the coast over the most arduous of terrain with roads wide enough to accommodate both the Supreme Inca's runners and llama caravans laden with trade goods and tribute.

KEY DATES

trackways	4th millennium BC, northern Europe
caravan routes	5000 years ago, Mesopotamia
Appian Way	312 BC, Italy
road network	late 3rd century BC, China
plank roads	later 2nd century BC, Ireland & Germany
road network	1460s, Andean region

Inca roads formed a network 25,000 km (15,535 miles) long, crossing deep valleys, high mountains and fast-flowing rivers. They were used by those engaged in the business of the emperor, armies, caravans of llamas and the runners who carried messages from one end of the empire to the other. This winding section leads up to Machu Picchu.

Bridges & Canals

… as many bridges are vantage points for long and entrancing views of natural beauty, so, too, are they vantage points for … views of human lives and endeavours.

F. W. ROBINS, 1948

Right *The great bridge of Apollodorus, with timber arches, built for Trajan across the Danube in about AD 104, as depicted on Trajan's Column.*

Below *A natural stone bridge at Moffat Beach, Queensland, Australia.*

Below right *Diagram of the bridge built in the 13th century BC to link defensive walls around the Hittite capital of Hattusas in Asia Minor. The timber deck is supported on stones which are cantilevered part of the way across the gorge.*

Bridges had a natural origin – from the tree fallen across a stream, the vine draped across a gorge or the stone slab spanning a gap. Only stone has a long life and the oldest surviving bridges are of stone.

Timber bridges

The first artificial bridges were probably built of timber, however. King Nabopolassar reputedly built one, 115 m (377 ft) long, across the River Euphrates at Babylon before 605 BC. Another was built even earlier, in around the 13th century BC, at Hattusas, the Hittite capital in Asia Minor, to link protective walls around the city. The deck was timber, with a clear span of about 6.7 m (22 ft) on stone supports built out from the natural rock walls to reduce the gap. This technique was used to a

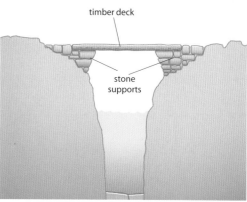

timber deck

stone supports

greater extent in early bridges with timber supports, such as in the Hindu Kush, with four layers of support logs extended out progressively to about the quarter-point of the span; such supports are described as cantilevers and the bridges are cantilever bridges. There are also Chinese examples from about the 4th century AD.

The Romans built many wooden bridges. The Pons Sublicius in Rome, built initially about 600 BC and defended by Horatius in 510 BC, was an early example. In 55 BC, Julius Caesar built a timber bridge across the River Rhine in 10 days, destroying it 18 days later on his return (by his own account). Columns dedicated to Trajan (AD 113) and Marcus Aurelius (AD 193) in Rome carry reliefs showing at least 13 log girder bridges. One has six spans, timber piles braced by diagonal stays, a crosshead and parallel timber girders; others have handrails on transverse decking and longitudinal timber girders. The most remarkable was built across the Danube in c. AD 104 for Trajan by Apollodorus, with 21 arch spans, each about 32 m (105 ft).

Another method of spanning stretches of water was to build floating bridges. The Assyrians built ones as early as 700 BC; in 480 BC, Xerxes used two to cross the Hellespont, and in about 320 BC, Alexander the Great floated another across the Indus River. The columns of Trajan and Marcus Aurelius also show floating bridges, with timber girders on boats.

Suspension bridges

Simple bamboo and vine suspension bridges were used in many countries, such as Burma, Java and Peru, but the most important developments were in China. In their simplest form such bridges consisted of two bamboo cables forming handrails and a third tread-rope, with creepers plaited between them to form a V; spans up to 240 m (787 ft) have been recorded between Assam and Tibet.

Later bridges had up to six deck ropes supporting transverse bamboo planks, connected to hand ropes made of plaited bamboo strips on each side. Most were single-span but the An-Lan bridge at Kuanhsien had eight spans up to 60 m (197 ft), with a total length of 320 m (1050 ft). In its original form it may date from the 3rd century BC. The Chinese also used iron chains, possibly as early as the 1st century AD, with heavy stone abutments and cables stretched to a slight sag. The use of a flat deck hung from suspension cables dates from about AD 1420.

The Pons Fabricius was one of ten early bridges across the Tiber in Rome. Built in 62 BC, it carries the name of the builder, Fabricius, above the arch, and has a flood arch above the central pier.

The oldest known stone bridge, at Knossos in Crete, dates from about 1900 BC; the lower portion is still intact. The upper portion was built in the form of a primitive corbelled arch.

Stone bridges

Stone slab bridges, although difficult to date, were used in many countries; the oldest known example, with a series of rudimentary corbelled arches (see p. 70), dates from about 1900 BC at the Palace of Knossos on the island of Crete.

The Romans used the classic arch, a good example being the Pont du Gard in the south of France, carrying water to the town of Nîmes (p. 83), with semicircular arches, radial joints, protruding stones supporting temporary timber falsework, and three tiers of arches. It was completed about

When completed about AD 100, this bridge across the Tagus at Mérida in Spain was the longest Roman stone bridge, with 62 spans in a length of 790 m (2590 ft). The central part was built first and then after a flood cut through the city approach, the bridge was extended; the same thing then occurred at the far end.

18 BC. The earliest known Roman bridge still standing is the small Ponte di Nona near Rome, built possibly around 173 BC and later incorporated into a larger bridge. The Pons Fabricius of 62 BC crosses the Tiber in Rome and is interesting both for its inscriptions and the flood arch above the pier.

The Romans' largest single span was 35.6 m (116.8 ft), in the Pont St Martin, near Aosta. This arch is not a full semicircle but includes an angle of about 144° – and is therefore said to be segmental. The Romans used markedly segmental arches at Alconéta in Spain and Limyra in Turkey.

A great Chinese bridge is the Zhao-Zhou or Anchi bridge, built about AD 605 with a single segmental arch of 37 m (121 ft), with open spaces above. The segmental arch has been included in the list of inventions introduced to Europe by Marco Polo, but this is incorrect.

Canals

The first artificial waterways were built for irrigation or drainage. According to Egyptian tradition (p. 99), in about 3100 BC, King Menes built a canal to carry water from the Nile to his new capital at Memphis, and by the Middle Kingdom a vast irrigation system

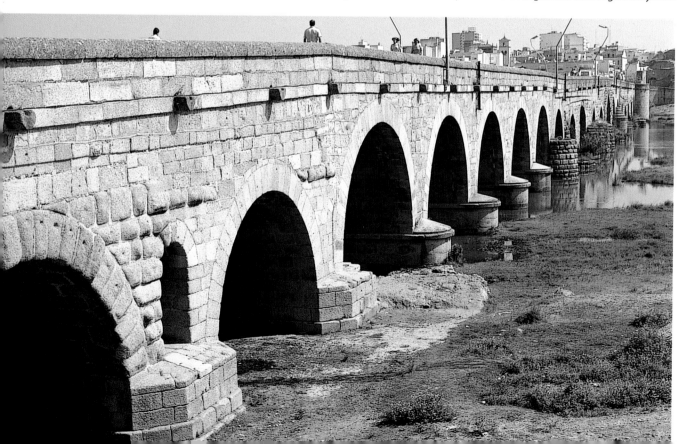

had been built. Similar channels in Mesopotamia carried water from the Euphrates and the Tigris; by about 1800 BC Hammurabi's law code spoke against a man who opened his canal for irrigation and then neglected it.

It seems probable that these early waterways could also be used by vessels. Writing in the mid-5th century BC, Herodotus describes the work of the pharaoh Necho II (610–595 BC) and the Persian ruler Darius I (521–486 BC): 'It was Necos who began the construction of the canal to the Arabian gulf, a work afterwards completed by Darius the Persian. The length of the canal is four days' journey by boat.... The water is supplied from the Nile and the canal ... runs ... on to the Arabian Gulf (the Red Sea).' This early forerunner of the Suez Canal shows that the use of canals for transport may date from this time.

Early canals were close to sea level but by the 1st century BC flash or staunch locks were introduced in China to control stream flow. Part of a barrier across the stream could be removed, enabling boats to shoot downstream through the gap or be towed upstream. They tended to be wasteful of water and Chinese engineers built slipways to allow boats to be dragged from one level to another.

KEY DATES

stone bridge, corbelled	*c.* 1900 BC, Crete
timber bridge	13th century BC, Turkey
floating bridge	700 BC, Assyria
Pons Sublicius	600 BC, Rome
flash locks	1st century BC, China

A great early canal was the Chinese Grand Canal. Inaugurated in AD 605 and based on earlier networks, by AD 1327 the Grand Canal extended from Beijing to Shanghai and Hangchow in Zhejian, with a total length of about 1700 km (1056 miles). Its first section, from the Yellow River to the Huai Valley, dates from at least the 4th century BC. Although possibly begun as an irrigation system, it was soon used for long-distance transportation. In AD 983 an engineer for the Grand Canal built the first ordinary or pound-lock with two sets of gates opened one at a time, enclosing a pound or basin long enough to take a boat. Such locks, when coupled with an adequate water supply, enabled a canal to climb and descend. The Grand Canal eventually rose about 42 m (138 ft) above sea level. Similar locks were used in Holland as early as AD 1065.

A section of the Chinese Grand Canal at Suzhou. Although perhaps begun for irrigation purposes, it soon became an important transportation network, eventually stretching for around 1700 km (1056 miles). The first pound-lock was built on this canal, in AD 983.

Camels & Camel Saddles

Hamlet: Do you see yonder cloud that's almost in shape of a camel?
Polonius: By th'mass, and 'tis like a camel indeed.
SHAKESPEARE, HAMLET, III, II, 400

Above *A camel, laden with carpets, and its rider, from China; Wei dynasty, 4th–5th centuries AD.*

Below *A dromedary wearing a saddle, on a relief from Palmyra, Syria, 3rd century AD. Palmyra was an important city on the caravan trade routes.*

For all their curmudgeonly temperament, camels are ideal beasts of burden for desert travel. They can absorb heat by allowing their body temperature to rise 6 degrees above normal in a single day without perspiring; in addition, they conserve water through an efficient kidney system and can distribute immense amounts of it through their body tissue within 48 hours.

The two-humped or Bactrian camel appears to have been domesticated in the border region between northeastern Iran and Turkmenia. A potsherd bearing an image of a two-humped camel from the city of Sialk, south of Tehran, is dated to between 3000 and 2500 BC, but the animal may be wild. Camel bones and clay models of wagons

bearing camels' heads date to between 2500 and 1600 BC at other sites. A clay jar made of camel dung and hair comes from the Sistan region of eastern Iran from the same period.

Camel domestication seems to have taken hold independently in Arabia and areas to the south at least 4000 years ago. Camels were probably rare before 1500 BC, after which Bactrians spread widely. They were well known to the Assyrians, appearing on the famous bronze gates of Balawat in northern Iraq. The two-humped camel became an important beast of burden on the Silk Route after the 1st century AD, but was never used for basic subsistence, as was its Arabian relative.

Single-humped Arabian camels, dromedaries, were probably first domesticated in southern Arabia sometime before 2500 BC, but more than ten centuries passed before they came into common use. Why, then, did the camel not immediately revolutionize desert travel? The problem was the saddle, an invention that taxed camel owners' ingenuity for centuries.

Saddle design

The first Arabian camel saddle was mounted over the animal's hindquarters. Seated near the rear of the beast, the rider had to use a stick to control the mount. This lost a major strategic advantage of the camel – the height of its rider above the ground. Nevertheless, dromedaries travelled the incense route to Israel as early as 1200 BC.

A major breakthrough was the development of the North Arabian saddle between 500 and 100 BC. This was a rigid, arched seat mounted over the camel's hump, distributing the rider's weight evenly, not on the hump but on the beast's back.

KEY DATES

camel domestication	3000–2500 BC, Iran/Turkmenia
	before 2500 BC, S. Arabia

A load could be slung from either side of the saddle. Even more important, a warrior could fight from camel-back with sword or spear.

The North Arabian saddle, with its military potential, was a dramatic shift in the balance of commercial and political power in southwestern Asia. Originally, control of the lucrative Arabian frankincense trade lay with the buyers – the owners of the beasts were unimportant. Now, the camel breeders found themselves in control, and profits flowed to them. Petra, in the Jordanian desert, founded before 312 BC, was the first great caravan city. Wheeled carts effectively vanished from southwestern Asia for many centuries – the camel, with a North Arabian saddle, was more efficient.

Large numbers of camels arrived in Egypt with the invasions of the Assyrians and then Persians in the 7th and 6th centuries BC. In the 2nd and 1st centuries BC, Egyptian records tell of camel caravans travelling 800 km (500 miles) between the Red Sea and Upper Egypt. With their North Arabian saddles acquired from Arabia, they dominated the lucrative trade routes that linked the Red Sea with the Nile. To the south, the city of Meroë in present-day Sudan, founded in 539 BC, lay at a great crossroads, where trade routes from Egypt, the Ethiopian highlands and the Red Sea met. From Meroë, camel tracks stretched westwards into the Sahara.

Camels were still rare in North Africa when the Roman general Julius Caesar captured 22 of them from the king of Numidia in the 1st century BC. The camel population multiplied during the next three centuries, so much so that the Romans placed a levy of 4000 beasts on the city of Leptis Magna in Tripolitania (modern Libya). But they did not use camels for desert travel, employing them only to haul carts and to form defensive corrals for soldiers. The Romans did not have the necessary saddles.

A catalyst of history

Long-distance desert travel required a different saddle design – the key factors were load-carrying

Detail of a relief from the North Palace of Ashurbanipal at Nineveh, c. 645 BC, showing Assyrian troops on horseback pursuing Arab tribes on camels. The Arabs used the one-humped camel or dromedary for long-distance travel and rapid movement.

capacity, endurance and easy control on long marches. The Saharan saddle was mounted on the animal's shoulders, so the rider could control his mount with a stick or his toes. This design in various forms developed in the desert, where there were no Roman cavalry or other enemies to worry about.

With the Saharan saddle, the camel reached its full potential. For centuries, the Saharan saddle carried peaceful loads across the desert. Then, in the 7th century AD, Arab armies introduced the North Arabian military saddle to the desert. By that time, the camel had become the 'ship of the desert', the vehicle of a lucrative trade in Saharan cake salt, so highly prized in West Africa that chiefs would pay with the equivalent weight in gold. Thus it was that the ingeniously designed camel saddle became one of the great catalysts of African history.

A modern Berber camel saddle in use today in Tunisia. It was the invention of a suitable camel saddle that opened the Sahara Desert to long-distance trade.

Rafts & Logboats

The many devices upon which men, living in various states of culture,
launch themselves afloat upon river, lake and sea.

JAMES HORNELL, 1946

The oldest known boat in the world: the pine logboat from Pesse, in the Netherlands, dated to c. 7200 BC. This simple boat, made by hollowing out a log and shaping it externally, is 3 m (9.8 ft) long and around 44 cm (17 in) wide.

There were seamen before there were farmers, and boatbuilders before there were wagon-makers. Scientific dating techniques now show that Australia was first peopled before 40,000 BC (and possibly as early as 60,000 BC). These early migrants must have used some form of water transport to voyage through the archipelago which lay between mainland Southeast Asia and the island continent of Australia. The earliest date when water transport was first used on lakes and rivers may never be known, but presumably it was well before 60,000 BC.

Most finds of early water transport are from Egypt, the eastern Mediterranean or Europe. They are relatively late in date: the earliest excavated boat, a logboat, is from *c.* 7200 BC, and the earliest raft dates to the 2nd century AD. Most of the vessels excavated to date are either logboats or plank boats (p. 156) – boats made from other materials, and rafts of all types, are almost invisible. Early illustrations and descriptions can supplement excavated evidence, but these depictions and descriptions are often general rather than specific.

Each of the basic types of float, raft and boat was probably invented on more than one occasion in different parts of the world, as the need arose, as the environment required, as available raw materials facilitated, and as human ingenuity and technological competence determined.

In the 15th to 19th centuries AD, for example, Europeans noted that indigenous Americans had independently developed a wide range of water transport. Similar types were found at widely separated locations: log rafts off both the west and the east coasts; hide boats and bark boats in both North and South America. This American scene may well reflect what happened in other continents during the early millennia of human settlement.

Floats & buoyed rafts

Floats are individual aids which directly support a person in the water and have been in use worldwide into recent times. Swimmers aided by sealed pots and hide floats are depicted crossing rivers in 9th-century BC Assyrian reliefs. A similar use of hide floats is shown on the 1st-century BC stupa at Sanchi in India. In the 17th and 18th century AD log floats were used in Australia and Tasmania to cross rivers and visit offshore islands. In the 19th century, planks (prototype surf boards) were used off Hawaii and Easter Island.

Calabashes (gourds) netted together were used as rafts in the Americas; more widespread is the use of hide floats or sealed pots linked together by a light wooden framework. Hide float rafts are depicted on 7th-century BC Mesopotamian reliefs, and they were used to cross rivers in 1st century BC/AD China. A raft buoyed by pots appears on a 6th-century BC Etruscan gem; and they were also used in medieval China and 17th-century AD India.

Log rafts

Two log rafts recovered from the River Rhine are dated to the 2nd century AD. Two centuries earlier, Julius Caesar noted that Celts used log rafts to cross rivers in Gaul. Widespread use at a much earlier date seems likely. A simple log raft is depicted on an early 7th-century BC Mesopotamian stone relief. They were used on Chinese rivers in the 5th century BC, and sailing log rafts were known off Taiwan and the Fujian province in the 12th/13th century AD.

Sailing log rafts traded between the Coromandel and Travancore coasts of southern India in the 1st century AD. In the 16th and 17th centuries, off America's west coast, Europeans sighted great cargo-carrying sailing log rafts which used adjustable leeboards (*guares*) to assist in steering. *Guares* have been excavated from Peruvian graves which suggests that sailing log rafts were used in 300 BC (p. 165), and probably much earlier.

The ocean-going log rafts of Oceania were first noted in the 16th century. It is possible that similar sailing rafts were one means by which remote Oceania was settled between the mid-2nd millennium BC and the late 1st millennium AD.

Simple log rafts seen in Australia when the Europeans arrived there are unlikely to have been suitable for the voyages undertaken by the first settlers in 40,000 BC or earlier. Nevertheless, it is generally agreed that seaworthy log rafts of bamboo were probably used.

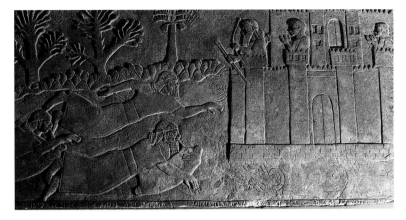

Bundles & bark

Rafts of pole bundles are still used today in eastern India, Uganda and on the Upper Nile. In the 19th century Europeans noted that Tasmanians made boat-shaped rafts from bark bundles. Otherwise, bundle rafts are made of reeds, or similar material, lashed together into a flat or a boat-shaped form.

Illustrations on Egyptian pottery and a linen fragment of *c.* 3500 BC are probably of reed-bundle rafts. Boat-shaped bundle rafts are subsequently

Above *Enemy soldiers crossing a river towards a fortress, aided by inflated skin floats: a scene from the Northwest Palace of Ashurnasirpal II at Nimrud, Iraq (c. 883–859 BC).*

Below *Reconstruction of a Manteño balsa sailing raft, Ecuador.*

depicted in use as ferries and for fishing, fowling, fighting and hunting. The earliest Mesopotamian evidence is a Sumerian pictogram from late-4th-millennium BC Uruk.

In South Asia bundle rafts are depicted on a baked clay amulet and a seal from Mohenjo-daro, both dated to around 2000 BC. Pliny the Elder noted that bundle rafts were sailed from the River Ganges along India's east coast to Sri Lanka in the 1st century AD. There is no early evidence for such rafts in Europe. However, they were used in recent centuries at sea off Corfu, Sardinia and Morocco, and also on lakes in both Hungary and Ireland, which suggests wider use in earlier times.

A Chilean model reed bundle boat dated to the early years BC/AD is the earliest evidence in the Americas; Peruvian pottery models of reed bundle rafts are dated to the 12th to 13th centuries AD. During the early 1530s European seamen sighted reed bundle fishing rafts off the west coast of America. They were later found on rivers and lakes, mostly on the west side of the continent.

Bundle boats are made of reed bundles linked together by coiled basketry and made watertight with bitumen. A light wooden framing is then inserted. Europeans noted round and boat-shaped

boats of this type in Iraq in the mid-17th century. They had been described 1600 years earlier by Strabo, and a Mesopotamian inscription of c. 2300 BC may refer to them.

Fragments of bitumen with impressions of reed bundle coiled basketry have recently been excavated from sites in Turkey (near the River Euphrates), Kuwait and Oman: these are probably the remains of reed bundle boats. Dates range from the 6th to the 3rd millennia BC, the earliest being those from As-Sabiyah in Kuwait.

In the 16th to 18th centuries, European explorers found bark boats in three regions of the Americas: across northern North America; on the rivers of Guyana and Brazil; and on the southern coast of Chile. In the 19th century Australians were using bark boats on rivers and in coastal waters; they were also used in recent centuries in Southeast Asia, northeast China, Siberia and East Africa. Earlier use seems likely in these and other regions.

Hide boats

Hide boats (also known as 'skin' or 'leather' boats) consist of a watertight envelope of hides on a framework of wood, bamboo or (in Siberia) whale bones. Boats are usually circular (for lakes and rivers) or 'boat-shaped', but *kayak/baidarka* of the northern circumpolar region have an elongated lanceolate shape.

Whether Mesopotamian clay models from Eridu of the 5th millennium BC represent hide boats is debatable; however, stone reliefs of c. 700 BC clearly depict round hide boats.

Classical authors describe the use of hide boats in Iberia and the Po Valley in Italy, though there is little evidence of their subsequent use. In northwest Europe, on the other hand, round and boat-shaped hide boats are still used today in Wales and Ireland, and there are documentary references to their use, at sea as well as on rivers, back to the 1st century BC. Furthermore, a 4th-century AD poem appears to describe 6th-century BC trading voyages by hide boat between Brittany and Ireland.

Ivory models of hide boats, full-size paddles and fragments of framing excavated in Alaska and the Aleutian Islands indicate that hide boats were used there in the 1st century BC/AD. When Europeans first

Below *Binding reed bundles together to make a boat-shaped bundle raft. A scene from the tomb of Ptah-Hotep, c. 2400 BC at Saqqara, Egypt.*

arrived, simple hide boats were found in use on lakes and rivers in both North and South America. Complex ones were used in the sub-Arctic region from eastern Siberia to eastern Greenland. Hide boats are mentioned in 4th-century AD Chinese documents, and references to their use in southern India can be traced back to the 14th century AD.

Basket boats

Baskets boats are circular or near-elliptical, and consist of a closely woven basketry hull of split bamboo made watertight by a resin mixture and coconut oil. The hull is supported internally by bamboo framing. No examples have been excavated, but they were used recently in eastern Java, and have been used in Vietnam from the early 19th century until today. Earlier use in this region is likely.

Logboats

A logboat ('dugout canoe') is made by hollowing out a log and shaping it externally. Unless the parent log has the great breadth found in parts of the Americas, such a boat has limited stability. Breadth can be increased, however, with methods including expansion – forcing out the sides of the boat; adding stabilizers or outriggers to the sides; or pairing – linking two logboats alongside one another. The resultant increase in stability may be sufficient for use at sea, possibly under sail. Adding strakes (planks) to the sides of a logboat allows more crew and/or cargo to be carried; this process may have been one of the ways in which plank boats were first developed.

Logboats have been excavated in Europe, North America, Southeast Asia and China; one is also known from Sri Lanka. The oldest, from Pesse, the Netherlands, is dated to c. 7200 BC, while one from Noyen-sur-Seine, France, is dated to c. 6900 BC. Logboats much earlier than this can hardly be expected since sizeable trees were not available in northwest Europe in earlier times.

Interpretation of excavated remains is never straightforward and is sometimes controversial. Conservative estimates for the earliest European logboats with extra capacity and stability suggest that strakes were in use possibly by the 4th/3rd millennium BC and certainly by 300 BC; while expan-

KEY DATES

seagoing watercraft	before 40,000 BC, SE Asia/ Indonesia
logboat	c. 7200 BC, Netherlands
log raft	7th century BC, Mesopotamia

sion possibly dates to the 1st–3rd centuries AD. Paired logboats may be as early as the 2nd/1st millennium BC, more probably from c. 300 BC; and were certainly in use by the 1st century BC when the Celts used them on rivers.

A 5th-century BC logboat excavated in Sri Lanka may have had an outrigger. In the 2nd/1st millennium BC logboats were used as coffins in Sarawak. The earliest Chinese logboats are c. 4250 BC; while in Japan they are a little later, at c. 3500 BC.

Excavated American logboats are mainly simple, for use on rivers and lakes: the oldest is from Florida and is dated to c. 5120 BC. In the early centuries of European colonization, large seagoing logboats were noted on both east (Honduras-Caribbean) and west (British Columbia-Washington State) coasts; some were under sail, many were paddled. In Alaska, Brazil, Guyana, Tierra del Fuego, and latterly in Nootka territory on the North American west coast, logboats were expanded. Colombian and Chilean logboats had stabilizer logs.

Opposite above & centre
A fragment of bitumen with impressions of reeds on one side and barnacles on the other, from As-Sabiyah, Kuwait, is some of the earliest evidence of boat building in the world, dating to around 5000 BC. The model boat from the same site may help understand the construction of vessels at this time: the raised prow and stern perhaps reflecting reed-bundle construction.

Modern basket coracles still in use today for fishing in Vietnam, with an internal framework made of bamboo.

Planked Boats & Ships

The invention of the frame-first ship made possible the great 15th-/16th-century western European exploration of the world, and the development of international commerce.
BASIL GREENHILL, 1976

Above *The* Helek: *a 20th-century reconstruction of a Chumash California Indian sewn plank boat known as a* tomol. *Note the double-bladed paddles.*

Right *The oldest plank vessel in the world. In c. 2550 BC, this large, oared ship was dismantled and entombed in a pit at the foot of the Great Pyramid of Khufu at Giza. After its excavation it was reassembled and is now on display in a museum built above its former burial pit.*

Known at an early date in all continents except Australia, the plank boat is the most versatile method of boatbuilding and the only form of water transport that can be increased in size to become a ship. When fitted with a sail (p. 159), boats (subsequently ships) had an enormous impact on overseas contacts and trade, and greatly increased geographical and oceanographical knowledge of the world.

Plank boats developed in different ways and at different times in various regions of the world: possibly from the bark boat in the Americas, the bundle

raft in Egypt, the log raft in China, the hide boat in Atlantic Europe, and the logboat in Scandinavia. In the Americas, the sewn plank boat became established in two widely separated regions: in the Santa Barbara Channel north of Los Angeles among the Chumash; and around the Chronos archipelago in Chile. That this occurred without any external stimulus indicates independent invention.

It is not possible to date such inventions exactly, but the first may have been in Egypt, where the earliest known plank ship has been excavated. This ship, measuring 45.4 m

(148 ft) long when reassembled, was buried in a pit next to the Great Pyramid of the pharaoh Khufu and dates to *c.* 2550 BC. Its size and complexity suggest that the Egyptians had been able to build plank vessels for some considerable time. Indeed, there are partially excavated plank boats buried in special graves at Abydos, dating from *c.* 3000 BC, which are 23 m (75.5 ft) long.

The next oldest excavated plank boats come from Dover, and the Humber and Severn estuaries in Britain. The planks of Khufu's ship and later Egyptian craft were fastened together by mortice and tenon joints and by rope stitching. The British planking was fastened only by rope: the earlier ones (ranging in date from 2000 to 1200 BC), by individual ties; the later ones (from 1100 to 800 BC), by stitching. There is also a sewn plank boat from 4th-century BC Denmark.

Plank-first & frame-first

The planking of these sewn boats was fastened together to form the hull and then framing was inserted. This 'plank-first' technique appears to have been the method used to build early boats worldwide. The earliest known use of the alternative sequence – with a framework constructed to create the hull shape and planking then fastened to it – is in the nail-fastened, Romano-Celtic vessels of the 2nd and 3rd centuries AD from Guernsey and the Thames and Severn estuaries. Seventh-century AD ships built 'frame-first' have been excavated from the central and eastern Mediterranean.

Frame-first methods gradually superseded plank-first in much of Mediterranean and Atlantic Europe, and led to the ships of the explorers who sailed the world's oceans in the 15th and 16th centuries, transferring aspects of European culture and technology with consequences that we see today. Chinese Admiral Zheng He's voyages throughout the Indian Ocean, as far west as Arabia and the east coast of Africa, during the early 15th century, may similarly have been undertaken in independently invented frame-first ships. A Chinese pictogram of the late 2nd millennium BC may denote a plank boat, but this is far from certain. The earliest excavated plank boats, from Yanghe near Shanghai, are dated 200 BC to AD 200.

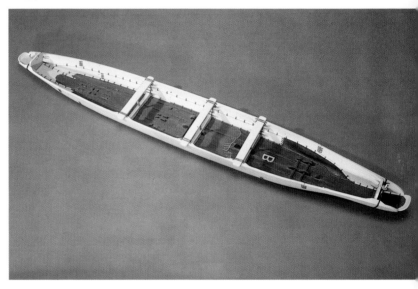

Jointing & sewing

The planking of the earliest known Mediterranean ships was fastened together by locked mortice and tenon joints, an improvement on the Egyptian unlocked joints. Two ships, excavated in the sea off southwest Turkey (at Uluburun and Gelidonya) and dated to *c.* 1300 and 1200 BC, are thought to have been built in the Levant, and it may be that the locked joint (used widely in the Mediterranean for the next 1500 years) was invented by the Phoenicians. Sewn plank boats have also been excavated from the Mediterranean: the earliest is dated *c.* 600 BC, but there are good reasons for thinking that sewn boats were in use as early as the 3rd millennium BC.

Top *The third Bronze Age Ferriby sewn plank boat as discovered in the mud of the Humber estuary in northern England.*

Above *A reconstruction model at 1:10 scale of the first Ferriby boat. The parts coloured black represent elements excavated, the remainder is conjectural.*

Right *Locked mortice and tenon plank fastenings as used on Mediterranean vessels from the mid-2nd millennium BC to the late 1st millennium AD.*

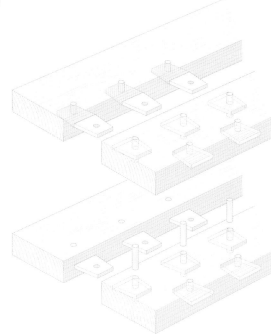

KEY DATES

plank boats	*c.* 3000 BC, Egypt
sewn plank boats	2000–1200 BC, England
locked wooden joints	*c.* 1300 BC, Levant
frame-first	2nd/3rd centuries AD, Britain

region. Plank boats with two outriggers appear on Javanese carvings of the 8th/9th century AD. Sixteenth-century Europeans regarded paired outriggers as a distinguishing feature of Southeast Asian seagoing vessels: they are also used in Madagascar, which was settled from Borneo in the 5th–6th century AD.

Boats with a single outrigger featured largely in early European reports from Oceania. Outriggers were possibly invented in western Melanesia and spread both eastwards and westwards. Other Oceanic plank boats noted at first European contact were boats on a logboat base, and paired boats. All three types had stitched planking.

Far right *The oldest depiction of a planked vessel in South Asia, on a 2nd-century BC carving from Bharhut, India. The planks are fastened together with double-dovetail shaped wooden clamps.*

The earliest known Southeast Asian plank boat is dated to the 4th century AD: its planking was fastened by individual rope ties and treenails (wooden dowels). Treenail fastenings subsequently became the principal method in this

It is possible that a graffito on a Mohenjo-daro potsherd of *c.* 2000 BC represents a plank boat. Otherwise, the earliest depiction from India is on a 2nd-century BC carving from Bharhut; the planks are fastened by double-dovetail wooden clamps, which are known elsewhere but not at such an early date. Sewn plank boats, a feature of both the western and eastern coasts of southern India in recent times, are not mentioned until the 16th century AD.

Right *Looking down into the mid-2nd century AD Romano-Celtic ship during its excavation from the River Thames at Blackfriars, London, in 1962. Large iron nails fastened the oak planking to the oak frames. This is the earliest known vessel built 'frame-first'.*

Sailing Vessels

*Few utilitarian creations of man were so spectacularly
handsome as a working sailing ship.*
BASIL GREENHILL, 1962

Sail has been used on every type of raft or boat from early times in every continent except Australia. But its use developed most in conjunction with plank boats and ships: for nearly 5000 years such vessels were at the forefront of warfare, communications, exploration and trade. Sailing ships are still used commercially today: for example, the 3-masted Tuticorin *thoni* (a sailing ship of 250–650 tonnes capacity) plies a regular route between southern India and Sri Lanka.

Types of sail

North American Indians occasionally used the wind to propel their boats by simply holding up a leafy bush, or by fastening a blanket, a skin or piece of bark to a paddle. Generally speaking, the use of sail leaves some evidence on a boat: a mast stepped in a special fitting and supported by rigging made fast to the boat, and a sail with running rigging. If it is not intended to sail across or into the wind (when greater stress is imposed on the boat), a simpler rig may be used. Balance boards and leeboards (including *guares*, see p. 165) also imply the use of sail.

The rectangular sail known as a 'square sail' (because it is generally set at right angles to the ship's heading) was widely used and is the earliest type known. Sails set nearer the fore-and-aft line of the vessel came later, and there appears to have been regional specialization. In the eastern Mediterranean and Indian Ocean the triangular lateen is found; in Southeast Asian the canted rectangular sail. The Chinese favoured the battened lugsail (a four-cornered sail); in Oceania 'claw-like' sails were used, and the peoples of the Americas had their own distinctive sails.

A measure of a sailing vessel's effectiveness is whether she can be sailed across the wind, or even at an angle into the wind. Based on iconographic evidence, it seems that Egyptian ships could prob-ably be sailed across the wind by the mid-2nd millennium BC; in other regions this ability is likely to have been later. Using the scanty information available, it seems that, even by the end of the period under consideration, the effective angle that ships could sail into the wind was never more than around 20 degrees. Sailing significantly closer to the wind had to await new materials and the competitive environment of racing.

Sails are even more perishable than wood and there are only two surviving examples: a linen fragment with a wooden brail ring re-used as a shroud in 2nd-century BC Egypt; and a 12th- to 13th-century AD fragment of matting sail with bamboo battens from China.

Depictions of sail, however, date back as far as Predynastic Egypt – the earliest representation being a pole mast with a square sail on a pot dated

Above *The earliest evidence for sail in the Mediterranean comes from Minoan seals, one dating to c. 2000 BC (top). The Minoans were a great sea-faring people and had extensive trading contacts around the Aegean and with Egypt.*

Left *The earliest depiction of sail: a vase from Naqada, Egypt, dating to c. 3100 BC. The exact type of water transport shown is not clear.*

found off Cyprus, was stepped well forward suggesting that she may have had a lateen sail.

Sailing ships around the world

From the 6th century BC onwards Mediterranean ships are depicted with two masts – so far this is the earliest evidence anywhere for multi-masted vessels. They are also depicted or described in India in the 2nd century AD; in Southeast Asia in the 3rd century; and, later, in China, Arabia and northwest Europe, in the 12th–14th centuries. South American log rafts and Oceanic paired boats with two masts were seen and recorded by European explorers.

A *periplus* (a narrative of a voyage) dating to the 6th century BC and incorporated into a 4th-century AD poem, *Ora Maritima*, describes how Breton seamen sailed to Ireland in two days. The earliest artifactual evidence for sail in northwest Europe is the gold model from Broighter, Ireland, of the 1st century BC. Caesar attests to sail on Breton ships in the same century. A mast is stepped amidships on the Broighter model, as it is on ships depicted on the 1st-century AD coins of Cunobelin of eastern England: this suggests that these vessels had a square sail.

Above *The reconstructed Kyrenia sailing vessel, based on a wreck found off Cyprus dating to around 300 BC. The mast was well forward, suggesting the use of the triangular, lateen sail.*

On the other hand, three excavated Romano-Celtic vessels dating to the 2nd to 3rd centuries AD found in the Severn and Thames estuaries in England and the island of Guernsey, had mast steps set well forward, while the mast depicted on the 1st-century AD Rhineland monument to the Celt Blussus (p. 164) is similarly stepped: this suggests that a fore-and-aft sail such as a lugsail may have been used – if so, this would be the earliest evidence for a fore-and-aft sail outside the Mediterranean.

to *c.* 3100 BC. It is possible that sail is mentioned in Mesopotamian documents of the later-3rd millennium BC; more convincing evidence comes from two Bahrain seals of *c.* 2000 BC, on which ships are depicted with a mast amidships.

Engravings on Minoan seals are evidence for sail in the eastern Mediterranean around 2000 BC. Square sails remained the rule in Mediterranean iconography until the 2nd century BC, when the fore-and-aft spritsail is depicted; the lateen, another fore-and-aft sail, is depicted in the 2nd century AD. The mast of the *c.* 300 BC Kyrenia ship,

A graffito of *c.* 2000 BC on a Harappan potsherd from Mohenjo-daro is the earliest evidence for sail in South Asia. A 3rd-century AD text describes large Southeast Asian ships with sail. The evidence for Chinese sail is not so clear: dates from before 1200 BC to 300 BC have been suggested. The most convincing evidence is a description of matting

KEY DATES

depiction of sail	c. 3100 BC, Egypt
two-masted ships	6th century BC, Mediterranean
oldest surviving sail	2nd century BC, Egypt

sails in a dictionary dated to *c.* AD 100. Sail was first noted in Oceania and in the Americas early in the 16th century.

The origin of sail

A superficial assessment of these dates might suggest that sail originated in Egypt and subsequently was diffused northwest (Mediterranean, Atlantic Europe and the Baltic) and southeast (Arabia, Indian Ocean and the China Seas). Indeed, sail, like the wheel, is its own advertisement. However, Egypt was certainly not the sole origin of sail: Europeans found a variety of sailing rigs on the rafts and boats of America, from the Arctic to Brazil and Peru.

A more sustainable hypothesis is that there may have been several places where the idea of using a sail originated, with diffusion around each centre of innovation. It may be that these regions are those which subsequently developed a distinctive form of sailing rig: the eastern Mediterranean and Indian Ocean; Southeast Asia; Oceania; and China; with possibly more than one region in the Americas.

Left *The earliest artifactual evidence for sail in northwest Europe: a gold model of a boat (possibly representing a hide boat) with a mast, of the 1st century BC from Broighter, Co. Derry, Ireland. Note also the 14 oars and the steering oar, and two forked poles inside the boat.*

Paddles, Poles
& Oars

*Unless there is something sticking out of a boat (paddle, pole or oar)
she can't be moved through the water.*
CDR ERIC MCKEE RN, 1983

The use of tides and river currents as a form of propulsion for boats is widespread today, and early use is likely but difficult to demonstrate since no artifact (apart from a steering device) is needed and no evidence is left on the craft itself. Paddling also leaves no sign on the vessel; poling ('punting') may again leave no trace, but special walkways are sometimes fitted. Oars need a pivot, and specialized fittings may also be used for towing, though it can be done from any available strong point.

A type of propulsion little known elsewhere is the Chinese treadmill paddlewheel, said to have been invented before the 10th century AD. Illustrations of the 12th/13th century are known, showing river vessels with between 2 and 22 paddlewheels on each side.

Paddling & poling

The earliest known paddles are dated to around 7500 BC and come from both Germany and Britain. Some Danish paddles, from 5500 BC onwards, are decorated, as is one of the 5th millennium BC from China. The lengths of excavated paddles show that most would have been used while sitting or kneeling, but some would have been used from a standing position.

Paddle use is first illustrated in 4th-millennium BC Egypt, late-3rd-millennium BC Arabia and in 2nd-century BC India. Medieval travellers reported their use in Southeast Asia. They were noted at first European contact in Australia, Oceania and the Americas. Uniquely, American kayaks, sewn plank boats and small rafts were propelled by double-bladed paddles (p. 156).

Poling using a forked pole is shown on a Mesopotamian cylinder seal of *c.* 3200 BC, and is also depicted on Egyptian paintings of the 3rd to 2nd millennia BC. The earliest European evidence

Model of a riverboat, found in the tomb of Meketre, Thebes, Egypt, early 12th dynasty, c. 1985 BC. At the stern is a median rudder and the oars are being worked 'sit-pull'. The man at the prow may be holding a sounding weight.

comes in the form of forked poles found with the gold model boat of the 1st century BC from Broighter, Ireland (pp. 160–61), and pole terminals of that date have been excavated from the Rhine region. The 1st- to 2nd-century AD Pommeroeul boat 4 from Belgium had a poling walkway, as had a 1st-century AD boat model from Guangzhou, China. Poles were in use in Oceania and in America at first European contact.

Left *Paddles and paddle fragments found with the 4th-century BC sewn plank boat from Hjortspring, Denmark.*

Rowing & towing

Oarsmen can ply their oars either from a standing or sitting position, and oars may be pulled or pushed. From the mid-3rd millennium BC onwards there are Egyptian depictions of rowing, with the oarsmen sitting and pulling their oars, which are pivoted in a rope grommet. Some oarsmen on the mid-2nd millennium BC Akrotiri frescoes from the Aegean island of Thera use a similar style. Homer tells us that oars were worked against a wooden pin through a leather grommet. Mesopotamian and Phoenician oarsmen of the 9th century BC are shown in four different styles: stand-push; stand-pull; sit-pull; and sit-push. A late 8th-century BC relief from the palace of Sargon at Khorsabad shows oars being worked stand-push.

Two model oars were excavated with the 5th-century BC boat model from Dürnberg in Austria. And from 1st-century BC China comes a wooden

Below *Detail of a relief from the palace of Sargon II (721–705 BC) at Khorsabad, showing sailors rowing a boat, towing timber, possibly cedarwood. Here the oars are being worked 'stand-push'.*

model boat complete with oars. At First Contact it was noted that the oars of the *umiak*, a seagoing hide boat of northern America, were pivoted against bone tholes or in thong loops.

Sculling, the technique of working an oar from side to side within a groove in a boat's stern, is widely used today. This technique was perfected in China by an ingenious auto-feathering arrangement (*yuloh*) which was documented in the 17th century and may be shown on a brick dated to the 1st century BC/AD.

Towing from river banks is described in late 3rd-millennium BC Mesopotamian documents, and a swimmer towing a bundle raft is depicted on an early 7th-century BC Mesopotamian sculpture. This technique has been widely used in recent centuries: for example, small hide boats and rafts of

On this Rhineland monument to Blussus, of the 1st-century AD, the helmsman is holding the tiller of a steering oar pivoted at the stern. The two crew near the stern are pulling oars; the fourth man may be assisting steering from the bow. The mast is stepped well forward and may be for towing, although there is no sign of a rope.

KEY DATES

paddles	*c.* 7500 BC, Germany
poling	*c.* 3200 BC, Mesopotamia
rowing	mid-3rd millennium BC, Egypt
towing	late 3rd millennium BC, Mesopotamia
steering oar	?4th millennium BC, Egypt
side rudder	mid-3rd millennium BC, Egypt
median rudder	later 3rd millennium BC, Egypt

netted gourds were propelled in this way in the Americas. Boats have also been widely used to tow ships: an Egyptian mid-2nd-millennium BC relief depicts a large vessel loaded with two obelisks being towed downstream by 30 oared boats.

Below Guares – *long wooden boards – were used in the Americas to assist steering; this one, dating to c. 300 BC, is from Ica, Peru.*

Steering

Steering a vessel may be achieved at the same time, and by the same means, as propulsion when paddling, poling or stand-push rowing. The different devices include steering oars used against a single pivot at the stern or on the quarter; side rudders used on the quarter and turned around their own long axis; and median rudders used astern on the centreline.

A steering oar may be shown on an Egyptian 4th-millennium BC linen fragment, but the earliest certain depiction comes from the mid-3rd millennium BC. Paired steering oars are shown on a seal and on a baked clay amulet from Mohenjo-daro, dated to *c.* 2000 BC, and the steering oar is still widely used in South Asia today.

The marvellously detailed frescoes from Akrotiri (see p. 200) also show steering oars, and there is one with the Broighter model boat. A Rhineland monument and a Netherlands altar, both of the 1st century AD, also depict examples. Steering oars of the early centuries AD have been excavated from the Low Countries and Switzerland. Dated to the same period is a Chinese model boat from Chang-sha which has a steering oar pivoted in a notch in the stern. Except for steering oars used in *umiaks*, steering in the Americas appears to have been by the same means as propulsion, sometimes with the assistance of *guares* (a leeboard).

Rudders

In Egypt, Khufu's ship of *c.* 2550 BC (p. 156) and boats from Dahshur of *c.* 1850 BC have a side rudder on each quarter. Also in Egypt, a relief dated to the late-2nd-millennium BC shows ships of the 'Sea Peoples' (from the Aegean or the Levant) with paired side rudders, and this method of steering continued to be used in the Mediterranean for millennia.

Marks on ships engraved on two 1st-century BC coins of the Briton Cunobelin may represent a side rudder. Fourth-century AD boats excavated in southern Scandinavia have a single side rudder: this appears to be an innovation independent of Roman influence, and a rudder on the starboard quarter became a defining characteristic of the medieval Viking ship. Some early Indian depictions, for instance on 2nd-century AD coins from Andhra and a 6th/7th-century cave painting at Ajanta, may show side rudders rather than steering oars.

Median rudders with tillers, pivoted over the stern and against a stanchion further forward, are found on Egyptian tomb models of the later 3rd millennium BC. They became increasingly common but do not seem to have superseded paired side rudders, nor do they appear to have influenced Mediterranean practice. A 1st-century AD pottery model boat from Guangzhou, southern China, has a median rudder slung under the stern, an arrangement widely used in China during recent centuries.

Navigation, Harbours & Lighthouses

And all I ask is a tall ship and a star to steer her by.

JOHN MASEFIELD, 1900

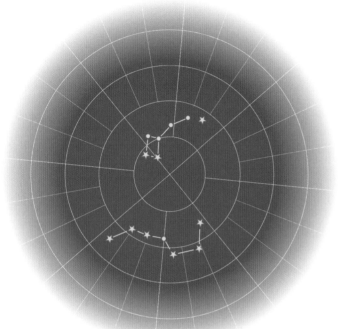

Above *The night sky in the northern hemisphere as it would have appeared around 1000 BC, showing the position of the pole star in relation to Ursa Minor (top, with the pole star to the right) and Ursa Major. The pole star was further away from the celestial pole (centre) than it is today – as seen in the photograph (**above right**, in the upper centre) – and the position of the celestial pole (a fixed point in space) required careful estimation.*

During the earliest voyages it is likely that seamen remained within sight of land. On such voyages a mental reckoning would have been kept of the boat's position relative to natural landmarks. Descriptions of landmarks and seamarks sighted on such routes were probably learned by rote and passed on from pilot to apprentice. Such oral descriptions were subsequently incorporated into the *periploi* (sailing directions) of the Classical world and the medieval sailing manuals of the Mediterranean and Atlantic Europe. The use of the sounding pole is illustrated in 3rd-millennium BC Egypt. Sounding weights are seen on Egyptian boat models dated around 2000 BC (p. 162) The earliest excavated leads, and an account of their use, are from the mid-1st millennium BC Mediterranean (see sidebar, p. 169).

Navigation without instruments

In the mid-2nd millennium BC, seamen in the South Pacific, the eastern Mediterranean and the Indian Ocean undertook voyages out of sight of land. How did they do this without navigational instruments? Fortunately, non-instrumental techniques were still being used when Europeans first entered the South Pacific. In the late 18th century Captain James Cook commented on the accuracy of these Oceanic navigators and noted: 'In these navigations the sun is their guide by day and the stars by night. When these are obscured they have recourse to the points from whence the wind and the waves of the sea come upon the vessel.'

This form of navigation is known as 'environmental' since the navigator uses visible information such as sun, stars, constellations, wind, swell and the flight line of migrating birds for directions; the sun's changing bearing and the relative position of the circumpolar stars are used as a measure of time. Indirect references to such methods can be found in Homer's *Odyssey* and in medieval texts such as the *Life of St Brendan*.

In southern Europe the position of the celestial north pole was known relative to the constellation Ursa Major, at the latest by the time of Homer. Subsequently the Phoenicians recognized that Ursa Minor gave a more accurate position. It may be that estimates of star altitudes were made in handspans, but this is not possible to demonstrate. Environmental navigation would have been used worldwide before the late 1st millennium AD when instruments began to be introduced.

Scientific navigation

By Classical times, the Greeks could estimate their latitude on land using the equinoctial sun's noon shadow cast by a gnomon (a vertical rod); this is unlikely to have been practicable at sea, but it is possible that star altitudes were measured against the mast in the 1st century AD. Ninth-century Arabs in the Indian Ocean appear to have been the first to use instruments at sea: they measured star altitudes using a 'staff', subsequently developed into the *kamal*, a series of wooden tablets on a knotted string with which estimates of latitude could be made. It is likely that this development was based on Persian knowledge which in turn had been influenced by Greek learning and practices.

The Chinese, who had been steering by the pole star since the early centuries AD, first used the mariner's compass in *c*. AD 1100. Around a century later it was in use in the Mediterranean and Arab world, possibly independently invented. The sand glass came later, being used by Mediterranean seamen for time measurement (hence for distance/speed) from the late 12th century, followed by the sea chart in *c*. AD 1250. Arab and Chinese navigators first used charts during the 14th century. It was not until the early 15th century that Genoese and Iberian seamen began to measure star altitudes with the mariner's astrolabe and the quadrant.

By 1492, when Christopher Columbus crossed the Atlantic from Europe to the Americas, Chinese,

Above *Drawing to show steering by the position of stars (including Polaris, centre, and Ursa Major, right) in relation to the ship's rigging, in the South Pacific. Star altitudes were possibly measured against the mast by the 1st century AD.*

Left *Diagram showing the method of using a* kamal *to measure the altitude (vertical angle) of a star to estimate latitude. The line is calibrated in knots for harbours in Sri Lanka and the eastern coast of India.*

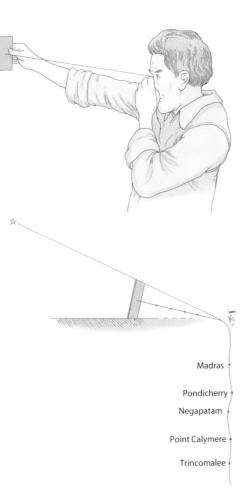

Madras

Pondicherry

Negapatam

Point Calymere

Trincomalee

Arab and European seamen had charts, scientific tables and a range of instruments which enabled them to undertake oceanic voyages. In essentials, these 15th-century techniques continued to be used until they were overtaken by satellite navigation in the late 20th century. No one region can be said to have invented navigation using instruments: Chinese, Arabs and Europeans all played their part.

Harbours

Boat landing places within natural harbours in the Red and Arabian seas are mentioned in the 1st-century AD *Periplus of the Erythraean Sea*. By that date such informal sites would already have been in use for millennia the world over. At these landing places boats are anchored, made fast to a mooring post or hauled on to the foreshore, which may be consolidated to facilitate beaching and the movement of goods and animals to and from the boats. Examples of such informal landing places include a mat of light timbers (a 'hard') that was pegged to the Humber estuary foreshore at North Ferriby, northern England, in the early 2nd millennium BC; while in Christchurch harbour, southern England, gravel was used to achieve a similar effect in the 1st century BC.

Above *A busy harbour scene, with boats carrying horses, from Trajan's Column, 2nd century AD.*

Below *A 3rd-century AD Roman slab carved with a ship and a lighthouse.*

In the 9th/8th century BC stone structures were built on offshore reefs and islands to protect natural harbours on the Levant coast of the eastern Mediterranean. At about the same time, a breakwater of dressed stone on top of rubble was built at Delos, an island in the Aegean. These first steps led to the complex harbours of the Greek and Roman world with their quays, jetties, cargo-handling facilities, warehouses and ship building sites, and their victualling and fresh water supplies.

Such a complex harbour was built at Alexandria in Egypt in the 3rd century BC. From a site just to the west of the westernmost branch of the Nile, a causeway was built out to the island of Pharos. Two harbours were thus formed, one protected from the east, the other from the west. A third waterfront on Lake Mareotis to the south gave access to the Nile.

The *Periplus* noted above mentions 13 harbours on a 450-nautical mile stretch of the southwest coast of India; these all appear to be informal landing places, including Kalliena which, centuries later, became the port of Mumbai.

The shipbuilding 'factory' said to have been established in the 7th to 5th centuries BC at Fuzhou on China's southeast coast and the 3rd-century BC shipyard with a slipway excavated at Guangzhou in southern China may be examples of proto-ports. The excavation of wharfs and a shipyard at Ningbo, and Song dynasty references to Chinese 'state shipyards' demonstrate that formal harbours of some size were in use by medieval times.

Lighthouses

During the siege of Troy, the bones of Achilles, Menoetius and Antilochus were buried under a mound on a promontory. Such artificial landmarks were built, according to Homer, so that they 'might be seen far out to sea by the mariners of today and future ages'. Homer also mentions temporary beacon fires which by then had probably been used for millennia to guide vessels to a harbour. In the 16th century AD beacons may well have been similarly used on Maya shrines and watchtowers on the Yucatan coast of Central America.

The first specialist landmark with a light was built in the mid-3rd century BC at an entrance to Alexan-

KEY DATES

environmental navigation	mid-2nd millennium BC, South Pacific, east Mediterranean, Indian Ocean
sounding-pole	3rd millennium BC, Egypt
sounding-leads	*c.* 2000 BC, Egypt
complex harbour	3rd century BC, Egypt
lighthouse	mid-3rd century BC, Egypt

dria's harbour on Pharos island, close to the Nile's westernmost branch. The Pharos lighthouse was so renowned that it became one of the Seven Wonders of the ancient world, and the word *pharos* (for lighthouse) was taken into the Italian, Greek and French languages.

The emperor Claudius built a lighthouse in Ostia, the port of Rome, in AD 50 and this led to others, so that by the end of the Roman empire in the West, there were 30 around the Mediterranean and the Black Sea; others were found on the Atlantic coast at La Coruña in northwest Spain, Boulogne in northwest France, and two were built at Dover in southeast Britain. Lighthouses were subsequently built on prominent sites around the Indian Ocean by Arabs and Indians, and also on the Chinese coast.

SOUNDING-LEADS

The sounding-lead, the most important navigational instrument before the invention of the compass, was used to determine the depth of water and the nature of the sea bed, hence giving an approximate position relative to a river mouth, a sandbank or other unknown underwater features. The typical Greek or Roman lead was a bell-shaped casting weighing about 5 kg (11 lb), with a lug at its apex for a line. Soft tallow was inserted into a hollow in the base, and with this a sample of the sea bed could be recovered. A sailor, standing towards the bows of the vessel, would cast the lead forwards, then waited for it to strike the sea floor, and noted the depth from knots or coded tags on the rope when it was vertical as the ship passed overhead. The seabed sample adhering to the tallow could then be identified. The lead sounding-weight may have been invented in the 6th century BC, but stone weights may well have been used in earlier times.

Hunting, Warfare & Sport

Hunting is as old as humanity itself. Humans have been predators for more than 2.5 million years. First scavengers, then hunters, early hominids raided kills by fellow predators, ran down small antelope, and used clubs and stones to kill disabled quarry. No one knows when the first wooden spear came into use, but it was at least half a million years ago, probably much earlier. The hunter required expert stalking skills, the ability to approach so close to the quarry as to be almost able to touch it. Any form of hunting, indeed survival, depended on an intimate knowledge of animals' habits and movements. The chances of success rose sharply when the prey was helpless, so people dug pits along well-frequented paths and wove nets of vegetable fibres to trap animals in their dens.

By at least 20,000 years ago, hunting weaponry had achieved considerable sophistication, with the development of the spearthrower, a throwing stick that extended the range and velocity of a spear. Then came the bow and arrow, invented during the late Ice Age, a portable weapon that could kill or wound at greater range. A hunter could shoot several arrows, often with poisoned tips, within a few seconds.

Warfare, too, is as old as humanity; for thousands of years it was little more than a matter of short-lived, volatile confrontations between individuals and small bands. Disputes erupted over territory and food resources, over women or prestige. The weapons were those of hunting – spears for long-range duels, simple knives and daggers for hand-to-hand fighting.

Detail of an Assyrian relief showing a warrior with a bow and arrow and a sword at his side, while another protects them both with a shield; from the Northwest Palace of Ashurnasirpal at Nimrud, Iraq, 9th century BC.

With the first civilizations came more specialized weapons of war which took advantage of copper, bronze and then iron, to fashion tough-edged daggers, swords and throwing spears. Hammered metal gave protection, too, fashioned into armour, helmets and shields, tough combinations of leather, bronze or iron sheet, and other materials, that allowed mobility and some defence against arrows and thrusting weapons.

The first standing armies coincided with the earliest cities, carefully fortified communities girdled by high defensive walls. As weaponry became more sophisticated, and siege technology more menacing, so fortifications were elaborated with bastions and towers, deep ditches and high ramparts. Such works offered protection against attacking infantry, catapults and showers of deadly sling shots. Despite such technology, fortresses and cities were formidable strongholds capable of withstanding sieges and inflicting numerous casualties on attacking infantry, witness the regiment of soldiers killed by arrows during a siege buried near pharaoh Mentuhotep's mortuary temple in Upper Egypt in about 2010 BC.

The invention of the chariot and the domestication of the horse introduced a new mobility into ancient warfare. Horse-drawn chariots looked magnificent as monarchs and great lords paraded before their subjects and their armies. They were also effective on battlefields in open terrain, for they provided a platform for archers, a better viewpoint of the battlefield and a good base for hurling spears. Cavalry were a much more enduring innovation, for they provided great mobility, considerable strategic advantage on open battle fields, even against massed infantry, and above all speed – the ability to execute a lightning raid and then move away to safety. Like stolid legions, they became a vital component in the Roman war machine.

No one knows when armies took to the sea. The Egyptian pharaohs regularly moved their regiments by ship up and down the Nile, both within Egypt itself and deep into Nubia. But their battles were mostly fought on land. The first actual warships were little more than platforms for archers and close combat, but by the mid-1st millennium BC, naval warfare was well established. In an era when sailing ships were only effective downwind, everything depended on well-trained oarsmen, many of them slaves, for the rise of slavery and the use of galleys in Mediterranean waters went hand-in-hand.

War and sports have always gone together, for both are competitive activities where the swift, the aggressive and strong, and the adept sharpshooter, do well. Warfare calls for teamwork; so do many sports. The casual competitions of earlier times gave way to organized events. The Olympic Games, a neutral arena of international competition, were traditionally first staged in Greece in 776 BC. Sports also had a strong ritual undercurrent, especially in Mesoamerica, where the ceremonial ball game re-enacted cosmic struggles and the losers were often sacrificed to the gods. Mental games too were important – the quiet strategic battles waged on boards that were the forerunners of today's chess.

Four players engage in the Mesoamerican ball game, wearing the elaborate protective equipment necessary for this contest, as depicted on a Maya vase of c. AD 600–800. It was against the rules to touch the hard rubber ball with hands or feet, and the central figure is down on one knee, ready to hit the ball with his padded yoke. The ball game had great symbolic significance, and the losers of the contest on the court sometimes also lost their lives.

Animal & Fish Traps, Fishing Nets

42

*For he that beats the bush the bird not gets
But who sits still and holdeth fast the nets.*
EDWARD DE VERE, EARL OF OXFORD, 1573

Traps and nets are invaluable hunting and fishing aids allowing people to capture greater numbers of animals and fish than would be possible without such aids. Some traps are simple, others are large and ingenious, and hunters and fishers have used them for millennia.

Traps for land animals are of two types. The first involves driving the animals into a pound or corral. Once they are herded together inside, it is much easier to kill the animals. Such drives might hunt just a few animals, or they could take many more. In North America, Plains Indians drove hundreds of bison over cliffs, funnelling the animals in the desired direction by lines of cairns while harrying them from behind. At Head-Smashed-In, a drive site in Alberta, excavation reveals that this method goes back at least 6000 years. Early travellers in the Near East record hundreds of gazelle being driven into pounds up to 100 m (330 ft) in diameter. Diverging walls extended up to 1 km (0.6 mile) from the corral, forming a funnel into which the animals were driven. These examples were built of stone and are difficult to date, but the method probably goes back thousands of years.

The second sort of trap is the snare, which operates passively, without humans having to drive the animals. Snares tend to catch single animals, often fur bearers. They are made exclusively of organic materials which hardly ever survive, but Upper Palaeolithic inhabitants of Ice Age Europe did use cord made of sinew and most probably set snares – they would certainly have needed the furs.

Fish traps & nets

Fish traps in recent times display an incredible variety of forms, suited to different situations and types of fish. In tidal estuaries simple stone traps may be built consisting of walls that are covered at high tide, so that fish drift in over them. As the tide recedes the fish are trapped. The antiquity of such traps is unknown but their simplicity suggests it could be very great. In less tidal waters fences are built out perpendicular to the shoreline, with a catching chamber at the outer end. Fish encountering the fence swim along it towards the deep water, and enter the catching chamber. Several Mesolithic examples are known from Denmark, dating to before 4000 BC. Such traps usually catch large

*One form of hunting was simply to drive a herd of animals over a cliff to their death. At the bison drive sites of Head-Smashed-In and Calderwood, in Alberta, Canada, this method dates back around 6000 years (**below left**); below are some of the thousands of bison skulls that were discovered there in the deep deposits that accumulated over the centuries.*

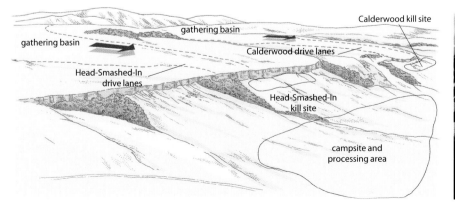

gathering basin

Calderwood kill site

gathering basin

Calderwood drive lanes

Head-Smashed-In drive lanes

Head-Smashed-In kill site

campsite and processing area

KEY DATES

animal drives	Palaeolithic
snares	Upper Palaeolithic, Europe
basket traps	Mesolithic, Scandinavia
net	Mesolithic, Russia
fish traps	before 4000 BC, Denmark

Above *Fishermen in a boat haul in a large catch of fish in their net, in a 4th-century AD Roman mosaic from Sidi Abdallah, near Bizerta, Tunisia.*

Right *In this relief scene from the North Palace of Ashurbanipal at Nineveh, c. 645 BC, a herd of deer are being chased into a net that has been stretched across their escape route.*

numbers of quite small fish; the thousands of bones from Danish coastal settlements show that cod, flounder and mackerel were commonly caught.

In the tighter confines of rivers, traps are often set for migratory species such as salmon. These may be in the form of weirs spanning the river, either with basket traps set into gaps or platforms from which fish could be speared. The most skilful exponents of this technology in recent times were the Northwest Coast Indians of British Columbia and southeast Alaska, who used many different types of salmon traps. This high level of development argues that the methods originated long ago, although no date can be given. Basket traps suitable for narrow streams have been recovered from a variety of Mesolithic sites in Scandinavia (p. 27).

Nets are made purely of cord. They may be suspended and catch fish swimming into them, or act as barriers to confine fish so that they can be speared or lifted out of the water with hand nets. One Mesolithic example from Antrea, in Karelia in northern Russia, measured some 30 m (98 ft) in length. Made of bast (cordage from the inner bark) of lime trees, it had floats of birch bark along the top and stone weights along the bottom. Finds in Peru indicate that nets made of cotton were in use several thousand years ago.

But these finds may not be the earliest in either region. Nets and most traps are made entirely of organic materials which survive only under excep-

tional circumstances. None have survived from the Ice Age, leading some to argue that fish only began to be heavily exploited in the postglacial period. Others, however, think that European Upper Palaeolithic hunter-gatherers probably did use such devices even though no trace of them has survived. Ice Age coasts (where most of the evidence would be) are now far below modern sea level due to rising water levels around the globe following the melting of the ice sheets .

If Ice Age peoples did indeed use such devices, there are important implications. Nets and fish traps commonly catch more fish than can be eaten on a day-to-day basis; so such catches are usually stored. There are two outcomes. Firstly, nomadism and big food stores are not very compatible: people cannot easily carry the store and so have

to stay put and guard it. Recent hunter-fishers with stores remained in one place for several months, or lived in the same settlement all year. Secondly, such stores belong to individuals or families – not the whole group. Some individuals might thus become wealthier than others, leading to social inequalities. We often assume that sedentary settlement and social hierarchies are a feature of the more recent past; but if fish traps were used in the Upper Palaeolithic, these developments might go back far further among modern humans.

Spearthrowers, Boomerangs & Bows & Arrows

Bring me my bow of burning gold:
Bring me my arrows of desire:
Bring me my spear: O Clouds unfold!
Bring me my chariot of fire.
WILLIAM BLAKE, 1804–18

Our primate cousins frequently throw things, and no doubt our hominid ancestors would have done the same. Modern humans, however, developed methods of projecting objects further than can be achieved by simple unaided throwing. This has both brought a wide variety of prey into easy reach, and has also improved our ability to kill each other.

The spearthrower (or *atlatl* in North America) is a lever that in effect extends the length of the thrower's arm, allowing greater momentum to be imparted to the spear. Held in the hand, it has a hook at the other end that fits into a hole in the base of the spear. This simple piece of equipment extends the potential range of a spear up to fourfold – although accuracy depends on practice.

Spearthrowers were most often made of wood, which rarely survives well in the archaeological record, though some were made of other materials, in particular antler, which fortunately survive better.

In recent times the spearthrower was used by many hunter-gatherers around the world, probably indicating that it is an ancient invention, perhaps even spreading across the world with the earliest modern humans. The oldest surviving examples come from French Upper Palaeolithic caves, inhabited during the last Ice Age. The main prey here was reindeer and wild horse; if killed during the autumn migrations their meat could be stored to help people survive the long cold winter.

Just how important these implements were is shown by the fact that some are decorated with beautiful and lifelike carvings of animals and birds. Such fine examples may have been purely for display and never intended for actual use. Spearthrowers are probably just as ancient in other parts of the world – they are commonly shown in Australian rock art, for example, but it is difficult to date the carvings.

Left *Upper Palaeolithic spearthrower, 17,000 to 13,000 years old, from Mas d'Azil, France. This beautifully carved example is made of reindeer antler and depicts a young ibex, with two birds perched on one end. One of the birds forms the hook on which the butt of the spear would be placed. Ornate examples like this may have been intended for show rather than use.*

Below *The spearthrower adds extra length to the arm, and can help propel a spear up to four times the distance of an unaided throw.*

Above *An Australian Aborigine launches a boomerang. When thrown with skill and speed an aerofoil effect is created, making it fly further and sometimes it returns to the thrower.*

Right *A boomerang held in the correct attitude for throwing. This example from Australia was decorated using a stone tool and was probably made around the middle of the 20th century.*

The boomerang

The boomerang is another hunting weapon, but one that works on a completely different principle. Flat and curved, it is thrown so that it spins fast, creating an aerofoil effect which makes it fly further, and in some cases even return to the thrower; it kills by impact. Identified primarily with Australia, occasional ancient wooden tools from other parts of the world have been claimed as boomerangs, but these may just be ordinary throwing sticks (which do not use the aerofoil principle) or pieces of natural wood never used by humans.

As boomerangs are made of wood, very few archaeological examples survive, so the history of boomerangs is also incomplete. Some returning boomerangs have been found in Wyrie Swamp in Australia which date to 10,000 years old, making them the world's oldest convincing examples.

The bow & arrow

The bow and arrow is the pre-firearm weapon system recognizable to everyone. Not only was it widely used by hunting and farming peoples, it was a major element in the armies of the ancient world. The bow is basically a spring which stores energy when the bowstring is drawn; this energy is transferred to the arrow when the string is released. Some prehistoric bows from Europe are made of elm staves, which are naturally springy. Others are made of yew, the preferred wood of later times. Yew sapwood resists stretching, while the heartwood resists compression; a bow made of a strip of wood from the sapwood-heartwood transition, with the sapwood on the side away from the archer, is exceptionally powerful.

Contrary to popular myth, not all hunter-gatherers used bows and arrows. Australian Aborigines for example did not, although those in contact with the Torres Strait Islanders in the north must have been acquainted with it. Arrows may have a head of stone or metal mounted on the shaft, or may simply be whittled to a point; if they are used on fur bearing animals, where an undamaged skin is the target, the head may be a blunt bolt designed to stun rather than penetrate.

As with boomerangs and spearthrowers, bows and arrows are mostly made of organic materials that do not usually survive. The earliest European evidence for archery takes the form of probable stone arrowheads from Spain, some 18,000–20,000 years old and belonging to the Solutrean culture. But bows may be much older than this. In the Howieson's Poort culture of southern Africa we find many small tools of the kind later used as arrow points and barbs. If these really were arrow armatures (and we have no proof), this takes archery back to 60,000–70,000 years ago.

Definite arrows from northern Germany date from about 12,000 years ago, the end of the Upper Palaeolithic. The earliest actual bows are from the early Mesolithic of Denmark, a millennium or so later. There are interesting differences between them: Upper Palaeolithic arrows are heavy, designed for killing by penetration, evidently specialized for use on reindeer. Mesolithic equipment was lighter and more general purpose, suitable for a variety of animals – although this could include the very largest: a spectacular skeleton of an aurochs (a wild ox that could reach 1.8 m or 6 ft at the shoulder) from Prejlerup in Denmark had been hit by some nine arrows containing 16 armatures, but even then had escaped the hunters. Although Mesolithic hunters were very efficient, many animal bones in their settlements show healed wounds, testifying to earlier hunting episodes when the animal escaped.

Hunters also used bows for warfare. The cemetery of Jebel Sahaba in Sudan dates from 10,000 years ago and contains 58 skeletons, about one third of which had arrowheads stuck in them. Bows continued to be used for both hunting and warfare after the appearance of farming. Composite bows are made of several pieces, some of which resist extension, while others resist compression; they are thus remarkably powerful manufactured equivalents of the yew bows described above. They rose to prominence after the 16th century BC when palace workshops could turn them out in large numbers.

In Egypt they were used by soldiers wearing plate armour, riding in war chariots (pp. 182 and 196). The Hittites used this weapons system to develop the first 'combined arms' army, uniting chariot-based mobility and fire power with manoeuvre. Composite bows were later used by mounted archers such as the Scythians and other nomads from the northern steppes; their military successes continued until the days of Genghis Khan and beyond.

Missile weaponry that extended the human range of action beyond that of simple throwing was one of humankind's earliest technological triumphs, and may have been responsible for giving us a competitive edge over other hominids in two ways – firstly as more efficient hunters of game; and secondly, as and when necessary, as killers of other hominids.

KEY DATES

spearthrower	Upper Palaeolithic, France
possible arrow points	60,000–70,000 years ago, South Africa
stone arrowheads	18,000–20,000 years ago, Spain
arrows	12,000 years ago, Germany
bow	10,000 years ago, Denmark
boomerang	10,000 years ago, Australia

Left *A bow made from elm, found at Holmegaard in Denmark. It dates to around 8000–7000 BC, and is perhaps the world's oldest bow.*

Below *Probable arrowheads from Parpalló cave in Spain; Solutrean, c. 18,000 to 20,000 years old.*

Right *A bolt-headed wooden arrow from Holmegaard IV, Denmark, for stunning fur-bearing animals without damage to the skin; and an arrowhead from Sweden, with flint insets.*

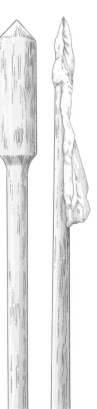

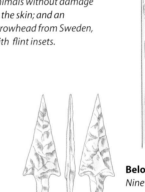

Below *Assyrian relief from Nineveh, 7th century BC, with an archer and slingers advancing behind a shield.*

44

Swords, Daggers & War Spears

The history of the Sword is the history of humanity.

RICHARD BURTON, 1884

Right *This dagger, with a flint blade and a bone hilt carved in the image of a snake, was found at Çatalhöyük in Turkey and dates to the 6th millennium BC. It is remarkable in that it retains its organic hilt.*

The origins of swords, daggers and war spears go back to the first stone tools. The path towards the superlative craftsmanship of the Japanese *katana* (the Samurai long sword) or the delicately wrought rapiers of the medieval period began with an early hominid choosing a bit of stone for its sharp edge. Over the millennia, hominids and then humans gradually learned to work with stone, flaking and grinding it down to the desired shape. As humans became sedentary and began to produce surpluses of food and goods, there came the need to defend their territory from outsiders, and so the development of weapons increased dramatically.

Right *A depiction of an Aztec Eagle Knight, from the Codex Ixtlilxochitl, shows him carrying a feather mosaic shield (see p. 184 for an actual example) and an obsidian-edged* macuahuitl *wooden sword, and wearing some form of organic protective armour.*

Stone tools & weapons

It is not possible to distinguish between a stone spearhead for warfare and one for hunting – both would have been used in much the same manner, whether the victim was human or animal. The first stone knives were also multi-purpose tools. Utility, and the high degree of craftsmanship required, sometimes meant that stone rather than metal was employed even when the technology existed, and occasionally non-metallic replicas were made. Remarkably well-made flint daggers and swords have been found in Denmark which are thought to date from the 3rd and 2nd millennia BC.

An important step in the development of martial items came with composite technology: combining two materials in one tool. The earliest knives were probably simple stone blades, but when they were first attached to some form of haft or handle, the development of true knives, spears and swords began. As the preservation of organic materials is not good at most archaeological sites, such handles and binding materials generally do not survive. A fine example of a hilted flint dagger was found at Çatalhöyük in Turkey, dating to the 6th millennium BC, with a carved bone hilt in the form of a snake.

In the absence of developed copper or iron metallurgy, the Aztecs of Mexico developed a tremendously effective alternative. A form of wooden sword, approximately 1 m (39 in) long, had pieces of worked obsidian (a volcanic glass) set along its edge. This weapon, traditionally called the *macuahuitl*, was wielded with devastating effectiveness against the Spanish conquistadores in the early 16th century AD. The Aztecs also used spears with obsidian-edged broad blades (*tepoztopilli*), strong enough to be used even for slashing blows. Accounts by the Spanish conquistadores record that the Aztecs also used simple obsidian blades in their daily life; they were so sharp that some Spanish soldiers took to shaving with them, like the local inhabitants.

Spears

Long blades of stone might be either daggers or spearheads; there is rarely any evidence of how, or if, they were fixed to a handle or shaft. Because of their use for hunting, it is likely spears came before swords. A spear is, in its most basic form, a knife blade on a long handle. One advantage of this is that the target is kept further from the hunter or warrior, thus providing an additional margin of safety. Spears are not suited to fighting at close quarters, however. Their most effective use is when large numbers of individuals work together.

The soldiers on the Vulture Stela (from Telloh, Mesopotamia, *c.* 2500 BC; see p. 185) are shown in a very early, and probably very effective, phalanx formation, with spears and large rectangular shields. On the same stela lightly armed troops wield an axe in one hand and a shorter spear in the other, suggesting that there were at least two different methods of using the spear in mid-3rd-millennium BC Mesopotamia.

A troop of model Middle Kingdom Egyptian infantry from the tomb of Mesehti in Egypt. The soldiers are shown marching in formation and are all equipped in the same manner, with long spears and hide shields.

Above *A drawing of a Mainz-type* gladius, *the typical Roman infantry sword of the 1st century* AD.

Opposite above left
Drawing of a Roman spatha *and the blade of an actual example of this type of sword found at Newstead, Scotland. The* spatha *was a cavalry sword – it was longer and slimmer than the* gladius, *giving the rider a longer reach.*

Right *The Warrior Vase from Mycenae, 13th century* BC, *showing a line of soldiers armed with long spears and round shields.*

Daggers & swords

Changes in the form of edged weapons came with the arrival of the sword. Although it is rather arbitrary, scholars have categorized edged implements by the length of the blade, distinguishing between dagger, dirk and sword. Categories based strictly on length are somewhat imprecise, and do not take into consideration the method in which the weapon was used. The sword is shorter than the spear, which makes it more suitable for fighting at close quarters; however, as the sword is longer than the dagger it serves to keep an enemy more at a distance and also offers greater force on impact.

Hafting a long stone blade on to a hilt or handle would have given a rudimentary and very early form of short sword, and this method continued for many centuries. The long thin metal swords of the Middle Bronze Ages of the Near East (*c.* 2200–1600 BC) and Europe (*c.* 1100–900 BC) are generally considered to be rapiers used only for thrusting, since the method of attaching the hilt to the blade, via several rivets, was relatively weak and would not long withstand being used for slashing blows. A great technological step forward occurred with the development of a sword cast with the blade and hilt in one piece. Swords made in this way were considerably stronger, and suitable for slashing strokes as well as thrusting.

With the decline in the use of bronze towards the end of the 2nd millennium BC, iron technology grew in importance. In Greece, bronze swords began to fall out of use in the 9th century BC and were replaced with iron ones. In the eastern Mediterranean there was a heavy reliance on the spear at this time, and the Spartans of Greece were one of the few peoples to use the sword as the primary weapon. The Classical Greek Hoplite sword was quite similar to Late Bronze Age swords

in style, but was formed of an early type of pattern-welded steel. This was created by repeatedly folding and forge-welding hard, high-carbon steel together with soft, flexible iron to get a more homogeneous and durable type of steel. Swords made of such steel maintained a sharp edge even after repeated use, and were also tough and flexible enough not to bend or break.

The Greek style of sword was used widely across Europe and the Mediterranean for several centuries, but was gradually replaced by a variety of local styles. One particular form that proved very popular was the *gladius hispaniensis*, the short utilitarian 'Spanish sword' adopted by the Romans most likely around the time of the first Punic Wars (*c.* 264–241 BC). The Greek historian Polybius (writing *c.* 150 BC) refers to the sword used by the Roman army as being a 'Spanish' sword; however, no definitive examples exist of early Roman prototypes or developmental forms.

In ancient China a style of short, slightly curved single-edged fighting knife (the *xiao*), with an animal-head pommel, came into use in the late

KEY DATES

hilted flint dagger	6th millennium BC, Turkey
bronze rapiers	Middle Bronze Age, Near East & Europe
curved knife	*c.* 11th century BC?, China
iron sword	9th century BC, Greece
'Spanish sword'	3rd century BC, Roman empire

Shang dynasty period (*c.* 1600–1100 BC). Similar ring-pommel styles were also used in the Shang and Zhou (*c.* 1100–221 BC) dynasties which gave rise to the later ring-pommel swords of the Han dynasty (*c.* 206 BC–AD 220).

An early style of straight double-edged sword, the *jian* style, had leaf-shaped bronze blades and integral round grips and pommels. This type of sword came into common use at about the same time as cavalry (around the 8th century BC), and continued in various forms, gradually increasing in length and crossing the technological boundary from bronze to iron.

Weaponry was, from the beginning, invested with a sort of potency. Over the last several millennia the sword has come to be associated with both bravery and authority, as seen, for instance, in the conferral of a British knighthood by the tap of the sword on the shoulder. In many cultures and regions, the arms and armour of the warrior were buried with him, and in some cultures swords and daggers became objects of veneration and often had a 'soul' of their own, such as the *katana* in Japan and *kris* in Southeast Asia.

Above *Decorated bronze sword from China, Eastern Zhou, Warring States Period.*

Left *Carefully crafted stone weapons often copied known metallic examples. Here, two Danish swords from the 2nd millennium BC are shown, one made of metal, the other of stone. The stone example would originally have had a wooden core, and is in principle not unlike the obsidian-edged Aztec macuahuitl (p.178).*

Armour, Helmets & Shields

45

And there went out a champion out of the camp of the Philistines, named Goliath, of Gath …. And he had an helmet of brass upon his head, and he was armed with a coat of mail; and the weight of the coat was five thousand shekels of brass. And he had greaves of brass upon his legs, and a target of brass between his shoulders.

1 SAMUEL 17: 4-6

Much of the history of humankind has seen an arms race, with different groups continually developing better and more effective weapons; body armour was then developed as a response and a countermeasure. It is not possible to determine when the first body armour was invented, although any form of clothing would provide some protection.

Examples could readily be found in nature, such as the shell of a tortoise, the scales of a snake or the hard chitin of a beetle. But exactly when early humans created a garment designed specifically to prevent injury from animals or other humans is unknown; what is certain, however, is that the earliest

Left *Reconstruction of the armour of a Scythian warrior of the 5th–4th century BC.*

Right *A sleeveless corselet made of rawhide scales on a linen backing, as found in the tomb of Tutankhamun in Egypt, c. 1322 BC.*

armour was made from organic materials, which unfortunately do not usually survive.

Our knowledge of early body armour is therefore based on depictions and ancient texts. Some of the earliest illustrations of body armour appear on the Standard of Ur, dating from the middle of the 3rd millennium BC in Mesopotamia. Soldiers are shown wearing heavy capes, probably of leather, fastened at the collar and decorated with circles or discs. Although quite simple, these capes would have provided protection against cuts and blunt trauma; any heavy padding or thick garment would help to absorb the force of a blow.

Body armour in China was also made first from organic materials. The earliest known Chinese armour dates to the Shang dynasty (*c.* 1600–1100 BC) and was found in tomb 1004 at An-Yang. Little survives of this armour aside from the yellow, black,

red and white pigments which remained in the earth after the leather background, a single-piece breastplate, had decomposed. A later, and extremely important discovery consists of 12 coats of lacquered leather armour from a tomb at Sui-hsien in Hupei, dating to c. 443 BC. These were made of numerous small leather plates laced together, a forerunner of the style of armour used in China and the orient for the next two millennia, and similar to armour found at different times in many parts of the world.

Not unlike such Chinese armour, the coat of mail that the Philistine champion Goliath wore was made of a large number of small leather or bronze scales. This is the style that was used by the military elite of the Late Bronze Age Near East (c. 1600–1150 BC). Even a simple sleeveless vest of scale armour often took over 1500 scales to make. The scales were laced together in rows so that they overlapped like the scales of a fish or reptile, and the rows were then attached to a garment made of leather or several layers of linen. A complete coat of such scale armour was found in the tomb of Tutankhamun (c. 1322 BC), made of several thousand small rawhide (untanned leather) scales attached to a linen backing. Texts from the Late Bronze Age site of Nuzi, near Kirkuk in Iraq, tell us of several different styles of scale armour that were available at that time, some of which used both bronze and leather scales together.

Perhaps the earliest surviving example of full plate armour comes from the site of Dendra in

Greece. Made of bronze, this armour shows a level of technology in working sheet metal which rivals the skills of medieval European armourers of the 15th and 16th centuries AD. However, it was not very practical for foot combat and was probably a coat of parade armour. It is quite possible that it emulates the style of contemporary leather or organic armour.

Another very early form of metallic armour is chainmail, which is made of interlaced rings of iron, with each ring passing through four others. Although often attributed to the Romans, it was most likely an innovation of the Gauls of western Europe in approximately the 3rd century BC. After the Roman army adopted the technology, chainmail spread to the furthest reaches of the Roman empire

In the New World in the 16th century AD the Aztec warriors made use of body armour made of organic materials, primarily heavy quilted cotton or heavy woollen tunics. These coats of armour, called *ichcahuipilli* and *onka* respectively, were sufficient to help protect the soldiers from arrows and darts, as well as provide some protection against the tremendously effective obsidian-edged *macuahuitl* wooden swords.

Helmets

The earliest helmets were also probably made of organic materials. Well-made metal examples appear as early as c. 2500 BC, at Ur in Mesopotamia, where six were found still in place on the heads of guards who accompanied their ruler to the grave. This same style of helmet appears to be

A warrior wearing partial scale armour, from the terracotta army of Qin Shihuangdi, China, 210 BC.

Left *A coat of plate armour found at Dendra in Greece, dating to approximately 1500 BC, with a helmet made of boars' tusks. Although it was more likely used for parade rather than combat, it may have imitated actual armour made of leather.*

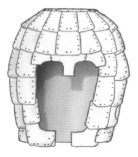

Above *Drawing of a helmet found at I-hsien, China, from the late Warring States period (c. 475–221 BC): it is the earliest example of an iron helmet found in China.*

Below *Drawing of a Roman Coolus-pattern helmet, early 1st century AD, similar to the Montefortino type, with wide cheekpieces and back neck guard. The peak at the front was to deflect blows.*

Above right *This crushed skull with copper helmet, found in a burial pit at Ur, Iraq, is from one of six soldiers who followed their king to the grave. It demonstrates that some metallic armour was in use in the middle of the 3rd millennium BC, though no metallic body armour was found.*

Right *An Aztec featherwork shield, c. AD 1500, with the depiction of an animal, probably a coyote. The symbol in front of the animal combines fire and water, an Aztec metaphor for war.*

depicted on the Standard of Ur, discovered in the same burial. Although these helmets were made of metal, they very likely followed the style of the leather helmets also in use at the time. A simple leather cap would not have afforded much protection – but some protection was certainly better than none at all.

The presence of metal helmets but no metallic armour in the burial pit at Ur may indicate a turning point in the development of body armour. This burial included some 60 individuals, and buried with them were chariots, weapons, a large selection of jewelry and household artifacts, many made of precious materials such as gold and silver. If metallic body armour, other than helmets, was being used in Mesopotamia at this time, it would have been almost certainly have been included in this rich assemblage of burial goods. Perhaps this is an indication that at *c.* 2500 BC in Mesopotamia, metallic defences for the body were just beginning to be developed.

Another early form of helmet made from organic materials are the boar's tusk helmets from Late Bronze Age Mycenaean Greece, *c.* 1250 BC. These were probably formed of a leather cap reinforced with slices of boar's tusks. Helmets of a lamellar construction were also used in ancient China, where an early iron example from I-hsien, Hopei, dates to the late Warring States period (*c.* 475–221 BC), although earlier examples of metal helmets are thought to have existed also.

There are many different styles of Roman helmet and these evolved from earlier European examples. The typical Montefortino-style helmet, a basic rounded helmet with a slight point and finial on the top and cheek-pieces, which dates

to the 4th and 3rd centuries BC, is very similar to Minoan examples found at the palace of Knossos, Crete, which are much earlier, dating to approximately 1400 BC.

Shields

The shield probably predated body armour as the first stage in the development of defensive equipment. It is all but impossible to determine at what point in prehistory the earliest shields were made, but it is likely that they began simply as the first available item that came to hand which could be used to fend off attack. Early hunters would quickly have recognized that the skins of certain animals which were tougher and more difficult to kill could be stretched over a wooden or wicker frame.

Many soldiers in the ancient world had no body armour aside from a helmet, but carried a large shield which would cover them, essentially, from head to foot; a pair of greaves protected the lower legs (see p. 180). This approach was used by much of the Qin period Chinese infantry (*c.* 3rd century BC), Aztec soldiers (*c.* 16th century AD), as well as the Hoplites of ancient Greece. In fact, it is probable that the same can be said of many military organizations in many periods. A simple shield would be much easier and less costly to manufacture than

The Vulture Stela from Telloh (c. 2500 BC) shows Eannatum of Lagash leading a group of armoured soldiers, each carrying a spear and large rectangular shield. The shields are shown placed side by side as the soldiers advance, providing a very early example of a shield wall and formation fighting.

tory, humans realized that the body needed protection. First came shields, then armour which would leave both hands free. The complex nature of body armour, and cost of manufacture, generally confined its use to a wealthy elite, leaving the common soldier to use a helmet and shield.

Above *A battle scene from Trajan's Column, 2nd century AD, with ranks of Roman auxiliary and allied troops with their shields held in front advancing on the Dacian enemy.*

Right *A Greek red-figure krater by the Berlin Painter showing a Hoplite with little body protection apart from a helmet and a large round shield. It seems probable that many soldiers in the ancient world would have fought like this.*

body armour, which usually needs to be closely fitted to the user. For tasks where the soldier had a hand free, a shield would provide substantial protection, but when the task required the use of both hands, armour had the advantage.

The form of shield used would be governed in part by the style of fighting. Fast-moving infantry or skirmishers would benefit from a smaller shield which would allow them to move and react quickly to their environment, whereas heavy infantry fighting in formation would be best protected by large rectangular shields which could be lined up to present a defensive wall to the enemy. This latter tactic is shown on the Vulture Stela dating to *c.* 2500 BC, on which a group of soldiers is depicted holding their large rectangular shields close together, with gaps left for their spears.

The precise origins of body armour, helmets and shields are uncertain. At some point in prehis-

Fortifications

46

The Stranger. This is an old British camp, I believe, sir?
The Rev Dr. Folliott. Roman, sir; Roman: indeniably Roman. The vallum is past controversy.
It was not a camp, sir, a castrum, but a castellum, a little camp, or watch station.
ROBERT BAGE, 1796

The first defences were built for protection not from other humans, but against animal predators. They were brightly blazing hearths, a firebrand and menacing shouts, perhaps a crude fence of thorny brush fencing off a cave entrance or a hunting camp. Once people herded cattle, goats or sheep, they constructed stout corrals and substantial thorn fences to protect their beasts from carnivores, and also from cattle raiders.

The entire dynamic changed with the development of weapons with longer ranges, especially the bow and arrow (p. 175), which allowed an archer to stand at a distance and pick off his targets. A village needed fortifications, at first perhaps simple wooden palisades, then a ditch and earthen rampart, to give the defenders a strategic advantage against bowmen.

The earliest known fortifications protected the town of Jericho and its spring around 8000 BC: a stone wall complete with a solid masonry watch-tower with central spiral staircase, and a rock-cut ditch. The wall and ditch were defences in depth, creating a distance between attackers and defenders. Whether they were actually built against enemies or as flood works is now a matter of some debate, but the watch-tower is certainly suggestive of a military purpose.

These simple defences were the ancestors of the more sophisticated fortifications devised by eastern Mediterranean civilizations with standing armies. Sumerian city-states maintained such forces and bickered constantly amongst themselves. Compact, walled cities with mud-brick fortifications were commonplace by the 3rd

The stone wall and tower at Jericho, the earliest known fortifications in the world, dating to around 8000 BC.

millennium BC. They were formidable obstacles for besiegers, especially in the days before sophisticated siege engines.

Egyptian forts

Walled cities and forts were lethal for attacking infantry. Almost all of the 60 soldiers buried with honour beside the mortuary complex of Egyptian pharaoh Mentuhotep (c. 2010–1960 BC) had died from arrows shot from above. They had presumably come under enemy fire from the fortifications they were attacking.

Egyptian kings were serious about fortifications. The Middle Kingdom pharaoh Senwosret III (c. 1836–1818 BC) fortified the Nile trade routes above the First Cataract with a row of fortresses. The most impressive was Buhen, at a strategic point by the Second Cataract. This was a vast mud-brick construction that had much of the sophistication and impregnability of a European medieval castle. By this time, military architects were well aware of the damage that could be done by siege engines (p. 192).

The Buhen fortress faced the river, surrounded by a massive mud-brick enclosure wall up to 8.5 m (28 ft) high and 3.9 m (13 ft) thick, with external towers. Two parallel walls with their own towers and drawbridge protected the entrance on the desert side, so that an attacker was automatically under fire from the flanks. A ditch and rampart with a parapet defended the base of the enclosure wall, which was equipped with small towers and loopholes for archers. Buhen was to all intents impregnable. Further upstream, the royal architects tailored the fortifications to rocky outcrops by the river, erecting smaller versions which were heavily defended against ever more sophisticated siege machinery. Outlying watch-towers provided an early warning system.

Fortified towns

Small towns with fortifications appeared early in the Bronze Age of the eastern Mediterranean. We still know little about the initial history of fortifications among the civilizations that competed with one another in this region during the Late Bronze Age in the mid- to late 2nd millennium BC. The lords of Mycenae in southern Greece built a formidable citadel of huge, roughly carved boulders – so large that later Greek legends attributed them to the Cyclops, mythical one-eyed giants.

Each Mycenaean citadel – there are more than a hundred of them – had a main gate and smaller postern gates concealed with brush that were used for surprise forays against the enemy. The Mycenaeans also took pains to protect their water supplies by locating their fortresses near streams, or cutting tunnels under the walls to underground streams (p. 80).

Across the Aegean Sea, in what is now Turkey, the Hittites built remarkably similar cyclopean for-

tifications. They may in fact have invented this style of protection, which is well represented at their great citadel and capital, Boghazköy. Both Mycenaeans and Hittites were primarily concerned with protection against archers, so their fortifications were relatively straightforward, making frontal assault a virtual impossibility.

Extensive town walls appeared in the 6th and 5th centuries BC, usually constructed of mud brick with a stone facing, or with a rubble filling, as for instance Classical Athens' famous Long Walls built between 461 and 456 BC. By the 4th century, architects were increasingly concerned about siege warfare, so they improved the structure of walls by dividing them into compartments and using binding courses throughout the walls – mud-brick fills were vulnerable to battering rams. Walls became thicker, towers more frequent; these were also used for defensive artillery and catapults. The defenders relied on extensive ditches and ramparts to keep attackers and their catapults at a distance.

Below *The Bronze Age citadel at Mycenae, Greece, with its massive stone walls of cyclopean masonry – some of the individual stones are so large that in the past it was thought that the walls could only have been built by the mythical giants, the Cyclops.*

Above *The serried earthworks of the Iron Age hillfort at Maiden Castle, Dorset, England; its final form dated to c. 250 BC.*

Below *The impressive gateway, guarded by lions, of the massive fortifications at Boghazköy, Turkey, the capital of the Hittites.*

Roman defences

The Romans developed fortifications of all kinds to a high degree of refinement, deriving their ideas from earlier Etruscan and Greek practice. As much as possible, their architects made use of strategic locations, and, if practicable, upgraded any existing defences of cities they occupied. Earthworks were often constructed when the Roman legions campaigned in Gaul and Britain, where they confronted hillforts such as Maiden Castle, with their multiple earth ramparts, deep ditches, carefully defended entrances and stout palisades to guard against catapults and sling shots.

Hadrian's Wall in northern Britain is the most famous of all Roman frontier fortifications. Erected under the governor A. Platorius Nepos in AD 122–26 on Hadrian's instructions, it stretched for about 193 km (120 miles) from Pons Aelius (modern Newcastle upon Tyne) on the North Sea to the Cumbrian coast. With space on top for two soldiers to walk abreast, Hadrian's Wall was like a raised highway. Its defensive system also included 9-m (30-ft) wide ditches on either side, fortified gateways every Roman mile (1481 m/4860 ft) and garrison forts behind the wall, connected to it by a road.

After the 3rd century AD, Roman defences usually consisted of thick, high walls with regular protecting towers, small gateways and large ditches. Except for Rome, urban defences tended to enclose relatively small areas – often less than 20 ha (50 acres).

China & the Great Wall

Roman efforts were puny compared with the massive efforts of Chinese military strategists. Rectangular defensive enclosures first appear in the Longshan period, between 2700 and 2000 BC. The architects used a special construction method known as *hang tu*, or 'rammed earth'. Regular layers of loose earth, some 10–15 cm (4 to 6 in) thick, were poured between parallel lines of timber shuttering – rather in the way that concrete is poured today. The layers were then compacted by pounding them with long wooden poles. When one layer was finished, another would be poured and the process repeated until the desired height was reached. Some Longshan walls were as much

stone wall & tower	*c.* 8000 BC, Jericho
walled cities	3rd millennium BC, Mesopotamia
cyclopean masonry	13th century BC, Greece

as 10.6 m (35 ft) thick, with rectangular guard-houses on either side of the entrance.

Chinese fortifications involved hundreds, if not thousands, of workers. One Shang civilization enclosure at Zhengzhou of 1500 BC boasted walls 7.25 km (4.5 miles) long. Later fortifications were even more massive. The rammed earth walls of the Han capital, Chang'an, were 16 m (52 ft) thick at the base and surrounded an area 6 × 7.6 km (3.7 × 4.7 miles), with three gates on each side of the huge rectangle and heavily garrisoned watch-towers.

The Great Wall of China, in total some 10,000 km (6214 miles) long, is the ultimate in fortifications. Some of the earliest stretches date to the Warring States Period (475–221 BC). The Qin emperors (221–207 BC) joined and strengthened the surviving fragments of the earlier fortifications into a wall meant to protect their domains from marauding nomads. Some 300,000 soldiers

and 500,000 conscripted peasants and convicts laboured on the Qin wall. Subsequently, the Han emperor Wudi (141–87 BC) strengthened the wall and extended it a further 480 km (300 miles) across the Gobi Desert to gain greater control of Silk Road trade routes. The Wall that survives today was reorganized and refurbished by the Ming Dynasty emperors (1368–1644). Millions of labourers toiled on sections of the wall for many generations, constructing a fortification of stone, bricks and stamped earth.

Above *The 'playing-card shaped' fort at Housesteads, on Hadrian's Wall in northern England is a classic example of Roman fortification.*

Below *A section of the Great Wall of China, snaking across the hilly countryside, as restored by the Ming emperors. On top is a broad walkway guarded by a crenellated parapet.*

47 Siege Engines, Catapults & Crossbows

The engines of all legions were masterpieces of construction, but none were equal to those of the Tenth; their quick-loaders were more powerful and their stone-throwers bigger, so that they could repulse not only the sorties but also the fighters on the wall.

JOSEPHUS, 1ST CENTURY AD

Above *The siege of a city, probably during the campaigns of Tiglath-pileser III (745–727 BC), in a relief from the palace at Nimrud, illustrating the use of scaling ladders.*

The rise of siege techniques and technology is tied intricately to both the rise of civilization and more importantly the creation and improvement of fortifications (p. 187). It is hard to say when sieges began, as many techniques leave little in the way of material remains, but we can assume that siege techniques were in use as early as the Neolithic. Siege warfare can be divided into those techniques which are fairly simple (the use of fire and regular weapons in siege settings) and the more complex use of siege engines which would have required an organized military. It is the invention of the latter that leave more substantial remains.

Some of the earliest siege techniques were directed at settlement walls. Escalade involves the scaling of walls by hand, rope or scaling ladders, or the use of siege towers. All these methods seem to have been utilized fairly early in the Near East and Mesopotamia. Assyrian reliefs display the use of siege towers to overrun city walls, notably the representations of the campaigns of Shalmaneser III of Assyria (mid-9th century BC). Equipment was also specifically designed to breach walls: battering rams may have been in use earlier than 2000 BC. Egyptian wall paintings (c. 1900 BC) depict soldiers breaching walls and gates with poles or rams, and battering rams and siege shields (shields to protect sappers who were attempting to breach walls)

are depicted in both Egyptian wall-paintings and Assyrian reliefs.

Such devices were not the only way to overcome fortifications: the Babylonians constructed large earthen ramps against enemy walls to gain access, and the massive Roman siege ramp at Masada, in Israel, is still an impressive feature at the site today. A siege's primary function was to blockade the besieged, cutting them off from receiving supplies and aid. Circumvallation, or the surrounding of a fortification with an offensive wall, was often employed in Roman sieges; famous examples include Numantia (133 BC), Alesia (52 BC) as well as Masada (AD 72–73).

Catapults

The Bible alludes to the use of catapults as early as the reign of Uzziah (*c*. 800 BC). The first definite mention of the catapult dates to *c*. 400 BC in Sicily, under Dionysius, tyrant of Syracuse, who ushered in a new era of siege equipment. These first catapults were based on bows and would have shot arrows or bolts. Later, under Philip of Macedon (360–336 BC), catapults were developed which utilized torsion, making them more effective than earlier versions. Catapults could also be used by the defenders, the first example coming from the siege of Perinthus in 340 BC. Under Alexander the Great (336–323 BC) the use of catapults intensified and they began to shoot stones as well as bolts.

Catapults also began to be used in naval warfare and were mounted on siege towers. Sometimes novel ammunition was used, such as dead animals, live snakes, incendiaries like Greek fire and even plague victims, in an early form of germ warfare. The Greek writer Diodorus described the early catapults and the sieges of Dionysius, but it was Heron of Alexandria who discussed their construction in his artillery manual.

The Greeks and later the Romans made extensive use of catapults in expanding their territory. The ballista, an extremely large crossbow-like catapult that fired bolts and stones up to 460 m (1500 ft), became an important tool of siege and field warfare for the Roman military. The onager, or 'scorpion' as it was also known, was a catapult that launched stones much in the manner of a sling rather than a

Above *A relief from the Northwest Palace of Ashurnasirpal at Nimrud, 9th century BC, depicting the use of a battering ram to knock down fortifications; behind it is a high siege tower with archers on top.*

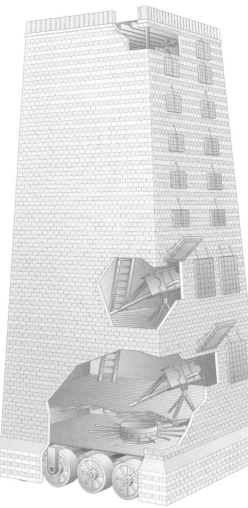

Left *A reconstruction drawing of a large Greek siege tower, with catapults inside.*

Opposite below *This Egyptian wall-painting from the tomb of Khety at Beni Hasan (c. 1900 BC) shows a city under siege: note the use of a simple battering ram by the three men protected behind the shielding.*

Right *A modern reconstruction of a Roman light ballista – a large crossbow-like catapult that fired bolts with great speed and accuracy over large distances.*

Below *A modern full-size reconstruction of a Roman catapult known as an onager, or 'wild ass', from its violent kick.*

bow. While it is hard to be sure when this design was first invented, it was definitely in use by the Romans, as attested by Ammianus (*c.* AD 380).

Catapults were also developed in China during the 1st millennium AD, but unfortunately little is

known about these; they may have used counter-weights like later medieval catapults. In addition to being extremely powerful and accurate, these ancient catapults and siege engines also had a devastating psychological effect on the besieged, which made their use even more effective.

Crossbows

Bows and arrows, in the traditional sense, have been in use from prehistoric times (p. 175). The crossbow, however, seems to have been a later development, the origins of which are not easily determined. It is possible that crossbows were in use from the 5th century BC in China; however, the earliest Chinese historical reference to the use of crossbows is the Battle of Ma-Ling in 341 BC. The earliest archaeological remains of a Chinese crossbow, using the lock mechanism, were found in the tomb of Wu-Yang, which has been dated to 228 BC.

Historical depictions show the Japanese *oyumi* crossbow was in use in the 6th to 7th century AD, but saw only limited employment, while the design is believed to have originated somewhat earlier, with the Chinese examples. This weapon could have taken several different forms, but it is noted in Japanese texts that there were often only two *oyumi* within a 50-man military unit, suggesting that they may have been heavy weaponry requiring more than one man to operate. Although the *oyumi* saw use in earlier periods in Japan, its use in siege warfare is thought to have ended around the time of the 'Former Nine Years War' in the middle of the 11th century.

Crossbows have two main advantages over standard archery: first, the crossbow may be kept drawn for a much longer time than an archer can hold a drawn bow; and secondly the crossbow can be made substantially more powerful, thus being able to deliver a projectile with greater force. The crossbow also afforded the user a greater degree of accuracy at short to medium ranges with less training than required for a longbow. The maximum strength of a normal bow is limited by the strength of the archer, while the strength of a crossbow can be much greater than that of the user, as mechanical devices could be used to draw the bow. The main disadvantage of the crossbow is that it is quite slow to operate compared to the normal hand-held bow, particularly the very heavy crossbows used in later periods, some of which required complex mechanical aids to draw the string.

The earliest crossbows resembled smaller catapults, and it was probably not a difficult step to make them portable and usable by a single soldier. The Romans have the first explicit textual reference to hand-held crossbows, which were certainly being used by the Roman military by the 4th century AD, as attested by Vegetius in his military treatise *De Re Militari*. As the strength of the prod (the 'bow' of the crossbow) increased, various mechanical devices needed to be developed to draw the string and to hold it once drawn.

Some of the earliest Mediterranean crossbows employing mechanisms to aid in drawing the string were the *gastraphetes* or 'belly bows' of ancient Greece, but these were described as siege weapons which confuses the distinction drawn between catapults and crossbows in the ancient Mediterranean. These bows had a series of ratchet stops which would keep the string drawn as the user put his weight on the belly arch in order to draw the string.

Later forms of crossbows used a simpler system, whereby a stirrup was attached to the front of the crossbow into which the user placed a foot while drawing the string. The foot stirrup was effective, but eventually, as the strength of crossbows increased, other mechanisms had to be developed, including the 'goat's-foot' lever and a rack-and-pinion gearing system – known as the crannequin.

The earliest crossbows likely relied on a simple crosswise groove on the stock which would hold the drawn string. To shoot the crossbow, one would have had to pry the string out of the groove by hand. Eventually, a mechanism was developed to force the string out of the groove by means of a small peg attached to a long trigger. At the end of the 12th century AD a notched cylinder and latch system was devised, which improved the efficiency of the crossbow considerably.

KEY DATES

battering ram	1900 BC, Egypt
siege ramp	Babylonia, 1st millennium BC
catapult	c. 400 BC, Sicily
circumvallation	2nd century BC, Roman
crossbow	5th century BC, China
onager	4th century AD, Roman

Below *A drawing of the Greek gastraphetes, or 'belly bow', the earliest recorded catapult and a precursor to the crossbow. The string was drawn back by the archer using his weight against the belly arch.*

Below *The strength of crossbows meant that mechanical devices, such as the goat's-foot lever seen in this drawing, had to be invented to draw the string back.*

Below *A Japanese soldier using an* oyumi *(crossbow). The design of this crossbow is thought to have been developed from Chinese originals. The earliest known example of a catapult found in China dates to 228 BC.*

48 Chariots & Cavalry

*As the great Achilles rampaged on, his sharp-hoofed stallions trampled shields
and corpses, the axle under his chariot splashed with blood, blood on the
handrails sweeping round the car, sprays of blood shooting up from
the stallions' hoofs and churning, whirling rims …*

HOMER, 8TH CENTURY BC

Above *A line of four-wheeled battlewagons, each drawn by four onagers, as depicted on the Standard of Ur (c. 2600–2400 BC).*

Cumbersome, solid-wheeled battlewagons were in use by the first half of the 3rd millennium BC. They are depicted on the Standard of Ur, each drawn by four onagers. A thousand years later the war chariot with spoked wheels had superseded the battlewagon. Horses – larger, more powerful and temperamentally better – were becoming more numerous and replaced the onager. The normal hitch was now two animals, but three- and four-horse hitches were not unknown. Chariots were in use in Egypt, the Near East, Assyria, Anatolia, Urartu and Iran. China came relatively late to chariot use: it is first recorded under the Shang King Wu Ding (early 12th century BC). Early chariot numbers were small: in Anatolia King Anittas (c. 1750 BC) fielded 40, Hattusilis I (1650–1620 BC) 80; by the Battle of Kadesh, c. 1285 BC, Muwatallis II commanded 2500.

Variations in chariot types

Chariot construction constantly improved. Egypt's light chariot had a rear axle which facilitated rapid turns. Experiments were made there with four, six, and eight spokes per wheel, six being favoured, although some pharaohs are shown using a chariot with eight spokes per wheel. Other cultures varied the number of spokes per wheel, but most had six. Chariots were drawn by the central pole, with horses attached by the ox-type yoke.

At first the normal chariot crew was driver plus fighter. The three-man crew developed in both Hittite and Assyrian armies. The Assyrians, who continuously developed their chariots, eventually used an extremely heavy vehicle with very large eight-spoked wheels and a crew of four in the chariot box. Ashurnasirpal II (c. 883–859 BC) experimented with a three-horse hitch. Two horses were yoked, while the third was attached as a replacement for an injured or exhausted horse. Shalmaneser III (c. 858–824 BC) reverted to a two-horse hitch. The use of four yoked horses is first documented under Sargon II (c. 721–705 BC). Persia and China also used four-horse hitches.

Below *An Egyptian light chariot drawn by two horses – a hunting scene from the tomb of Userhat, 15th century BC.*

A pair of bronze chariots, each with four terracotta horses and a charioteer, discovered in a pit associated with the Tomb of China's first emperor, Shihuangdi, who died in 221 BC, at Xi'an. Each part of the gold, silver and bronze harnesses on the chariot horses varies according to the strain it would bear.

Chariots in battle

The weaponry of chariot fighters included a bow, arrows, spear, sword and shield. Such weapons indicate long- and short-range fighting. However, the idea that chariots closed in a head-on charge is false. Chariots were primarily mobile firing platforms, and horses and their equipages were too valuable and too vulnerable to injury and wreckage to risk in a frontal assault. A multi-vehicle pile-up would have created chaos, making infantry ineffective as they clambered over the wreckage. Chariotry's task was to intimidate, transport warriors, harry and provide flanking protection. All injured horses are shown shot in the side, none in the chest or head. Undoubtedly some chariots got enmeshed in close-order combat as units lost cohesion.

Documents from 15th-century BC Alalakh in Syria reveal the infrastructure of the chariot corps. Census lists indicate which villages supplied *maryannu* (chariot warriors), some of whom owned chariots, and by extension horses. The tablets also list which villages supplied horses for chariot use. Alalakh had several chariot workshops.

The literature

Important literature on chariot and cavalry training has survived. A 14th-century BC treatise by the Mitannian Kikkuli, who was in Hittite employ, outlines 184 days of incremental training for chariot horses. Cavalry training is outlined by Xenophon in his book *The Art of Horsemanship* and in *The Cavalry Commander*. Kautilya, advisor to Chandragupta (*c.* 324 BC) of the Indian Mauryan empire, wrote a very comprehensive treatise on both chariotry and cavalry.

A model chariot from the Oxus Treasure of the 4th–5th centuries BC. The two figures in the chariot wear the dress of the Medes, from the Achaemenid empire in Persia. Four horses pull the chariot, which has wheels with eight spokes.

Above *Assyrian relief from the North Palace at Nineveh showing King Ashurbanipal (c. 669–630 BC) hunting. The quality of the carving is extremely good: the forms and proportions of the horses are realistic and many details of the bridles and saddle cloths are visible.*

Cavalry

Cavalry increased the mobility of ancient armies. The first cavalry corps is traditionally accorded to Assyria under Tukulti-Ninurta II (*c.* 890–884 BC). However, the ridden horse appeared regularly, if in small numbers, from at least the reign of Thut-

Right *Over 3000 miniature cavalry and foot soldiers were discovered in this Han royal tomb, c. 179–141 BC, at Yangiiawan, Xianyang, China, giving a vivid and detailed picture of accoutrements and cavalry formations of the time.*

mose IV (*c.* 1400–1390 BC) in Egypt. Such horses would have been mounts for couriers and scouts, though Egyptian reliefs show riders equipped for war in a battle context. Tablets from Nuzi (modern Kirkuk) of the 15th century BC record ridden horses in a military context. A 12th-century BC plaque from Syria reveals a line of Canaanite cavalry, and a Canaanite horseman is shown on an Egyptian battle relief at Karnak of the early 13th century BC.

Assyria has the best reliefs showing cavalry. At first the Assyrian cavalryman wielded his weapons, while a second horseman led his horse. At this stage the riders' position on their horses was still precarious. By Sargon II's reign horsemanship had improved and cavalrymen rode independently, using a more secure balanced seat. The reliefs of Ashurbanipal (*c.* 668–627 BC) are superb: they show the armament of riders, the barding of mounts and the good balanced seat used. Equally revealing are the king's chariot reliefs. The horses of both chariotry and cavalry are quality mounts, with stocky conformation and are of considerable size; no rider appears underhorsed. As the proportions of equine anatomy are so correct the sizing is believable.

The Achaemenid Persians (560–330 BC) took cavalry to a new high, with both horse and man armoured in the heavy cavalry. Elite cavalry rode huge, ram-headed Nisaean horses bred in the Plain of Nisaya south of Ecbatana (Hamadan). Persia's satrapies supplied excellent horses and cavalrymen, many from the Turanian swathe. After the Battle of Plataea in 479 BC, Xerxes' commander Mardonius wintered in Thessaly and Macedonia. His cavalry included units from Iran, the Saka, India and Bactria. An equid legacy surely persisted, as would have happened with the horses rounded up by the Greeks after their victory at Plataea.

Philip of Macedon (360–336 BC) made great improvements in his cavalry arm. His son Alexander the Great (336–323 BC) took its use to its apogee, using it as a hard-hitting force in battle and in relentless pursuit of defeated enemies, notably Darius III. Alexander drew heavily for his chargers on Thessaly, Macedonia, Greece and Paeonia. Later, he acquired the Nisaean herds and cavalry from Persian satrapies. The Seleucids and Parthians increased the use of cavalry, but in the Roman era infantry once more came to the fore.

Rome's cavalry

Rome's use of cavalry is well documented from the legendary days of Romulus, who according to Livy founded Rome in 753 BC, to the last days of Justinian (AD 527–65), Maurice (AD 582–602) and Heraclius (AD 610–40). Livy recounts its early days from only three centuries under Romulus to Tarquin's strike force of 1800. It took Hannibal and his massive victories on Roman soil, especially at Cannae in 216 BC, and his expert use of cavalry, to convince the Romans that their cavalry needed augmentation. Julius Caesar (d. 44 BC), horseman and breeder of note, used Roman and allied tribal cavalry to effect, but it was under Augustus (27 BC–AD 14) that cavalry began major expansion. The cavalry of beaten enemies was drafted into Roman service, and allied client kingdoms provided numerous horsed contingents.

The format changed from massed tribal horse to contingents – *alae quingenaria* and *milliariae*. By the later Roman empire the Sarmatians, Celts, Thrace, Spain, Gaul and Syria all supplied superb cavalry. Some had been so doing in the early empire. Eventually Gothic and other mounted incursions frequently punctured the empire's

battlewagon	3rd millennium BC, Mesopotamia
war chariot	16th century BC, Egypt
ridden horse	14th century BC, Egypt
war chariot	12th century BC, China
cavalry corps	9th century BC, Assyria

expanding borders. Under Diocletian (AD 284–305) cavalry assumed an even more important and independent role. Strong cavalry detachments stationed at critical points around the empire moved fast and independently to quash localized trouble before it could erupt into full-scale rebellion.

Cavalry continued as a major force in the Oriental sphere, but had to begin a slow rise to eminence in the Occident. In all the horse has served man in his military exploits for over 4000 years.

Longinus Sdapeze, a Roman cavalryman, is depicted trampling on a fallen, naked enemy, on his tombstone from Colchester, England, late 1st century AD. He is wearing scale armour and rides without stirrups.

Galleys & Warships

It is the people who row the ships who give the city its power,
together with the helmsmen and the rowing masters
and the under-officers and the bow officers and the shipwrights.

PSEUDO-XENOPHON, *c.* 425 BC

In the ancient world, galleys – sea-going ships powered by oar – were essentially a Mediterranean phenomenon, because the unreliability of the winds made sailing unpredictable. Outside the Mediterranean, the use of oars was largely restricted to small vessels and inland waterways. The earliest sea-going warships were probably paddled like large canoes, but by the 3rd millennium BC, in Egypt at least, ships were being rowed, with the crew seated facing sternwards and pulling on an oar attached to the side by means of an oarloop.

Single-level galleys

Paddling continued alongside rowing into the 2nd millennium in the Minoan culture of Crete and the Aegean, but by the Mycenaean era in the later part of that millennium oared ships (using sails for secondary propulsion) had become the norm. Such vessels are likely to have been rowed at a single level, with the oars fitted over the topwales. The evidence from writing tablets found at the palace of Pylos suggests that a typical crew would have numbered 30 men. In the 8th century BC, evidence from both Geometric-style vase paintings and the epic poems of Homer suggests that ships varied in size, and were powered by between 20 and 40 or 50 oars.

It is likely that these ships would have been privately rather than state owned, and would have been used as merchant vessels or raiders (the two would not necessarily be mutually exclusive). They would have been able to carry armed men to protect themselves from pirates or to double as

A procession of ships from the Bronze Age Aegean being paddled by crewmen bending over the side; a detail from a miniature fresco at Thera (Santorini), mid-2nd millennium BC.

warships when required by the state's rulers, although their principal role would have been to transport warriors to fight on land rather than to engage in fighting at sea. The 5th-century BC historian Thucydides says that in the past the troops on ships were *auteretai*, that is they did the rowing as well as the fighting.

The pentekontor

While ships with around 30 oars (triakontors) were undoubtedly rowed at a single level, the larger 50-oared ships (pentekontors) may reflect an important new development of the 8th century. This was the distribution of oars at two levels, with an upper level of rowers (*zygioi*) sitting on the main cross-beams (*zyga*) of the ship and rowing over the topwales as before, and a lower level (*thalamioi*) seated in the hold (*thalamos*) and working their oars through holes cut in the hull. The advantage of such an arrangement would be that compared with the earlier single-level ships the same or an even greater number of oars could be placed within a hull which was significantly shorter and had a much smaller wetted area. This would have produced a ship which was significantly faster and more manoeuvrable than its predecessors. This in turn implies that fighting capability, particularly in ramming, was beginning to be favoured over carrying capacity, and perhaps signals a less peaceful era and a growth in piracy.

Two oval clay bases, around 24 m (79 ft) long and 4 m (13 ft) across, found on the island of Samos and dating from around 650 BC, may have supported such vessels dedicated in the sanctuary of the goddess Hera. Vase-paintings of the later 6th-century BC may indicate that galleys gradually became longer and incorporated more oars, possibly up to 100 in total, although pentekontor apparently continued to be the generic term for such ships.

Above *A Greek black-figure vase of the 6th century* BC, *showing a galley powered by rowers.*

The *trieres* or trireme

The two-level pentekontor appears to have remained the principal warship type from the 8th until the end of the 6th century BC, when arguably the most important technical development of all took place. This was the creation of a three-level ship, the *trieres* or trireme. A third level of oars was added either to a pentekontor or perhaps to one of the large oared merchant vessels used by the Egyptians and known as *kerkouroi*. In 5th-century and later Greek triremes, the top level of oars was

A Hellenistic plaster model of a warship, 4th century BC: *the warriors' shields are attached to the rail, and the helmsman stands at the stern.*

The trireme, powered by three levels of oars, formed the core of the Greek fleet which defeated the Persians at Salamis in 480 BC and was the basis on which Athens then went on to build a maritime empire. The diagrams (**far right**) show the arrangement of the three tiers of rowers. The top level rowed through an outrigger, while the oars of the lower two levels were worked through holes cut in the hull. In addition to rowers, the trireme also had sails.

Right & below No wrecks of triremes have been found, but the Olympias is a full-scale reconstruction based on literary and artistic evidence, as well as the remains of ship sheds in Greece. In trials at sea, the Olympias demonstrated that this arrangement of oars was entirely successful.

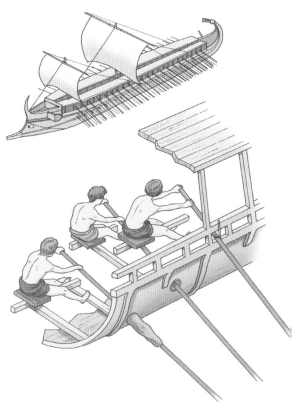

worked through outriggers, which allowed the hull itself to be kept narrow, but it is unclear when and where the outrigger (*parexeiresia*) was invented, and whether Egyptian and Phoenican triremes also made use of it. With or without an outrigger, the result was a ship powered by 170 oars, as manoeuvrable as a large pentekontor, but even faster and more destructive.

Thucydides attributes the introduction of the trireme into the Greek world to a Corinthian shipwright, Ameinocles, in the late 8th century BC. However, recent scholarship has plausibly suggested that it was actually invented either by the Egyptians or by the Phoenician subjects of the rival Persian empire at the end of the 6th century.

In 483/2 BC Athens used the fortunate discovery of silver mines on her territory to fund the construction of a fleet of 200 of this expensive new type of vessel, and it was these which formed the core of the Greek fleet which defeated the Persians at Salamis in 480 BC. Athens then went on to build a maritime empire in the Aegean based on the power of her trireme fleet.

Our knowledge of these ships is limited by the total absence of ancient warship wrecks (unlike cargo-carrying merchantmen, they had positive buoyancy when holed), but has been considerably increased by the *Olympias* project of the mid-1980s. A full-scale reconstructed trireme was built, based on the evidence of ancient depictions, inscriptions, literary texts and the remains of the sheds at Zea harbour in the Piraeus, in which the Athenian trireme fleet was housed in the 4th century BC – these suggested dimensions of *c.* 40 m (131 ft) long and 6 m (20 ft) wide. When the principles of naval architecture were applied to all these data, they were found to restrict the design within sufficiently narrow parameters to justify the building of the *Olympias* as a 'floating hypothesis'.

Five seasons of sea trials between 1987 and 1994 established that a three-level oar system is entirely viable (despite doubts expressed by earlier scholars) and proved the design to be both fast (just under 9 knots was attained under oar) and highly manoeuvrable. It is now widely accepted that the *Olympias* is likely to be a generally accurate representation of a Greek trireme of the period.

Fours, fives & polyremes

A final major development in galley design appeared at the beginning of the 4th century BC, with the construction at Syracuse in Sicily of the first ships manned by more than one man at an oar. These were fives, known as *pentereis* or quinqueremes, which were three-level ships with two men to an oar at the top level, two to an oar in the middle, and one to an oar at the bottom, giving an oarcrew of around 300 men. Such ships were not quite as fast as triremes, but could carry far more troops as well as the new catapult artillery pieces which were being developed for land warfare. From this time, boarding tactics gradually came to be used alongside, and even instead of, ramming. Within a few years, the Syracusans had developed three-level sixes (*hexereis*), and the Carthaginians smaller, two-level fours (*tetrereis* or quadriremes).

From the end of the 4th century BC, triremes were no longer the most important warship. While a few cities specialized in smaller oared vessels for raiding, the major states built ever larger ships – sevens, eights, nines and tens – with more and more men to an oar and greater capacity to carry troops, artillery and fighting towers. Still larger vessels were built to besiege coastal city walls, or to break through harbour chains, culminating in the impractical (but hugely impressive) forty of Ptolemy IV Philopator of Egypt (221–204 BC), which was essentially two twenties fixed together to form a massive catamaran.

The middle section of a trireme depicted on the so-called Lenormant relief of the late 5th century BC, found on the Acropolis of Athens. The top level of oarsmen is clearly visible, seated under a canopy and rowing through an outrigger. The shafts in the middle and the lowest level of oars can also be seen emerging from the hull.

Right *A naval battle between warships powered by oars, depicted in a wall-painting from the House of the Vettii, Pompeii, 1st century AD. The soldiers carrying shields are visible on board.*

Roman fleets

By the later 2nd century BC, as Rome conquered the Mediterranean world, the monster polyremes were obsolete. Rome had built her first major fleet during the First Punic War (264–241 BC) by copying a wrecked Carthaginian five, and thereafter continued to rely mainly on fives, although larger vessels were also used. By the 1st century AD, the mostly unemployed imperial fleets consisted of fives, fours and threes, as well as small two-level liburnians. The bigger ships appear from depictions to have had all their rowers seated above a deck and

rowing through an enclosed oarbox protruding from the side. Triremes are last heard of being used in a civil war of AD 324, and the 5th-century AD writer Zosimus tells us that by his time the secret of three-level ships had been forgotten.

KEY DATES

pentekontor	8th century BC, Greece
trireme	6th century BC, Egypt or Phoenicians
quinquereme	4th century BC, Sicily

Below *A Roman warship carrying troops on a relief of the mid-1st century BC from Praeneste (Palestrina), Italy. Note the fighting tower in the bows.*

Ball Games & Competitive Sports

50

The man who sent the ball through the stone ring was surrounded by all. They honoured him, sang songs of praise to him, and joined him in dancing. He was given a very special reward of feathers or mantles and breechcloths, something highly prized. But what he most prized was the honour involved: that was his great wealth. For he was honoured as a man who had vanquished many and had won a battle.

DIEGO DURAN, 16TH CENTURY AD

These lines, written by the Spanish friar Diego Duran, have a timeless quality. The celebrations recall the mobbing of the star striker who has sealed victory for his team in a modern soccer game. The honour (and material rewards) paid to the winner provides echoes of the adulation (and sometimes large quantities of olive oil, clothing or even cash prizes) accorded a victor in the games of the ancient Greek world.

In fact Duran was describing a unique form of ball game, practised only by civilizations in the New World. Thus the familiarity of his picture of an afternoon at the Mexican ball-court confirms the idea of sport as a universal human activity, springing up independently, but in similar guises, all over the globe. His words also reflect a broadly accepted definition of sport, as opposed to play or recreation. Sport involves physical exertion and, above all perhaps, competition, regulated by a set of rules which leads to comparison between performances and the identification of winners and losers.

Tracing the origins of sport archaeologically, however, is extremely difficult. The simplest forms of competitive running, spear throwing or rock tossing, perhaps little more than training or preparation for the essential activities of prehistoric life, will leave few traces. It is not surprising then that, to date, no credible evidence for the existence of Palaeolithic sport has been discovered. Yet studies have shown that groups of hunter-gatherers can have considerable leisure time to meet up with other bands for communal activity. Ethnographic descriptions of the log races, wrestling bouts and tree-climbing competitions of 19th- and 20th-century Stone Age societies may thus serve as speculative models for sport in the Palaeolithic.

Sport in the Old World

The earliest unambiguous evidence of competitive sport comes from Mesopotamia, where a small number of images of wrestling and boxing, along with brief textual references on cuneiform tablets indicating bouts with defined rules, survive from the early 3rd millennium BC.

From the walls of Egyptian temples and tombs comes a much clearer and richer picture of a range of sports and pastimes. These include archery, along with gymnastics, acrobatics and dancing.

The Discobolus – *the ideal of athleticism personified. A Roman copy in marble of a lost Greek original in bronze by Myron, this statue probably originally commemorated a victor in the pentathlon at one of the major Greek games in the 5th century BC.*

Female acrobats playing a ball game: two of the girls throw a ball back and forth, each sitting on the back of another girl. This charming detail comes from a wall-painting in the tomb of Baqt, at Beni Hasan, Egypt, c. 1970 BC.

Two young boys engaged in a boxing match in a fresco from Thera (Santorini), mid-2nd millennium BC. They each wear one glove and a belt, and their heads are shaved, apart from long reserved locks.

There are also elegant sculptures of girl swimmers and depictions of female participants in perplexing ball games, usually regarded as juggling or games of catch, documented around 2000 BC in wall-paintings at Beni Hasan. Balls, made of pieces of coloured leather stitched together and stuffed with straw, have been found in a number of tombs.

Wrestling was another favoured sport in Egypt, and the Beni Hasan paintings also show ranks of contestants in a range of throws and holds that look remarkably modern. A more distinctively Egyptian sport was 'stick-fighting' in which two opponents hold a short stick in one hand and often wear a protective covering on the other forearm. Stick-fighting endured along the Nile until at least the 18th century and is still practised today by the Nuba of Sudan.

So in Egypt, as in Mesopotamia, the principal documented forms of competitive sport were paramilitary, encouraged, perhaps, to maintain the fitness and preparedness of the military elite. We still know very little about sports or team games that might have been played by the bulk of ordinary people.

Bronze Age sites in the Aegean have produced some dynamic sculptural representations of boxing matches, with participants wearing a range of protective clothing, including calf-high boots and helmets. One of the most famous images from the early Mediterranean world is that of Minoan 'bull-leaping', depicted in bronzes and on ancient seals but best known from a fresco from the palace at Knossos. However, it is hard to interpret exactly what this performance represents. Is it legendary, part of a religious ceremony, or is it both ritual and sports contest? Forms of bull-leaping also seem to have been practised on the Greek mainland. Most scholars today tend to interpret it as a real event, but more of a circus performance than a sport, originating perhaps in the hunt and representing the remote ancestor of the bull-fighting that survives in Mediterranean countries today. Overall, there is little evidence at this time of organized public contests held to celebrate outstanding individual achievement. It is the institutionalization of competitive sport which makes the Greek contribution unique.

Greek sport & the Olympic Games

The Mycenaean Greeks of the Bronze Age appear to have held athletic contests, perhaps associated with funerary ceremonies; this has led to the suggestion that funeral games were the ancestors of

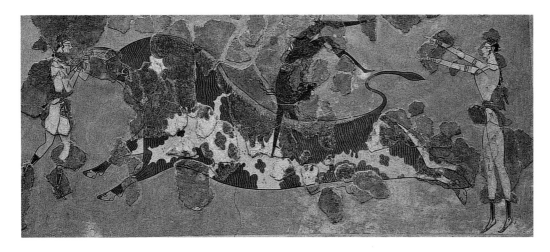

The well-known Minoan bull-leaping fresco from the Palace at Knossos, Crete, c. 1500 BC. There are numerous images of youths engaged in this dangerous activity from the Bronze Age Aegean world and elsewhere, but it is not certain whether it was a religious ceremony or sport.

the Olympics. The Games certainly evolved as part of a religious festival in honour of Zeus, the father of the gods.

The traditional date of the founding of the Olympic Games is 776 BC. This is in fact the year of the first recorded Olympic victor, Koroibos of Elis, who was winner of the *stade* race, a sprint of about 200 m (656 ft), or one length of the original *stadion* at Olympia, thought to be the only event that existed at the time. The sanctuary at Olympia developed rapidly, however, and the number of events increased. By the 5th century BC, the four days of competition included a 400-m (1312-ft) foot-race, a longer distance race, wrestling, boxing, *pankration* (a kind of free fight with few rules), chariot races and a pentathlon involving running, jumping, wrestling and throwing the discus and javelin.

Events now considered essential to the Olympics had no part in the original games. There was no marathon and no water sports nor ball games, no team events nor participation by women, though they had their own more modest competition at a different time of year.

Extensive documentation, in the form of texts and images, survives to show the Greeks' infatuation with sport. Lyric poets wrote in honour of their heroes and an astonishing corpus of art celebrated the physical perfection, nobility and moral worth of the successful athlete. Records also reveal their individualistic and intensely competitive attitude. Only the winner of an event was acclaimed – there was no recognition for runners-up. It is evident that, in theory at least, sport was open to all social classes – the goatherd Polymnestor of Miletus won the sprint race at Olympia in 596 BC and Amesinus, a herder of cows, was the wrestling champion in 460.

Over time much of the original religious significance of the ancient games appears to have been lost. They became more devoted to competition for competition's sake and noted for the fervent

Warfare and sport have close connections: on this Attic black-figure vase of the late 6th century BC, the upper band shows a scene of a battle between the gods, in chariots, and giants; below are athletes wrestling and engaged in other sports, watched over by their trainers.

partisan support of local sporting superstars, who had sponsorship and material rewards lavished upon them.

The only Greek city that differed in its attitude to competitive sport was Sparta, which developed its own forms of brutal team games as training for war. Rome, another society permanently on a war footing when a fledgling state, followed much the same pattern, regarding the Greek games as indulgent and decadent. Their principal sports largely involved physical training for military activity.

Sport further afield

Evidence for the early development of sport along the Indus Valley and in the Indian sub-continent is limited. Scenes of bull-fighting and acrobatics on 3rd-millennium BC seals from Mohenjo-daro and Harappa have parallels with Minoan Crete. There are references in the Vedic literature, first set down around 500 BC, to boxing and wrestling, which presumably were also practised in earlier times. By the Hellenistic period, invasions and influence from the West into what is now Pakistan and northern India had introduced such sports as chariot racing and javelin-throwing, though not, it would seem, the idea of public games.

Polo probably first emerged on the plains of Central Asia and then spread into Persia, northern India and China during the early centuries AD. Polo's origins are to be found in the hunt, the wooden mallets used today being descended from the clubs employed in the mounted pursuit of game animals. In China, competitive archery was established by the Zhou dynasty (c. 1100–221 BC). A form of boxing, without gloves and including elements of wrestling much like the Greek *pankration,* was established in China by 600 BC. It is said that the sport was taken up enthusiastically by Buddhist monks in order to defend their monasteries.

Perhaps the most interesting early sporting development in China was the emergence

Bronze statuette of a female runner, from Sparta, c. 500 BC. Women could compete in their own special games in honour of the goddess Hera at Olympia.

by at least 300 BC of various forms of football, although the rules remain unclear. Two opposing teams kicked and even dribbled the ball, but the major contrast with the soccer of today was that there was only one goal, which could itself take different forms – from posts 9 m (30 ft) high joined by a silk cord over which the ball had to be lofted, to a section of net nearer the ground pierced by a hole through which the ball was propelled. The earliest Chinese football was made of leather stuffed with hair, later superseded by an improved, air-filled model. In pre-Columbian America, however, sportspeople had the benefit of rubber, a natural material that eventually revolutionized the practice of sport throughout the world

New World ball games

Ethnographers have documented a rich variety of traditional sports among the indigenous peoples of both North and South America. Foot races, log-carrying competitions, archery, tug-of-war and wrestling are but a few of the sports whose true antiquity we cannot gauge, but which may date back many hundreds or even thousands of years.

Fortunately, we can say rather more about the most renowned of all native American sports, known simply as 'the ball game' – a team game played with a rubber ball in a rectangular court. It appears to have originated in Mesoamerica around 2000 BC, or even earlier, making it probably the earliest team game in the world. It then spread south to the Caribbean and north into what are now the southern states of the USA. The Olmecs, the first major civilization of Mesoamerica, played the game and it is in their homeland along the Gulf Coast of Mexico that ancient balls, boiled and solidified spheres of latex, have recently been found preserved in waterlogged conditions.

There were local variations in the layout of ballcourts, but by Aztec times the playing alley, flanked by parallel walls, was some 8 to 10 m (26 to 33 ft) wide, up to 40 m (131 ft) long, and opened out into two end zones that gave the court an I-shape. There is still uncertainty surrounding the rules, but as recorded by Spanish chroniclers the game was played by two teams of up to four players. The aim was to keep the ball in the air by striking it with the hips, thighs or upper arms and bouncing it off the side walls. Use of the hands or feet was forbidden and the ball must not touch the ground. Around 10 to 15 cm (4 to 6 in) in diameter, the ball was extremely hard. Injuries were commonplace and players wore protective clothing in the form of gloves, pads on the knees and upper arms, and a large protector for the hips and waist. By the time of the Spanish conquest stone rings, not much bigger than the diameter of the ball, had been mounted vertically into the side walls of the court and anyone who passed the ball through them was at once declared the winner. But such a feat was very rare and simply making contact with the ring or propelling the ball into the end zone of the opposition also seem to have been elements in scoring.

The game was evidently played on a number of different levels. It was a contest between highly trained athletes and drew passionate popular support from crowds who gambled heavily on the outcome. It also offered all the drama and bloodshed of a Roman gladiatorial encounter. For a gruesome end often awaited the loser, whose head would be impaled on a 'skull-rack' adjacent to the court, and whose blood would be offered as food for the gods. In contrast to the more secular role that sport has played over the centuries in most Old World societies, in Mesoamerica the ball game attained a quite fundamental, sacred importance. The Classic Maya, for example, appear to have conceived of the court as a magical threshold between the everyday world and the supernatural.

KEY DATES

wrestling/boxing	3rd millennium BC, Mesopotamia
juggling/catch	2000 BC, Egypt
the ball game	2000 BC, Mesoamerica
bull-leaping	2nd millennium BC, Crete
Olympic Games	776 BC, Greece
polo	c. 600 BC, Central Asia
football	300 BC, China

Ball-courts were given a central place in the layout of their cities and here kings and priests would ritually participate in the re-enactment of origin myths that featured titanic struggles in the ball game between the precursors of human beings and the lords of the Underworld. Sport thus provided a metaphor for cosmic struggle and the very origins of human existence.

Below *The court at Xochicalco, Mexico, where the Mesoamerican ball game was played: the stone rings would originally have been mounted high up on the side walls and the aim of the game was to pass the heavy rubber ball through the ring, without using hands or feet.*

Bottom *Two teams face each other on either side of the large rubber ball, while onlookers with rattles watch, depicted on a Late Classic Maya vase, AD 600–900, from Guatemala.*

Board Games

Woe, woe, my knucklebone,
my knucklebone.
BABYLONIAN TEXT, 500 BC

The above extract from a Babylonian school text in cuneiform from about 500 BC is probably part of a literary *Gambler's Lament*. A player is addressing the knucklebones used to determine the moves of the pieces in a betting game which have betrayed him, and he has lost all.

Games, in their very broadest sense, are as old as mankind, and there is scarcely an attested society, ancient or modern, that has flourished without some form of board game, played with pieces on a prescribed surface, often with the help of dice. Board games can thus be proposed as a defining element of human society, whose primary function has perhaps always been entertainment – what in India is known as 'time-pass'.

For this reason, it is hardly possible to speak of 'invention' as such with regard to board games, and indeed the circumstances under which they evolved remain obscure. Conceivably their origin ran in parallel with divination or ritual processes using pieces with specific movements. It has also been argued that games involve the safe sublimation of competition and rivalry. It is likely that the factors were multi-layered and complex.

Archaeology provides the first evidence for game boards in the Neolithic of the ancient Middle East, around 7000 BC. This was a period of communal settlement and shared responsibility, before writing or even pottery in the region, and it is likely that their appearance at this time is due to the first manifestations of social leisure, if not security.

These earliest boards are a conundrum. Stone slabs with two or three parallel rows of regular holes, they are attested at Beidha and 'Ain Ghazal in Jordan, Wadi Tbeik in the Sinai Peninsula, El Kowm in Syria and Chagha Sefid in southwest Iran. Later examples from such sites as Arad in southern Israel have been found distributed in many adjacent houses. Without writing of course there is no evidence as to their use, but some scholars have seen them as ancestral to the modern and highly widespread family of counting games known as Mancala, in which seeds are sown by two players in rows of between two and four holes. Such a mechanism suggests that Mancala at least ultimately derived from a fertility ritual designed to promote crop yield.

From race games to chess

The archaeological record is then completely blank for over 4000 years. All the games which appear in subsequent periods up to the advent of chess in the 1st millennium AD are race games, in which dice play a crucial role. The classic type, the two-handed Game of Twenty Squares, perhaps developed in India, spreading around 2600 BC through Iran to the Middle East and achieving remarkable distribution, being found in Egypt, Mesopotamia, Iran, Israel, Jordan, Lebanon, Turkey and even Crete, for at least the next two and a half millennia.

Another game, sometimes called the Game of Fifty-Eight Holes, achieved less persistent popularity, and relied on moving peg men along a track of holes that has sometimes, although most erroneously, been claimed as a relative of the 18th-century game of Cribbage. In contrast, the Egyptian 'national' game of Senet, played for some

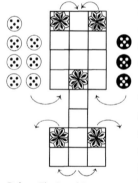

Below *Diagram to illustrate the route followed by the pieces in the Royal Game of Ur. Rosettes probably gave a second throw, and were also safe squares, while the pieces were at war along the central aisle.*

Below *The Royal Game of Ur, dating to around 2600–2400 BC, with inlays of shell, stone and lapis lazuli. It was used to play the Game of Twenty Squares.*

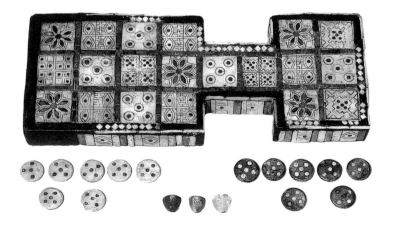

game boards	7000 BC, Middle East
Senet	c. 3000 BC, Egypt
Game of Twenty Squares	c. 2600 BC, India
rule book	177 BC, Babylonia
chess	1st millennium AD, India

Left *A set for playing Senet, with game board and counters, dating from the 14th century BC. The most popular game in ancient Egypt, Senet was played from Predynastic times on and tomb paintings often depict people engaged in a game.*

Below *A modern reconstruction of the board and pieces for the Roman game Duodecim Scripta, or Twelve Lines, the probable ancestor of backgammon.*

3000 years on a board of 3 × 10 squares, achieved religious funerary significance beyond the bounds of a pure game, but hardly spread beyond the limits of that country.

Traditionally in Indian stories the invention of chess is attributed to the ingenuity of an individual, and made the subject of an international competition. A plausible interpretation now sees the game developing on an existing 8 × 8 board with figurative pieces as a means of instructing young knights in the arts of warfare.

Although the 'inventors' of all early – pre-commercial – games are lost to history, the evolution of board games is gradually becoming clearer, and modern research is attempting to furnish family trees to sketch in the processes, although there is much contention about the correct classification of board games. Backgammon, for example, one of the world's most successful games, is evidently a descendant of the two-row Roman dice game of Duodecim Scripta, or Twelve Lines, itself a refinement of an early three-row version, although the intermediate phases are unknown.

Obviously, certain individuals must have contributed telling input to the development of all early games, but they will forever remain anonymous. An exception is a single board-game name, that of the Babylonian scholar-scribe Itti-Marduk-Bal-tu, who codified the rules for the Game of

Twenty Squares on a cuneiform tablet in 177 BC, adding details to enliven it for the contemporary gambler. This stands in contrast to their modern counterparts, such as Alfred M. Butts, who perfected Scrabble in his garage by 1946, or Lizzi Magie, whose innocent Quaker Landlord's Game, patented in 1903, turned into the world-conquering game of Monopoly.

Below *A Han dynasty tomb model from China showing two men playing liubo, the rules of which are still unknown.*

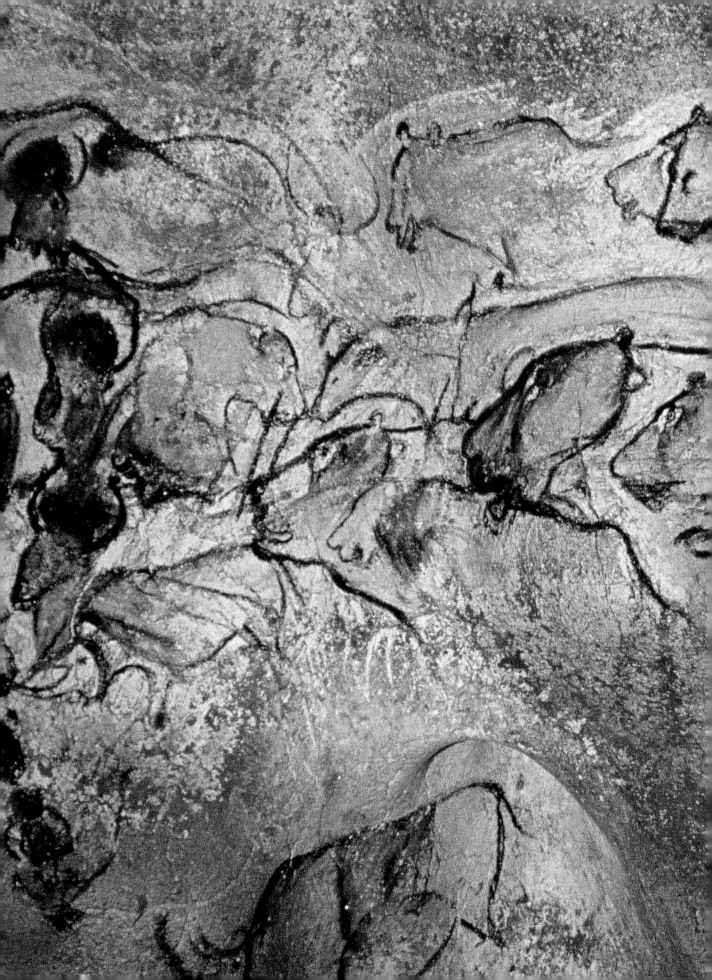

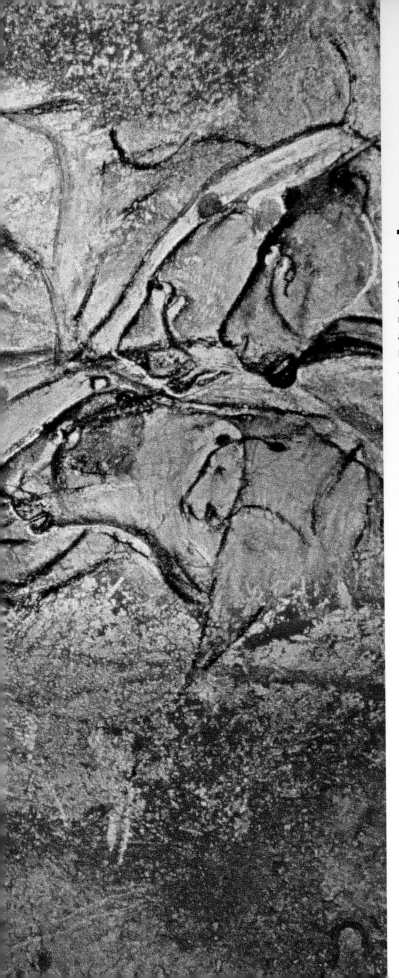

Art & Science

The full creativity of *Homo sapiens* bursts into view around 30,000 years ago, with the dramatic appearance of the world's earliest art traditions. Only a fraction of this ebullient art survives on rock walls, sometimes far from daylight in narrow defiles, or in the form of delicately carved and engraved bone and antler artifacts. We do not know for certain when or where the first art appeared. Cave art flourished in Australia, and perhaps South Africa, almost as early as it did in Europe, so it seems that artistic expression was a reflection of a surge in human creativity. The motives for the art are the subject of intense debate; much of it may have been connected with solitary vision quests, shamanism and altered states of consciousness. It may have denoted rank or group affiliation, communicating information of many kinds. But so much more is lost, painted or carved on wood and hide,

Chant and dance, simple music and song, all were an integral part of human existence in worlds where all knowledge was passed orally from one generation to the next. The drum and the simple flute were part of musical tradition as early as the late Ice Age, the forerunners of the more sophisticated music making of the early civilizations.

Music was, and still is, a form of communication. Writing developed as a way of passing information from one person to another, and as an aid, also, to human memory. One popular theory argues that the simple clay tokens found by the dozen in early farming villages were the forerunners of the cuneiform tablets that recorded commercial transactions in early Mesopotamian cities. Cuneiform became the standard diplomatic script of the eastern Mediterranean world, while

The lion frieze from Chauvet Cave, France; this remarkable painting dates to around 30,000 years ago. At this early date the animals depicted are often dangerous ones.

others served the Egyptians and Minoans, the Mycenaeans, Harappans and Chinese. The intricate Maya glyphs of lowland Mesoamerica doubled as calendrical symbols, and as a formal script that commemorated the deeds of rulers and their genealogies. To be literate in any script was to have access to information; information meant power, and so it is hardly surprising that codes and ciphers soon developed to preserve state secrets and to restrict information among an ever-widening circle of people who could read and write. It was no coincidence that Maya lords cut off the fingers of scribes from conquered cities.

Clay and wax tablets, papyrus, bamboo strips and even slivers of bark, were the materials used to preserve and disseminate information before the advent of books and paper. Early libraries, such as that at Alexandria in Egypt, stored books on rolls, while Aztec scribes wrote on deer skin to create codices as *aides memoires* for official orators. Much of this transmitted information included records of calendrical events and the movements of the heavenly bodies, laboriously passed from one generation to the next by long apprenticeships.

Astronomy was all-important to early farming societies, whose lives revolved around the passage of the seasons, the solstices and equinoxes, measured by observing the heavenly bodies. Sacred places like Stonehenge and the megalithic tomb at Newgrange, Ireland, were aligned with the heavenly bodies, with special significance attached to the turning points of the year. Early calendars also depended on astronomical observation, developed by the ancient Maya and Inca to a fine art. Time measurement itself was a more arcane art, which became increasingly important for the scheduling of major ceremonies and other events on a more accurate timetable. The first attempts at time measurement are attributable to Babylonian astronomers.

Scientific and medical knowledge developed rapidly with the growth of civilizations, as life became more complex and royal courts supported scholars and physicians. We explore some facets of the resulting information explosion – the invention of maps and cartography, the increasing importance of counting devices of all kinds, and also of coinage as a way of regulating complex transactions and tribute. This in turn also necessitated sophisticated, and standardized, ways of measuring and weighing commodities of all kinds. The urban markets of Chinese cities and of Aztec Tenochtitlán depended on standard measurements, rigorously enforced. International trade at the Harappan cities of Harappa and Mohenjo-daro on the Indus also relied on accurate units.

Some of the greatest advances came in medicine, fields in which Egypt and China led the way with such methods as acupuncture and sophisticated surgeries, as well as an impressive array of folk remedies for medical conditions of all kinds. Egyptian anatomical expertise is reflected in the increasingly complex methods of mummification, a classic manifestation of a civilization with a strong belief in the afterlife.

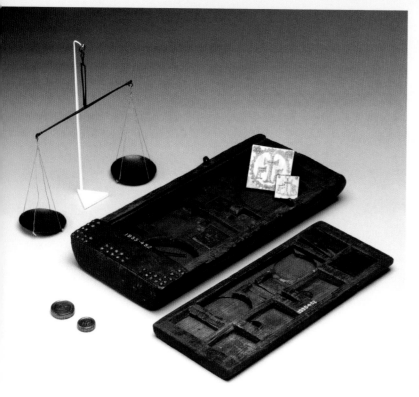

A Roman equal-arm balance made of bronze and dating to AD 350. Symmetrical balances of this type are the simplest and earliest method of weighing, and consist of a bar with pans or hooks suspended at either end. To weigh an object in one pan, weights are added or removed from the other until the beam is level.

The Earliest Art

*It's pretty,
but is it Art?*
RUDYARD KIPLING, 1895

Around 30,000 years ago people living in Ice Age Europe began to paint cave walls with pictures of tundra-living animals and enigmatic signs and stencils of their own hands. They were also carving ivory and bone into figurines, including supernatural creatures, part human and part animal, such as the 'lion-man' from Hohlenstein-Stadel, Germany. At approximately the same time, people on the other side of the world – the Aborigines living in the deep interior valleys of Tasmania – were also painting their cave walls. These are the earliest known examples of representational art; but whether 30,000 years ago marks a true turning point in human expression or merely a date after which art has survived remains highly contestable.

One problem is that a great deal of art made by traditional peoples was on perishable materials – such as paintings on bark and skin – and so would not survive in the archaeological record. And very simple marks, which might easily be either overlooked or neglected by archaeologists, are known to carry complex symbolic meanings.

The capacity to create art is often taken to be a distinguishing characteristic of our species alone, *Homo sapiens*; hence its presence or otherwise among premodern humans, such as the Neanderthals, lies at the heart of questions about our own identity as a species.

But is it art?

There have been several claims for art having been made by pre-modern humans; few – if any – stand up to rigorous scrutiny. One of the most contentious is in the form of a small piece of volcanic rock, no more than 35 mm (1.4 in) in length, that is claimed to have been carved by a flint tool into a female form. This is the so-called Berekhat Ram 'figurine', from a site of the same name in Israel. It is believed to date to around 250,000 years ago, which would mean it would have been made during the Acheulian.

Two questions need to be asked: first, was the piece of stone really modified by a human hand; second, was there the intent to create a female form? Microscopic study has indicated that grooves on the stone have the diagnostic shape of incisions made by flint blades, but whether there was any intent to impose a specific form is the subject of much debate. Many archaeologists believe that the similarity to a female form is purely coincidental and that the stone had simply been used to blunt the edge of a blade or as a small wedge or some other mundane, practical implement. While the Berekhat Ram 'figurine' has been claimed to be the earliest known piece of representational art, the first abstract images may come from Bilzingsleben, a site in southern Germany, dating to some 350,000 years ago. This site has provided several pieces of bone that carry incisions from flint blades which are claimed to form patterns of such regularity to suggest that they were deliberately made. The excavator has suggested that they might carry a symbolic code.

The Berekhat Ram 'figurine', from Israel – a 35-mm (1.4-in) piece of volcanic stone that has been incised by a flint tool with a possibly deliberate but more likely coincidental resemblance to a female figure.

would have been made by a member of *Homo sapiens* and the key question is not why it is present, but why such art objects are so rare if making art is indeed a characteristic feature of our species? It is possible that a great deal of art might have been made in South Africa at this time since the cave deposits provide many samples of red ochre, in the form of pigment, crayons and palettes. The ochre may have been used for painting bodies or objects that have since perished.

Cave paintings & their meaning

Before the discoveries in Blombos Cave, the cave paintings of southwest Europe were the earliest, unambiguous examples of art. These were discovered in the late 19th century and academics were at first reluctant to accept that they were the work of 'prehistoric savages' owing to their technical brilliance and emotive power. We now know that they were first made about 30,000 years ago, soon after the first modern humans had spread into Europe from their African home.

The very earliest paintings, such as those in Chauvet Cave in France, have an emphasis on 'dangerous' animals, such as lions and woolly rhino, but this is replaced by a focus on larger herbivores as climatic conditions deteriorated towards the height of the Ice Age at 20,000 BC. Consequently, in caves such as Lascaux, Pech Merle (France) and Altamira (Spain), images of horse, bison and deer are dominant. These are found with a wide array of abstract signs, occasional depictions of humans and striking prints or stencils of hands. Along with the cave paintings, and more widely distributed, are carvings in bone, stone and ivory depicting a similar range of imagery.

Archaeologists have vigorously debated the meaning of this art for more than 100 years. Many theories have been put forward – that it was simply 'art for art's sake', hunting magic or a 'tribal encyclopaedia' that encoded information critical to survival within its

Above *A small engraved piece of red ochre from Blombos Cave, South Africa, dating to 70,000 years ago.*

Below *An ivory horse, under 5 cm (2 in) long, carved some 30,000 years ago, from Vogelherd, Germany.*

Opposite *The lion-man from Hohlenstein-Stadel, Germany, carved from a single piece of mammoth bone and measuring c. 29 cm (11 in) tall.*

An alternative suggestion is that marks like these were the accidental by-product of other activities, such as cutting meat or plants on a bone support. These objects might then easily become unintentionally incised with patterns that appear to us to form geometric designs.

Far more persuasive abstract images come from cave sites in South Africa, notably Blombos Cave, dating to 70,000 years ago. These were made on small pieces of bone and lumps of red ochre. One piece of the latter, discovered in 2001, bears a crisscross pattern and seems to defy any explanation other than it constitutes some form of artistic activity. This

Left *Hand prints and especially hand stencils are a frequent motif in certain caves, and perhaps bring us closest to the ancient artists. The stencils may have been produced by spitting paint, either directly from the mouth or through a tube, around a hand pressed against the cave wall. This example is from the Panel of the Hand Stencils, from Chauvet Cave, France.*

Below *Part of the Panel of the Horses, in Chauvet Cave, France, dating from around 30,000 years ago. The use of shading creates a vivid impression of three-dimensions and movement.*

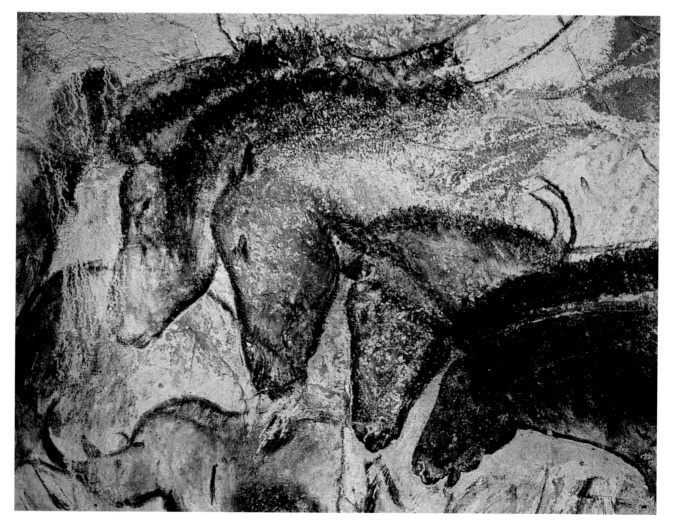

pictorial representations and associated stories. As the art was made over a period of 20,000 years and reached from the Urals to southern Spain, it seems unlikely that a single all-encompassing explanation is sufficient.

Indeed, when archaeologists have studied the rock art of recent hunter-gatherers, such as the Australian Aborigines, they find that any one image can have several different meanings, depending on who is looking at it. And so it seems likely that the Ice Age cave paintings may have served both functional purposes, as repositories of hunting information, and symbolic ones, in representing supernatural beings.

Art around the world

By the time the caves of Ice Age Europe were being painted, modern humans had dispersed throughout Africa, Asia and Australasia. A collection of painted slabs have come from Apollo Cave, Namibia, depicting a giraffe-like creature, a rhino and a wild cat that some believe to have human legs. Archaeologists remain unsure whether these date closer to 20,000 or 30,000 BC; whichever is the case, these are the earliest known representational art from South Africa.

The most dramatic recent discoveries have come from the remote interior valleys of Tasmania. These are now covered with dense, temperate rainforest and are uninhabited. In 1981 the first traces of prehistoric occupation were identified within Kutikina Cave; over the next two decades remarkable evidence was revealed of Ice Age wallaby hunting by people who occupied the valleys before the forests grew, between 30,000 and 12,000 years ago.

In 1986 the first Tasmanian art was discovered: a panel of 16 hand stencils, from at least five separate individuals, in the deep recesses of what became known as Ballawinne Cave in the Maxwell River Valley. Iron oxide had been ground, mixed with water and sprayed across hands placed flat against the wall. More hand stencils were discovered in Wargata Cave, 85 km (53 miles) to the southeast. Both adults and children, using human blood as one of their pigments, had left this remarkable record of their presence.

KEY DATES

abstract images	?350,000 years ago, Germany
earliest figurine	?250,000 years ago, Near East
abstract images	70,000 years ago, South Africa
cave paintings	30,000 years ago, Europe
carvings	30,000 years ago, Europe

PAINT PIGMENTS

The study of Ice Age art has been transformed during the last decade by the application of scientific techniques that analyze microscopic samples of pigment. These have revealed an unsuspected degree of complexity as to how the paints were made. Two colours dominate the cave paintings – red and black. The red, in a wide variety of hues from browns to orange, derives from minerals containing iron oxide, otherwise known as haematite or red ochre. In the cave at Cougnac, France, traces of red pigments were found on the cave floor (**above**). The black comes from either manganese oxide or charcoal. The minerals were ground and mixed with a binder; this was sometimes nothing more complicated than water from the caves themselves, but in other cases animal and plant fats were used, so some Ice Age artists were engaging in oil painting.

Additional minerals may have been added. Analysis of paintings in Niaux Cave, France, showed that three pigment 'recipes' had been employed, one containing potassium feldspar, one talcum and one biotite. There seemed to be no relation between the type of image painted and the recipe used, nor with the location of the image in the cave. It seems likely that different recipes were used in different periods; fortunately it is now also possible to directly date minute samples of charcoal taken from the paintings by accelerator mass spectrometry (AMS) radiocarbon dating. When combined, these new techniques will provide many insights into the mysteries of Ice Age art.

53 Music & Musical Instruments

It is very difficult to say anything about the origin of music,
because the phenomenon is quite outside the range of our observation.
MARIUS SCHNEIDER, 1957

Above *The oldest musical instrument discovered so far, and the earliest tangible evidence for music: a flute carved from a bear femur, dated somewhere between 43,400 and 67,000 years old.*

The invention of music itself is lost to us. The uniquely intangible nature of music before the age of recording is such that we cannot ever know when and where music first appeared, or what it sounded like. Prehistorians have speculated that music developed from human imitation of animal sounds, forms of early speech, as a means of signalling or from children at play. The assumption behind these theories is that the earliest music was vocal in nature, followed by the eventual use of tools – instruments – to make some kind of accompanying sound. About the invention of musical instruments we are on slightly firmer ground, since remains of prehistoric musical instruments do survive. The evidence suggests that they were 'invented' in a number of locations independently of each other.

The earliest direct evidence for music is a bear femur carved into a wind instrument somewhere between 43,400 and 67,000 years old, recently found in the former Yugoslavia, a remnant of the Mousterian (Neanderthal) culture. This flute has holes suggesting that it was designed to play the notes of a diatonic scale (the seven-note scale on which modern Western music is based). It is considerably more elaborate than the various single-note whistles from about 20,000–30,000 years ago that

were previously thought to be the oldest musical instruments.

Evidence for the increasing complexity of prehistoric music comes from China, where the earliest playable musical instruments have been found. Archaeologists discovered six multi-holed flutes made from the bones of the red-crowned crane that date to around 7000 BC at the early Neolithic site of Jiahu. These flutes, with their differing scales and fingering, suggest the development of multiple styles and traditions of music within a single

Right *The earliest known playable musical instruments are these flutes made from the bones of the red-crowned crane, from the Neolithic site of Jiahu, China, dating to c. 7000 BC. With their different fingerings and scales, they suggest that music was already quite complex.*

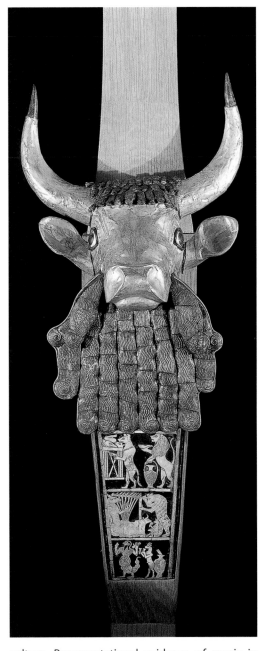

Mesopotamia & Egypt

The most extensive evidence for the early development of music and musical instruments can be found in the ancient Near East, in the cultures of Mesopotamia and Egypt. Although the earliest fragments of Mesopotamian instruments are whistles and flutes of types known from other prehistoric cultures, representational evidence shows that a complex and sophisticated musical culture had developed in these regions by 3000 BC.

The lavish and striking harps from the royal tombs at Ur are the most dramatic surviving evidence of the early development of stringed instruments in Mesopotamia, but an extensive body of pictorial evidence shows a wide variety of stringed, wind and percussion instruments, as well as their use in ensembles and to accompany singers. Remains from Anatolia, including bronze cymbals, rattles and bells, supplement what is

Left *The magnificent 'Great Lyre' was found in the King's Grave at Ur. It is decorated with a bull's head of gold and lapis lazuli and a panel inlaid with shell, and dates from c. 2600–2400 BC. The instrument was found with the bodies of sacrificed women, possibly court musicians and singers.*

Below *An Egyptian relief depicting two women musicians, one playing the harp, the other singing; from the tomb of Nikaure, Saqqara, c. 2300 BC. The harp was a very popular instrument in ancient Egypt and often features in art.*

culture. Representational evidence of music in prehistory comes from various Neolithic and Chalcolithic sites (*c.* 7000–5000 BC) in Anatolia, where representations of ceremonial activity accompanied by drums and other percussion instruments have been found, providing hints of the complex roles music had begun to play. Clearly music and the use of musical instruments was developing in different places and ways throughout the later Stone Age.

A young man plays the aulos, the double reed flute, in a procession of musicians and dancers in a wall-painting in the Etruscan Tomb of the Triclinium at Tarquinia, c. 470 BC. Etruscan flautists were highly renowned among the Greeks and Romans for their skill and virtuosity.

Below right *The elaborately decorated top of a bronze Vietnamese Dong Son drum, c. 700 BC–AD 200.*

Below *Terracotta figures of dancers playing hand drums from Roman Egypt (c. AD 100). Dancers frequently provided their own rhythmic accompaniment.*

language (*c.* 1400 BC). The lyrics are placed above musical instructions that provide the notation. Although there is some disagreement among scholars as to exactly how this notation is to be interpreted, the accumulated evidence shows that a complex, and most likely polyphonic, musical tradition existed in the Near East.

Ancient Egypt developed a complex music culture of its own, but one with less emphasis on theory and writing, and more on performance and representation. By the time of the great pyramid builders of the Old Kingdom (*c.* 2650–2450 BC), Egyptians had taken basic instruments of the types common in Mesopotamia and elaborated on them in unique ways. The harp in particular underwent considerable change into a complex and subtle instrument, played by professional entertainers and amateurs alike.

The climate of Egypt has preserved a much wider range of musical instruments than Mesopotamia, and these remains, along with extensive visual representations, allow us to reconstruct a rich musical ensemble, including harps, lyres, lutes, reed flutes (single and double), as well as a wide variety of percussion instruments. The tomb of

known of the range of early instruments used in the ancient Near East.

Cuneiform tablets from Mesopotamia provide perhaps the earliest song lyrics, including the compositions of the priestess Enheduanna (*c.* 2300 BC). Lexical lists reveal an extensive musical vocabulary, while literary compositions describe the skills needed by musicians at this time. Old Babylonian (*c.* 1800–1600 BC) cuneiform tablets preserve the beginnings of musical theory in Mesopotamia: treatises on stringed instruments and their parts, the nature and variety of scales they produced and tuning systems.

Given the especially literate character of much of the evidence for music in Mesopotamia, it is not surprising that cuneiform tablets preserve early examples of musical notation. Excerpts from songs can be reconstructed from theoretical texts, but the earliest example of a complete piece of notated music is a tablet from Ugarit (Ras Shamra, Syria). This is a hymn written in the Hurrian

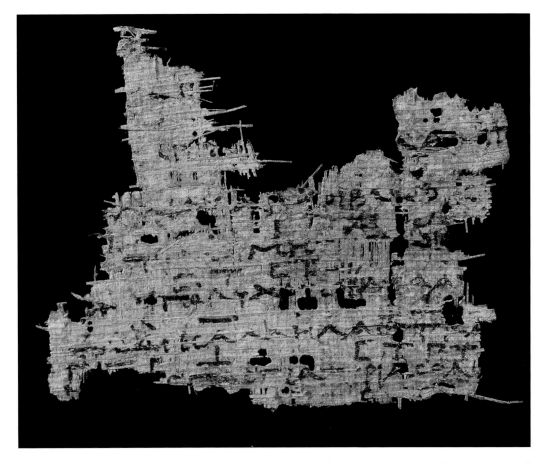

An early papyrus with musical notation found in Egypt and dating to c. 250 BC. It consists of a fragment of a musical score for a Greek tragedy.

New Kingdom ruler Tutankhamun (*c.* 1332–1322 BC) yielded the oldest playable instruments from Egypt, including a silver trumpet whose sound was recorded in 1939.

Egyptian evidence documents the uses and contexts in which music was made, with representations of music at social or celebratory occasions being especially common. Harpists were popular as professional entertainers, and we begin to know individual musicians, such as the lute-player Harmose who was buried with his instrument. Music played an important part in temple ritual in Egypt, where elite women often served as 'musicians' of a particular god or goddess, for whom they would perform ritual music on the sistrum, a ceremonial rattle.

Lyrics for religious duets sung by singers disguised as goddesses have survived as part of funerary rituals. But lyrics are nearly all that survives of Egyptian music in writing – there are only a very few cases of apparent notated music from Egypt before the introduction of Greek systems of musical notation.

Greece & Rome

These Greek systems of notation are part of one of the most complex music cultures found in the ancient world. Both professional and amateur musicians in Greece played on a wide range of musical instruments, of which the most highly esteemed were the *kithara*, one of a number of developments from the lyre, and the *aulos*, a double reed flute in which one pipe played the melody while the second provided a droning accompaniment. Many related stringed and wind instruments developed, as well as a full complement of percussion instruments, including hand drums and castanets, which provided rhythmic accompaniment.

To accommodate the new musical instruments and styles, a complex set of systems for notating vocal and instrumental music developed in

Above *A Maya processional 'orchestra' from the murals of Bonampak, Mexico, c. AD 790.*

Below *An Aztec vertical drum, huehuetl, c. AD 1500, almost 1 m (3 ft) tall.*

Greece, the earliest witnesses of which are found in inscriptions and also in papyri found in Egypt. The surviving examples of notated Greek music attest to its great importance in the theatre. But the Greeks' most substantial and lasting contribution to music was surely their extensive body of literature on music theory, where philosophy, mathematics and music met to explore questions about the nature of music that still continue to influence us today.

The Romans, with their reverence for Greek culture, adopted many of the Greek musical traditions, while adding elements of their own. Military music was an area of innovation, resulting in the development of new varieties of trumpet, along with theories on the military uses and importance of music. Although invented earlier, the wider use of the *hydraulis* – a pipe organ with air forced through by water pressure – came about under the Romans, who found its loudness useful in their larger theatres.

The New World

Music and musical instruments developed in the prehistory of the New World along similar lines to those we have already

noted. Pottery wind instruments are known from as early as AD 500 among the Maya of Central America. A broad range of whistles, flutes and ocarinas (small, egg-shaped wind instruments) have been discovered in the archaeological record, while trumpets are known to have been made of gourds, wood and conch shells.

Percussion instruments in use included rasps, rattles, wooden gongs or slit-drums, and a variety of hand drums made of wood and animal skins. Some song lyrics have been found, suggesting complex traditions of vocal music, but no pre-contact musical notation appears to have survived, and stringed instruments do not appear until brought by Europeans.

Early New World music appears most often in religious, ceremonial, celebratory and military contexts, but its manifestations are as diverse as the many different cultures in which it appeared.

KEY DATES

flute	67,000–43,400 years ago, Balkans
playable flute	7000 BC, China
harp	c. 2500 BC, Mesopotamia
song lyrics	c. 2300 BC, Mesopotamia
musical theory	c. 1800–1600 BC, Mesopotamia
musical notation	c. 1400 BC, Ugarit

Writing

*Writing put agreements, laws, commandments on record. It made the growth of states larger
than the old city states possible. It made a continuous historical consciousness possible.
The command of the priest or king and his seal could go far beyond his sight and
voice and could survive his death.*

H. G. WELLS, 1922

54

Writing is among the greatest inventions in human history, perhaps *the* greatest, since it made history possible. Yet it is a skill most writers take for granted. We learn it when young, building on the alphabet, or, if we live in China or Japan, the Chinese characters. As adults we seldom stop to think about the mental-cum-physical process that turns our thoughts into symbols on a piece of paper or video screen, or bytes of information in a computer memory. Few of us have any clear recollection of how we learnt to write.

No one knows how writing was invented. The favoured explanation, until the Enlightenment in the 18th century, was divine origin. Today many, probably most, scholars accept that the earliest writing evolved from accountancy – though it is puzzling that accountancy is little in evidence in the surviving

writing of ancient Egypt, India, China and Central America (which is no guarantee that there was not such bureaucratic record keeping on perishable materials in these civilizations).

Some time in the late 4th millennium BC, the complexities of trade and administration in the early cities of Sumer in Mesopotamia, the 'cradle of civilization', reached a point where they outstripped the power of memory of the governing elite. To record transactions in a form that was permanent and beyond dispute became essential.

Above *A Maya plate of the Late Classic period with Hunahpu, one of the Hero Twins, depicted as a scribe. Hieroglyphs of the Young Maize God are written at the edges of the plate.*

Left *A temple receipt on a cuneiform tablet of c. 2100 BC. It seems that the growing complexities of trade and administration led to the invention of writing.*

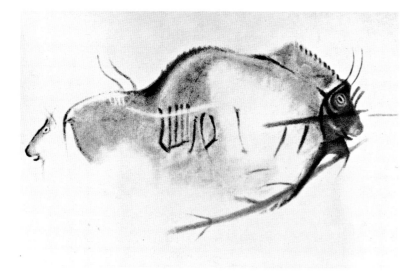

accidental discovery. Many regard it as the result of evolution over a long period, rather than a flash of inspiration.

One widely held theory states that writing grew out of a long-standing counting system of clay 'tokens' (p. 247). Such 'tokens' – varying from simple, plain discs to more complex, incised shapes whose exact purpose is unknown – have been found in many Middle Eastern archaeological sites. The substitution of two-dimensional symbols in clay for these three-dimensional tokens, with the symbols resembling the appearance of the token, was a first step towards writing, according to this theory. One major difficulty is that the 'tokens' continued to exist after the emergence of Sumerian cuneiform writing; another is that a two-dimensional symbol on a clay tablet might be thought to be a less, not more, advanced concept than a three-dimensional 'token'. It seems more likely that 'tokens' accompanied the emergence of writing, rather than gave rise to it.

'Proto-writing' & 'full' writing

Apart from the 'tokens', numerous examples exist of what might be called 'proto-writing'. For example, there are the Ice Age symbols found in

There are many examples of cave paintings which contain unexplained signs and symbols. In fact, such 'non-figurative' marks are much more frequent than the recognizably figurative paintings. **Above** *This bison from Marsoulas, southern France, drawn by Abbé Breuil, has linear signs added.* **Right** *Enigmatic dots painted on the wall of Chauvet Cave, France, next to a rhinoceros. This is from the Panel of the Hand Stencils, dating to around 30,000 years ago. Dots such as these are frequently found in painted caves, often in groups as here, though their significance is unknown.*

Administrators and merchants could then say the Sumerian equivalent of 'I'll put this in writing' or 'May I have this in writing?'.

Some scholars believe that a conscious search for a solution to this problem by an unknown Sumerian individual in the city of Uruk (biblical Erech), in about 3300 BC, produced writing. Others think writing was the work of a group, presumably of clever administrators and merchants. Still others say it was not an invention at all, but an

caves in southern France, up to 30,000 years old, such as a stencilled hand and a pattern of red dots. What does this mean? 'I was here, with my animals' – or is the symbolism deeper? Other images show animals overlaid with signs; and notched bones have been found that apparently served as lunar calendars (p. 239).

'Proto-writing' is not writing in the sense of the word as we use it today. A distinguished scholar of writing, John DeFrancis, has defined 'full' writing as a 'system of graphic symbols that can be used to convey any and all thought'. By this definition, 'proto-writing' includes, as well as Ice Age cave symbols, the Middle Eastern archaeological 'tokens', Pictish symbol stones and tallies such as the fascinating knotted Inca *quipus*, contemporary sign systems such as international transportation symbols, computer 'icons', and mathematical and musical notation. None of these systems is capable of expressing 'any and all thought', but they are each very good at specialized communication.

To express the full range of human thought we need a system intimately linked with spoken language. For as Ferdinand de Saussure, the founder of modern linguistics, wrote, language may be compared to a sheet of paper. 'Thought is on one side of the sheet and sound the reverse side. Just as it is impossible to take a pair of scissors and cut one side of the paper without at the same time cutting the other, so it is impossible in a language to isolate sound from thought, or thought from sound.'

The symbols of what may have been the first 'full' writing system are generally thought to have been pictograms: iconic drawings of, say, a pot or a fish, or a head with an open jaw (to represent the concept of eating). These have been found in Mesopotamia and Egypt dating to the mid-4th millennium BC, shortly after in the Indus Valley, and even earlier in China, according to the (not proven) claims of some Chinese archaeologists. In many cases, their iconicity soon became so abstract that

Cuneiform tablet, concerning the study of lucky and unlucky days, c. 600 BC. The pictograms of the earliest Mesopotamian writing system – iconic drawings which represented the concept expressed in a recognizable form – evolved into such abstract cuneiform signs made up of wedges produced by a reed stylus.

the meaning is barely perceptible to us – as in the cuneiform signs derived from pictograms.

But pictograms were insufficient to express the kinds of words, and their constituent parts, that cannot be picturized. Essential to the development of 'full' writing, as opposed to limited, purely pictographic 'proto-writing', was the discovery of the *rebus* principle. This radical idea, from the Latin meaning 'by things', enables phonetic values to be represented by pictographic symbols. Thus in English, a picture of a bee with a picture of a figure 4 could represent 'before', while a picture of an ant next to a buzzing bee hive might (less obviously) represent 'Anthony'. Egyptian hieroglyphs are full of rebuses, for instance the 'sun' sign – a disc – pronounced *R(a)* or *R(e)*, is the first symbol in the hieroglyphic spelling of the pharaoh Ramesses. In an early Sumerian tablet we find the abstract word 'reimburse' represented by a picture of a reed, because 'reimburse' and 'reed' shared the same phonetic value, *gi*, in the Sumerian language.

Once writing of this 'full' kind, capable of expressing the full range of speech and thought, was invented, accidentally discovered or evolved, did it then diffuse throughout the globe from Mesopotamia? The earliest Egyptian writing dates from about 3100 BC (recent claims suggest even as early as 3250 BC), that of the Indus Valley from 2500 BC, that of Crete from 1750 BC, that of China from 1200 BC, that of Central America from 500 BC – all dates are approximate.

On this basis, it seems reasonable that the *idea* of writing, but not the symbols of a particular script, could have spread gradually from culture to distant culture. It took 600 or 700 years for the idea of printing to reach Europe from China, and paper-making even longer (p. 232): why should writing not have reached China from Mesopotamia over an even longer period? Nevertheless, in the absence of solid evidence of the transmission of the idea (even in the case of the geographically closer civilizations of Mesopotamia and Egypt), a majority of scholars prefers to think that writing was invented independently in the major civilizations of the ancient world.

The Seated Scribe: a painted limestone statue found at Saqqara, Egypt, dating to the mid-3rd millennium BC. He has a papyrus scroll partially opened on his lap and his hand would once have held a pen.

Above *A glazed tile of the Egyptian pharaoh Ramesses II (13th century BC), made of blue faience inlaid with white. The hieroglyphs, enclosed in a cartouche, the oval frame used to enclose a royal name, represent the 'praenomen', or throne name, of Ramesses – Usermaatre-setepenre. The discs represent the sun, Re, and the seated figure with a feather on her head is the goddess Maat.*

Right *The Phoenician alphabet has 22 letters, the names of which were the same as those used by the Hebrews – the first letter was* aleph *and the second* beth. *Since the Phoenicians were great merchants who traded all round the Mediterranean, their alphabet probably travelled with them.*

Left *The earliest Chinese inscriptions are on oracle bones, dating from the Shang dynasty, 12th century BC. These were divinatory in purpose, but the symbols used were the precursors of some Chinese characters.*

KEY DATES

writing system	late 4th millennium BC, Mesopotamia	
	3100 BC, Egypt	
	2500 BC, Indus Valley	
	1750 BC, Crete	
	1200 BC, China	
	500 BC, Central America	
alphabet	2nd millennium BC, Near East	

THE ALPHABET

The invention and early development of the alphabetic concept, which most of the world uses for writing today, is shrouded in mystery. That the alphabet reached the modern world via the ancient Greeks is well known – the word alphabet is derived from the first two Greek letters, *alpha* and *beta* – but we have no clear idea of how and when it appeared in Greece, how the Greeks thought of adding letters for vowels as well as consonants, and how, even more fundamentally, the idea of the alphabet first occurred to the pre-Greek societies at the eastern end of the Mediterranean during the 2nd millennium BC.

The discovery in Sinai in 1905 of a sphinx dated about 1500 BC bearing apparently alphabetic signs resembling Egyptian hieroglyphs (**below**), suggested an Egyptian origin for the alphabet. But later discoveries of indisputably alphabetic inscriptions in what was then the land of Canaan (Palestine) date somewhat earlier, to the 17th and 16th centuries. However, discoveries in Egypt in the 1990s suggest that an alphabet may have been in use there as early as 1900 BC. It is certainly likely that the first alphabet was influenced by the scripts of the great empires of the time in Egypt and Mesopotamia (and perhaps Crete). Probably it was invented by merchants to provide a simpler and quicker means of recording transactions than, say, cuneiform and hieroglyphs, and also a convenient way to write the babel of languages used by traders at the eastern end of the Mediterranean.

Codes & Ciphers

Like the god whose hand Einstein saw behind the workings of the natural world,
[ancient writing systems] may be subtle, but they are not malicious. …
What cryptographic systems lack in subtlety, they make up for in malice:
it is their purpose to conceal information.

WHITFIELD DIFFIE, 1999

Right *A 'cryptographic' scarab from Egypt, Late Period (664–332 BC): the symbols of the sun disc, the cat, the basket and the vase can be read either as 'Someone favoured of Amun', from the initials of each of the words in Egyptian, or, more literally, as the cat as a manifestation of the sun god, sitting on the sign for lordship in front of an offering vase.*

Below *The Rosetta Stone, which was used by Jean-François Champollion in his famous decipherment of hieroglyphs, also contains the figurative or riddling use of hieroglyphs.*

Cryptography (or cryptology) is the study of the transformation of information – so-called 'plaintext' – by encoding and decoding for the purpose of keeping it confidential. Although 'codes' are often used loosely to include ciphers, the two terms should be distinguished, even if ciphers shade into codes as they grow larger. Encoding is a process that operates on linguistic entities in the plaintext, such as words and syllables, while enciphering uses meaningless elements as letters. In a code, a word such as 'the' might be represented by a single symbol; in a cipher, by three symbols.

Encryption is first found in ancient Egypt, at least as far back as 1900 BC, yet it is remarkably rare considering the antiquity and longevity of that civilization. Nor is it used for the sending of messages, but rather the figurative or riddling use of hieroglyphs. Thus, on the Rosetta stone, two different signs depicting a hole and a snake, which are normally phonemic (indicating *gs* and *f*) not pictographic in significance, are visually combined to show a snake leaving its hole so as to represent pictographically the word 'to go forth' (*prj*), which plainly has no phonemic resemblance to its two constituent signs. Another example from Egypt is a kind of crossword, carved on a large stone stela from Karnak, in which the hieroglyphs can be read both horizontally and vertically.

Other figurative transformations occur in a hymn to Thoth, a chapter of the Book of the Dead, in pharaonic titles displayed at Luxor, and elsewhere. While they do not appear to have been designed for confidentiality – unlike the earliest-known encrypted cuneiform clay tablet, dated to about 1500 BC, which contains an enciphered formula for making pottery glazes – these Egyptian writings were undoubtedly intended to challenge the reader to decrypt them.

Transposition & substitution ciphers

The first known military use of cryptography comes from Sparta, in Greece, from the 5th century BC. It involved a *scytale*: a wooden staff with a leather strip wound spirally around it. The message was written across the leather, and then unwound and sent as a strip – perhaps concealed as a leather belt – which would have then appeared as a scrambled string of letters. The recipient, as long as he possessed his own *scytale* of the same diameter, could decipher the message by re-wrapping the strip around the staff.

The algorithm for this kind of simple substitution cipher has 25 possibilities, involving letter shifts from 1 to 25 places along the 26-letter alphabet. If, in addition, we complicate matters and operate the substitution on alternative permutations of the English letters, not just on our familiar alphabetic order of A to Z, then it is possible to create an astronomically large number of more complex substitution ciphers – and furnish a daunting challenge for would-be decipherers, even if they were assisted by today's high-speed computers.

KEY DATES

encryption	1900 BC, Egypt
military cipher	5th century BC, Greece
substitution cipher	1st century BC, Rome

Left & above *The badly damaged 'crossword' stela of Paser, which was found near the Temple of Amun at Karnak, Egypt, dating from the late 12th century BC. Below a frieze of deities is a grid of squares filled with hieroglyphic signs (detail above) which can be read both horizontally and vertically, though an inscription on the stela itself says it can be read in three different ways.*

Below *Drawing of a Spartan scytale, 5th century BC: a strip of leather or parchment is wrapped around the scytale and the message written across. Once unwound the strip makes no sense – until rewound on a scytale of the same diameter.*

This is an example of a 'transposition' cipher, in which the letters of the plaintext are transposed according to a rule (known as an algorithm) into a new, enciphered pattern. The alternative technique is a 'substitution' cipher, in which the plaintext letters are *replaced* by other symbols according to some quite different algorithm. The first military leader known to have used such a cipher was the Roman commander Julius Caesar, both in war operations and in his private correspondence. He substituted the required Latin letter with the letter three places further along the Latin alphabet. Using the English alphabet this would entail the following 'Caesar cipher' transformation of letters:

plain a b c d e f g h i j k l m n o p q r s t u v w x y z
cipher D E F G H I J K L M N O P Q R S T U V W X Y Z A B C

231

56 Books & Paper

*The worm thinks it strange and foolish
that man does not eat his books.*
RABINDRANATH TAGORE, 1928

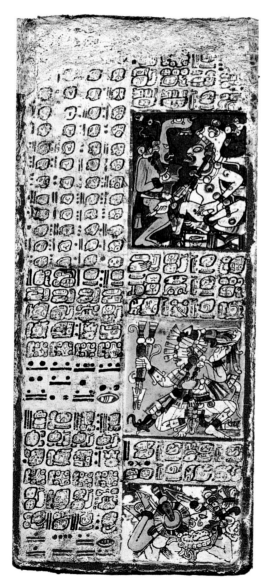

A page from the Dresden Codex, 15th century AD. Maya scribes painted such codices on skin using a brush or feather pens; the skin was then folded and had covers added, often of jaguar skin.

Despite the widespread use of computers and electronic means of communication and information storage, our consumption of paper and our production of printed books continues to increase. Indeed, it is well-nigh impossible to imagine how modern civilization could function without both paper and books. However ephemeral much of the flood of new material published worldwide may be, books remain the chief intellectual and cultural storehouse of a nation. That is why usurpers of power and conquerors have often burned books, as happened in China in 213 BC under the emperor Shihuangdi, in the 16th-century Spanish conquest of Mexico and in 1930s Germany under the Nazis.

Yet there is nothing in the concept of the 'book' that requires it to consist of pages, with text printed or written on paper, still less sewn or glued together between cardboard covers like present-day examples. A cache of Babylonian clay tablets, an Egyptian papyrus roll, a vellum codex from medieval Europe, a folding Maya codex with jaguar-skin covers from Central America, a microfilm and an electronic book all qualify as books, as much as a printed paper volume. They are all made for public circulation, enjoy a considerable degree of permanence and are relatively portable (compared, say, to a monumental inscription); through their different media, they are all capable of knowledge transmission transcending space and time. Of course, printing with movable type, which was invented much later than the book, vastly increases its potential readership – but it does not define the concept.

The book therefore dates not from the arrival of the printing press in the 15th century AD but to the early part of the 3rd millennium BC, soon after the invention of writing (p. 225). The earliest books were both the clay tablets of Mesopotamia, handwritten in cuneiform script using a reed stylus and then baked, and, more importantly, the papyrus rolls of Egypt written in ink with a brush, such as the famous Book of the Dead. The oldest known of these rolls, which is uninscribed, was found in the 1st dynasty tomb of Hemaka at Saqqara, dating to 3035 BC.

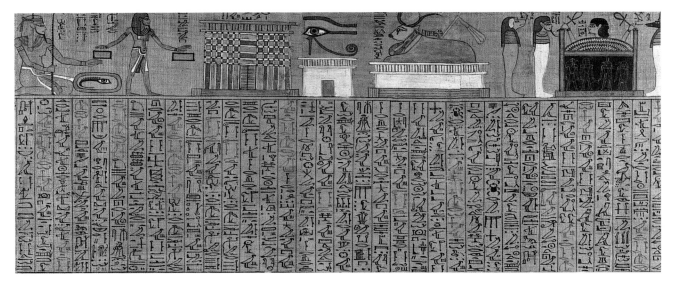

During the 2nd millennium BC in China, books were made of wood or bamboo strips bound together with cords, while around the Mediterranean writing tablets were created from one to ten pieces of wood or ivory held together by a clasp or hinge, or a cord strung through holes drilled in the edges – such as the pair of ivory-hinged boxwood writing tablets discovered in the Uluburun shipwreck off Turkey. Later still, the ancient Greeks and Romans used both writing tablets (often waxed) and rolls made of papyrus or parchment. To the Greeks, papyrus was known as *khartes* (hence English 'card', 'carton', 'chart' etc.), but a papyrus roll was a *biblion*, from the Greek *biblios* meaning 'papyrus pith' (hence English 'bible'); the Romans called it a *volumen* (hence English 'volume').

Papyrus & paper

The word paper, which is attested in English since the 14th century, is derived from the Latin word for papyrus. But although papyrus has an arguable claim to be the world's first paper, a distinction is normally drawn between papyrus and paper in modern usage. Sheets of papyrus were made by stripping and slicing up sections of the stems of the papyrus plant found in the Nile Delta. Many thin, soaked strips of the pith were then overlapped in layers at right angles to each other; the layers were pressed together so that the gluey sap ensured adhesion; and the strips were left to dry into strong and flexible sheets. Sheets of paper, by contrast, were derived from cotton, flax, wood and other plant materials, which had been treated with water and sometimes heat and then beaten into a pulp to release the cellulose fibres. These were collected as a mat on a woven screen, compressed and dried into sheets. (Various chemicals, such as bleach and size, are now added during this process, for whitening and coating to reduce absorbency.)

Credit for discovering how to make paper is traditionally given to Cai Lun, a eunuch at the imperial court in China. In AD 105, he is said to have made *zhi*,

Above *The Book of the Dead of Ani, c. 1250 BC. Such 'books' consisted of papyrus rolls containing religious spells and illustrations to assist the deceased in the afterlife.*

Below *This hinged writing tablet made from boxwood was recovered from the Uluburun shipwreck, off Turkey, dating to the 14th century BC. The rectangular recesses were filled with wax for writing on.*

233

A scrap of hemp paper found in a Western Han tomb near Xi'an, China, dating to c. AD 109 – the earliest known example of hemp paper in the world.

KEY DATES

cuneiform tablets	3rd millennium BC,	Mesopotamia
papyrus roll	3035 BC,	Egypt
bamboo strips	2nd millennium BC,	China
writing tablets	2nd millennium BC,	Mediterranean
paper	2nd century BC,	China

defined by a contemporary dictionary as 'a mat of refuse fibres', from tree bark, the remnants of hemp, rags of cloth and old fishing nets. But archaeological evidence, in the form of very early specimens of paper found at several arid sites in western China, suggests that paper-making probably started earlier than this, during the 2nd century BC, in the tropical regions of south and southeast China. It is even possible it began in the 6th or 5th century BC, when the washing of hemp and linen rags is attested; someone might have stumbled on the possibilities while drying some wet refuse fibres on a mat.

From China, the idea of paper reached Korea, Vietnam and Japan, which were producing their own paper within a few centuries. Its diffusion to far-off Europe was much slower; paper was not made there for nearly a millennium, until the 11th century. The idea followed the Silk Route and was

transmitted to Europe via the Arab rulers and Islamic civilization. Again, tradition has it that at a battle in Central Asia in 751, Muslim soldiers captured some Chinese paper-makers and took them to their base at Samarkand, where they started a celebrated paper industry. But it looks more likely from other evidence – not least the fact that 8th-century papers from western China are made mainly from mulberry, paper mulberry and ramie, while 'Islamic' papers consist predominantly of rag fibres – that paper reached Central Asia well before the Islamic conquest. What is certain, though, is that it was the Moorish rulers of Spain who established paper mills and introduced Christian Europe to the ancient Chinese invention. The English word ream, used today to describe 500 sheets of paper, comes from the Old French *rayme* via the Spanish *resma*, itself from the Arabic *rizma*, meaning 'bale or bundle'.

Below A merchant's letter written on paper in the Sogdian script, discovered by Aurel Stein near Dunhuang on the Silk Route, and dating to the 4th to 6th centuries AD.

Right A fragment of paper from the 2nd century AD, discovered in the Gobi Desert. Surviving examples show that paper was probably invented in south and southeast China during the 2nd century BC – though it is possible it may date back even further, to the 6th or 5th century BC.

Astrology & Astronomy

… hereditary prince and count, sole companion, wise in sacred writings, who observes everything in heaven and earth, clear-eyed in observing the stars, among which there is no erring; who announces rising and setting at their times, with the gods who foretell the future … and [who contents] the lands with his utterances.

INSCRIPTION ON THE STATUE OF ANCIENT EGYPTIAN ASTRONOMER-ASTROLOGER HARKHABI, *c.* 2100 BC

Astronomy, the study of the stars, is the oldest of the sciences. Its goal is to give an accurate mathematical account of how the universe and its component parts came to be. In contrast, astrology is a form of divining – looking into the future by consulting the superior forces held to reside in the wandering denizens of heaven above, believed to influence whatever happens here below. The word 'influence' is key, for in its original medieval guise the power conveyed from above to below was characterized by a flow or flux of rays – a radiance or energy.

Until the 18th-century Age of Enlightenment, when Western culture (and only Western) abandoned belief in the linkage between the powers of mind and matter, astrology was the driving force behind astronomy, for the more precisely one could predict the positions of celestial bodies, the better one could know what their subtle actions might portend.

The beginnings of astronomy go back at least as far as the written record. For example, the cuneiform Tablet of Ammizaduga (Enuma Anu Enlil), dated to the 17th-century BC reign of an Assyrian king, is a thorough astronomical compendium that follows the motion of Venus with omens attending every kink and bend in the celestial love goddess' course:

If on the 28th day of the month of Arahsamna Venus disappeared (in the west), remaining absent in the sky three days, and on the first of the month of Kislev Venus disappeared (in the east), [then] hunger for grain and straw will be in the land; desolation will be wrought.

Modern, scientifically educated people may be troubled by the link between the 'if' and 'then' in this statement, but it is the norm in astrological texts across the world. Take an example from a Maya codex from Mexico written some three

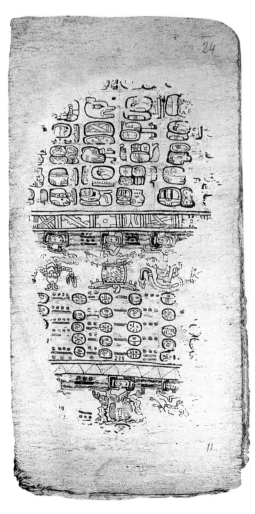

Above *Engraved eagle bones from Le Placard, France, c. 13,500 BC: the notches may be lunar notation. Humans have long been interested in the movements of the planets and stars, the basis of both astronomy and astrology.*

Left *A page from the Paris Codex: the Maya zodiac is represented in this 14th-century codex by various beasts (scorpion, tortoise, vulture, etc.), shown hanging from the segmented body of a serpent representing the sky. In contrast to the Old World 12, there are 13 divisions of the Maya zodiac.*

lion and bull, comprise most of the 12 zones, each of 30 degrees in extent, that go round the sky.

The zodiacal constellations have received a lot of attention in history because they also mark the way of five other bright lights, the planets, or 'wanderers' as the Babylonians called them: swift Mercury, bright white Venus, red Mars, slow and steady Jupiter, and lethargic Saturn. Each has its own periodic cycle and each came to acquire complex attributes. For example, Babylonian Mars was Nergal, who brought the red feverishness of the summer sun that destroyed the crops. Venus, always close to the sun and periodically lost in its

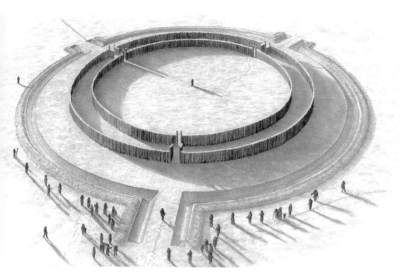

Above *A possible astronomical observatory at Goseck, Germany, dating around 4900 BC and consisting of concentric rings of wooden palisades with three entrances. Some scholars believe the site was designed for the observation of astronomical phenomena such as the movements of the sun, moon and stars, and for keeping track of time.*

Right *The Nebra sky disc, dating from 1600 BC and found at the Mittelberg hill in Germany, in the same region as Goseck. Made from bronze, with gold attachments depicting the moon, the sun's solstices tracked on the horizon and possibly the Pleiades, it is the oldest known astronomical depiction of the night sky in the world.*

millennia later, about the very same celestial object, a male deity in the Mesoamerican pantheon: 'And then on 9 Cimi, in the west, Venus reappears, from the north, having been absent 90 days … woe to the moon, woe to the man, the disease of the second maize crop … woe to night'; or this one from the Tang dynasty in China, 'when the sparkling Deluder [Mars] enters the Southern Dipper and its colour is like blood, then there will be a drought.'

The zodiac

The rationale for astrology is really quite simple. It developed in prehistoric times out of the recognition that the position of the sun influences the seasons, and the phases of the moon affect the tides and the menstrual cycle. Might not then other celestial bodies influence the affairs of men and women?

Astrology focuses primarily on the astronomy of a star-studded corridor that encircles the heavens – a skyway traversed in a year by the sun and in a month by the moon. The Greeks called it the zodiac, a word that means 'circle of animals', for animals, such as the scorpion, light, was the resurrected morning star, Quetzal-coatl, to the Aztec/Mixtec cultures of Mexico who thought of him as a wandering demi-god. Mercury, a wing-footed celestial messenger, with an ear always close to the ground, became the Greek god of gossip.

This assignment of attributes led to further associations; thus metals, herbs, specific organs of the body, even different types of discharge and bodily fluids each came to have specific cosmic associations.

Horoscopic astrology

Ancient civilizations invented their universes to parallel what they experienced in their own terrestrial lives. The Babylonian hierarchical model imitated the social order from royalty through merchant to peasant. It consisted of a series of vertical layers, each occupied by a planet. Because it moved slowest, Saturn lay in the highest; consequently, it was believed to possess the greatest influence. Next came less powerful Jupiter, then Mars, the sun, Venus, Mercury and, weakest of all, the moon.

The seven moving lights also gave their names to the days of the week (p. 239). Like night and day, and like the good and bad times we all experience, the hierarchy of celestial power also followed a bad-good-bad principle of alternation; thus Saturn became the all powerful evil, followed by Jupiter good, Mars evil, etc.

Today's astrology is a remnant of the Greek nativity horoscopic system ('horoscope' literally means to 'observe the hour'), which sought to offer indications about the course of one's life based on aspects of the sky at the place and time of one's birth. This system of astrology relied on predictions not only of a wanderer's whereabouts in the zodiac, but also with respect to a

system of Houses. The first House (affecting yourself, your appearance and your beginnings) is the first 30-degree segment of the zodiac beneath the eastern horizon. It is called the House of the Ascendant and it contains the celestial objects that are just about to cross the local skyline and come into view. Second came the House of Riches; other houses were dedicated to Love, Marriage, Death, Honour, etc. The idea of segmenting the ecliptic by the horizon and according prominence to the first segment below it likely had a practical basis: early agricultural people were all aware that the sun's rays had different effects on their crops at different times of day. Some gardeners still insist that their plants must bask in the morning sun and sun worshippers in many lands are required to face the sun's first rays which appear in the east at dawn – and so they must 'orient' themselves.

How astronomy nurtured astrology

The quest for precision in observational astronomy was aided by two developments. First, especially in the Old World, sophisticated instrumentation was

The late Egyptian zodiac ceiling of a chapel on the roof of the temple at Dendera (c. 30 BC) depicts 12 constellations and shows Venus in Pisces, Jupiter in Cancer, Mercury in Virgo, Saturn in Libra and Mars in Capricorn.

The Egyptian merkhet *was used as a shadow clock to mark the hours of the day, or at night as a device to sight the meridian and the stars crossing it. This example, of c. 600 BC, belonged to an Egyptian priest called Bes, son of Khonsirdis, who was the Observer of Hours at the Temple of Horus in Edfu, Upper Egypt.*

developed. It began in the Greek world and rose to great heights in Islam, which inherited and enhanced the astronomical and astrological texts and instruments of the Classical world. A second and much earlier development took place in 6th-century BC Babylonia. Arithmetic techniques were invented for predicting celestial phenomena, largely for producing astrological omens relating to affairs of state. This included techniques for the separation of complex motions into components that could be expressed by mathematical functions that could then be recombined to make a more precise prediction. The Greeks further honed this rational, abstract approach by devising earth-centred geometrical models, the forerunners of the heliocentric (sun-centred) model devised by Copernicus during the 15th-century scientific Renaissance.

Meanwhile, Chinese astronomy was an activity of bureaucrats rather than scholars or priests. Star catalogues appeared there as early as 400 BC and later epochs saw the development of large sundials and celestial spheres. However, the direction of such studies was unmis-

takably astrological. Chinese astronomers developed elaborate indications for different kinds of planetary conjunctions. For example, *chou*, *cheng* and *ling* referred, respectively, to one planet passing around another, descending from above, and moving upward from below. Each connoted a different omen.

Judged by modern standards, given the crudeness of both the equipment and the techniques employed, we can only marvel at the accuracy of planetary tables in both East and West produced before the invention of the telescope (in the early 17th century), an impression that is only reinforced when we confront Maya eclipse prediction tables, which were also based on the invention of a higher form of mathematics. These artifacts stand as a testimony to the fruits of dogged persistence and repeated observation without recourse to a sophisticated technology upon which we have become so dependent that we are often blinded to the possibility of ancient human achievement.

Right *A drawing of the Mithraeum of Sette Sfere, Ostia, near Rome, a 1st-century AD place of worship for a military cult that competed (unsuccessfully) with early Christianity. Zodiacal symbols carved on the benches are in the order in which they stood the night the world was created.*

Calendars & the Measurement of Time

58

Time rules life

Motto of the US National Association of Watch Manufacturers

If there is a human invention heaven sent it must surely be the calendar. Throughout the world the development of the calendar in its various guises (it was invented many times in different places) is rooted in astronomical observation (p. 235). People created the ordered plan for human activity that we call the calendar for a host of reasons, ranging from the natural demands of agriculture to the more rigid dictates of a state religion. Behind it all lay the desire to predict the future. But in order to set future dates we must learn from the past and the most reliable, periodically predictable events derived from record-keeping are those that take place in the clockwork sky.

If we dissect the calendar we discover specific celestial bodies behind the machinery. The year is marked by the return of the rising sun to the same position on the horizon, the shortest length of shadow cast by a stick, or the reappearance of a bright star lost in the light of the sun. These events can be correlated with more unwieldy phenomena on which life depends, such as the budding of a certain plant, the advent of the rains or the onset of of a river's inundation.

While most ancient civilizations based their calendars on direct observation, for instance sighting the first visible crescent moon to begin a month, those with complex social hierarchies that included systems of notation, such as the Maya of Mesoamerica and the Babylonians of the Near East, honed the calendar into a work of precision, thus requiring less direct dependence on viewing the natural world. As culture processed nature, particularly in the Western world, it encapsulated time in the mechanical clock, which, rather than merely aiding humanity in making life's plan, would ultimately evolve into the personal timepiece now strapped to our wrist – a simulacrum that has come to rule us, as the epigraph quoted above suggests. The waterclock (p. 242) is an excellent example of early time control.

The first calendars

The earliest calendars may have been simple notched sticks or fragments of bone used to count the 29 or 30 days between visible new or full moons. Kept by a hunter, such a record might have served to mark out intervals when moonlit night-time hunting could take place. In a pregnant mother's hands the same record could have been used to tally the months between the conception and birth of her child.

The highly organized chiefdom that built Neolithic Stonehenge on Salisbury Plain (*c.* 3000 BC) constructed a calendar in stone by erecting the main axis of the megalithic circle to mark sunrise on midsummer's day, the summer solstice. This is the longest day of the year when the sun god ranges highest in the northern sky, thus bringing a bountiful harvest. It has also been suggested that the midwinter sunset may have been of significance to the builders of Stonehenge. A connection between the sun's seasonal movement and funerary rites can be found at a contemporary site in Ireland. At Newgrange, the rising sun at winter solstice illuminates a narrow, 19-m (29.5-ft) long passageway that leads to a burial chamber. The December solstice (now Christmas) was marked by a Roman festival to celebrate the return from the southern climes of *Sol Invictus*, the unconquerable sun. The turning points of humanity's ultimate source of light and life have always been holidays to celebrate.

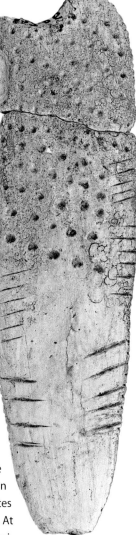

Bone plaque from Les Eyzies, France, 25,000 to 30,000 years old and marked with rows of holes and notches. These have been interpreted as lunar calendars and may therefore represent an early attempt at organizing and recording time.

*Stonehenge, at midwinter sunset. This megalithic monument, first built around 3000 BC and developed in several stages, can be seen as a giant calendar in stone. Viewed from the centre, the summer solstice sun rises over the Heelstone (diagram, **below**), and other alignments to the sun and full moon at midsummer and midwinter also probably figured in its design.*

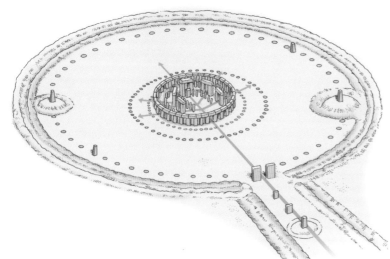

at 29.53-day rather than 30-day intervals, fell out of line with the year, nor by the misalignment of the 365-day canonic year within the actual seasonal year of 365.24 days. The invention of the leap year to take account of the latter maladjustment between nature and culture did not take place until the time of Julius Caesar.

Not all years have lunar months. For example, perfect geometry combined with an accident of geography conspired to create a native calendar that baffled 18th-century Dutch anthropologists working in Indonesia. In tropical latitudes the celestial guideposts for setting up the year are not

The year

Ancient Egypt gave Western civilization the 365-day numerical count that makes up the year of the seasons. Early Nilotic people had noted that the annual flooding of their river occurred very close to the time the brightest star in the sky, Sothis (Sirius to us), was glimpsed for a few moments in the eastern twilit sky, having been blotted out for the previous few weeks by the solar glare. This first sighting event, coupled with the summer solstice, constituted a reliable double time check indicating that the year clock needed to be reset and the count of the months begun anew.

The Egyptians divided their year into 12 months of 30 days, with five extra days tacked on at the end. They seem to have been bothered neither by the fact that the phases of the moon, which repeat

__Right__ Javanese calendar keepers used an unusual sundial that divided up the year by following the noontime shadow created by a gnomon (vertical rod), over equal intervals of length (rather than time) on the base plate; result: unequal months.

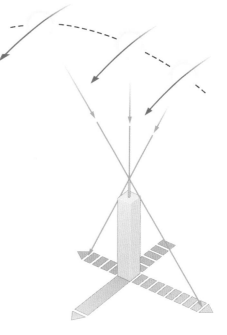

the same as those in temperate climates, consequently the calendars developed in this region of the world can be quite different.

In Java (latitude 7° S), the sun crosses the overhead point, or zenith, twice a year. When it stands on the meridian north of the zenith at noon on the June solstice, the shadow length of a gnomon (vertical rod) measured to the south is exactly double the length when the sun at noon lies at the December solstice south of the zenith, then projecting the shadow to the north. Javanese chronologists halved the shorter length segment and quartered the longer; this yielded a 12-month calendar with months ranging in length between 43 and 23 days, for the solar shadow does not cover equal lengths in equal periods of time. Once they had captured the perfect spatial symmetry of their unique timepiece, calendar keepers altered particular intervals by a day or two to correspond more precisely to agricultural practices and other human activities.

The week

If the calendar year is marked by a denizen of the sky, the week is an invention that may have been guided as much by the stomach. The period of the week, be it eight days as reckoned by the Inca of Peru, the seven of the Western calendar, or the 10 of Egypt, is a good measure of the time it takes to harvest a manageable load of fruits or vegetables, take them to a nearby market, dispense them before they overripen and then return to the field for another round. This so-called 'market week' was likely adjusted to seven days in the 1st-millennium BC Sumerian world to accommodate heavenly connections. Not only is seven days the interval between quarter phases of the moon (e.g. first quarter to full), but also it corresponds to the number of visible planets (Mercury, Venus, Mars, Jupiter and Saturn), plus the sun and the moon, that move about the zodiac (p. 236).

The months & years

Years need not be 365 days long. The Trobriand Islanders of the South Pacific began their year with the time of appearance of a spawning marine annelid, *Milamala*, after which they named their first month. In late October (our time) the worm

turns up on the surface of the sea to release its genital product. This phenomenon served as a signal to begin the gardening season. Islanders celebrated by gathering the worm in vast quantities, toasting and eating it. The Trobriand calendar ran 10 months, counted from the first full moon following the worm's appearance; then it expired. The remaining time in the yearly cycle went uncounted, for the fields lay fallow: without human activity there simply was no time. When the worm reappeared they reset the year clock. The Inca of Peru did much the same, marking a 327-day agricultural year by the first sighting of the Pleiades, which they named *collca*, or the storehouse; the remaining 37 days of the year cycle, literally dead time, was not tallied.

Above *A Roman calendar, with the months (the circle in the centre), the dates (at the sides) and the seven days of the week (at the top) marked with pegs. The concept of the leap year was invented in the time of Julius Caesar.*

Below *In Mesoamerica the oldest and most important calendar was the sacred 260-day cycle, with 20 day names and 13 day numbers, represented by the figures and dots in this codex from Mexico. In the centre is the fire god Xiuhtecuhtli, who was also god of the year and by extension of time itself.*

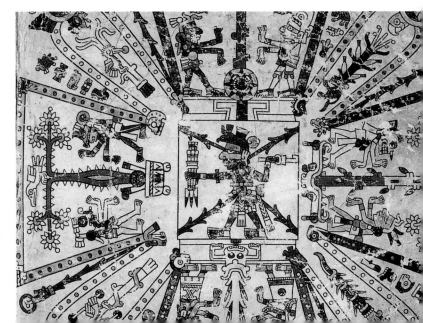

Right A Roman sundial of the 1st century AD. While such devices grew increasingly precise, they yielded unequal hours at different seasons of the year. And as Seneca (AD 65) remarked: 'I cannot tell you the hours exactly: it is easier to get agreement among philosophers than among clocks'.

KEY DATES

365-day year	ancient Egypt
sundial	15th century BC, China
7-day week	1st millennium BC, Sumer
calendar	600 BC, Mesoamerica

Though the Chinese developed sundials, just as in the West (their earliest mention dates from the 15th-century BC Shang Dynasty), the moon figured more prominently in setting up the ancient Chinese calendar. Han (1st-century AD) star charts indicate a division of the sky into 18 lunar mansions or houses. Unlike the zodiacs of the West these are centred along the celestial equator rather than the ecliptic.

Time is life, and the notion that the calendars we create reveal what we do in our lives resonates in the names given to the months by cultures all over the world, each reflecting the primary activity that takes place in that period. Likewise, the names of the days of the Maya 20-day month count refer to plants and animals that abound in the rain forest of Central America.

Below The Tower of the Winds, Athens, dating from the 5th century BC. Its interior workings apparently included a waterclock, with tanks of water dripping through at a measured rate; it also had an elaborate sundial on the exterior.

The Maya uniquely compounded their calendar cycles into units of 260-days, which may have originated in the recognition, at least as early as 600 BC (the earliest dated Mesoamerican calendar from the highlands of southern Mexico), that this interval contains a whole multiple of the numbers of fingers and toes on the human body as well as being a close approximation to the human gestation period. It also approximates to nine lunar months and the average period of appearance of the planet Venus, which they worshipped as a creator god, in the evening or morning sky. Finally the 260-day period beats in 3/2 harmony with the eclipse cycle: truly a calendar for all seasons.

The day

Our Western preoccupation for dividing up the day into hours came from the Babylonians, whose sexagesimal or base-six counting system (p. 247) split 24 hours into 60 minutes and each minute into 60 seconds. This penchant for precision, revealed in the development of the ever more precise Roman sundial and re-acquired in the 6th-century AD Christian monastery, where the Rule of St Benedict specified when to recite the hours, is not shared by all cultures.

Many seem instead content to point an extended arm in unmeasured angles skyward to indicate meal-time, milking-time or bringing-in-the-cattle time. Thus it is the human hand, rather than the hand of the clock that came to mimic it, that serves the same purpose in micro-time as the phases of the moon do in macro-time.

WATERCLOCKS

The mechanical clock, wrote one historian, was the single most influential invention in the West. Its invention early in the 12th century solved the problem of the variable and seasonally wandering hours that resided in the sundial's shadow. But sundials and mechanical clocks are not the only ways to measure duration. Banded candles, colour-coded to tally the hour of the day or night, and clepsydrae (waterclocks) were popular in China and Europe during the Middle Ages. The Tower of the Winds in Classical Athens was said to have housed a waterclock. Most operated via a falling float suspended in a tank, from the bottom of which water was allowed to drip. The float was attached to an arrow that moved over a calibrated scale. One drawback: because the pressure was

eased as the amount of water diminished, time ran fastest on a full tank. The Chinese managed to solve this problem by devising compensating tanks to yield a steady flow. They also developed an ingenious hybrid hydro-mechanical technology, essentially a mechanical clock powered by a mill wheel.

Maps & Cartography

59

Let our young men see and contemplate daily every land and all the seas and whatever cities, peoples, nations Rome's most invincible rulers either restore out of respect, or conquer by valour, or restrain by fear. ... Now, now at last it is a pleasure to look at a picture of the world, since we see nothing in it which is not ours.

ORATOR SPEAKING IN GAUL, AFTER BARBARIAN INCURSIONS INTO THE
ROMAN EMPIRE HAD BEEN REPULSED, LATE AD 290S

Maps reflect spatial awareness which may in turn be derived from a great variety of perspectives – local, regional, global, celestial. To judge by surviving artwork on rock and other durable surfaces, it seems credible that prehistoric craftsmen of the Old World sometimes sought to record such awareness, although to modern eyes their representations are so enigmatic as to defy confident interpretation.

We have a sounder understanding of the images preserved from the subsequent civilizations of the ancient Near East which developed writing. The Babylonians in particular made remarkable advances in mathematics and astronomy, as well as in surveying. Babylonian clay tablets from as early as the 2nd millennium BC preserve plans of buildings, estates and settlements, some just sketches, but others carefully drawn to scale. Other tablets represent the world and the stars. Egypt, too, offers a comparable range and sophistication of cartographic expertise from the Old Kingdom onwards, in the form of papyri and tomb reliefs, even including sketches of the underworld, marking farms and routes by land and water.

Mapmaking in China

The origins of mapmaking in China are elusive, not least because very few early maps survive. It is clear, however, that already by the 2nd century BC there was a grasp of scale, and that mapmaking tools had been developed – graduated rods, squares, plumb lines, compasses for drawing circles, sighting tubes. Moreover, maps of all kinds were highly valued by members of the educated elite, who were often sent to take administrative and military responsibility for areas not previously familiar to them; in fact some of the earliest surviving maps come from the tombs of senior officials.

As a medium, maps in China were closely integrated with other forms of expression.

Left *A Babylonian world map on a clay tablet, dating to c. 600 BC, designed to show the relationship of known regions with remote ones beyond the Ocean.*

Below *An Egyptian map drawn c. 1160 BC for a quarrying expedition in the Eastern Desert. Various rock types are distinguished by different colours.*

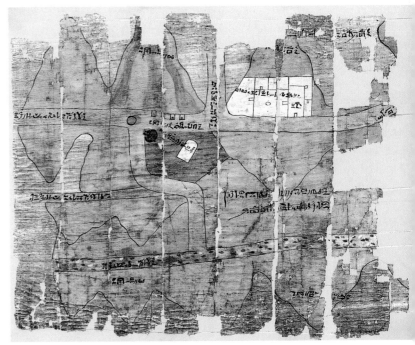

243

A topographic map on silk that was folded and placed in the tomb of a Chinese high official (possibly a general) who was buried at Mawangdui, near Changsha, in 168 BC.

Ideally, the mapmaker should be not only a draftsman and calligrapher, but also an expert on literary and historical texts, and even a poet. Multicoloured maps were drawn, inscribed and printed, on a great variety of surfaces – silk, wood, paper, bronze, stone, as well as the walls of caves and tombs; even three-dimensional relief models were also created.

The 'scientific' nature of maps covered by a grid should not be overstated, however, because such grids were merely a scaling device, not a latitude/longitude network such as the Greeks developed. In addition, Chinese mapmakers believed the earth to be flat, so they never addressed problems of projection.

Many Chinese maps were less concerned to be complete and accurate representations of reality than to render landscape – mountains and rivers especially – in a pictorial, impressionistic style; maps of this artistic type continued to be made in the traditional way right up to the end of the 19th

century. The Chinese noun *tu*, used to signify 'map', is itself an ambiguous term which can also mean 'plan' or 'picture'.

The Greek world-view & maps

A strong sense of spatial awareness infuses the earliest Greek literature – the two great epic poems, the *Iliad* and *Odyssey*, attributed to Homer. The vision of Earth here as a finite island-space encircled by boundless Ocean is one that – despite repeated refutation – persisted among many Greeks, and, later, Romans, throughout Classical antiquity. Greek world-view expanded at the time of the 'colonization' movement (8th to 6th centuries BC), when many migrated to settle in Sicily, South Italy, the Black Sea shores and even as far west as Spain. During the 5th century BC, the historian Herodotus tapped fresh knowledge of the Persian empire, North Africa and the western Mediterranean to challenge the belief that Ocean fully encircled the world as known to the Greeks (what he newly calls the *oikoumene*, literally the 'inhabited' world). He envisages the existence of other parts of the earth which may be inhabited, although the peoples there are unknown and quite impossible to contact because the *oikoumene* is bounded by water to the West and elsewhere by vast deserts.

Greek thinkers in Ionia, on the eastern seaboard of the Aegean, imagined the earth as a flattish, concave disc with a breadth three times its depth. A 'map of the world engraved on bronze, showing all the seas and rivers' is recorded as being in the possession of the ruler of Ionian Miletus *c.* 500 BC: how it would have looked, we have no idea. The concept of earth as spherical and forming part of a solar system stemmed initially from theories associated with the shadowy thinker Pythagoras, and over time gained much respect.

During the 4th century a layering of the globe by zones was first conceived – arctic, temperate, equatorial and antarctic – divided by two tropics and an equator. Concurrent efforts to measure the globe's circumference confirmed that the *oikoumene* was only small in relation to the whole, thus re-igniting speculation that there were peoples living elsewhere – across the western ocean, for example (in Atlantis, as imagined by Plato), or south of the equator as a mirror image of Europe, Asia and Africa (hence such names as Antipodes, or the 'counterworld' Antichthon).

The expeditions of Alexander the Great deep into the Persian empire and beyond during the late 4th century BC tremendously stimulated Greek interest in their surroundings. Above all, at the Museum in Alexandria, Eratosthenes devised a means of mapping the earth, addressing especially the issue of projection – the problem of representing the earth's curvature on a flat surface. His methodology was sound, and he grasped the need for precise physical and astronomical data. To obtain such information, however, was frequently impossible, not least because the units and the instruments to measure both time and distance accurately were lacking (in fact longitude could not be established with precision until the 18th century AD). The writings of Eratosthenes are lost, but his advances clearly underpin Ptolemy's surviving *Geography* of the 2nd century AD, which is (in modern terms) a Geographic Information Systems co-ordinates databank, offering the means to create a map of the entire globe, or parts of it, at the projection and scale chosen by the user. Any map that Ptolemy himself may have produced following his own instructions is lost, but many attempts by others from the Middle Ages onwards survive.

Ancient attitudes to maps

Ptolemy's *Geography* forms the foundation of modern Western cartography. In all likelihood, however, throughout antiquity few Greeks, and even fewer Romans, showed marked interest in maps. A map would not have baffled those who had received some education, but typically it would have no special appeal to them either. This may ultimately be a subjective matter of fashion and mindset. The fact remains that no regular standards for such fundamentals as how a map should be oriented and presented were ever developed. There was not even a specific term in either Greek or Latin to match our word 'map'. There were no general-purpose maps, nor mass production; in this era without printing, any but the simplest map would always be a challenge to copy. A set of maps comprising an atlas was unknown (the term dates to the 16th century), as was the notion of a discipline of cartography (a 19th century formulation). Between them, rulers, generals, sailors and traders evidently all but ignored the practical assistance that maps could offer.

Roman mapping

At the local level, large-scale maps or plans of landholdings were certainly made, and displayed, for legal and fiscal purposes. The practice was most widespread in Greek (Ptolemaic) Egypt and in Roman communities. Roman land surveyors (*agrimensores*) became a well-established professional group, whose extensive work is reflected in surviving plans on marble from Arausio (Orange, in France), and in a 'centuriated' (chequerboard) division of land still visible

A groma *reconstructed from metal parts found at Pompeii. This was the Roman surveyor's most important instrument, with which he was able to establish straight lines and right-angles with impressive accuracy.*

Below *The British Isles drawn according to Ptolemy's (inaccurate) co-ordinates.*

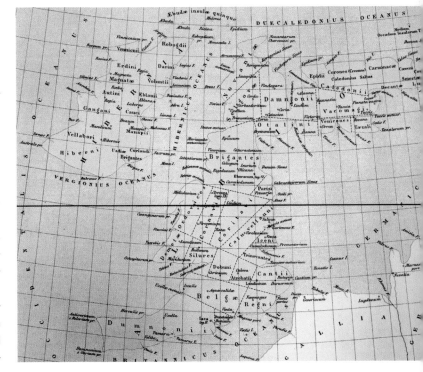

in many Mediterranean regions. There is much less evidence of corresponding activity in the Roman cities by surveyors, who typically worked to a scale of 1:240.

One outstanding example, however, is the (235-sq-m/2530-sq-ft) marble plan of Rome itself, made around AD 200, of which only about 10 per cent is known. It was oriented southeast, and its placement high on the wall of a temple indicates that it was made to impress viewers, rather than for any utilitarian function.

Lists of settlements and the distances between them along recognized routes were frequently compiled and used by travellers – termed *periploi*

KEY DATES

use of scale	2nd millennium BC, Babylonia
projection	3rd century BC, Alexandria
mapmaking tools	2nd century BC, China

in Greek for sea journeys, *itineraria* in Latin for land ones. To create maps using such data was evidently less common, although land routes do feature prominently on by far the largest known ancient map, an ingenious Roman masterpiece from perhaps the 4th century AD, surviving only in an incomplete medieval copy measuring 6.82 m x 34 cm (22 x 1 ft), usually referred to as Peutinger's Map, or Table. Its purpose was not least to glorify Rome's sway over the *oikoumene*. The same is true of the map at the school of rhetoric in Augustodunum (modern Autun, in France) praised at the head of this article.

Left *Reassembled fragments of the marble plan of Rome, c. AD 200, reflecting the detail of this painstaking, precisely scaled record. Even individual columns and steps are marked.*

Below *Section of Peutinger's Map (oriented north), with part of southern Asia Minor, Cyprus and Syria. Note the virtual elimination of open water in order to highlight land features and routes.*

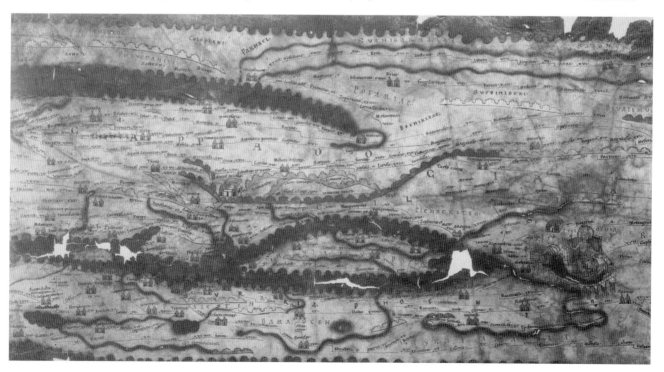

Mathematics & Counting Devices

Numeracy predates literacy by several thousand years. Across the Middle East, from Turkey to Iran, Neolithic societies used tiny clay or stone counters to keep accounts of stored or traded goods. By the 4th millennium BC counters were stored in clay envelopes, sometimes sealed or marked with impressions of the counters. They are typically found at ancient urban centres or outposts such as Susa, southwest Iran, Uruk, in southern Iraq, and Habuba Kabira in eastern Syria, as part of an assemblage of bureaucracy.

Counting was also a primary function of the written record in the earliest state societies of the late 4th millennium BC, as witnessed by the ivory labels counting prestige grave goods in Predynastic Naqada in Egypt, or the thousands of clay tablets recording the internal economies of large cities like Uruk and Susa, and even tiny agricultural settlements such as Jemdet Nasr in Iraq. Cuneiform numerical signs were simply stylized representations of the pre-literate counting tokens – which

may well still have been in use – with different number bases for different commodities. The first school mathematics exercises, from Uruk, are characterized by the use of conspicuously round numbers in problems to find the areas of fields.

Mathematical exercises

But the first large-scale evidence of mathematics as an intellectual activity appears in the Middle Bronze Age. From Egypt, the Rhind papyrus (*c.* 1560 BC) contains arithmetical tables and model problems. About a dozen mathematical papyri are known. Babylonia has left us many thousands of schoolboy exercises in the memorization of multiplication tables using the sexagesimal (base 60) place-value system and hundreds of mathematical problems in geometry, concrete algebra and other topics with no real-life applications. Intermediate calculations were mostly performed either mentally or on clay scratch-pads, although there is

Above *Early Egyptian kings, queens and nobles were buried with their belongings carefully inventoried and labelled. This ivory label from Naqada, c. 3000 BC, was originally attached to a necklace of 400 beads belonging to Queen Neithhotep.*

Left *Tiny clay accounting tokens were used by administrators in the nascent city states of the 4th-millennium BC Middle East to record economic transactions. Their standard shapes and sizes were the precursors to the first written numerals. On the left of the photograph is a sealed clay envelope, 65 mm (2.6 in) in diameter, from the Iranian city of Susa, marked to show how many counters it contained.*

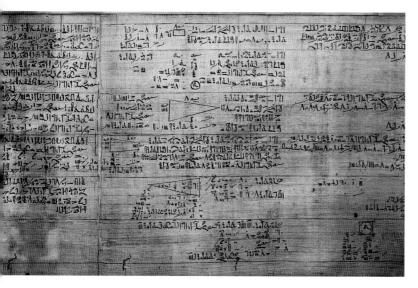

Above *The Rhind papyrus was copied by an Egyptian scribe named Ahmose in c. 1560 BC. This section shows exercises in plane geometry.*

Above *Babylonian schoolboys did their homework and rough exercises on small clay tablets in the 18th century BC. This example from southern Iraq, is an idealized problem on finding the areas of adjacent fields of lengths 1, 2 and 3. The student has left his tiny calculations underneath.*

Above right *Very few ancient copies of Euclid's* Elements, *written in c. 300 BC, survive. This fragment cites propositions from the beginning of Book I.*

some evidence for the use of counters with five-columned accounting boards.

The Indian numerical system, as witnessed by the Vedas (ancient Hindu scriptures) of the 1st millennium BC, seems always to have been decimal, with a little sexagesimal interference from Babylonia. The Vedas describe geometrical methods for constructing brick fire-altars and for transforming one design into another of equal area. In the 1st millennium BC, Buddhists and Jains considered mathematics to be a cosmological and philosophical tool. More prosaically, merchants used 'counting pits': counters in a row of shallow depressions, one for each power of 10. In AD 500 the Aryabhatiya, the earliest surviving Sanskrit mathematical treatise, presented rules for solving equations and summing series in the form of rhyming couplets for easy memorization.

The zero symbol has three different functions, two of which are necessary only in place-value systems (which do not use different numerical signs to represent numbers of different absolute value). Zero markers in the middle of numbers (e.g. 207) are first attested in cuneiform around 1600 BC; zeros at the end or beginning of numbers (e.g. 0.0045 or 27,000) are first attested in the astronomical works of Ptolemy in Roman Egypt, c. AD 150, who was using an adapted form of the Babylonian

sexagesimal place-value system. A notation for zero in the sense of 'nothing at all' did not develop until the early 7th century in the Indian Sanskrit mathematical tradition.

The earliest known Chinese numerals, which also use the decimal place-value system, are found on Shang oracle bones from 1500–1200 BC. From at least 500 BC ivory and bamboo counting rods were used for arithmetic and even algebra, by laying them out in standard arrangements with red for positive and black for negative numbers. Some ten Chinese mathematical treatises are known for the period 500 BC–AD 500, including the famous Nine Chapters on the Mathematical Arts. In common with many other early mathematical cultures they are concerned with the extraction of square and cube roots, the Pythagorean rule, linear and quadratic equations, astronomical calculations, as well as arithmetical rules and magic squares.

Greek & Roman mathematics

In this light, the mathematical traditions of the eastern Mediterranean are decidedly anomalous.

clay counters	4th millennium BC, Middle East
tables & problems	2nd millennium BC, Egypt & Iraq
decimal system	2nd millennium BC, China
	1st millennium BC, India

Left *A vase of the 4th century BC shows a bearded Persian tax collector calculating his income on a counting board. Letters on the abacus indicate the value of the counters. He holds a wax tablet with the words, 'a hundred talents', perhaps the weight of the tribute.*

The Greek-speaking world needed accountants, surveyors, merchants, engineers and tax assessors as much or as little as other ancient societies. But the extraordinary prestige and status accorded to the 5th-century BC formalization of mathematics is encapsulated in Aristophanes' satire quoted above. Strepsiades, misunderstanding the student to mean 'land for all', sees mathematics as a political tool for the redistribution of wealth; whereas the latter, intending 'land in the abstract', is presumably more concerned with questions such as the properties of circles and triangles. The diagram-theorem proof tradition of elite mathematics for leisured intellectuals culminated in Euclid's *Elements* in Egyptian Alexandria, *c.* 300 BC.

The numerically grounded, problem-orientated Asian tradition of mathematics resurfaced in the eastern Mediterranean soon after, hybridizing with the Euclidean tradition. Practical applications of mathematics to ballistics, architecture and mechanics came to the fore, as epitomized by the works of Archimedes, Vitruvius and Heron. Scholars such as Pappus and Hypatia re-edited the works of their predecessors, wrote learned commentaries on them and tried to piece together the history of mathematics.

Neither the Greek nor the Roman systems of decimal number notation lent themselves well to recorded calculation, as they lacked the concept of place-value. One solution was to use counting boards and, in Roman times, abacuses. Another, adopted by astronomers from Hipparchus on, was to adapt the sexagesimal place-value system to Greek notation. Thus we still measure time and angle in 60s, just as the Sumerians counted sheep with clay tokens in the 4th millennium BC.

Mathematics in the Americas

In Mesoamerica, Zapotec, Maya, Mixtec and Aztec mathematical activity mostly concerned complex calendrical calculations in base 20. The results of their calculations are recorded on monumental stone inscriptions and also on bark-paper codices, but it is not known exactly how the calculations were made. Zapotec-Maya notation denoted 5 by a bar and 1 by a dot, but from the 8th century AD onward the Maya also used elaborate 'head glyphs', each identified with a particular deity, for the numbers 1 to 13.

Centre *Many scenes on 8th-century Maya pottery show scribes doing mathematics. Here Pauahtun, the god of scribes, is teaching mathematics to two attentive students. He gestures to his codex with a brush pen, while speaking the numbers '11, 13, 12, 9, 8, 7'.*

Below *Ancient counting instruments bear very little resemblance to the later bead abacus, except for three small Roman examples in bronze. As seen in this modern replica they have separate columns for 1–4 and 5 in each power of 10 (I, X, C, etc from right to left) and two further columns to the right for money. The counters are attached for easy portability.*

Coinage & Money

Socrates tells Adeimantus that the ideal city will have coinage: 'Well then; in the city itself how will they exchange with one another what they make? It was, after all, for this purpose that we created a community and founded a city.' 'Clearly', he said, 'by buying and selling.' 'And from this there will come into being a market, and coinage as a token for the purpose of exchange.' 'Certainly.'

PLATO, 4TH CENTURY BC

Right *A silver tetradrachm of Athens, late 5th century BC. On one side is the head of Athena, the patron deity of the city, and on the other is an owl, the bird sacred to Athena, with the first three letters of the Greek word meaning 'of the Athenians'.*

Below *An electrum one-third stater, c. 650–600 BC, from Lydia, with a lion's head on the obverse and a punch mark on the reverse. The earliest coins were made of electrum, a natural alloy of gold and silver, that was found in the River Pactolus. Because the proportions of the metals could vary, electrum was soon replaced by silver as the most common coinage metal. All coins have two sides – obverse and reverse – and the earliest examples only have a design on one side, with a crude punch-mark on the other.*

Although coinage was not invented in the West until the 7th century BC, money has existed for a great deal longer than that. Some of the earliest written documents from ancient Mesopotamia and Egypt, dating back to the 3rd millennium BC, contain references to the making of payments in silver. Standards were established for weights in both Mesopotamia and Egypt (p. 253). Since metal was used to make payments by weight, the form it took could vary – ingots, wire or rings are all known.

Metal would only have been available to the wealthiest members of these societies, and other commodities, such as grain, could also be used as money. But most transactions at this time were probably conducted by barter.

The invention of coinage in the Greek world

The first coins, which were made towards the end of the 7th century BC in the kingdom of Lydia in western Turkey, were a natural development from the silver ingots of Mesopotamia and Egypt. What distinguished the earliest coins was that they bore designs indicating the issuing authority, thereby providing a guarantee of their quality, and they were made to consistent weight standards. People could use them in transactions without having to weigh them every time.

During the 6th century BC, coinage spread both eastwards to the Achaemenid empire and westwards across the Aegean Sea to the Greek islands and mainland. The Greek world at this time consisted of many small city states and in the space of a little over a hundred years over 250 cities, from Spain in the west to the Black Sea in the east, had started producing their own coins with designs reflecting the badge of each individual city. As we see from the quotation above, issuing coins was thought to be one of the normal functions of a city state.

During the 5th century BC Athens became the leading power in the Greek world. Much of the city's power was based on the wealth unlocked by the discovery of silver mines at Laurium, enabling the city to produce coins in large quantities which circulated widely across the eastern Mediterranean. In the following century, the power of Athens was eclipsed by the Macedonian kingdom of Alexander the Great, who established an empire stretching from Greece to the borders of India and produced the first world coinage.

China & India

Money was not the sole preserve of the cultures of the Near East and the Mediterranean. Chinese inscriptions show that cowrie shells were used as

250

money in the 13th century BC, and bronze copies of these shells date back to around 1000 BC. The first coins from China seem to date to the late 7th or early 6th centuries BC, when China consisted of several independent states. These were cast in bronze in the form of spades or knives. Later, at the end of the 3rd century BC, the Qin dynasty, which ruled a united China, started issuing round coins, also cast from bronze, with a square hole in the centre, known as 'cash'. These continued down to the 20th century AD and no precious-metal coins were issued in China until recent times. The copper 'cash' coins had a low value; for high-value transactions barter seems to have been the norm.

The earliest coins from the Indian subcontinent date to the 4th century BC and were made by the Achaemenid empire of Persia which at that time extended into India. The Achaemenid empire had itself first started issuing coins in its western provinces in about 600 BC. The first Indian coins are made of silver and are known as 'punch-marked', as the designs were applied, to one side only, with a series of small punches carrying symbols, but no inscriptions. A little later, in the 3rd century BC, we start to find copper coins cast in square moulds.

Rome

At the time of Alexander the Great, Rome was still a minor city at the periphery of the Greek world and it only began producing coins in the 3rd century BC. Rome's earliest coins reflect two entirely separate traditions: its earliest silver coins follow Greek models – some even have the name of the city in Greek. At the same time, however, Rome was also producing

unwieldy bronze currency, reflecting a totally separate Italic tradition. These did not, however, survive for long, and by 200 BC the coinage of Rome consisted of a silver coin, the 'denarius', supported by a range of six bronze coins, from an 'as' to an 'uncia', which circulated at a fixed exchange rate with the silver coin.

During the 2nd and 1st centuries BC Rome gradually annexed the whole of the Mediterranean world, as well as much of northern and central Europe. At this time Rome was still a republic and her coin designs follow in the tradition of Greek city coinages with designs that depict deities. In 31 BC, however, Augustus emerged the winner from a series of civil wars between generals. As the founder of the Roman empire, he established the tradition that all Roman coins should bear the emperor's portrait.

In its first two and a half centuries the Roman empire maintained a tri-metallic system with coins in gold, silver and bronze, circulating at a fixed exchange rate. This broke down during the 3rd century AD when the combination of a shortage of silver and external pressures on the frontiers of the empire led the imperial authorities to debase the silver coinage, so that by AD 270 it contained no more than 1 or 2 per cent of silver. This had two consequences: first, the bronze coinage became unviable and ceased to be issued and, secondly, the debased silver coins (known as 'radiates') were issued in ever greater quantities. It has been estimated that the emperor Tetricus I (AD 271–74) was issuing a million coins a day, a scale not equalled

Above *A bronze flat-handle spade of the Beiqui kingdom, China.*

Above left *A square copper cast coin of the Mauryan empire, India, 3rd century BC. This coin has the symbols of an elephant, bull's head and standard.*

A Chinese coin mould. The coins were round with a square hole in the centre; such coins were known as 'cash'.

payment in silver	3rd millennium BC, Mesopotamia & Egypt
cowrie shells	13th century BC, China
metal coinage	7th century BC, Turkey
cacao beans	pre-Columbian, Americas

Above *A cast bronze currency bar made in Rome about 280 BC and weighing around 1.5 kg (3.3 lb). Perhaps it was these objects that the Roman historian Livy had in mind when he wrote that upper-class Romans used to carry their money about with them in carts. The elephant design is likely to be a reference to wars the Romans fought against the Greek king Pyrrhus, who used elephants in battle.*

Right *Spondylus shell necklace, Peru, 15th century AD. The shell, with its rich orange colour, was highly prized by the Incas.*

Below *A gold 'solidus' of Constantine the Great, AD 307–37, minted in Siscia (modern Sisak, Croatia). This coin is unusual because Constantine's name and titles appear on the reverse of the coin and he is shown with his head upturned. Constantine was the first Christian emperor and it is probably this coin to which the church historian Eusebius refers when he states that the emperor 'directed his likeness to be stamped on a gold coin with his eyes uplifted in the posture of prayer to God'.*

until the Industrial Revolution. This debasement and increase in production led to price inflation that became endemic for the next 150 years, but its consequences were by no means all bad. The availability of large numbers of low-value coins meant that coin use became far more widespread among the inhabitants of the Roman empire.

Production on a massive scale continued during the 4th century, when the coinage comprised gold coins known as 'solidi' and debased silver or bronze coins. In the West, Roman coinage came to an end during the 5th century AD, as Roman rule was replaced by that of the barbarian successor states, many of which produced their own copies of Roman coins. In the East, however, Roman coinage continued for another thousand years until the fall of Constantinople to the Turks in 1453. The Islamic states, established from the 7th century AD onwards, derived their coinage from the Byzantine empire.

The Americas

Although the peoples of the Americas had developed advanced civilizations long before their first contacts with Europeans, our knowledge of their currency systems is based entirely on Spanish accounts, written a few years after Columbus' first arrival in the Americas. Aztec records show bagfuls of cacao beans – the raw ingredient of chocolate (p. 120) – being used to make payments, and early

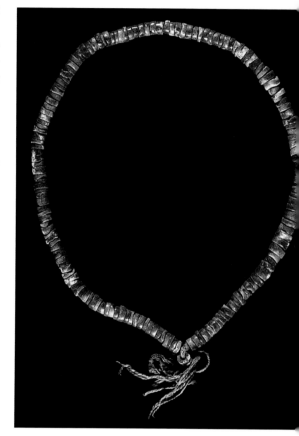

Spanish settlers in Mexico also report their use as money. Further south, among the Inca of Peru and Bolivia, the most valued item was the shell of the spondylus, the spiny oyster.

Gold was not used as money, although of course large quantities of jewelry and other artifacts were made from it in the Americas. In North America the first British settlers found that the native Americans of the northeastern woodlands made use of belts made from shell beads – known as 'wampum', 'peak' or 'roenoke' – in ritual payments, and the settlers made their own version of wampum to trade with the native Americans.

Balances, Weights & Measures

62

If a (female) innkeeper refuses to accept grain for the price of beer but accepts only silver measured by the large weight, thus reducing the value of beer in relation to the value of grain, they shall establish (the guilt of) that (female) innkeeper and they shall throw her into the river.

LAWS OF HAMMURABI, *c.* 1750 BC

While it is easy to compare the weights of two medium-sized objects by holding one in each hand, it is almost impossible to do so accurately and consistently. The earliest recognizable sets of weights, from the Nile and Indus valleys, thus seem to have been designed especially for small, valuable commodities such as precious stones and metals. From the early 4th millennium BC the Egyptian *beqa* system, with a base unit of 13 g (± 5 per cent), was used exclusively by court officials for weighing gold and other highly valuable materials. In Mohenjo-daro and Harappa, however, weights with a base unit of 13.7 g (± 2 per cent) are found even in ordinary houses, suggesting that weighing was not a socially restricted practice there.

In Mesopotamia, fixed weights of barley and silver became standard media of exchange from the mid-3rd millennium, using a sexagesimal system based on the *shekel* (*c.* 8.3 g) and *mina* (*c.* 500 g). Both textual and material evidence show that while professionals such as jewelers and innkeepers used and owned weights and balances, it was a royal duty to maintain sets of reference standards and to oversee the proper use of the differing weight standards. Ideas of balance, fairness

and divine justice became closely intertwined. Even after the invention of coinage (p. 250), weighing remained central to the concept of monetary value: the Greek weight names *obolos* (*c.* 1.04 g or 0.73 g) and *drachme* (*c.* 6.24 g or 4.36 g) became attached to coins of those weights.

Many weight systems were grounded on the fact that grains and seeds have remarkably consistent weights. In Mesopotamia the barleycorn was used, in Hindu India the carob seed. And in the 1st century AD all Chinese metrologies became defined by the number, capacity and weight (*liang*, *c.* 14 g) of black millet seeds that would fill a *huanzhong* musical pipe, in a system supposedly invented by the legendary Yellow Emperor.

Balances & steelyards

The earliest scales were simple, symmetrical balances which were made of wood or bronze, suspended or supported in the middle of the beam, with pans or hooks hung from either end. To weigh an object in a balance pan one simply added or removed weights on the other side until the beam was horizontal. Byzantine moneyers used

Above *Bronze weights were often cast in the shape of animals: gazelle, oxen and hippopotami in Egypt, eagles in the Hittite kingdom, goats in Pompeii. These bronze lion weights belonging to a set commissioned for King Shalmaneser V of Assyria (726–722 BC) were found in his throne-room at Nimrud. The largest is inscribed in cuneiform, 'Palace of Shalmaneser, king of Assyria, 5 royal mina', and in Aramaic '5 mina of the land' and '5 royal mina'. The smallest has had a rather inelegant collar fitted round its neck to bring it up to weight.*

Left *Stone weights are first attested in Egypt and the Indus Valley in the 4th millennium BC. Distinctive cuboid weights made of chert (a type of flint) are found not only in many of the Indus Valley cities, as seen here, but also on the coast of the Arabian Gulf and in southern Iraq until about 1500 BC.*

Right *According to the Egyptian Book of the Dead, entry to the underworld was permitted only after the deceased's heart was weighed against the feather of truth. Here the jackal-headed god Thoth weighs the heart of Ani, a royal scribe; c. 1250 BC.*

Far right *Body parts were often used as the basis for linear measures in ancient societies. The Ashmolean metrological relief probably formed part of the facade of an official weights and measures office in western Turkey or one of the Greek islands in the mid-5th century BC. It shows a foot (here 297 mm), various finger and hand measurements, a cubit (fingertips to elbow, here 520 mm) and a fathom (fingertips to fingertips, here 2.08 m).*

Below *Metrological accuracy began to be tightly controlled by the Chinese state in about 200 BC. This bronze capacity measure, with two attached measuring cups, holds about 2 litres of grain, and has an inscription dated AD 9. Such vessels typically bear warnings against abuse: 'If any official attempts to cheat he must be stopped. If he does not stop he shall be punished.'*

KEY DATES

weight system	4th millennium BC, Egypt & Indus Valley
steelyard	1st century AD, Rome

fine balances with highly accurate glass coin weights.

Many ancient cultures, whatever their basic unit of weight, manufactured reference weights in binary series; that is, by successive doubling or halving of the base unit. This was less a result of cultural transmission than of practical efficiency: only one weight stone of each kind is needed to cover the whole range from lightest to heaviest with equal precision.

Roman steelyards, however, did away with the need for large sets of weights by applying the principle that the downward force exerted by a load depends both on its weight and on its distance from the pivot point. The load on one end of the

suspended beam was balanced by moving a single counterpoise along the other end until equilibrium was reached, and the weight of the load read off from calibrated markings on the beam. The Roman base unit was the *uncia* (ounce, c. 27 g). First attested in the 1st century AD, the steelyard spread rapidly, reaching China within 200 years.

Other measures

Almost all other early metrologies (systems of measurement) were particular to the type of object being measured, just as today horses may still be measured in hands and sea depths in fathoms. And, like the hand and the fathom (the distance between the fingertips with arms outstretched), many of the length units used were based on body parts. But as individual human bodies are very variable in size it became necessary to choose standard reference measures against which to compare all others, and to fix ratios between the units. Thus across much of the Old World, from China to Europe, the cubit, or forearm, was fixed at about 50 cm (±10 per cent), and the fathom at 4 cubits or 6 or 7 ft. This says much less about cultural contact than it does about norms of the adult male body.

Capacity measures, on the other hand, varied much more widely across time and place as well as by commodity, being dependent only on preferred vessel types and sizes. Capacity measures thus had to be particularly rigorously controlled by central authority.

General Medicine

A society's attitude towards the health of its population and the development of medicine are reflections of both its social order and the quality of human development.

ROBERT ARNOTT, 1996

Medicine is defined as the science of preventing, diagnosing, alleviating or curing disease. Today, it has advanced to such an extent that, certainly in Western societies, most people live longer, suffering from diseases of old age, while infant mortality is not a major problem. People will always have suffered ill health, attempting to deal with disease with the resources they had to hand. However, unless there is a contemporary written record, their efforts remain invisible unless some imprint is left in the archaeological record.

Our main sources of evidence come from written and iconographic records, though there are mummified remains and skeletons that have been discovered with wound 'dressings' (and marks of trepanation and amputation; p. 260). Archaeological evidence comes in the form of the remains of hospitals and other institutions for the sick, and medical implements. We should remember that concepts of why a disease affected a person or population differed from modern Western thought and thus medical treatments often do not make sense to us today.

For very early prehistory for which there are no written records we can only surmise what types of medical treatments might have been available. It is possible that herbal remedies played a large part in alleviating symptoms, as well as the use of rituals, though there is extensive evidence for trepanation being practised (p. 260).

New World medicine

In the New World there is less available evidence for the practice of medicine in antiquity than in the Old. Following the arrival of the Spanish in the late 15th century, however, chroniclers began to document the native population's already well-developed knowledge of medicine. There were gods related to healing and disease, and a concept of sin being associated with illness (and treatment by confession) was well established. Astrology was used in diagnosis, and amulets and incantations in treatments.

*The Moche of the north coast of Peru produced ceramics that often depicted scenes of the activities of everyday life in great detail. Here (**left**) a healer attends to a sick person, perhaps in a curing ritual, and (**below**) midwives assist at a childbirth.*

255

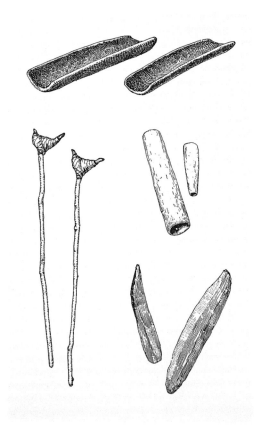

The Aztecs in Mexico were familiar with around 1200 medicinal plants, and also used fumigation, bathing, bloodletting and dietary remedies; an annual ceremony, the Citua, included a cleansing of homes, which must have contributed to public health. In the Inca empire in Peru, similar concepts of the causes of disease and treatment prevailed. Additionally, disease transference to animals from humans was also a known remedy.

Causes of disease & treatments

It is from Egypt that some of the earliest written evidence for medicine comes in the form of medical papyri. The most famous are the Edwin Smith (*c.* 1550 BC), Ebers (1550 BC), Hearst (1450 BC), and Berlin (1200 BC). The Edwin Smith papyrus contains details of methods of examination, diagnosis and treatment of different conditions, and is classed as an 'instruction book'.

The Ebers papyrus is a 110-page compendium of many sources of medical texts which seems to assume that a diagnosis has already been made.

It includes treatments using animal, vegetable, fruit and mineral concoctions for diseases of the eye, bites, skin complaints and injuries.

In Egypt, doctors' knowledge of anatomy must have come from the observation of embalmers preparing dead bodies during mummification (p. 264), and also from viewing victims of accidents. Because many diseases were thought to be caused by demons entering the body, discussion of magical remedies and medicine's association with religion go hand in hand with more conventional therapies. There is also evidence that many magicians also acted as physicians. In addition, there were pharmacists, nurses, midwives, physiotherapists and 'bandagers'.

China also claims early evidence of medicine, some dating as far back as 2000 BC. Texts include medical theory, diagnostic methods, drug use and prescriptions. The health and well-being of the living depended on their relationship with the dead; to identify a cause and treatment for a disease the dead were consulted. If the dead were not treated well then curses were put on the living. For instance, in the 1st millennium BC, a period of unrest was thought to be connected with demons entering the body, which were held responsible for

disease – cause and effect were important in Chinese medicine. Various manuscripts dating to before and after the unification of the Chinese empire in 221 BC indicate that China's health care consisted of a complex series of approaches associated with the socio-economic situation at the time.

One of the main sources of our knowledge of Chinese medicine is a great compendium known as the *Nei Ching* ('Manual of Physic'), dated to between 479 and 300 BC. Disease was viewed as being caused by the intrusion of an agent into the human body (a worm or insect), or as a result of a multiple functional disturbance. Diagnosis of disease included taking a person's pulse, observing their skin colour and smelling their breath.

Until the 13th century, medicine was concerned with drug therapy – the first herbal book dates from the 1st century AD (*Shen-nung pen-ts'ao Ching*) – and/or maintaining harmony in the body. Treatments involved massage, specific diets, magical cures and cautery (application of hot irons

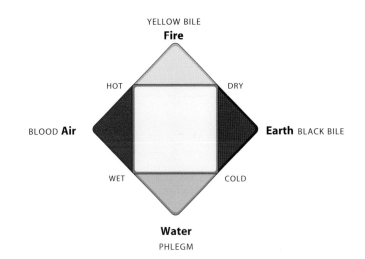

to the affected part), with the practice of acupuncture first described around 90 BC by Pien Ch'io.

Medical ethics

In 7th-century BC Mesopotamia, many clay tablets from the library of King Ashurbanipal document diseases and their treatments. Religion and medicine were linked, and astrology also played a large part in treatments. People who dealt with disease were of three kinds: first, those who predicted the course of a disease; second, those who drove out the evil spirits causing the disease; and third, those who administered drugs, using a compendium of 250 plants, 120 minerals and animal parts. Here, too, is the earliest evidence of a code of medical ethics for physicians in the Laws of Hammurabi (*c.* 2000 BC).

It was the ancient Greeks, however, who invented 'scientific medicine', around 500 BC, and provided most of our medical nomenclature. They are

Above *The four humours and their relationship to the elements and qualities. A belief in such a system was at the basis of much ancient medicine; illnesses were thought be caused by imbalances between the different humours.*

Left *Drawing of the interior of an Attic red-figure drinking vessel of c. 500 BC which depicts Achilles bandaging the wounded Patroklos. Patroklos, with his head turned away, holds one end of the bandage which Achilles is wrapping round his arm.*

Above *In the foreground of this scene from Trajan's Column soldiers are having their wounds dressed and attended to by medical orderlies.*

medical treatment, and the works of Aristotle (384–322 BC) in Greece were built upon. While the Alexandrian School was not as successful as the Hippocratic, advances in knowledge of anatomy and physiology undoubtedly helped to advance medicine.

Roman medicine

Rome became a centre for medical instruction in the 1st century AD. Medical works by Celsus indicate a Greek influence: *De Re Medica* (AD 30) was the first Classical medical book and was a compilation of the works of others. Galen (2nd century AD) was also famous for his synthetic works, diagnostic methods and anatomical observations derived from animal dissections. Probably the major contribution of the Roman empire to health was in preventing disease, for example by the provision of clean water and drainage, latrines, sewers and public baths (p. 84),

seen as a major contributor to the development of medicine in the Western world, particularly through the works of numerous followers of Hippocrates (460–377 BC), the 'father of medicine' (and founder of the medical school of Cos). The 'Hippocratic Collection' of medical works is believed to derive from numerous scholars at Cos, and documents cases of disease and treatment in detail.

Up to this time efforts had been made to treat the sick, but it was in the 5th century BC that a real concept of medicine developed. Emphasis was placed on the relationship of environment to the occurrence of disease, and adopting a lifestyle conducive to health. Letting nature heal was advocated and a healing system developed independent of religion and the supernatural. As in Chinese medicine, a 'balanced body' was key to health, and particularly a balance between the four humours – blood, phlegm, and black and yellow bile. Diet, drugs, rest and exercise, as well as cupping, were used to restore any imbalance.

In *c.* 300 BC in Alexandria in Egypt another medical school was founded: Herophilus was claimed to be the 'founder of anatomy' and Erisastratus the 'founder of physiology'. A good knowledge of these subjects is key to successful

Right *A set of Roman bronze cupping vessels, found in Bingen, Germany. Such cups functioned by suction, being applied either to speed up the flow of blood from a vein in bloodletting, or to extract humours in order to restore their balance.*

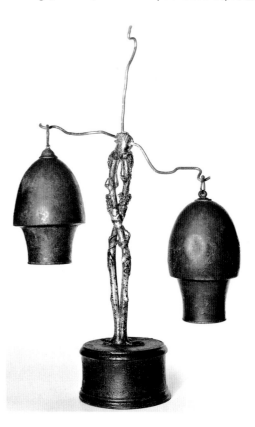

KEY DATES

ethical code	*c.* 2000 BC, Mesopotamia
medical texts	*c.* 1550 BC, Egypt
'scientific medicine'	*c.* 500 BC, Greece
acupuncture	90 BC, China
herbal text	1st century AD, China

Far left *A Roman oculist's stamp, found in the River Moselle, France. Oculists specialized in treating eye diseases, such as cataracts. Such stamps would have been used to mark and identify the pastes and preparations they used.*

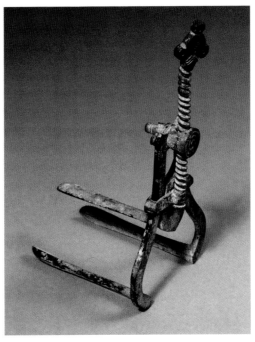

Left *A Roman vaginal speculum made of bronze, found in Lebanon. The screw mechanism allowed the instrument to be opened and closed, and demonstrates the sophistication of Roman medical equipment.*

all of which became part of everyday life. Rome also initiated the concept of the hospital/infirmary (*valetudinaria*) in towns, cities and military bases, thus paving the way for the development of hospitals as major institutions in later periods.

Indian medicine

Indian medicine was clearly different from that of Greece, Islam or China, although an imbalance of three humours (wind, bile and phlegm) was seen to result in disease. Termed Ayurvedic ('knowledge, or science, of life') or Hindu medicine, it was based on practical advice about all aspects of life. Rest, food, exercise, sex and medicines were recommended for achieving a healthy body. The earliest documents are from the 1st century AD and consist of plant and dietary remedies, and sometimes magic bound up with with religion. The most famous medical texts are the *samhitas*, compiled in the 1st and 4th–6th centuries AD.

Christianity & medicine

From around AD 400 the Christian church in Europe continued the commitment to medical care and learning. Disease was often seen as a punishment for sin, with shrines or saints becoming pilgrimage places, and religion and medicine were strongly linked. Nevertheless, monastic institutions did a considerable amount for the development of the care of the sick as 'preservers of learning', and much of their knowledge derived from translations of Graeco-Roman Latin medical texts.

FALSE TEETH

Losing teeth is usually linked to increasing age. In the past it likely happened earlier in life because of poor dental care. Replacing lost teeth must have been contemplated, maybe more for vanity than to enable mastication of food. The earliest false teeth come from the Etruscan population of Italy (Tuscany); in 700 BC, partial dentures were made using substitute teeth, set in a 3–5-mm gold band (**below**). Another example of early prosthetics is seen in a Phoenician grave at Sidon dated from the 4th-6th century AD; here gold wires were attached to carved ivory teeth.

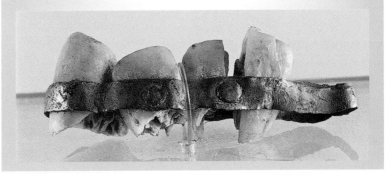

64 Surgery & Surgical Instruments

A surgeon should be youthful … with a strong and steady hand which never trembles, ready to use the left hand as well as the right; with vision sharp and clear, and spirit undaunted; filled with pity so that he wishes to cure his patient, yet not moved by his cries to go too fast or cut less than is necessary.

CELSUS, 1ST CENTURY AD

Above *A Bronze Age skull excavated at Jericho, dating to 2200–2000 BC, with circular trepanned holes produced using a drill. It appears that this individual survived the process as the bone shows signs of healing.*

People must have suffered from wounds, injuries and traumas since the dawn of time, and we may be sure that some form of treatment was a normal response. Much can be done with natural materials from the immediate surroundings, and the human hand is very dextrous, but the use of implements in surgical treatment is likely to have occurred early in prehistory. Because there were no written accounts, however, and because the implements used for surgery may have differed little, if at all, from other tools and utensils, it has not been possible to identify, unequivocally, a single surgical tool from the earliest periods.

Trepanation

Only rarely is it possible to distinguish surgical treatment in human remains, for soft tissue, the site of most surgery, seldom survives. A few operations, however, were located in, or actually penetrated to, bone. Evidence for one of the most dramatic, cranial trepanation – the surgical opening of the skull – has been found in skeletons dating as far back as the early Neolithic period – over 7000 years ago. This is the earliest confirmed surviving evidence for surgery, and many examples have been found worldwide.

It is likely that severe acute or chronic head pains, whether caused by disease or injury, or perhaps migraine, were the trigger for such painful and perilous surgery. The earliest trepanations in Europe were performed by incising the scalp and cutting or paring away the skull, probably with blades of flint. A freshly-struck flint blade is both very sharp and potentially aseptic and can be most effective. Certainly, healing and remodelling of the bone margins show that many prehistoric patients survived the operation.

Not until the 3rd to 2nd centuries BC do we encounter surviving purpose-made trepanning instruments: in a few La Tène C graves in Celtic Europe, small kits of iron instruments have been found that include a tanged saw with a small, finely toothed cutting edge, similar to the Hey's saws of early 19th-century trepanning sets. A unique survival from ancient times is a crown-trephining kit, consisting of two bronze cylindrical drills and a bronze folding bow-handle, which was found

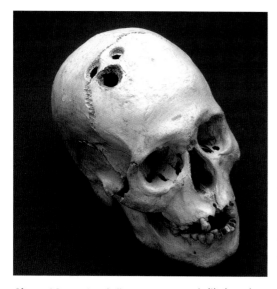

Right *A trepanning knife from Peru, with a scene of trepanation on the top.*

with other surgical tools in a grave of the early 2nd century AD at Bingen, in Germany.

Fractures & amputation

Much more common than cranial trepanation would have been the treatment of fractured limbs, and splinting was practised as far back as the 3rd millennium BC: splints made from tree-bark were found attached by means of linen bandages to broken, unhealed limbs of Egyptian mummies in rock-cut tombs of the 5th Dynasty (*c.* 2400 BC) at Naga ed-Deir (p. 256). The earliest surviving substantial surgical text from ancient Egypt, the Edwin Smith papyrus, is a kind of instruction manual for pharaonic healers, principally concerning the management of trauma to the upper part of the body. Most treatment comprised the setting of fractures, reduction of dislocations, and the stitching and bandaging of flesh wounds, but there are references in several of the Egyptian medical papyri to 'knife treatment'.

In the un-sterile world of the distant past, wound infection would have been an ever-present peril, with chronic ulceration and gangrene as the distressing and dangerous consequences. In the early 1st century AD the Roman author Celsus described the procedure for amputating a gangrenous limb, and evidence of a successful leg amputation dating to the 2nd century AD has recently been found at the Isola Sacra cemetery at Ostia, near Rome. The end of the femur of a tall man was found to bear the distinctive cut-marks of a saw, together with sufficient healing to suggest the patient survived for months, perhaps even years, after the operation. Traces of wear on the bone imply that the man had been fitted with an artificial leg, probably a simple wooden 'peg'.

Archaeological evidence for an artificial limb intended both to function and to look like the missing part, comes from a tomb at Capua in southern Italy, dated *c.* 300 BC. It had been made for a man who had lost his lower right leg and consisted of a wooden core covered with bronze sheet, which realistically depicted the shin and calf from the ankle to just below the knee. It was hollowed at the top to accommodate the stump of the calf and at the bottom for a substitute foot.

Surgical instruments

Although the medical texts from ancient Egypt and Greece demonstrate that both routine and complex surgery took place during the 2nd and 1st millennia BC, few of the instruments themselves have been identified. One exception is the bronze cupping vessel, examples of which have been found in Greece dating as far back as the 6th century BC. Cupping vessels were designed to function as suction cups, either to speed up the letting of blood from an incised vein (wet-cupping) or to extract perceived 'vicious humours' through the pores of the skin (dry-cupping). Such cups were the auxiliary of one of the most enduring disease theories of antiquity, as we have seen, that of the bodily humours (p. 258). Cupping, wet or dry, was the principal means of restoring the balance, and cupping vessels hardly varied in form throughout the Greek and Roman world from the 6th century BC to the 4th century AD.

The *Susruta Samhita* is an early Indian medical text, dated by some to the 4th century AD and by others to the 2nd century AD, though it was probably codified several centuries earlier and long transmitted orally. Surgical interventions were classified as excision, incision, scarification, puncturing, probing, extraction, drainage and suturing, and Ayurvedic healers used cutting instruments, blunt instruments, cauteries, needles and probes. Like Greek and Roman surgeons they performed plastic surgery on damaged ears and noses, operated for bladder stone, fistula and piles, and even couched for cataract. It is likely that the transmission of surgical knowledge was a two-way process

Above *A copy of the artificial leg from Capua, Italy, c. 300 BC. The original consisted of a wooden core covered with bronze sheet and was modelled in the shape of the leg. An artificial foot would have been added at the bottom.*

Below *The Roman crown-trephining kit (which cut the bone by circular action) from Bingen, Germany, early 2nd century AD. This kit consisted of two cylindrical drills and a folding bow-handle, made of bronze.*

One of the largest surviving sets of Roman surgical instruments. It includes scalpel handles, hooks, forceps, probes, needles, catheters, bone chisels, drug boxes and a rectal dilator. From Italy, 1st or 2nd century AD.

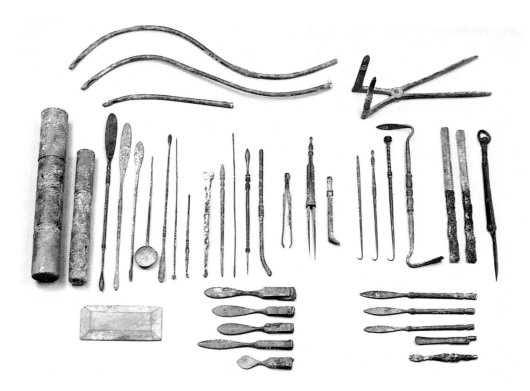

between the Indian and Classical worlds. Unfortunately, none of the early Indian instruments has yet been positively identified.

By the start of the Roman empire, however, in the early 1st century AD, recognizable, purpose-made surgical instruments begin to appear in the archaeological record. Not only are the instruments well-designed, many are also exceptionally finely crafted and often exquisitely decorated. Roman metalworkers manufactured sharp blades,

Below *The surgical instrument kit found at Stanway, Essex, dating to the mid-1st century AD. It contained all the basic tools used in ancient surgery.*

fine-pointed needles, catheters with an immaculately smooth surface, and many other precision tools. Most were made of copper and its alloys, principally bronze and brass. Iron was chosen especially for blades, and Roman blacksmiths were familiar with the technique of carburization to produce steel tools. Although new instruments were invented, many acquired a distinctive form that changed little over the centuries, and examples have been found throughout the empire. Their distribution implies widespread uniformity of surgical practice, even if the medical theories that lay behind the surgery differed.

Surgical kits

Individual instruments help to build up a picture of ancient surgery, but much more informative are the groups of medical instruments occasionally found in Roman period burials. At Stanway, near Colchester, in England a grave was found in 1996 dating to the mid-1st century AD containing 14 surgical instruments, comprising all the basic tools of ancient surgery. They include scalpels, forceps, needles, sharp and blunt hooks (used above all for retracting the margins of wounds or incisions) and a small saw. This is one of the earliest finds of a surgical kit, and was probably used by a native British healer both before and immediately after the Roman conquest of Britain in AD 43.

Even more informative are finds from sites overwhelmed by sudden catastrophes, such as Pompeii. Some healers were among the victims, including a man found near the amphitheatre with an instrument kit in a wooden case. Additionally, between 10 and 20 houses have yielded sufficient instruments to indicate the full-time or part-time practice of surgery by their occupants. Some were equipped with gynaecological and obstetrical instruments, some with surgical tools, and others combined pharmacy with surgery.

Pompeii is unique in allowing us a glimpse of the medical provision for a whole town, but a few other sites have provided equally vivid evidence of individual practitioners. Most spectacular of all is a healer's house at Rimini, Italy, burnt down in the middle of the 3rd century AD. Over 150 metal instruments were preserved, by far the largest number ever found. In addition to a wide range of the basic tools of surgery there are many instruments with a more specialized use: levers for elevating fractured bones; chisels and gouges for cutting and trimming bones, stout forceps for removing bone fragments and splinters, and folding handles for operating bow-drills; dental forceps for extracting teeth; a roughened scoop for the very dangerous operation of lithotomy (the removal of stone from the urinary bladder) and special forceps for throat operations and the removal of haemorrhoids. They provide some of the best evidence we have for the equipment of a Roman healer.

Of course it is impossible for us to gauge his skill and success, but we may be sure that he examined his patients, diagnosed their diseases and gave his prognosis, before offering advice on dietetics and regimen, prescribing a drug or carrying out surgery. His instruments, like those found in other parts of the Roman empire, clearly demonstrate the enormous potential of surgery in the ancient world and the striking continuity of surgical instrumentation up to recent times.

KEY DATES

trepanation	c. 5000 BC, Europe
splinting	3rd millennium BC, Egypt
cupping vessel	6th century BC, Greece
artificial limb	c. 300 BC, Italy
surgical instruments	1st century AD, Rome

Above *Part of the Roman instrument find from Rimini, Italy, including bone drills, bone forceps and a lithotomy scoop. In the ruins of the house of a healer burned down in the 3rd century AD, a kit comprising over 150 metal instruments was preserved, the largest ever found.*

Left *A unique Roman plunger forceps used in the operations to amputate the uvula in the throat, haemorrhoids and other growths. Roman surgical instruments were both extremely well crafted and often beautifully decorated, as well as being very functional. Most were made of copper, bronze or brass.*

263

Mummies & Mummification

The bodies were so intact that they lacked neither hair, eyebrows nor eyelashes. They were in clothes just as they had worn when alive … and weighed so little that any Indian could carry them from house to house in his arms or on his shoulders.

GARCILASO DE LA VEGA, 1609

Right *A mummy bundle of a Chiribaya infant with grave goods, c. AD 800–1000, from the Ilo region, southern Peru.*

The term *mummy* is usually applied to a body which retains its soft tissue, its skin, hair and nails. Although this can occur naturally when decomposition is impeded in dry, frozen or water-logged environments, the dead can also be preserved using artificial methods of mummification. Closely associated with ancient Egypt, where the term mummy originates, independent forms of mummification were actually practised on five continents and can be traced back 8000 years to South America.

The earliest mummies – South America

Below *Detail of a mummified Chinchorro boy with clay mask and human hair wig, c. 2600 BC, from the Camarones region of northern Chile.*

Discovered on the coastal edge of the arid Atacama Desert on the border between Chile and Peru, the world's earliest artificially created mummies date back to *c.* 6000 BC. They were created by small fishing communities of the Chinchorro culture,

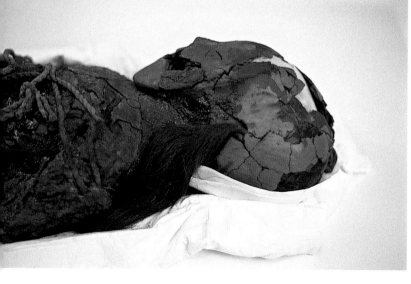

who preserved their dead using highly complex procedures. After defleshing the extended body, the internal organs were removed and the bones dried with hot ash before being reassembled with twigs and reeds as support. Then the original skin was replaced, sometimes coated with an ash paste, and the scalp hair reattached. Finally the face was covered in a clay mask and painted with either black manganese or red ochre.

Since some face masks show evidence of repainting and the feet area can be damaged, the mummies may originally have been stood upright as objects of veneration before final burial in family groups. As the earliest mummies are those of infants and foetuses, it has been suggested that Chinchorro women were the first practitioners of mummification as a means of keeping their dead children with them. This is supported by evidence which indicates that the women would have processed and prepared the daily catch of seals and fish brought by the men, who spent the majority of their time diving for food at sea, and thus used their anatomical knowledge to prepare their own dead.

Mummification techniques continued to evolve, and around 400 BC the farming communities of southern Peru began to bury their dead in the contracted position, with the knees drawn up under the chin enabling the bodily fluids responsible for decomposition to drain away. These compact and easily transportable bundles were wrapped in multiple layers of highly decorated textiles, typified by mummies of the Paracas and Nazca regions up to AD 600.

Similar mummy bundles of the Chachapoyas 'Cloud People', discovered in Peru's northern highlands, and more recent examples found in a large cemetery beneath the modern city of Lima, confirm the continuation of such practices under the expanding Inca empire. Although the well-preserved bodies found in the high Andes had been naturally mummified by freeze-drying, artificial mummification continued, and the extremely life-like appearance of Inca royal mummies was reportedly due to the application of various substances, named in Spanish accounts as Tolù balsam, calabash, muña plant as well as an unnamed, bitumen-like substance. Regarded as living beings, the mummified royals were fed, clothed, consulted and carried aloft at state occasions, a practice only ended after the Spanish conquest, when all the mummies found were burned during religious reforms.

Mummification in Egypt

By no means the first culture to practice mummification, the process remains inextricably linked with ancient Egypt where the body was preserved to provide a permanent home for the soul. The earliest Egyptian mummies are naturally preserved, having been buried in the foetal position directly into the hot desert sand which absorbed the bodily fluids responsible for decomposition. Still in a recognizable form, with skin, hair and nails intact, these bodies must have had a profound effect on those accidentally uncovering them. Perhaps trying to replicate the process with their own dead, examples of linen-wrapped bodies have been found as early as the Badarian Period, c. 4500 to 4100 BC. Following experimentation over the next few centuries, the linen was impregnated with a variety of resins or coated in plaster to retain the contours of the body.

Yet optimum preservation was only achieved with the removal of the internal organs where putrefaction begins: those of Queen Hetepheres (c. 2600 BC) were removed and preserved in a solution of natron salts (sodium carbonate and sodium bicarbonate). The practice of evisceration also meant bodies were no longer mummified in a foetal position, but were laid

The well-preserved mummy of the Egyptian pharaoh Sety I (c. 1290–1279 BC), found in the Deir el-Bahri cache burial of royal mummies at Thebes. This is perhaps the classic image of an Egyptian mummy.

Above *Small linen pouches containing natron and organic materials, such as this one from tomb KV39 in the Valley of the Kings, were used during the mummification process between the 18th and 21st dynasties in Egypt.*

it seems most likely that the word 'mummy' is in fact based on the ancient Egyptian word for wax ('mum') rather than the Persian word for bitumen ('mummiya'), since beeswax has been found in significantly greater quantities than bitumen.

With final life-like touches added using cosmetics and hairstyling, the mummified body was finally wrapped in layers of linen, with numerous protective amulets inserted between. The completed mummy, placed in a wooden coffin, could then undergo the funeral ceremonies needed to reactivate the soul prior to burial.

Mummification elsewhere

Although the quality of preservation greatly declined by the Graeco-Roman period, mummification had become ever more widely available, both to the Egyptian population and throughout much of the ancient world.

According to the Greek historian Herodotus, the Persians embalmed their dead using wax. The body of Alexander the Great was similarly preserved in Babylon after his death in 323 BC, using a mixture of wax, honey and spices. Following the political struggles between his successors, his body was finally interred some 30 years later in Alexandria, and was still in good condition almost three centuries later when visited by the Roman emperor Augustus.

Similar combinations of wax and plants were used to mummify Scythian leaders, *c.* 500 to 400 BC, and, with the internal organs removed, Herodotus states that the body cavity was filled with 'various aromatic substances, crushed galingale, parsley-seed and anise; it is then sewn up and the whole

out flat to enable the embalmers to remove the organs more easily.

As the Egyptians refined and developed their techniques, the 'classic' form of mummification was perfected as early as *c.* 1500 BC. In most cases the brain seems to have been liquidized using a long metal probe and drained out through the nose. The stomach, liver, lungs and intestines were removed through an incision on the left side of the abdomen made with an obsidian blade, and the cavity and organs sterilized with date palm wine. The body and entrails were then dried out for a standard 40 days beneath piles of dry natron before the desiccated skin was washed and finally sealed with complex blends of resins, waxes and oils, both for ritual purposes and to prevent moisture re-entering the body. With bitumen widely used for this purpose only by Graeco-Roman times,

Right *A rare representation of the final stages of the Egyptian mummification process, including possibly the application of molten resin to the exterior (bottom left), accompanied by the recitation of ritual texts. From the Tomb of Thoy, c. 1200 BC.*

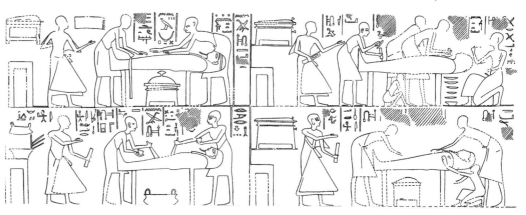

body coated in wax'. Although the majority of mummies from the Taklamakan region of China were naturally mummified, several bodies dated to *c.* 1000 BC showed signs of additional artificial preservation, a thin layer of a protein-based paste having been found over the surface of their skin.

Mummification techniques were also used in parts of the Roman empire between the 1st centuries BC and AD, with at least three artificially preserved bodies discovered in Rome itself. Recent research in Yemen has revealed artificial mummification was practised by the elite of southern Arabia between *c.* 1200 and 300 BC. Ongoing analysis has revealed the use of native plant-based desiccants, animal fat and mineral preservatives, and bodies wrapped in linen and leather.

Recent re-analysis of a child's eviscerated body wrapped in animal skins indicates that mummification was practised in southern Libya as early as *c.* 3500 BC, while as far west as the Canary Islands, the native Guanche culture were using mummification at the time of the Spanish invasions of the 15th century AD. After drying out the eviscerated body in the sun or over fire, locally available preservatives such as sand, powdered pumice stone, charcoal, pine needles and animal fat were employed prior to wrapping it in layers of animal skins.

Highly elaborate forms of artificial mummification involving evisceration have also been found

KEY DATES

earliest mummification	*c.* 6000 BC, South America
	c. 4500 BC, Egypt
	c. 1200 BC, Yemen
	c. 1000 BC, China
	c. 500 BC, Scythians
	c. 400 BC, Persia

A mummified adult male of the Guanche culture, wrapped in goat skins, from a cave burial at San Andres, Tenerife, Canary Islands.

amongst the Aboriginal populations of Australia, Melanesia and the Aleutian Islands, and although only dating back several centuries may well be a continuation of earlier practices.

A Yemeni adult male mummified in the foetal position and wrapped in a shroud, possibly camel skin, with the head exposed, from Shibam el-Ghiras, c. 400 BC.

267

Adorning the Person

We will never know when people first donned skins to keep themselves warm or crude sandals to protect their feet. They certainly did so when they settled in cooler climates with cold winters, when frost was on the ground for days on end. *Homo erectus* was the first to colonize such lands, perhaps before a million years ago. For hundreds of thousands of years, clothing was little more than furs and skins, which often doubled as containers for carrying seeds and nuts. Such garments did not offer sufficient protection to survive in extreme cold, which may be why the Neanderthals of 75,000 years ago never settled permanently on the vast, open steppe-tundra of northern Europe and Eurasia. As we saw earlier, the eyed needle changed all that (p. 31). Layers of tailored garments would then have allowed hunting bands to settle in environments with sub-zero temperatures.

In prehistoric times, when there were many fewer of us, encounters with others were unusual events – moments of caution, sometimes defiance, and often welcome. Body painting may be the oldest art of all, a simple way to distinguish one band from another, to identify fellow kin, or to record one's prowess as an elephant hunter. As ceremony and ritual became a central part of human existence after 50,000 years ago, body painting must have moved to centre stage as an integral part of initiation ceremonies and dances. Such markings never survive in the archaeological record, but they must have an enormous antiquity, assuming ever-greater importance in the more crowded world of the late Ice Age and early farmers. Body painting was, above all, a means of identification, of marking social roles and status.

Detail of a wall painting from the tomb of Nebamun, Egypt (c. 1350 BC), depicting women at a banquet, with elaborate gowns, jewelry and wigs topped by perfumed unguent cones.

Tattooing is more permanent marking, once again an art with important social and ritual implications. The Ice Man from the Similaun glacier in the Italian Alps bore tattoos behind his knees. The horsemen of Pazyryk in Siberia flaunted elaborate markings over much of their bodies. And we know from historic societies like the New Zealand Maori that such decorations on face and body were important gauges of social ranking.

Clothing and shoes began as practical necessities and remained so for many millennia. But we find traces of personal adornment as early as the late Ice Age – necklaces of predator claws and sea shells, the remains of garments buried with the dead marked by hundreds of small beads laboriously sewn to them. The big change came with more sedentary lifeways, especially with city life, when there were many more non-farmers and people of leisure and wealth, who could indulge their personal vanity with expensive clothing, shoes and accessories.

Clothing, and the correct regalia, also became marks of status, sometimes enforced with rigid sumptuary laws. The Aztecs of Mexico regulated the wearing of outer garments. Commoners wore coarsely woven yucca leaf capes, while nobles, war leaders and the ruler wore cotton capes adorned with special edging or feathers. Even the method of knotting them was prescribed.

Jewelry and ornaments of all kinds denoted status, too. Brightly shining metals, semiprecious stones, faience (glass) bead necklaces – all were signs of rank, privilege and power clearly displayed for all to see. Such distinctions were important on public occasions, and in battle, where leaders were rallying points for their troops. An Egyptian pharaoh's jewels and regalia had great symbolic significance, reinforcing his divine power, his close relationship to the gods and his leadership over the Two Lands. So did the lavish, feather-decked costumes of the Maya lords. Jade had profound importance for these lords, as it did to the Chinese. Han nobles were buried in suits of jade plaques to ensure their immortality.

Behind the lavish displays of rank and wealth lay personal vanity and ever-changing fashion – the subtle intrigues of the court and harem, status-conscious courtiers, officials and merchants, with disposable wealth and the ability to support artisans who catered to people of means. This was the realm of cosmetics and perfume, used as much by men as women in some ancient societies, such as the Egyptians or the Minoans of Bronze Age Crete. This, too was the realm of the mirror, used as much for vanity as for ritual purposes, for people have always been entranced by their own images – in still water or in the lustrous surface of volcanic glass. And in the world of the royal court, the contraceptive and the aphrodisiac were part of the eternal quest for fulfilment, youth and beauty that still preoccupies us today.

A Mixtec pendant in the form of the fire god Xiuhtecuhtli, from Monte Albán, Mexico, Postclassic period. The Mixtecs were highly regarded craftsmen and they supplied the Aztecs with much of their spectacular jewelry.

Body Art
& Tattooing

The Thracians ... consider tattooing a mark of high birth, the lack of it a mark of low birth.
HERODOTUS, 5TH CENTURY BC

There are numerous ways to change permanently the appearance of the human body –
the skin has been pierced, scarred, branded
and tattooed, and the bones distorted by skull
modelling and foot binding. In the ancient world
these modifications were used to express an individual's status and their relationship with society,
or applied for protective or therapeutic purposes.

Piercings

The most widespread form of body modification
involved piercing the lobes of the ears. The discovery of earrings in male and female graves in Ur's
royal cemetery shows the practice dates back at
least to the 3rd millennium BC. The fashion had also
spread from Nubia to Egypt by c. 1600 BC, and soon
became popular throughout society; pierced lobes
can be seen on the mummies of pharaohs such as
Thutmose IV and Tutankhamun, while certain elite
women have two holes in each lobe. Male and
female mummies from China's Taklamakan region
dating to around 1000 BC have perforated lobes, a
form of adornment also favoured by Assyrian kings
and Persian nobility. Roman women had their ears
pierced in infancy and early Hindus in India
believed the practice protected against evil spirits,
as well as having an aesthetic appeal which
increased with the size of the hole.

Found in South America as early as the Pre-
Ceramic Period (around 3000 to 1800 BC), greatly
elongated, perforated lobes were regarded as a
mark of high status amongst Inca men, whom the
Spanish called *orejones* ('big ears'). Nasal piercings
were similarly popular amongst elite males in pre-
Inca times, with the Peruvian Moche rulers piercing
the nasal septum to attach large decorative plates
(*narigueras*). Men and women of the Maya and
Aztec civilizations of Central America pierced their
own ears, tongues and genitals during bloodletting rites of self-sacrifice.

Scarification & branding

Skin can be marked by creating scar tissue, as noted
on the abdomen of a female mummy from Egypt of
c. 2000 BC. During Scythian mourning rites circular
designs were incised into the arms, and the face was

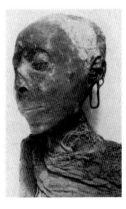

Above *The well-preserved
mummy of the Egyptian lady
Teye, with her earlobes
greatly distorted by the
regular insertion of heavy
earrings; c. 1000 BC, from
Deir el-Bahri, Thebes.*

Left *A decorated ceramic
'portrait vessel' in the form of
a Moche nobleman with a
large decorative metal plate
(nariguera) inserted through
the nasal septum as a mark
of high status; Early
Intermediate Period (c. 200
BC–AD 500), northern Peru.*

271

also gashed as a mark of grief. Branding was also used to mark out prisoners: the pharaoh Ramesses III, *c.* 1150 BC, described those he had 'branded and made into slaves, impressed with my name'.

Tattooing

Derived from the Polynesian word 'tattaw', tattooing was practised throughout the ancient world for a variety of decorative, social and protective reasons. The earliest examples date back around 5300 years and were found on the frozen Ice Man discovered in the Alps on the Italian-Austrian border. The tattooed dots on his spine and knee joints correspond to areas of strain-induced degeneration and are therefore thought to have been applied to relieve joint pain.

It is likely that the tattooing of Egyptian women had a similarly therapeutic role. Markings painted on figurines dating from

Right Predynastic ceramic figurine of a female painted with a series of geometric and semi-naturalistic tattoo designs; Gerzean/Naqada II period, c. 3500–3100 BC, Naqada.

Far right Detail of the ornate abstract tattoo designs on the detached right hand and arm of a mummified Chiribaya adult, c. AD 800–1000, from the Ilo region, southern Peru.

Below Elaborate tattoos preserved on the frozen body of a Scythian woman, buried in the Pazyryk region of Siberia, c. 400 BC. The tattoos seem to have been a sign of high status.

after *c.* 4000 BC are also found on female mummies, and were applied with sets of small bronze needles. With dotted patterns on upper bodies and thighs, extensive net-like designs across the abdomen and figures of the god Bes on the thighs, the use of tattoos as permanent amulets during pregnancy and childbirth seems a more likely explanation than their standard interpretation as simply charms against sexual diseases or marks denoting prostitution.

Women in parts of South America may also have been tattooed for similarly protective purposes, and both men and women of several pre-Columbian cultures used stylized designs on the torso, limbs and face as a mark of high status. The ornate tattoos on the mummies of Scythian leaders of around 400 BC found at Pazyryk likewise confirm Classical accounts which describe tattoos as evidence of their high birth. The ancient Britons were also reportedly tattooed with 'all kinds of animals', and as the fashion was adopted by Roman soldiers it spread rapidly across the Roman empire until the acceptance of Christianity.

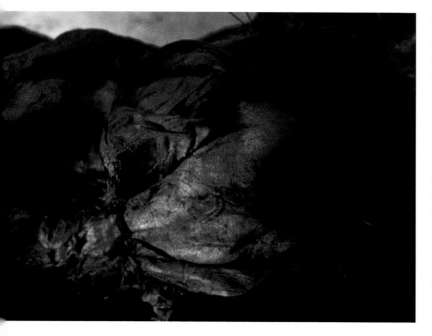

Under the influence of Christianity, tattoos were felt to 'disfigure that made in God's image' and so were banned by the emperor Constantine (AD 307–37). In Han dynasty China, only criminals were tattooed, whereas Japanese men began adorning their bodies with elaborate tattoos in the late 3rd century AD.

KEY DATES

cranial shaping	60,000 years ago, Iraq
elongated lobes	3000–1800 BC, South America
tattooing	3300 BC, Europe
pierced ears	2600 BC, Mesopotamia
scarification	2000 BC, Egypt
branding	12th century BC, Egypt

Skull shaping

Evidence for the practice of intentionally altering the shape of the skull dates back 60,000 years to Neanderthal skulls from northern Iraq. Although only one confirmed example has been found in Egypt, dating from the Christian period, the practice is widely found in the Americas, where skulls were reshaped in childhood using a range of wooden boards, bindings and cradling devices. The most exaggerated shapes are found in pre-Columbian cultures of South America, with the skulls of high-status men from Paracas of c. 200 BC showing an incredible degree of elongation. Pre-Inca cultures such as the Chiribaya also compressed skulls widthways using a facial sling device, while the Maya flattened the forehead.

Left *A set of seven bronze pins which may have been used for tattooing, from Gurob, northern Egypt and dating to c. 1500–1100 BC.*

Skulls of elite males of the Paracas-Nazca culture showing extreme cranial shaping, c. 400–200 BC, from southern Peru.

Clothing, Shoes & Wigs

Wealthy Indians … dye their beards white, dark blue, red, purple or even green. Their clothes are linen and they wear tunics down to the mid-calf, an outer mantle round their shoulders and another around their heads. They wear shoes of decorated white leather with thickened soles to make them seem taller, and all except the very poor carry parasols in the summer.

NEARCHUS, *c.* 326 BC

Right *One of several well-preserved silk robes found in the Han dynasty tomb of the wife of the Marquis of Dai, at Mawangdui, China, dating to around 145 BC. It is 1.6 m (5.25 ft) long and weighs just 49 g (1.75 oz).*

Above *One of more than 145 neatly folded linen loincloths belonging to Tutankhamun and found in his tomb in the Valley of the Kings, 14th century BC.*

First developed as a practical means of protecting the body against environmental conditions, the earliest tailored clothing dates back around 25,000 years ago, when the animal skins wrapped around the body for warmth were sewn into garments using bone needles (p. 31).

Skin & leather clothing

Male bodies at the Russian site of Sungir had been buried in shirts, trousers and hats of animal skin, decorated with ivory beads, around 23,000 BC, and a contemporary figurine from Siberia wears a fur suit. A male body dated to *c.* 7400 BC, found in Spirit Cave, Nevada, had a garment of rabbit skin, while later bodies from other sites in the American southwest were buried with fur or deerskins.

Predynastic Egyptian burials contained garments made of goat and antelope skin, fastened with bone or ivory toggles and sometimes coloured with mineral pigments. Coloured leather garments are also associated with the Nubian Pan Grave culture (*c.* 1640–1532 BC), the red leather fringed cloaks from female burials corresponding to Libyan examples described by Herodotus, and the pierced leather kilts of men appearing in Egyptian art. Fragments of a leather cuirass were found in the tomb of Amenhotep II and in Tutankhamun's (p. 182), while a ceremonial crocodile skin garment from Egypt has been dated to the 3rd or 4th century AD. The leather clothing of north European bog bodies of the 5th century BC to 1st century AD support Julius Caesar's description of Germanic animal skin garments, and a pair of leather 'bikini'-style pants of the 1st century AD were found in Roman London.

Textile clothing

The oldest woven garments known are made of linen, with part of a skirt dated to the 7th millennium BC found at Çatalhöyük in Turkey, and linen fragments dating to around 6500 BC from Nahal

According to Herodotus, the Persians adopted clothing 'they think more handsome than their own' and were especially fond of the tunic and trousers of the Medes. Yet when Alexander the Great adopted Persian dress to symbolize the diversity of his empire, he drew the line at trousers which the Greeks regarded as effeminate and Plutarch as 'barbaric and outlandish'. In 331 BC the robes of the Persian king found at Susa were valued at over 5000 talents, a hundred tons of them coloured with purple dye from the Gulf of Spetsae in Greece. As the colour of high status in much of the ancient world, purple

Above *A four-pointed woven hat decorated with symbolic motifs and worn by men of the Tiwanaku-Huari culture, c. AD 200–800, southern Peru.*

Far left *'The world's oldest dress', from the Petrie Museum – a linen dress with tightly pleated yoke and long sleeves, believed to have been worn by a teenage girl around 2800 BC. It was found in a tomb at Tarkhan, northern Egypt.*

Hemar in the Judaean Desert. Flax was introduced into Egypt by around 5000 BC, and linen appears in Neolithic burials in the Faiyum region. For the next five millennia linen forms the basis of the ancient Egyptian wardrobe since cotton was only introduced during the 1st century AD.

Egyptian garments were relatively simple. Men generally wore a skirt, or kilt, and women a dress – the world's earliest surviving example from the Egyptian site of Tarkhan is dated to c. 2800 BC. Linen loincloths and 'bag' tunics were also worn by both sexes, with shawls, cloaks, sashes, gloves and headscarves added in various combinations. Linen socks were found in Tutankhamun's tomb.

Although royal garments could be adorned with embroidery, beading and gold sequins, status was generally demonstrated by the quantity of linen, together with its quality, which ranged from ordinary coarse cloth to the gauze-like 'byssos' reserved for royalty and exported as diplomatic gifts. Foreign powers responded by sending pharaoh some of their own high-status garments, such as multicoloured shirts, leggings of shaggy wool and a purple woollen robe and matching cap.

Left *Part of the well-preserved woollen clothing of a female bog body known as 'Huldremose Woman', which included a woven shawl, skirt and headband, and two lambskin capes. Dating to c. AD 40, the body was found in Huldremose Bog, Djursland, eastern Jutland, in Denmark.*

robes were worn by Macedonian royalty, statues of divinities in 5th-century BC Egypt and Roman emperors, who donned the purple *toga picta*.

The flamboyant Roman emperor Elagabalus (AD 217–22) wore long silk robes as part of his Syrian-inspired dress. Silk was a highly prized luxury item exported from China – where a silk industry was established by at least 1500 BC – along the Silk Route as early as the 10th century BC, until the secrets of its manufacture reached Constantinople in AD 552. Robes, skirts, socks and mittens of silk were found in the Han dynasty tomb of the wife of the Marquis of Dai at Mawangdui. The Chinese also used thick mulberry paper for clothing as early as the 6th century BC – the philosopher Yuan Hsien is said to have worn paper clothing and a hat in the early 5th century AD. In the Tarim Basin, the earlier people in the Taklamakan region (*c.* 2000 to 1000 BC) wore cloaks, coats, shirts, trousers, dresses, hats and hoods predominantly made of sheep's wool and felt. Many are dyed a range of colours, with plaid designs so similar to contemporary Celtic plaids that a common origin has been suggested. Woollen clothes have also been found in Denmark in waterlogged Bronze Age burials (14th century BC) and on later Danish bog bodies.

In North America, shroud-like material made of plaited reeds was found with a male burial in Spirit Cave, Nevada, dated to 7400 BC, while in South America cloth was made from llama, alpaca and vicuña wool, and the cotton grown from *c.* 2500 BC. Such textiles, dyed by specialists and often adorned with feathers, shells and metal, played a vital role as currency, tribute and diplomatic gifts.

Their decoration was also a means of recording important information before the introduction of writing during the Spanish conquest; and since dress provided information about the wearer, it became an offence to wear clothing and headgear incompatible with one's status and origin. Although most people wore simple tunics and cloaks, there was a wide variety of headgear, from caps, hats, turbans to exotic feather crowns. The finest quality cloth woven by royal women (*acclla*) was reserved for the Inca king and the gods, whose clothes were either burnt as offerings or left with human sacrifices on mountain peaks.

Shoes

The earliest footwear was developed to protect against the cold, with 20,000 year-old animal skin moccasins found in Siberian burials. Boots of white deerskin were worn by mummies from the Taklamakan region around 1000 BC, and appliquéd felt boots were recovered from a Pazyryk burial of *c.* 500 BC. A male burial from Nevada had also been provided with moccasins of complex design made from three different kinds of animal skin, while yucca plant fibres were later used to make ornate, buckskin-fringed sandals for the dead, who would need them when resurrected.

In most ancient cultures, sandals were the most practical form of footwear. The earliest Egyptian

hair extensions dyed with henna had been knotted into natural hair. Hair extensions were worn by men and women of all classes throughout the pharaonic period; the earliest complete wig is from the tomb of the priestess Amunet *c*. 2000 BC.

Generally worn over shaven or cropped hair to reduce parasites, wigs were a hygienic way to have an elaborate hairstyle. They also protected the scalp from the sun, while their open-mesh foundation base kept the wearer cool. As well as their practical use, wigs were also worn as a mark of status by many of the rulers of the ancient world, including Egypt, Media, Persia and in Anatolia.

In Greece wigs were worn by actors to change their appearance, while wealthy Roman men and

Opposite left *Bronze statue of a young male charioteer, from Delphi, wearing a finely draped long robe, the* chiton; *c. 450 BC.*

Opposite right *A pair of Tutankhamun's sandals, with wooden soles overlaid with leather, bark and gold foil.*

Left *Detail of a Greek black-figure vase showing a sandal-maker at work.*

Below *Egyptian stone head of a priestess wearing a full-styled wig of crimped hair, bound with a lotus headband, c. 1320 BC.*

sandals date from the Predynastic period and were made of leather, while most later examples are of plant fibre. Sandals first appear in Egyptian art being carried by the royal sandal bearer around 3100 BC, and etiquette required that sandals were removed in the presence of superiors. Their decoration also had a symbolic role, with the enemies painted on the soles of royal sandals crushed with every step, a motif found among Tutankhamun's 93 sandals (at least 42 pairs and numerous single sandals), many of them richly decorated with gold and beadwork.

Decorated leather shoes were worn in 4th-century BC India, southern Arabia and across the Roman empire from Egypt to Britain, with shoe colour in Rome regulated according to profession. Hobnails were added to leather soles to increase durability, and well-preserved soles from Eboracum (York) preserve the impressions of the callouses and bunions of their ancient owners.

Wigs & hair extensions

Wigs and false hair have been used for millennia, with human hair reattached to the heads of South American Chinchorro mummies as early as *c*. 6000 BC. The earliest evidence for false hair to enhance the appearance of the living comes from Hierakonpolis in Egypt, *c*. 3400 BC, where dreadlock-type

KEY DATES

skin clothes	20,000 BC, Russia
shoes	20,000 years ago, Siberia
woven garments	7th millennium BC, Anatolia
hair extensions	c. 3400 BC, Egypt
fans	c. 3150 BC, Egypt
sandals	c. 3100 BC, Egypt
parasol	mid-3rd millennium BC, Assyria
wig	c. 2000 BC, Egypt
umbrella	AD 386–535, China

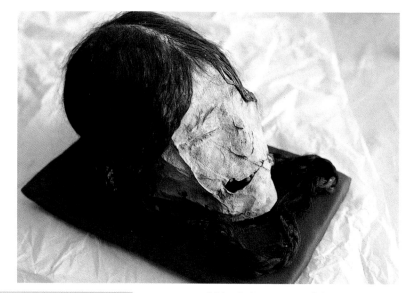

Below *Relief showing an Assyrian king with a sunshade; and Aztec feather fan, of the early 16th century, made with brighly coloured quetzal feathers.*

Right *A mummified head of a Chiribaya female with added simply dressed long hair and cheeks stained pink with a mineral pigment,* c. AD *800–1000, southern Peru.*

FANS, PARASOLS & UMBRELLAS

Fans, parasols and umbrellas were developed by cultures sufficiently sophisticated to consider matters of personal comfort. Fans first appear in Egypt, with the king of southern Egypt accompanied by fan bearers as early as c. 3150 BC. Examples are found in royal tombs: one of Tutankhamun's eight fans was made of ostrich feathers obtained by the king himself while hunting, while less costly examples made of palm leaves or woven plant fibres were used throughout society. The Aztecs of Mexico had glorious fans made from brightly coloured feathers.

Wealthy Egyptians also used sunshades, ranging from large tent-like canopies to the smaller portable examples represented in tomb and temple scenes. The sunshade of Tjekerbaal, prince of Byblos, was carried by his Egyptian butler in the Story of Wenamun c. 1080 BC. The warrior kings of ancient Iraq also appreciated their sunshades. Sargon of Akkad was accompanied by his sunshade bearer in scenes from the mid-3rd millennium BC and the Assyrian king Ashurbanipal around 645 BC stands in his chariot beneath the shade of a large parasol. In 4th-century BC India most people carried parasols, as did wealthy Athenian ladies and the Romans, whose *umbraculum* only protected against the sun. The waterproof umbrella was not invented until AD 386–535, when the Chinese discovered that oiled mulberry paper was an effective shield against rain.

women used false hair to create elaborate styles – and to disguise their baldness. They obtained blonde and red hair from Germany, and black hair from India, although some of the wigs found in Rome, Egypt and Britain also reveal wigmakers were using more economical vegetable fibres during the early centuries AD.

Below *A man's double-style wig of human hair dressed in curls and plaits set with a mixture of beeswax and resin,* c. *1400–1300 BC, from Deir el-Medina, Egypt.*

Jewelry

He who wishes to be acclaimed a good master must be a good universal master in several arts, for the different kinds of work that come to his hands to be done are infinite. Those who work in gold and silver must outdistance all other craftsmen in learning and achievement.

VANNOCCIO BIRINGUCCIO, 16TH CENTURY

S elf-adornment is a basic human instinct. Over the passing millennia love of jewelry has fuelled a disproportionate amount of conquest and trade in search of precious materials, engaged some of the greatest artists and craftspeople, and provided a continuous witness to man's vanity and greed. It seems likely that jewelry began as trophy and talisman. The lion's claw suspended on a thong about the neck demonstrated hunting prowess and strength and, no doubt, would be a warning to other beasts and other less tangible dangers to keep their distance. There was also the attraction of bright pebbles or sea shells, as appealing then as now. Necklets of shells and simple beads have been found in Stone Age habitation sites. In terms of the earliest surviving examples, there are possible pendants from Arcy-sur-Cure in France, dating from around 30,000 years ago, and an ivory bead necklace from Sungir, near Moscow dated to around 23,000 years ago.

With the gradual move to settled agriculture and the rise of permanent settlements, rank was measured in things other than hunting and fighting skills. The upper echelons of society had others to hunt for them. So how to express such rank? The answer lay in wearing clothes and ornaments made from exclusive materials and by skilled workers which only the privileged few had access to.

Gold, silver, jade

The primary jewelry metal has always been gold. There are various reasons for

this. First of all gold occurs as nuggets, dust or veins, it does not have to be converted from complex mineral ores (p. 43). It is deposited in river beds, from where it could be picked out by anyone attracted by its bright yellow glint. The resistance to chemical attack that allows gold to lie for millennia sparkling in a river bed also means that it does not tarnish or corrode in use. So, a gold vessel did not ruin the taste of the soup in life and could remain buried with its deceased owner to serve them in the afterlife, and, even, perhaps, transfer some of the metal's longevity. It was also reassuring that gold is the same colour as the

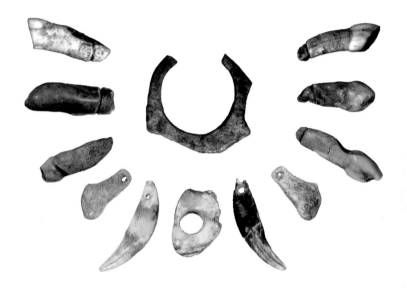

Above *Pendants, possibly talismans, made from animal teeth and bones which have been pierced and grooved for suspension. Found at the Grotte du Renne, Arcy-sur-Cure, France, they date to c. 30,000 BC.*

Left *The beads forming this necklace from Ur (mid-3rd millennium BC) are evidence of long-distance connections in luxury materials – the lapis lazuli is from Afghanistan and the technique of the etched carnelian beads originated in the Indus Valley.*

most primitive of gold jewelry had to wait until the Bronze Age (by 2500 BC in the Near East).

If gold was the metal of the sun, so the pale glint of silver was almost universally associated with the moon. An alternative was to use naturally occurring gold alloys that had enough silver present to give them a pale white colour. This was true of much early Egyptian 'silver'.

Silver can be worked using much the same techniques as gold, but with certain exceptions – such as Iron Age Spain – silver jewelry was never common. Even in Greek and Roman times the main use of silver seems to have been for tableware and other opulent symbols of wealth.

Most of the characteristic ancient gold working technologies – fine gold wires, chain manufacture, delicate soldering such as for granulation work, etc. – were well established in the Near East by about 2000 BC and for the next three millennia the advances lay more in the dissemination and application of these technologies than in the development of new ones. Nevertheless, there were some significant changes – such as the finer decorative wires and stamped work that followed in the wake of iron tools (by about 700 BC) and the greater predictability of composition and thus melting temperatures that were associated with the widespread refining of gold.

To the north of the Alps, Bronze Age goldwork was mainly produced by the simple smithing techniques of hammering or casting, although some ornaments were produced with consummate skill. Fine ornaments were also made of copper alloys, but silver was less common. The 'Near Eastern' approach to gold working – assembling ornaments from numerous separate and often minute components – only spread into northern Europe in the later Iron Age and was not common much before the Roman period, when copper alloy jewelry also was popular – often finely enamelled.

In the Far East, in China, there is little evidence for a sophisticated precious metal jewelry industry much before the mid-1st millennium BC. The technology suggests an introduction by way of the nomads of the Russian steppes, and ultimately from the Mediterranean region. But the jewelry material and technology that China can really claim

Above *The spectacular gold headdress and earrings of Queen Pu-abi of Ur, Iraq, mid-3rd millennium BC. Different layers of gold ornaments are combined, with circlets of gold ornaments imitating the leaves of willow and beech, as well as flowers, all topped by a comb. Such jewelry was a clear marker of status.*

sun, provider of all life. In addition, from the craftsperson's perspective, gold was easy to work, while its softness tended to exclude any more functional use.

A gold nugget could be worn as a pendant or hammered out into the shape of a small cup or talisman; but more often than not making something in gold meant melting together a quantity of nuggets or dust to give a larger ingot to form into ornaments. Simple cast or beaten gold ornaments were being made well before 4000 BC in parts of the Old World, such as the Balkans. However, more sophisticated gold working required tools made of metal rather than stone. So, by and large, all but the as its own is jade. Jade is very hard and tricky to work, but even so, examples of Chinese jade ornaments date back to around 3000 BC. Little appears to have been traded west as jade ornaments are essentially unknown in the Mediterranean world or Europe – even though jade from local sources was used for axes and other implements.

Jade was used in Central American jewelry by 1000 BC, but metalworking at this period was more characteristic of the Andean region. South and Central American craftspeople did not have access to sturdy metal tools and so their jewelry most typically relied on hammering into sheets or casting. They used the so-called 'lost-wax' casting process in which a model of the desired ornament is first shaped in wax – or perhaps more typically a natural wax-like plant extract – which is then coated in clay. The clay is fired, the wax melts out and molten gold is poured into the 'negative space'. Once all is cool and the gold solidified, the clay mould is broken and the gold ornament released. Pure gold is tricky to cast well, so they often used a more forgiving, though reddish-coloured, gold-copper alloy. The ornaments could be chemically treated to etch out the copper near the surface, leaving a rich gold appearance (p. 44).

Of course, throughout history, those who did not have the rank or money to possess gold jewelry could turn to gold-plated ornaments. The coating or 'gilding' of other materials with thin gold foil to give them the appearance of gold is a very ancient

Quadruple spiral beads, such as the ones in this necklace from Tell Brak, Syria (c. 2300–2159 BC), are found in an area ranging from the Aegean to the Indus Valley – though the majority are of gold rather than silver as here. Silver jewelry was rarer in the ancient world than that made of gold.

practice, but durable gilding, that is gold foil held in place by something more than glue or bent-over edges, is little in evidence much before about 1500 BC. The application of gold foil to silver or copper was largely superseded in Roman times – earlier in China – by what is called amalgam gilding. In this process gold is mixed with mercury to form a buttery amalgam; this is spread over the metal object which is then heated. The mercury is driven off as vapour to leave a gold coating.

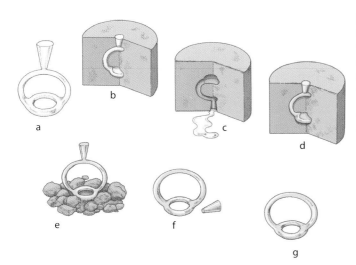

Right *A gold earring in the form of a siren playing a kithara, of around 330–300 BC. As is typical for Greek jewelry, it is assembled from numerous separate elements. The strings of the kithara are some of the thinnest Greek gold wire known.*

Left *The process of lost-wax casting. A model of the desired ornament is made in wax and coated in clay; the clay is fired, the wax melts and molten gold is poured in; once cool and solidified, the clay mould is broken and the gold ornament released.*

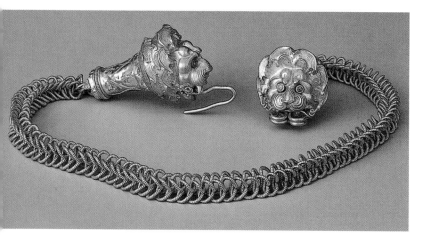

Gemstones, synonymous with jewelry from the earliest times, were originally worn as pierced beads or pendants strung on cords. The accuracy and often minute dimensions of the holes drilled through hard stones with the most primitive equipment elicit our amazement – as does the laboriousness of the work. The setting of coloured stones was only possible once a relatively sophisticated metalworking industry existed. The earliest examples include Old Kingdom Egyptian jewelry and that from the Royal Tombs at Ur in what is now Iraq. Most favoured were orangey-red carnelian, some at least from India, and royal-blue lapis lazuli from the remote mines of Badakhshan in what is now Afghanistan. These coloured stones were characteristically used as blocks of pigment – opaque stones cut to shape and inlaid into a metal form. It was only far later that settings began to suit the stone rather than the other way round.

Above *A gold chain necklace with lion-head terminals made of sheet gold, with eyes added in blue enamel. The chain is a massive but simple loop-in-loop form – the technique of which is shown in the diagram* **below**.

Roman 'imitation' jewelry is also often found made of copper-zinc alloys that have a gold-like colour and could be polished to a high shine. A huge number of such ornaments have survived, and these were usually produced by casting. Some of these alloys are near enough identical to the Pinchbeck and other copper-zinc alloys which have been used even into recent times as gold substitutes.

Right up to the beginning of the Christian era more northerly European jewelry was all-but devoid of coloured stones. One exception in northern Europe was amber – fossilized tree resin washed up on the beaches flanking the North Sea and Baltic. Some was traded south to be integrated into early Iron Age Greek jewelry, a fusion of European and Near Eastern materials and techniques. Jet, a hard, shiny black lignite, was another favoured substance for jewelry.

The gradual move to favour transparent gemstones occurred during the 1st millennium BC with the rise of the Persian empire, and was given a great impetus by Alexander the Great's conquests in the East. With the growth of a trade in pearls and gems, as well as the discovery of the direct sea-route to the gem island of Sri Lanka during Roman times, the modern gemstone industry was born.

Right *A belt hook – a typical ancient Chinese personal ornament – made of gilded copper alloy inlaid with silver in the form of a feline head, 3rd century* BC.

An important use of gemstones was for making seals, which by Greek and Roman times were often set in gold, most typically as signet rings. During the Bronze Age most of the gemstones used in jewelry, and for beads and seals, could be polished or cut using sand or a similar sili-

cate material – such as flint. With simple equipment, stones could be cut to shape as inlays, drilled as beads or engraved as seals. Highly intricate designs were produced, but a leap forward came with the move from a vertically worked drill to a small cutting wheel mounted horizontally. The small but strong components needed for such equipment might have necessitated iron, and indeed the introduction of the horizontal wheel cutting tool seems to coincide with the dawn of the Iron Age. The introduction of diamond-tipped engraving tools by the beginning of the Roman period allowed the drilling and engraving of even the hardest gems.

KEY DATES

cast/beaten gold	5th millennium BC, Balkans
jade working	3000 BC, China 1000 BC, Central America
gold wire/chains	2000 BC, Near East
gilding	1500 BC

Above *The so-called Carthage Treasure: the sapphires were from Sri Lanka, the emeralds probably from Egypt's eastern desert and the pearls from the Persian Gulf or India (c. AD 400).*

Left *An elaborate pectoral from the Popayán region of Colombia, c. AD 1100–1500. The various individual figures were cast separately using the lost-wax process. The large central figure is itself wearing a nose disc.*

69

Cosmetics & Perfumes

Since with paste my sides were adorned, since with balsam my mouth was coated,
since with kohl my eyes were painted …

INANNA'S SONG IN A HYMN OF KING SHULGI OF UR, *c.* 2094–2047 BC

A painted limestone statue of Nofret, her eyes of inlaid glass outlined in black eyepaint, her short hair covered by a thick wig; c. 2600 BC, from Meidum, Egypt.

Cosmetics and perfumes have been used to enhance and protect the body for more than 7000 years. Used equally by both men and women, they were regularly included in the grave goods of ancient cultures.

Cosmetics

In Egypt, cosmetic materials have been found in male and female burials of the Badarian period (5th millennium BC). Green malachite (copper ore), black galena (lead ore) and red ochre (iron oxide) have all been found in their raw state as well as in powdered form, having been crushed on slate (greywacke) palettes which are also found in burials. The powder was stored in shells, hollow reeds or purpose-made containers kept usually in small baskets or boxes; wealthy men and women had cosmetic chests with multiple compartments and pullout drawers.

The powdered minerals were mixed with water, fat or oil when required and applied with the fingers until the development of applicator sticks, around 2000 BC. Malachite formed the basis of the green eyepaint *wadju,* initially worn in a thick band across the eyes and upper cheeks until superseded by black galena-based kohl, known as *mesdemet*, and red ochre (*menshet*) to colour cheeks and lips.

Cosmetics formed an important part of religious ritual, with green eyepaint mentioned in the Pyramid Texts and associated with the amuletic eye of the god Horus. Eyepaints were applied to temple statues to allow them to see and this practice was extended to the dead – their eyes were outlined and lips and cheeks reddened to restore a life-like appearance. The same cosmetics were used by men and women in daily life as far more than simply beauty aids – eyepaint reduced the glare of the sun and its antiseptic qualities soothed problems caused by heat, flies and wind blown sand. Certain eyepaint containers were sometimes labelled with specific dates for their use, as opposed to 'everyday eyepaint'; others named their owner or the king in whose reign they had been distributed as gifts.

Female make-up artists, referred to as 'painters of the mouth', worked alongside manicurists and hairdressers. Henna paste was used to colour the hands, feet, nails and hair, and a whole variety of cosmetic preparations were listed in medical texts, from cleansing creams and face packs to rejuvenating oils such as one example, *c.*1500 BC, entitled 'How to make an old man into a young man ... found effective a million times'.

Cosmetics were also popular in 3rd millennium BC Mesopotamia. Green malachite, black kohl and

Above *Two glass perfume vessels and a glass eyepaint container shaped like a palm tree (right) in colours typical of the reign of the Egyptian pharaoh Amenhotep III, of the 14th century BC.*

other coloured pigments have been found in male and female burials, and the goddess Inanna paints her eyes with kohl in a hymn of King Shulgi. At the same date, the Indus Valley cultures were using white lead as a skin cosmetic, a fashion later adopted by Athenian women to emphasize their status and rare exposure to the sun. As the author of *On Painting the Face*, the Roman poet Ovid advocated white lead face powder, while Nero's wife Poppaea favoured red lips, cheeks and nails and black eyelids. The greatest exponents of Rome's cosmetic arts were the family of emperor Elagabalus, who himself wore blue and gold eyepaint, blue lip-paint and henna on his feet.

The early Europeans also painted their faces and bodies: the British Cruithni were renamed Picts (Painted People) by the Romans on account of their blue woad body paint. Propertius (*c.* 20 BC) criticized 'the painted Briton' and hated the use of 'Belgian rouge on Roman cheeks', but a glass vessel from Silchester shows the British were importing Italian face powder in the 1st century AD.

Elaborately painted faces were common throughout much of the ancient world. For instance, a female mummy from the Taklamakan region, of around 1000 BC, had yellow painted

Left *Multicoloured faience cosmetic container, 14th century BC, in the form of the Egyptian household god Bes, with pierced ears; the wooden stick used to apply the cosmetics is inside the jar.*

Below *A bronze Chinese censer inlaid with gold, Western Han dynasty, late 2nd century BC. The basin would have been used to burn aromatic substances.*

Right *A female banquet guest with eyes rimmed with black eyepaint and long full wig topped by a cone of semi-solid perfumed unguent; from the tomb of Nakht.*

spirals around her nose and Aztec women coloured their faces with yellow ochre or red cochineal. Red staining has also been found on the faces of a pre-Inca Chiribaya female mummy from Peru and a Colombian mummy of the Muisca culture of the early 13th century AD.

Perfume

Perfume was commonly used in ancient times to disguise low standards of personal hygiene. The Egyptians, however, were frequent bathers and used moisturizing oils perfumed with various flowers, herbs, spices, woods and resins. The earliest perfumes come from Predynastic burials (pre-3100 BC) and are made of imported conifer resin and vegetable fat.

Prior to the development of the distillation process in the 4th century BC, perfumes were created by steeping ingredients in oil or fat

A relief scene carved in limestone depicting women extracting the essential oil from lilies in order to make perfume; c. 380–343 BC, Egypt.

(enfleurage) or heating them together (maceration). Complex blends could take up to 365 days to prepare, and perfume and incense production are portrayed in tomb and temple scenes. Perfume laboratories are even incorporated into certain temple layouts.

Perfumes such as the Seven Sacred Oils played a vital role in Egyptian ritual. The gods were regarded as highly fragrant beings and their divine characteristics were replicated with perfumes. Scent also had a protective purpose: sweet odours were believed to repel evil and strong perfumes were used in funeral rites to restore the senses of the deceased. The mummification process involved perfumed ingredients too – the 'myrrh, cinnamon and every other aromatic substance' noted by Herodotus also hiding signs of decay.

Used around the home, perfume played an important part at social gatherings when guests were told to 'follow your heart as long as you live, put myrrh on your head and anoint yourself with oils fit for a god'. Exaggerated cone-shaped lumps depicted in paintings were used to indicate that figures were wearing perfume, the red-brown streaking showing that the perfumed oils rubbed over the body had soaked through clothing. Favoured courtiers were rewarded with perfume, and an army commander in around 1300 BC was advised to 'take heed to have full preparation made in front of Pharaoh, with incense and perfumed oils to anoint his soldiers and chariotry'. Yet such practices were not to everyone's

Left *A yellow faience perfume container naming the Egyptian pharaoh Amenhotep III and his great royal wife Tiy, of the 14th century BC.*

KEY DATES

cosmetic materials	*c.* 5500 BC, Egypt
obsidian mirrors	5000 BC, Anatolia
perfume	pre-3100 BC, Egypt
metal mirrors	3rd millennium BC, Egypt
perfume distillation	4th century BC

taste; perfume was banned in Sparta and the Spartan king Agesilaus is said to have stormed out of an Egyptian banquet in 361 BC since he felt the lavish use of perfume decadent and effeminate.

By Graeco-Roman times, the Egyptian capital Alexandria was the centre of world perfume pro-duction, combining ingredients from as far afield as Arabia, India and the Far East. According to Pliny, those employed in this highly lucrative industry were subject to rigorous security checks, with 'a seal put on their aprons … and before they are allowed to leave the premises they have to take off all their clothes'.

In his essay *De Odoribus* (*Concerning Odours*), Theophrastus stated that Egyptian perfume was the best in the world. One Greek merchant had had a batch in his shop for eight years and it was in better condition than fresh perfume. Even with the taxes and duty levied on perfume imports, merchants could still make a hundredfold profit. As well as being the largest importers of Egyptian perfumes, the Romans manufactured their own fragrances at Capua, exporting them across their empire in small glass phials known as *unguentaria*.

Perfumes were popular in India as early as 2000 BC, and although the Assyrians only used perfume for ceremonial events, Herodotus says the Babylonians 'perfume themselves all over'. Inscribed incense burners from southern Arabia show that frankincense was offered to the region's gods as early as the 8th century BC. The Chinese Su Ma Chien of the 2nd century BC refers to an incense made from a hundred ingredients 'harmoniously compounded', and the gimbal, described as 'a perfume burner for use among the cushions', was invented by the Chinese around 100 BC.

MIRRORS

Although obsidian mirrors over 7000 years old were found in female burials at Çatalhöyük and were used much later by the Maya and Aztecs, most mirrors were made of polished copper or bronze, the earliest dating to the early 3rd millennium BC in Egypt. They are shown beneath the chairs of male and female owners or held up for use. The mirror's reflective disc led to solar associations, enhanced by handles representing Hathor, goddess of beauty and daughter of the sun god. By reflecting the living image, mirrors were also associated with vitality and placed in burials, sometimes close to the mummy's face.

Metal mirrors were also made in the Indus Valley *c.* 2800–2500 BC and in China and Siberia *c.* 1500–1000 BC, where they served the requirements of vanity and conferred an ability to see into the spirit world. Later Chinese examples were worn on the belt. Highly ornate bronze mirrors were produced by the Celts in the 4th to 1st centuries BC, and the Etruscans – the stately figure of Seianti Hanunia Tlesnasa, who died *c.* 140 BC, reclines on her sarcophagus holding a mirror replicating in terracotta the silver example found in her tomb. The Greeks and Etruscans also used compact-style lidded mirrors made of metal, although Pliny states that the first true glass mirrors were developed in the Lebanese city of Sidon and then copied by the Romans.

Contraceptives
& Aphrodisiacs

Worn with a gem or even spoken, the following verse serves as a contraceptive:
'Would that you be fated to be unborn and die unmarried!' Write this on a
piece of new papyrus and tie it up with the hairs of a mule.

GREEK CONTRACEPTIVE RECIPE, 3RD CENTURY AD

Left & below *These two Moche pots from Peru,* AD *100–600, show couples enjoying non-reproductive sex, perhaps a common way of avoiding pregnancy in societies without reliable contraception.*

women take advantage of whatever contraceptive technology was on offer. The best evidence for it comes from Greece, Rome and Egypt, where medical knowledge was recorded; it is almost impossible to say anything about contraception in pre-literate societies.

Magic & medicine

Despite social imperatives for high birth rates, some contraceptives were available in antiquity – though of wildly variable efficacy. One that was not available was the condom. It is often claimed that condoms made of animal bladders or fine skins were invented in antiquity, but in fact they were unknown before the 16th century. The simplest contraceptive was to enjoy fellation, cunnilingus, anal sex or other non-fertile sexual positions.

The numerous 'magical' methods of birth control were unpredictable but perhaps not always completely useless, because medical or dietary therapies often accompanied the supernatural elements. One example is an Egyptian spell for prolonging lactation, which involved women wearing amulets of white stone and eating various high-protein foods. The prolactin produced while breast-feeding certainly suppressed fertility, and wearing amulets and reciting magical formulae might additionally have had a placebo effect.

Ancient contraceptives also included substances that induced abortion, which was not differentiated from contraception. However, the most reliable and seemingly 'scientific' birth control method was to

As the above magical spell suggests, the cultures of antiquity never developed reliable contraceptives. This was in part because there was no reason to do so: infant and maternal death rates were so high that female fertility had to be maximized rather than limited. Conservative estimates suggest that half of all live-born children would die before the age of 10, and consequently populations would decline dangerously unless women had multiple pregnancies. Practically, this might mean that the adult population could only remain stable if each fertile woman produced five or six live-born children. As ancient populations mostly experienced growth, effective birth control could never have been widely practised. Even so, the exhausting and potentially lethal prospect of spending much of one's adult life pregnant made

Right *An Egyptian charm in the form of the god Bes, who was regarded as warding off evil influences at childbirth, showing that for many women, birth control was not as important an issue as safe childbirth.*

Below *A Roman wind-chime made of bronze, from Pompeii, 1st century AD, in the form of a flying phallus. Such items were thought of as good-luck charms.*

insert physical barriers against sperm entering the cervix, along with mild spermicides such as honey, alum or cedar oil. Barriers could be anything from sponges, rag tampons or even small onions, to complicated pessaries that could only have been made in a well-equipped pharmacy. Chemists have recently analyzed some ancient contraceptive recipes, with surprising results.

A prototype Pill?

Some ancient Greek recipes for contraceptive pessaries use plants, such as pomegranates, with high natural levels of oestrogen, which stops the pituitary gland producing the hormone that stimulates ovulation. Seemingly, these ancient pessaries worked on the same principle as the modern oral contraceptive pill (though the ancient doctors could not have known this); but the picture is more complicated. Laboratory tests have showed that only the skin around the pomegranate seed lowered fertility, whereas the ancient recipe called for the rind and peel, which were quite ineffective. And tests on other plants with supposed contraceptive powers, such as coriander, tansy and willow, concluded that to have any effect these either had to be taken in enormous doses, or in very purified forms that could not have been manufactured in antiquity.

Also, it is crucial to remember that ancient doctors used plants as much for the powers conveyed by their mythological symbolism as for any scientific reason. Pomegranates, for instance, were associated with infertility because in myth the goddess Persephone had to spend six months in Hades, having eaten some pomegranate seeds,

and thus caused the earth's seasonal sterility. Another example is the recipe for a contraceptive pessary made of crocodile dung known from an Egyptian medical papyrus. As a pessary base, crocodile dung might have been mildly effective as a barrier, but it was used because of its association with Seth, god of every kind of disorder and infertility, including abortion. All in all, modern assertions that some ancient contraceptives were developed from empirical scientific testing fall down when they are considered in the broader reasoning that underpinned the pharmacologies of antiquity.

Aphrodisiacs: ancient Viagra?

Unlike contraceptives, which were made for women and mostly applied vaginally, most ancient aphrodisiacs were made for men, to be taken orally or applied direct to the penis. Aphrodisiacs were men's business, reflecting the ideology, common in patriarchal cultures, that women are more lustful than men and have no need of stimulants to the libido. Roman aphrodisiac recipes illustrate this. Men were recommended to drink wine infused with pine-kernels and pepper, or celery and rocquette seeds; or to anoint the penis with honey and pepper, or carrot juice.

Ancient aphrodisiacs did include substances that are still used to enhance sexual performance, as well as those with culturally specific mythological associations that now seem the opposite of sexually stimulating. So, the properties of the dried cantharides beetle (modern 'Spanish fly') were well known, but lettuce was also thought to be an aphrodisiac, the milky sap it exuded when cut supposedly encouraging sperm production. Other pleasant-smelling substances were not gender-specific, such as the Egyptian resin *kyphi*, which induced a state of muscle relaxation and overall well-being that was conducive to sexual activity.

Further Reading

Technologies

1 Stone Tools

Boesch, C. & Boesch, H., 'Tool-use and tool-making in wild chimpanzees', in Berthelet, A. & Chavaillon, J. (eds), *The Use of Tools by Human and Non-Human Primates* (Oxford, 1990), 158–74

Toth, N., 'The Oldowan reassessed: a close look at early stone artefacts', *Journal of Archaeological Science* 12 (1985), 101–20

Whittaker, J., *Flint Knapping, Making and Understanding Stone Tools* (Austin, 1994)

Johanson, D. & Edgar, B. (eds), *From Lucy to Language* (New York & London, 1996)

2 Fire

Bellamo, R. V., 'A methodological approach for identifying archaeological evidence of fire resulting from human activities', *Journal of Archaeological Science* 20 (1993), 525–55

Mellars, P. & Dark, P., *Star Carr in Context* (Cambridge, 1998)

Rehder, J. E., *The Mastery and Uses of Fire in Antiquity* (Montreal, 2000)

3 Wooden Tools

Boesch, C. & Boesch, H., 'Tool-use and tool-making in wild chimpanzees', in Berthelet, A. & Chavaillon, J. (eds), *The Use of Tools by Human and Non-Human Primates* (Oxford, 1990), 158–74

Burov, G. M., 'The use of vegetable materials in the Mesolithic of Northeast Euope', in Zvelebil, M., Dennell, R. & Doman'ska, L. (eds), *Harvesting the Sea, Farming the Forest* (Sheffield, 1998), 53–64

Mercader, J. & others, 'Excavation of a chimpanzee stone tool site in the African rainforest', *Science* 296 (2002), 1452–55

Thieme, H., 'Lower Palaeolithic hunting spears from Germany', *Nature* 385 (1997), 807–10

4 Composite Tools, Blades & Chisels

Bordes, F., *The Old Stone Age* (New York, 1968)

Fagan, B., *The Journey from Eden* (London & New York, 1990)

Gamble, C., *The Palaeolithic Societies of Europe* (Cambridge, 1999)

Mithen, S., *The Prehistory of the Mind* (London & New York, 1996)

Stringer, C. & Gamble, C., *In Search of the Neanderthals* (London & New York, 1993)

5 Bone & Antler Tools

Gamble, C., *The Palaeolithic Societies of Europe* (Cambridge, 1999)

Hoffecker, J., *Desolate Landscapes* (New Brunswick, 2001)

Mithen, S., *The Prehistory of the Mind* (London & New York, 1996)

White, R., *Dark Caves, Bright Images* (New York, 1996)

6 Grinders, Polishers & Polished Axes

Fullagar, R. & Field, J., 'Pleistocene seed-grinding implements from the Australian arid zone', *Antiquity* 71 (1997), 300–07

Wright, K., 'Early Holocene ground stone assemblages in the Levant', *Levant* 25 (1993), 93–111

Bradley, R. & Edmonds, M., *Interpeting the Axe Trade: Production and Exchange in Neolithic Britain* (Cambridge, 1993)

7 Baskets & Basketry

Berns, M. & Hudson, B. R., *The Essential Gourd: Art and History in Northeastern Nigeria* (Los Angeles, 1986)

Capistrano-Baker, F. H., *Basketry of the Luzon Cordillera, Philippines* (Los Angeles, 1998)

Guss, D. M., *To Weave and Sing; Art, Symbol and Narrative in the South American Rain Forest* (Berkeley, 1989)

McGregor, R., *Prehistoric Basketry of the Lower Pecos, Texas* (Madison, Wisconsin, 1992)

Wendrich, W. Z., 'Basketry', in Nicholson, P.T. & Shaw, I. (eds), *Ancient Egyptian Materials and Technology* (Cambridge, 2000)

8 Pottery

Barnett, W. K. & Hoopes, J. W., *The Emergence of Pottery: Technology and Innovation in Ancient Societies* (Washington DC, 1995)

Cooper, E., *Ten Thousand Years of Pottery* (London & Philadelphia, 2000)

Freestone, I. & Gaimster, D. (eds), *Pottery in the Making: World Ceramic Traditions* (London & Washington, DC, 1997)

Kenrick, D. M., *Jomon of Japan: The World's Oldest Pottery* (London, 1995)

Rice, P. M., *Pottery Analysis: A Sourcebook* (Chicago, 1987)

Rice, P. M., 'On the Origins of Pottery' *Journal of Archaeological Method and Theory* 6(1) (1999) 1–54

Sentance, B., *Ceramics* (London & New York, 2004)

9 Copper, Bronze, Gold & Silver

Craddock, P. T., *Early Metal Mining and Metal Production* (Edinburgh, 1995)

Craddock, P. T., 'From Hearth to Furnace: Evidences for the Earliest Metal Smelting Technologies in the Eastern Mediterranean', *Paléorient* 26.2 (2001), 151–65

Craddock, P. T. & Lang, J. (eds), *Mining and Metal Production Through the Ages* (London, 2002)

Hauptmann, A., Pernicka, E., Rehren, Th. & Yalçin, Ü., *The Beginnings of Metallurgy, Der Anschnitt*, Beiheft 9 (Bochum, 1999)

Maddin, R., *The Beginning of the Use of Metals and Alloys* (Cambridge, MA, 1988)

Ramage, A. & Craddock, P. T., *King Croesus' Gold* (London, 2000)

Tylecote, R. F. *The Prehistory of Metallurgy in the British Isles* (London, 1986)

10 Iron & Steel

Coghlan, H. H., *Notes on Prehistoric and Early Iron in the Old World*, Pitt Rivers Occasional Paper 8 (Oxford, 1956)

Craddock, P. T., *Early Metal Mining and Production* (Edinburgh, 1995)

Craddock, P. T., 'Cast iron, fined iron, crucible steel: liquid iron and steel in the ancient world', in Craddock, P. T. & Lang, J. (eds), *Mining and Metal Production Through the Ages* (London, 2002), 233–48

Rostocker, W. & Bronson, B., *Pre-Industrial Iron*, Archaeomaterials Monograph 1 (Philadelphia, 1990)

Tylecote, R. F., *A History of Metallurgy* (London, 1976)

Wagner, D. B., *Iron and Steel in Ancient China* (Leiden, 1993)

11 Glass

Grose, D. F., *Early Ancient Glass* (New York, 1989)

Henderson, J., *The Science and Archaeology of Materials* (London, 2000), 24–108

Newby, M. & Painter, K. (eds.), *Roman Glass,* Society of Antiquaries of London, Occasional Papers XIII (London, 1991)

Nicholson, P. T., *Egyptian Faience and Glass* (Aylesbury, 1993)

Tait, H. (ed.), *Five Thousand Years of Glass* (London, 1991)

Saldern, A. von, Oppenheim, A. L., Brill, R. H. & Barag, D., *Glass and Glassmaking in Ancient Mesopotamia* (Corning, 1970)

Tatton-Brown, V. & Andrews, C., 'Before the invention of glass blowing', in Tait, H. (ed.), *Five Thousand Years of Glass* (London, 1991), 20–61

12 Textiles & Weaving

Barber, E. J. W., *Prehistoric Textiles* (Princeton, 1991)

Barber, E. J. W., *Women's Work: The First 20,000 Years* (New York, 1994)

Broudy, E., *The Book of Looms: A History of the Handloom from Ancient Times to the Present* (Providence, 1979)

Emory, I., *The Primary Structures of Fabrics* (Washington, DC, 1962)

Gervers, V. (ed.), *Studies in Textile History* (Toronto, 1977)

Good, I., 'Archaeological textiles: a review of current research', *Annual Reviews of Anthropology*, 30 (2001), 209–26

Rutt, R., *A History of Handknitting* (Loveland, CO,1987)

Shelter & Subsistence

13 Houses

De Laet, S. J. (ed.), *History of Humanity*, Vol. I (Paris & London, 1994)

Johnson, M., 'Studying Structures', in Barker, G. (ed.), *Companion Encyclopedia of Archaeology* (London, 1999), 310–43

Oliver, P. (ed.), *Encyclopedia of Vernacular Architecture of the World* (Cambridge, 1997)

Preston Blier, S., *The Anatomy of Architecture; Ontology and Metaphor in Batammaliba Architectural Expression* (Cambridge, 1987)

14 Stone Architecture

Adam, J. P., *Roman Building. Materials and Techniques* (London & Bloomington, 1994)

Arnold, D., *Building in Egypt: Pharaonic Stone Masonry* (Oxford, 1991)

Coulton, J., *Ancient Greek Architects at Work. Problems of Structure and Design* (New York, 1977)

Nicholson, P. T. & Shaw, I. (eds), *Ancient Egyptian Materials and Technology* (Cambridge, 2000)

Oliver, P. (ed.), *Encyclopedia of Vernacular Architecture of the World* (Cambridge, 1997)

Scarre, C. (ed.), *The Seventy Wonders of the Ancient World* (London & New York, 1999)

15 Furniture

Baker, H. S., *Furniture in the Ancient World: Origins and Evolution 3100–475 BC* (London & New York, 1966)

Killen, G., *Ancient Egyptian Furniture, Vol. I, 4000–1300 BC* (Warminster, 1980; repr. 2002); *Vol. 2, Boxes, Chests and Footstools* (Warminster, 1994)

Killen, G., *Egyptian Woodworking and Furniture* (Princes Risborough, 1994)

Killen, G., 'Wood turning in ancient Egypt', *The Journal of the Tool and Trades History Society*, 10 (1997)

Richter, G. M. A., *The Furniture of the Greeks, Etruscans and Romans* (London, 1966)

Simpson, E. & Spirydowicz, K., *Gordion, Wooden Furniture* (Ankara, 1999)

Simpson, E., 'Early evidence for the use of the lathe in antiquity', in *Meletemata, Studies in Aegean Archaeology Presented to Malcolm H. Wiener* (Liège, 1999)

16 Lighting & Heating

Forbes, R. J., *Studies in Ancient Technology*, vol. 6 (Leiden, 1966, 2nd ed.)

Humphrey, J. W., Oleson, J. P. & Sherwood, A. N., *Greek and Roman Technology: A Sourcebook* (London & New York, 1998)

Szentléleky, T., *Ancient Lamps* (Chicago, 1969)

17 Water Supplies & Plumbing

Dalley, S., 'Water management in Assyria in the ninth to seventh centuries BC' *ARAM* 13/14 (2001/2), 443–60

Evans, H., *Water Distribution in Ancient Rome* (Ann Arbor, 1993)

Hodge, A. T., *Roman Aqueducts and Water Supply* (London, 1992)

Koloski-Ostrow, A. (ed.), *Water Use and Hydraulics in the Roman City* (Dubuque, 2001)

Wikander, Ö. (ed.), *Handbook of Ancient Water Technology* (Leiden, 2000)

18 Bathing & Sanitation

Fagan, G. G., *Bathing in Public in the Roman World* (Ann Arbor, 1999)

Forbes, R. J., *Studies in Ancient Technology*, vol. 2 (Leiden, 1965, 2nd ed.)

Jansen, G. C. M. (ed.), *Cura Aquarum in Sicilia* (Leiden, 2000), 275–312

Yegül, F., *Baths and Bathing in Classical Antiquity* (Cambridge, 1992)

19 Security

British Museum, *A Guide to the Exhibition Illustrating Greek and Roman Life* (London, 2nd ed., 1920)

Pitt-Rivers, A. H. L-F., *On the Development and Distribution of Primitive Locks and Keys; illustrated by specimens in the Pitt-Rivers Collection* (London, 1883)

Manning, W. H., *Catalogue of the Romano-British Iron Tools, Fittings and Weapons in the British Museum* (London, 1985)

20 Cereal Agriculture

Mithen, S., *After the Ice: A Global Human History* (London, 2003; Cambridge, Mass., 2004)

Smith, B. D., *The Emergence of Agriculture* (New York, 1995)

Stordeur, D., Helmer, D. & Willcox, G., 'Jerf el-Ahmar, un nouveau site de l'horizon PPNA sur le moyen Euphrate Syrien', *Bulletin de la Société Préhistorique Française* 94 (1997), 282–85

21 From Digging Sticks to Ploughs

Fowler, P. J., *The Farming of Prehistoric Britain* (Cambridge, 1983)

Glob, P. V., *Ard og Plov i Nordens Oldtid [Ard and Plough in Prehistoric Scandinavia]*, (Aarhus, 1951). With lengthy English summaries

Sherratt, A., 'Plough and pastoralism: aspects of the secondary products revolution', in Hodder, I., Isaac, G. & Hammond, N. (eds), *Pattern of the Past* (Cambridge, 1981), 261–305

Tools and Tillage (periodical)

22 Irrigation

Adams, R. McC., *Heartland of Cities: Surveys of Ancient Settlement and Land Use on the Central Floodplain of the Euphrates* (Chicago, 1982)

Butzer, K. W., *Early Hydraulic Civilization in Egypt* (Chicago, 1976)

Butzer, K. W., 'Irrigation' and 'Nile', in Redford, D. B. (ed.), *The Oxford Encyclopedia of Ancient Egypt* (New York & Oxford, 2001), 183–88 & 543–51

Eyre, C. J., 'The water regime for orchards and plantations in Pharaonic Egypt', *Journal of Egyptian Archaeology* 80 (1994), 57–80

Landels, J. G., *Engineering in the Ancient World* (Berkeley, 2000)

23 Handmills, Watermills & Pumps

Frankel, R., 'The Olynthus Mill, its origin and diffusion', *American Journal of Archaeology* 107 (2003) 1–21

Lewis, M. J. T., *Millstone and Hammer: The Origins of Water Power* (Hull, 1997)

Oleson, J. P., 'Water-Lifting', in Wikander, Ö. (ed.), *Handbook of Ancient Water Technology* (Leiden, 2000), 217–302

Wikander, Ö., 'The Water-Mill', in Wikander, Ö. (ed.), *Handbook of Ancient Water Technology* (Leiden, 2000), 371–400

24 Gardens

Carroll, M., *Earthly Paradises. Ancient Gardens in History and Archaeology* (London & Los Angeles, 2003)

Farrar, L., *Ancient Roman Gardens* (Stroud, 1998)

Gothein, M. L., *A History of Garden Art*, 1, trans. L. Archer-Hind (New York, 1966)

Moynihan, E. B., *Paradise as a Garden* (London, 1980)

Shoemaker, C. A.(ed.), *Encyclopedia of Gardens, History and Design*, 3 vols (Chicago & London, 2001)

Thompson, D. B., *Garden Lore of Ancient Athens* (Princeton, 1963)

Wilkinson, A., *The Garden in Ancient Egypt* (London, 1998)

25 The Domestication of Animals

Clutton-Brock, J., *Domesticated Animals from the Earliest Times* (London, 1981)

Collins, B. J. (ed.), *A History of the Animal World in the Ancient Near East* (Leiden, 2002)

Foster, K. P., 'Gardens of Eden: exotic flora and fauna in the ancient Near East', in Albert, J., Bernhardsson, M. & Kenna, R. (eds), *Transformations of Middle Eastern Natural Environments: Legacies and Lessons* (New Haven: Yale School of Forestry and Environmental Studies, Bulletin 103, 1998), 320–29

Houlihan, P. F., *The Animal World of the Pharaohs* (London & Cairo, 1996)

Sherratt, A., 'The secondary exploitation of animals in the Old World', *World Archaeology* 15 (1983), 90–104

Smith, B. D., *The Emergence of Agriculture* (New York, 1995)

Speed Weed, W., 'First to ride', *Discover* (March 2002), 54–61

Zeder, M. A. & Hesse, B., 'The initial domestication of goats (*Capra hircus*) in the Zagros Mountains 10,000 years ago', *Science* 287 (24 March 2000), 2254–57

26 Cooking

Bode, W., *European Gastronomy: The Story of Man's Food and Eating Customs* (London, 2000)

Brothwell, D. & P., *Food in Antiquity: A Survey of the Diet of Early Peoples* (London, 1969; Baltimore, 1998)

Rossotti, H., *Fire* (Oxford, 1993)

Schick, K. & Toth, N., *Making Silent Stones Speak: Human Evolution and the Dawn of Technology* (New York, 1993)

27 Fermented Beverages

Huang, H.-T., 'Biology and biological technology, Part V: Fermentations and food science', in Needham, J. (ed.), *Science and Civilization in China*, Vol. 6 (Cambridge, 2000)

Katz, S. H. & Voigt, M. M., 'Bread and beer: The early use of cereals in the human diet', *Expedition* 28 (1986), 23–34

McGovern, P. F., *Ancient Wine: The Scientific Search for the Origins of Viniculture* (Princeton, 2003)

McGovern, P. E., Fleming, S. J. & Katz, S. H. (eds), *The Origins and Ancient History of Wine* (New York, 1995)

McGovern, P. E. & others, 'A feast fit for King Midas', *Nature* 402 (1999), 863–64

McGovern, P. E. & others, 'The beginnings of winemaking and viniculture in the ancient Near East and Egypt' *Expedition* 39 (1) (1997), 3–21

McGovern, P. E. & others, 'Neolithic resinated wine', *Nature* 381 (1996), 480–81

Michel, R. H., McGovern, P. E., & Badler, V. R., 'The first wine and beer: chemical detection of ancient fermented beverages', *Analytical Chemistry* 65 (1993), 408A–413A

28 Food Preservation

Forbes, R.J., *Studies in Ancient Technology: Heat and Heating – Refrigeration, The Art of Cooling and Producing Cold-Light* (New York, 1997)

Kurlansky, M., *Salt. A World History* (New York & London, 2002)

Mack, L., *Food Preservation in the Roman Empire* (Chapel Hill, NC, 2001)

Shephard, S., *Pickled, Potted, and Canned: How the Art and Science of Food Preserving Changed the World* (London, 2000)

29 Chocolate & Tea

Chow, K. & Kramer, I., *All the Tea in China* (San Francisco, 1990)

Coe, S. D. & M. D., *The True History of Chocolate* (London & New York, 1996)

Schafer, E. H., 'T'ang', in Chang, K.C. (ed.), *Food in Ancient China* (New Haven & London, 1977), 85–140

Howstuffworks, 'What is chewing gum made of?' http://science.howstuffworks.com/question86.htm

Sahagún, Fray Bernadino de, *General History of the Things of New Spain, Book 10 – The People* (Santa Fe, 1961)

Tagalder Technology Corporation, *China's Tea Culture* http://www.index-china-food.com/tea-culture.htm

Wild Things, Inc. 'The botany and ecology of *chicle, Manilkara zapota* http://www.junglegum.com/Chicle/botany.html

30 Drugs & Narcotics

Emboden, W. A., *Narcotic Plants: Hallucinogens, Stimulants, Inebriants, and Hypnotics, Their Origins and Uses* (London & New York, 1979)

Furst, P. T. (ed.), *Flesh of the Gods: The Ritual Use of Hallucinogens* (London & New York, 1972)

Goodman, J., Lovejoy, P. E. & Sherratt, A. (eds.), *Consuming Habits: Drugs in History and Anthropology* (London & New York, 1995)

Rätsch, C., *The Dictionary of Sacred and Magical Plants* (Bridport, 1992)

Rudgley, R., *The Encyclopaedia of Psychoactive Substances* (London, 1998; New York, 1999)

Schultes, R. E. & Hofmann, A., *Plants of the Gods: Origins of Hallucinogen Use* (New York & London, 1980)

Transportation

31 Skis, Snowshoes, Toboggans & Skates

Burov, G. M., 'Some Mesolithic wooden artifacts from the site of Vis I in the European North East of the U.S.S.R.', in Bonsall, C. (ed.), *The Mesolithic in Europe* (Edinburgh, 1989), 391–401

Clark, J. G. D., *Prehistoric Europe: the Economic Basis* (London, 1952)

Helm, J., *Handbook of North American Indians: vol. 6 Subarctic* (Washington, DC, 1981)

Trigger, B., *Handbook of North American Indians: vol. 15 Northeast* (Washington, DC, 1978)

32 Wheels & Carts

Littauer, M. A. & Crouwel, J. H., *Wheeled Vehicles and Ridden Animals in the Ancient Near East* (Leiden/Köln, 1979)

Needham, J., *Science and Civilization in China*, Vol. 4: *Physics and Physical Technology* (Cambridge, 1965)

Piggott, S., *The Earliest Wheeled Transport: From the Atlantic Coast to the Caspian Sea* (London, 1983)

Piggott, S., *Wagon, Chariot and Carriage: Symbol and Status in the History of Transport* (London, 1992)

33 Horses & Horse Equipment

Hyland, A., *Equus. The Horse in the Roman World* (London & New Haven, 1990)

Marsha, L., 'The origins of horse husbandry on the Eurasian Steppe', in *Late Prehistoric Exploitation of the Eurasian Steppe* (Cambridge, 1999)

Meadow, R. H. & Uerpermann, H. P. (eds), *Equids in the Ancient World*, (Wiesbaden, vol. I 1986; vol. II 1991)

Postgate, J. N., *Taxation and Conscription in the Assyrian Empire* (Rome, 1974)

Potratz, J., 'Die Pferdetrensen des Alten Orients', *Analecta Orientalia* 41 (Rome, 1966)

34 Tracks & Roads

Chevallier, R., *Roman Roads* (London & Berkeley, 1976)

Coles, B. & Coles, J., *Sweet Track to Glastonbury: the Somerset Levels in Prehistory* (London & New York, 1986)

Coles, B. & Coles, J., *People of the Wetlands: Bogs, Bodies and Lake-Dwellers* (London & New York, 1989)

Coles, J. M. & Lawson, A. J. (eds), *European Wetlands in Prehistory* (Oxford, 1987)

Hyslop, J., *The Inca Road System* (New York, 1984)

Raftery, B., *Trackway Excavations in the Mountdillon Bogs, Co. Longford, 1985–1991*. Irish Archaeological Wetland Unit, Transactions: Vol. 3. (Dublin, 1995)

Raftery, B. & Hickey, J. (eds), *Recent Developments in Wetland Research*. Seandálaíocht, Vol. 2/ WARP Occ. Paper 14 (Dublin, 2001)

Whitfield, S., *Life Along the Silk Road* (Berkeley, 2000)

35 Bridges & Canals

Hopkins, H. J., *A Span of Bridges: an Illustrated History* (Newton Abbot, 1970)

Needham, J., *Science and Civilization in China*, Vol.4: *Physics and Physical*

Technology, part III: Civil Engineering and Nautics (Cambridge, 1971)

O'Connor, C., *Roman Bridges* (Cambridge, 1993)

Payne, R., *The Canal Builders: the Story of Canal Engineers through the Ages* (New York, 1959)

Robins, F. W., *The Story of the Bridge* (Birmingham, 1948)

Smith, N., *Man and Water: A History of Hydro-Technology* (New York, 1975)

36 Camels & Camel Saddles

Bovill, E. W., *The Golden Trade of the Moors* (Princeton, 1995)

Bulliet, R., *The Camel and the Wheel* (New York, 1990)

Wilson, R. T., *The Camel* (London & New York, 1984)

37 Rafts & Logboats

Adney, E. T. & Chapelle, H. I., *Bark Canoes & Skin Boats of North America* (Washington, DC, 1964)

Edwards, C. R., *Aboriginal Watercraft on the Pacific Coast of S. America* (Berkeley & Los Angeles, 1965)

Greenhill, B., *Archaeology of Boats & Ships* (London, 1995)

Hornell, J., *Water Transport* (Cambridge, 1946; Newton Abbot, 1970)

Johnstone, P., *Seacraft of Prehistory* (London, 1988)

McGrail, S., *Boats of the World from the Stone Age to Medieval Times* (Oxford, 2002)

38 Planked Boats & Ships

Casson, L., *Ships & Seamanship in the Ancient World* (Baltimore & London, 1995)

Haddon A. C. & Hornell, J., *Canoes of Oceania* (Honolulu, 1936–38/1975)

Hudson, T., Timbrook, J. & Rempe, M. (eds), *Tomol: Chumash Watercraft*, Anthropology Papers 9 (Santa Barbara, 1978)

Jones, D., *Boats (Egyptian)* (London, 1995)

McGrail, S., *Boats of the World from the Stone Age to Medieval Times* (Oxford, 2002)

Steffy, J. R., *Wooden Shipbuilding & the Interpretation of Shipwrecks* (College Station, 1994)

39 Sailing Vessels

Casson, L., *Ships & Seamanship in the Ancient World* (Baltimore & London, 1995)

Doran, E., *Wangka: Austronesian Canoe Origins* (College Station, 1981)

Haddon, A. C. & Hornell, J., *Canoes of Oceania* (Honolulu, 1936–38/1975)

Johnstone, P., *Seacraft of Prehistory* (London, 1988)

McGrail, S., *Boats of the World from the Stone Age to Medieval Times* (Oxford, 2002)

40 Paddles, Poles & Oars

Casson, L., *Ships & Seamanship in the Ancient World* (Baltimore & London, 1995)

Johnstone, P., *Seacraft of Prehistory* (London, 1988)

McGrail, S., *Boats of the World from the Stone Age to Medieval Times* (Oxford, 2002)

41 Navigation, Harbours & Lighthouses

Casson, L., *Periplus Maris Erythraei* (Princeton, 1989)

Lewis, D., *We the Navigators* (Honolulu, 1994)

McGrail, S., *Boats of the World from the Stone Age to Medieval Times* (Oxford, 2002)

Taylor, E. G. R., *Haven-Finding Art* (London, 1971)

Taylor, E. G. R. & Richey, M., *Geometrical Seaman* (London, 1962)

Waters, D. W., *Art of Navigation in England in Elizabethan and Early Stuart Times* (London, 2nd ed., 1978)

Hunting, Warfare & Sport

42 Animal & Fish Traps, Fishing Nets

Bateman, J., *Animal Traps and Trapping* (Newton Abbot, 2nd ed., 1988)

Pedersen, L., '7000 years of fishing: stationary fishing structures in the mesolithic and afterwards', in Fischer, A. (ed.), *Man and Sea in the Mesolithic* (Oxford, 1995), 75–86

Stewart, H., *Indian Fishing. Early Methods on the Northwest Coast* (Vancouver, 1977)

43 Spearthrowers, Boomerangs & Bows & Arrows

Bleed, P., 'The optimal design of hunting weapons: maintainability or reliability', *American Antiquity* 51 (1986), 737–47

Clark, J. G. D., 'Neolithic bows from Somerset, England, and the prehistory of archery in North-western Europe', *Proceedings of the Prehistoric Society* 29 (1963), 50–98

Peterkin, G. L., Bricker, H. & Mellars, P. (eds), *Hunting and Animal Exploitation in the Later Palaeolithic and Mesolithic of Eurasia*. Archaeological Papers of the American Anthropological Association no. 4 (1993)

Rausing, G., *The Bow. Some Notes on its Origin and Development* (Lund, 1967)

Torrence, R., 'Hunter-gatherer technology: macro- and microscale approaches', in Panter-Brick, C., Layton, R. & Rowley-Conwy, P. (eds), *Hunter-Gatherers. An Interdisciplinary Perspective* (Cambridge, 2001), 73–98

44 Swords, Daggers & War Spears

Coe, M. D. & others, *Swords and Hilt Weapons* (London & New York, 1989)

Oakeshott, R. E., *The Archaeology of Weapons* (London & New York, 1960)

Stone, G. C., *A Glossary of the Construction, Decoration and Use of Arms and Armour in All Countries and in All Times* (Portland, 1934, repr. New York, 1999)

Yadin, Y., *The Art of Warfare in Biblical Lands* (London & New York, 1963)

45 Armour, Helmets & Shields

Benitez-Johannot, P. & Barbier, J.P., *Shields* (London & Munich, 2000)

Dien, A. E., 'A study of early Chinese armour' *Artibus Asiae*, vol. 43, 1 & 2 (New York, 1981/82)

Oakeshott, R. E., *The Archaeology of Weapons* (London & New York, 1960)

Robinson, H. R., *The Armour of Imperial Rome* (London & New York, 1975)

Stone, G. C., *A Glossary of the Construction, Decoration and Use of Arms and Armour in All Countries and in All Times* (Portland, 1934, repr. New York, 1999)

Woolley, C. L. & Moorey, P. R. S., *Ur of the Chaldees* (London & Ithaca, 1982)

Yadin, Y., *The Art of Warfare in Biblical Lands* (London & New York, 1963)

Zettler, R. L. & Horne, L. (eds), *Treasures from the Royal Tombs of Ur* (Philadelphia, 1998)

46 Fortifications

Hogg, I. V., *The History of Fortification* (New York, 1981)

Johnson, S., *Hadrian's Wall* (London, 1991)

Mulvihull, M., *Roman Forts* (New York, 1990)

Qiao Yun, *Defense Structures: Ancient Chinese Architecture* (Princeton, 2002)

Toy, S., *A History of Fortification from 3000 BC to AD 1700* (London, 1955)

47 Siege Engines, Catapults & Crossbows

Alm, J. & Wilson, G. M. (ed.), *European Crossbows: A Survey*, trans H. Bartlett Wells (Leeds, 1994)

Kern, P., *Ancient Siege Warfare* (London, 1999)

Marsden, E. W., *Greek and Roman Artillery: Historical Development* (Oxford, 1969)

Payne-Gallwey, R., *The Book of the Crossbow* (New York, 1995, repr. of 1903 ed.)

Van Creveld, M., *Technology and War: From 2000 BC to the Present* (New York, 1989)

Yadin, Y., *The Art of Warfare in Biblical Lands* (London & New York, 1963)

48 Chariots & Cavalry

Hyland, A., *Training the Roman Cavalry from Arrian's 'Ars Tactica'* (Stroud, 1993)

Kendall, T., *Warfare and Military Matters in the Nuzi Tables* (Michigan, 1974)

Littauer, M. A. & Crouwel, J. H., *Wheeled Vehicles and Ridden Animals in the Ancient Near East* (Leiden/Köln, 1979)

Xenophon, *The Cavalry Commander* in *Scripta Minora*, trans. E. C. Marchant (Loeb Classical Library; London, 1925)

Xenophon, *The Art of Horsemanship,* trans. M. H. Morgan (London1962 (1979))
Yadin, Y., *The Art of Warfare in Biblical Lands* (London & New York, 1963)

49 Galleys & Warships
Casson, L., *Ships & Seamanship in the Ancient World* (Baltimore & London, 1995)
Gardiner, R. & Morrison, J. S. (eds), *The Age of the Galley. Mediterranean Oared Vessels since Pre-Classical Times* (London, 1995)
McGrail, S., *Boats of the World from the Stone Age to Medieval Times* (Oxford, 2002)
Morrison, J. S. & Coates, J. F., *Greek and Roman Oared Warships 399–30 BC* (Oxford, 1996)
Morrison, J. S., Coates, J. F. & Rankov, N. B., *The Athenian Trireme. The History and Reconstruction of an Ancient Greek Warship* (Cambridge, 2nd ed., 2000)

50 Ball Games & Competitive Sports
Blanchard, K., *The Anthropology of Sport. An Introduction* (Westport, 1995)
Gardiner, E. N., A*thletics of the Ancient World* (Oxford, 1930)
Gutmann, A., *From Ritual to Record* (New York, 1978)
Mandell, R. D., *Sport. A Cultural History* (New York, 1984)
Poliakoff, M. B., *Combat Sports in the Ancient World* (Yale, 1987)
Sansone, D., *Greek Athletics and the Genesis of Sport* (Berekeley, 1988)
Swaddling, J., *The Ancient Olympic Games* (London, 2nd ed., 1999)
Whittington, E. M. (ed.), *The Sport of Life and Death. The Mesomerican Ballgame* (London & New York, 2001)

51 Board Games
Murray, H. J. R., *A History of Board Games other than Chess* (Oxford, 1952)
Parlett, D., *The Oxford History of Board Games* (Oxford, 1999)

Art & Science

52 The Earliest Art
Bahn, P. & Vertut, J., *Journey Through the Ice Age* (London & Berkeley, 1997)
Clottes, J., 'Paint analyses from several Magdalenian caves in the Ariège region of France', *Journal of Archaeological Science* 20 (1993), 223–35
D'Errico, F. & Nowell, A., 'A new look at the Berekhat Ram figurine: implications for the origins of symbolism', *Cambridge Archaeological Journal* 9, 1999
Henshilwood, C. & others, 'Emergence of modern human behaviour: Middle Stone Age engravings from South Africa', *Science* 295 (2002), 1278–80
Jones, R., 'From Kakadu to Kutikina: The southern continent at 18,000 years ago', in Gamble, C. & Soffer, O. (eds), *The World at 18,000 BP, Vol. 2, Low Latitudes* (London, 1990), 264–95
Lewis-Williams, D., *The Mind in the Cave. Consciousness and the Origins of Art* (London & New York, 2002)
Mithen, S., *The Prehistory of the Mind: A Search for the Origins of Art, Religion and Science* (London & New York, 1996)

53 Music & Musical Instruments
Landels, J. G., *Music in Ancient Greece and Rome* (London & New York, 1999)
Manniche, L., *Music and Musicians in Ancient Egypt* (London, 1991)
Stevenson, R., *Music in Aztec and Inca Territory* (Berkeley, 1968)
Wellesz, E., *Ancient and Oriental Music,* Oxford History of Music 1 (London, 1957)

54 Writing
DeFrancis, J., *Visible Speech: The Diverse Oneness of Writing Systems* (Honolulu, 1989)
Harris, R., *The Origin of Writing* (London & La Salle, 1986)
Healey, J. F., *The Early Alphabet* (London & Berkeley, 1990)
Marshack, A., *The Roots of Civilization* (New York, 2nd ed., 1991)

Naveh, J., *Origins of the Alphabet* (London, 1975)
Nissen, H. J., Damerow, P. & Englund, R. K., *Archaic Bookkeeping* (Chicago, 1993)
Robinson, A., *The Story of Writing* (London & New York, 1995)
Schmandt-Besserat, D., *How Writing Came About* (Austin, 1996)

55 Codes & Ciphers
Kahn, D., *The Codebreakers* (New York, rev. ed., 1996)
Parkinson, R., *Cracking Codes: The Rosetta Stone and Decipherment* (London & Berkeley, 1999)
Robinson, A., *Lost Languages: The Enigma of the World's Undeciphered Scripts* (New York, 2002)
Singh, S., *The Code Book* (London, 1999)

56 Books & Paper
Bloom, J. T., *Paper Before Print* (New Haven & London, 2001)
Chiera, E., *They Wrote on Clay* (Chicago, 1975)
Hooker, J. T. & others, *Reading the Past: Ancient Writing from Cuneiform to the Alphabet* (London & Berkeley, 1990)
O'Donnell, J. J., *Avatars of the Word: from Papyrus to Cyberspace* (Cambridge, MA, 1998)
Parkinson, R. & Quirke, S., *Papyrus* (London, 1995)
Steinberg, S. H., *Five Hundred Years of Printing*, new ed. revised by J. Trevitt (London, 1996)

57 Astrology & Astronomy
Aveni, A., *Conversing with the Planets* (Boulder, 2003)
Pannekoek, A., *A History of Astronomy* (London & New York, 1961)
Tester, J., *A History of Western Astrology* (Wolfeboro, NH, 1987)

58 Calendars & the Measurement of Time
Aveni, A., *Empires of Time* (London, 2000; Boulder, 2002)
Lippincott, K. (ed.), *The Story of Time* (London, 2000)
Walker, C., *Astronomy Before the Telescope* (London & New York, 1996)

59 Maps & Cartography
Adams, C. & Laurence, R. (eds), *Travel and Geography in the Roman Empire* (London & New York, 2001)
Berggren, J. L. & Jones, A., *Ptolemy's* Geography: *An Annotated Translation of the Theoretical Chapters* (Princeton & Oxford, 2000)
Campbell, B., *The Writings of the Roman Land Surveyors: Introduction, Text, Translation and Commentary* (London, 2000)
Harley, J. B. & Woodward, D. (eds), *The History of Cartography, vol. 1: Cartography in Prehistoric, Ancient, and Medieval Europe and the Mediterranean* (Chicago & London, 1987)
Harley, J. B. & Woodward, D. (eds), *The History of Cartography, vol. 2.2: Cartography in the Traditional East and Southeast Asian Societies* (Chicago & London, 1994), chaps. 3–9 (by C. D. K. Yee)
Lewis, M. J. T., *Surveying Instruments of Greece and Rome* (Cambridge, 2001)
Rihll, T. E., *Greek Science* (Greece & Rome New Surveys in the Classics 29, Oxford, 1999), chapter V, 'Geography'
Selin, H. (ed.), *Encyclopaedia of the History of Science, Technology, and Medicine in Non-Western Cultures* (Dordrecht, Boston, London, 1997), 'Maps and Mapmaking in China'

60 Mathematics & Counting Devices
Cuomo, S., *Ancient Mathematics* (London & New York, 2001)
Closs, M. (ed.), *Native American Mathematics* (Austin, 1986)
Grattan-Guinness, I. (ed.), *Companion Encyclopedia of the History and Philosophy of the Mathematical Sciences. Part 1: Ancient and non-Western traditions* (London, 1994), 17–165
Nissen, H. J., Damerow, P. & Englund, R. K., *Archaic Bookkeeping* (Chicago, 1993)
Pullan, J. M., *The History of the Abacus* (London & New York, 1968)
Robbins, G. & Shute, C., *The Rhind Mathematical Papyrus* (London, 1987)

61 Coinage & Money
Burnett, A., *Coinage in the Roman World* (London, 1987)
Carradice, I., *Greek Coins* (London & Austin, 1995)
Cribb, J. (ed.), *Money. From Cowrie Shells to Credit Cards* (London, 1986)
Grierson, P., *Numismatics* (Oxford,1975)
Howgego, C., *Ancient History from Coins* (London & New York, 1995)
Williams, J. (ed.), *Money. A History* (London, 1997)

62 Balances, Weights & Measures
Dilke, O. A. W., *Mathematics and Measurement* (London & Berkeley,1987)
Kisch, B., *Scales and Weights: A Historical Outline* (New Haven, 1965)
Kletter, R., *Economic Keystones: The Weight System of the Kingdom of Judah* (Sheffield, 1998)
Powell, M. A., 'Weights and measures', in Meyers. E. M. (ed.), *The Oxford Encyclopedia of Archaeology in the Near East* (New York & Oxford, 1997), vol. 5, 339–42
Selin, H. (ed.), *Encyclopaedia of the History of Science, Technology, and Medicine in Non-western Cultures* (Dordrecht, Boston & London, 1997), 'Weights and measures' 1005–28
Skinner, F. G., *Weights and Measures: Their Ancient Origins and Their Development in Great Britain up to AD 1855* (London, 1967), 1–80

63 General Medicine
Ackerknecht, E. H., *A Short History of Medicine* (Baltimore & London, rev. ed., 1982)
Kiple, K. (ed.), *The Cambridge World History of Human Disease* (Cambridge, 1993)
Porter, R., *The Greatest Benefit to Mankind. A Medical History of Humanity from Antiquity to the Present* (London, 1999)
Porter, R. (ed.), *The Cambridge Illustrated History of Medicine* (Cambridge, 1996)
Singer, C. & Underwood, E. A., *A Short History of Medicine* (Oxford, 2nd ed., 1962)
Vogel, V. J., *American Indian Medicine* (Norman & London, 1970)

64 Surgery & Surgical Instruments
Bliquez, L. J., *Roman Surgical Instruments and Other Minor Objects in the National Museum of Naples* (Mainz, 1994)
Jackson, R., *Doctors and Diseases in the Roman Empire* (London & Norman, 1988)
Jackson, R., 'Medical instruments in the Roman World', *Medicina nei Secoli* 9:2 (1997), 223–48
Künzl, E., 'Forschungsbericht zu den antiken medizinischen Instrumenten', *Rise and Decline of the Roman World*, Pt II, 37.3 (Berlin & New York, 1996), 2433–39
Künzl, E., *Medizen in der Antike. Aus einer Welt ohne Narkose und Aspirin* (Stuttgart, 2002)
Majno, G., *The Healing Hand. Man and Wound in the Ancient World* (Cambridge, MA, & London, 1975)
Nunn, J. F., *Ancient Egyptian Medicine* (London & Norman, 1996)
Roberts, C. & Manchester, K., *The Archaeology of Disease* (Stroud & Ithaca, 1995)

65 Mummies & Mummification
Arriaza, B., *Beyond Death: the Chinchorro Mummies of Ancient Chile* (Washington, DC, 1995)
Barber, E. W., *The Mummies of Urumchi: Did Europeans Migrate to China 4,000 Years Ago?* (New York & London, 1999)
Brothwell, D., *The Bog Man and the Archaeology of People* (London & Cambridge, MA, 1986)
Cockburn, A, Cockburn, E. & Reyman, T.A. (eds), *Mummies, Disease and Ancient Cultures* (Cambridge, 1998)
Reid, H., *In Search of the Immortals*, (London, 1999; New York, 2001)
Taylor, J., *Death and the Afterlife in Ancient Egypt* (London & Chicago, 2001)

Adorning the Person

66 Body Art & Tattooing
Cockburn, A, Cockburn, E. & Reyman, T. A. (eds), *Mummies, Disease and Ancient Cultures* (Cambridge, 1998)
Fletcher, J., 'The decorated body in ancient Egypt: hairstyles, cosmetics and tattoos', in *Proceedings from The Clothed Body in the Ancient World Conference*, (Oxford, 2003)
Fletcher, J., *Ancient Egyptian Cosmetics and Tattoos* (Austin, forthcoming)
Longhena, M. & Alva, W., *Splendours of the Ancient Andes* (London & New York, 1999)
Spindler, K., *The Man in the Ice* (London & New York, 1993)
Stone-Miller, R., *Art of the Andes from Chavin to Inca* (London & New York, 1995)

67 Clothing, Shoes & Wigs
Barber, E. W., *The Mummies of Urumchi: Did Europeans Migrate to China 4,000 Years Ago?* (New York & London, 1999)
Longhena, M. & Alva, W., *Splendours of the Ancient Andes* (London & New York, 1999)
Nicholson, P. T. & Shaw, I. (eds), *Ancient Egyptian Materials and Technology* (Cambridge, 2000), chapters on 'Textiles', 'Leatherwork', 'Hair'
Stone-Miller, R., *Art of the Andes from Chavin to Inca* (London & New York, 1995)
Vogelsang-Eastwood, G., *Pharaonic Egyptian Clothing* (Leiden, 1993)

68 Jewelry
Aldred, C., *Jewels of the Pharaohs* (London & New York, 1971)
Antonova, I., Tolstikov, V. & Treister, M.,*The Gold of Troy* (London & New York 1996)
McEwan, C. (ed.), *Precolumbian Gold* (London, 2000)
Ogden, J., *Jewellery of the Ancient World* (London & New York 1982)
Ogden, J., *Interpreting the Past: Ancient Jewellery* (London & Berkeley, 1992)
Tait, H. (ed.), *Seven Thousand Years of Jewellery* (London & New York, 2nd ed., 1986)
Williams, D. & Ogden, J., *Greek Gold* (London & New York, 1994)

69 Cosmetics & Perfumes
Brovarski, E., Doll, S. K. & Freed, R. E., *Egypt's Golden Age: The Art of Living in the New Kingdom 1558–1058 BCE* (Boston, 1982)
Fletcher, J., *Oils & Perfumes of Ancient Egypt* (London, 1998)
Lilyquist, C., *Ancient Egyptian Mirrors from the Earliest Times through the Middle Kingdom* (Munich, 1979)
Nicholson, P. T. & Shaw, I. (eds), *Ancient Egyptian Materials and Technology* (Cambridge, 2000)
Simpson, S. (ed.), *Queen of Sheba: Treasures from Ancient Yemen* (London, 2002)
Zettler, R.L. & Horne, L. (eds), *Treasures from the Royal Tombs of Ur* (Philadelphia, 1998)

70 Contraceptives & Aphrodisiacs
Hopkins, K., 'Contraception in the Roman Empire', *Comparative Studies in Society and History* 8 (1965), 124–51
King, H., *Hippocrates' Woman: Reading the Female Body in Ancient Greece* (London & New York, 1998), 147–51
McLaren, A., *A History of Contraception from Antiquity to the Present Day* (Oxford, 1990)
Riddle, J., *Contraception and Abortion from the Ancient World to the Renaissance* (Cambridge, MA, & London, 1992)

Sources of Illustrations

1 SSPL; 2–3 Scala; 4 Ashmolean Museum, Oxford; 5l WF; 5r Simon Nicholls; 6l WF; 6r Scala; 7l Florida State Museum; 7r Egyptian Museum, Cairo; 12 Photo © RMN – J. G. Berizz; 13a Photo © RMN – R. G. Ojeda; 13b © CORBIS; 14l © Lowell Georgia/CORBIS; 14ar WF; 15a © Zev Radovan; 15b The Kisterman Collection, Aachen; 16a WF; 16bl Metropolitan Museum of Art, New York, Classical Purchase Fund, 1978; 16c National Museum, Athens; 17a Ediciones Turisticas QAPAC, Peru; 17b Sally Nicholls; 18–19 David L. Arnold/National Geographic Society Image Collection; 20 © V. Vitanov/AA&A; 21 RHPL; 22ar © Mary Jelliffe/AA&A; 22cl, bl PB; 22br SSPL; 23al Photo © RMN; 23ar PB; 24a PB, after Bellamo, R. V., in J. S. Oliver et al. (eds), *Early Hominid Behavioural Ecology* (1994), 175; 24b Dr Michael J. Rogers; 25ar John Sibbick; 25b Dr Ofer Bar-Yosef; 26a © Gallo Images/CORBIS; 26r Dr Hartmut Thieme; 27a Dr Hartmut Thieme; 27b *Acta Archaeologica Lundensia* series 8, no.12; 28c PB; 28br Photo © RMN – J. G. Berizz; 29a Photo © RMN – J. G. Berizz; 29b © Warren Morgan/CORBIS; 30a Photo © RMN – Jean Schormans; 30b Musée de l'Homme, Paris. Photo: B. Hatala; 31a&b Photo © RMN – Loic Hamon; 32 J. Field, University of Sydney; 33al&r Dr Ofer Bar-Yosef; 33b Dr Philip Edwards; 34a PB, after Willeke Wendrich; 34b Landesmuseum Trier. Photo: Th. Zühmer; 35al Griffith Institute, Ashmolean Museum, Oxford; 35r PB, after Willeke Wendrich; 35b Petrie Museum, University College, London; 36 bl PB, after Willeke Wendrich; 36br BM; 37a&b Jean Vertut; 38al © Sakamoto Photo Research Laboratory/CORBIS; 38br Museo Arqueológico Rafael Larco Herrera, Lima; 39 Historical Museum, Beijing; 40a Bill Sillar; 40c BM; 40b P. Newberry, *Beni Hasan*, 1893; 41 akg-images/Erich Lessing; 42a P. T. Craddock; 42bl Staatliche Museen zu Berlin, Preußischer Kulturbesitz, Antikensammlung; 42br PB, after W.B. Dinsmoor, in J. Camp, *The Athenian Agora* (1986), fig. 115; 43 Hubei Provincial Museum, Wuhan; 44a Museo del Oro, Bogota; 44bl AA&A; 44br P. T. Craddock; 45 BM; 46b State Historical Art Preserve, Periaslav-Khmel'nyets'kyi; 46r Egyptian Museum, Cairo; 47b © David Cumming/Eye Ubiquitous/CORBIS; 47a PB, after J. Allan & B. Gilmour, *Persian Steel* (2000), fig. 3; 48 PB, after Li Jinghua, *Bulletin of the Metals Museum* 25 (1996), fig. 30; 49ar BM; 49b PB, after D. Foy & M. D. Nenna, *Tout Feu, Tout Sable* (2001), 38; 50l PB, after P. T. Nicholson; 50b Corning Museum of Glass; 51a&b BM; 52a Corning Museum of Glass; 52b Denise Allen; 53 Courtesy Museum of Fine Arts, Boston; 54 Metropolitan Museum of Art, New York/WF; 55l Courtesy Museum of Fine Arts, Boston, Mrs Samuel Cabot's Special Fund; 55r Jingzhou Regional Museum, Hubei Province; 56al PB; 56ar Metropolitan Museum of Art, New York, Fletcher Fund, 1931 (31.11.10); 56b WF; 57bl WF; 57r PB; 58–59 © Alison Wright/CORBIS; 60 GL; 61 PB, after J. Wymer, *The Palaeolithic Age* (1982); 62a Colin Ridler; 62b PB, after Çatalhöyük Research Project; 63 Heidi Grassley, © Thames & Hudson Ltd; 64a E. Naville, *The Temple of Deir el Bahari*, Pt III (1898), pl. 69; 64b GL; 65a PB, after P. Oliver (ed.), *Encyclopedia of Vernacular Architecture of the World* (1997), 61; 65c&b Henan Provincial Museum, Zhenzhou; 66 Michael Jenner; 67a&b Kate Spence; 68 Jeremy Stafford-Deitsch; 69 Simon Nicholls; 70a Heidi Grassley, © Thames & Hudson Ltd; 70b © Roger Wood/CORBIS; 71 Crown Copyright reproduced by courtesy of Historic Scotland; 72 Griffith Institute, Ashmolean Museum, Oxford; 73 WF; 74a BM; 74b Metropolitan Museum of Art, New York, Rogers Fund, 1903 (03.14.13); 75bl Metropolitan Museum of Art, New York; 75br Geoffrey P. Killen; 76al Griffith Institute, Ashmolean Museum, Oxford; 76ar PB, after H. Carter, *The Tomb of Tut.ankh.Amen*, III (1933); 76b Photo © RMN – J. Schormans; 77 Hebei Provincial Museum, Shijiazhuang; 78a&b Soprintendenza Archaeologica di Pompeii; 79a PB; 79b GL; 80a Photo Hirmer; 80b BM; 81a PB, after F. Glaser in Ö. Wikander, *Handbook of Ancient Water Technology* (2000), fig. 19; 81b Soprintendenza Archaeologica di Pompeii; 82 GL; 83 akg-images; 84 © B. Norman/AA&A; 85a Archivi Alinari, Florence; 85b Roger Wilson; 86 GL; 87a Kevin Gould/Janet Delaine; 87b The J. Paul Getty Museum, Malibu, California; 88a&b W. H. Manning; 89a Griffith Institute, Ashmolean Museum, Oxford; 89b BM; 90a BM; 90bl PB, after R. E. M. Wheeler, *London in Roman Times* (1946), fig. 16; 90br PB, after W. H. Manning, *Bulletin of the Board of Celtic Studies* 22 (1968),

fig. 3; 91 Dr Mordechai Kislev; 92&93b WF; 94 © CNRS. Photo: Magali Roux; 95a Paul Sillitoe, Department of Anthropology, University of Durham; 95b Royal Library, Copenhagen; 96a Staatliche Museen zu Berlin, Preußischer Kulturbesitz, Antikensammlung; 96bl Scala; 96br National Museum of Denmark, Copenhagen; 97 WF; 98 WF; 99a Egyptian Museum, Cairo; 99b PB; 100a PB; 100b WF; 101a SSPL; 101b Bodegas Centrales del Instituto Hondureño de Antropologia e Historia, Tegucigalpa; 102a I Musei Vaticani, Rome; 102b Jingzhou Regional Museum, Hubei Province; 103a PB; 103b Museum of London; 104 Michael Jenner; 105a PB; 105b BM; 106 Scala; 107a Sussex Archaeological Society; 107b Scala; 108 © Gianni Dagli Orti/CORBIS; 109 John G. Ross; 110 Jingzhou Regional Museum, Hubei Province; 111a WF; 111bl BM; 111br © Zev Radovan; 112a Museo Arqueológico Rafael Larco Herrera, Lima; 112b Sally Nicholls; 113a Staatliche Museen zu Berlin, Preußischer Kulturbesitz, Antikensammlung; 113b Hubei Provincial Museum, Wuhan; 114a&b © Zev Radovan; 115a Norman de Garis Davis, *Tomb of Antefoqer*, 1920; 115b Art Archive/Dagli Orti; 116a Courtesy of Hasanlu Project, University of Pennsylvania Museum, no. 69-12-15 & David Parker/Science Photo Library, London; 116b Courtesy of Juzhong Zhang & the Institute of Archaeology, Zhengzhou; 117a BM; 117b Courtesy of the Gordion Project, University of Pennsylvania Museum of Archaeology and Anthropology; 118a D.A.I., Cairo; 118b Norman de Garis Davis, *The Tomb of Nakht at Thebes*, 1917; 119a GL; 119b Norman de Garis Davis, *The Tomb of Nakht at Thebes*, 1917; 120a © James L. Amos/CORBIS; 120b Brooklyn Museum of Art, Museum Collection Fund 40.16; 121a&b © Justin Kerr; 122a © Justin Kerr; 122b, 123a Michael Coe; 123b Famensi Museum, Fufeng, Shaanxi Province; 124a *Antiquity* 198, 1976; 124bl R. S. Merrilees; 124c Photo Hirmer; 125a Photo Nimatallah/Agenzia Luisa Ricciarini; 125b *Antiquity* 198, 1976; 126l Museo Nazional de Antropologia, Mexico City; 126a PB; 127 © Gianni Dagli Orti/CORBIS; 128–29 WF; 130 GL; 131bl&r Copyright © 2004 by WARA, Centro Camuno di Studi Preistorici, 25044 Capo di Ponte, Italy; 132a PB, after David G. Mandelbaum, *The Plains Cree* (1979), fig. 12; 132b © Canadian Museum of Civilization, catalogue no. III-L-185 a–b, photographer Ross Taylor, 1993, image no.S93-7877; 133a © Canadian Museum of Civilization, catalogue no. III-H-100, negative no. J5412; 133b Chapin Collection, Department of Anthropology, University of Winnipeg; 134a H.A. Shelley in S. Piggott, *The Earliest Wheeled Transport* (1983), fig. 8; 134b © Ronald Sheridan/AA&A; 135a Centrale Fotodienst de Rijksuniversiteit Groningen; 135c Inštitut za arheologijo ZRC SAZU, Ljubljana. Photo Marko Zaplatil; 136a Stuart Piggott; 136cl J. P. Mallory; 136b PB, after J. P. Mallory; 137al Courtesy of the American Museum of Natural History; 137ar Sichuan Provincial Museum, Chengdu; 138 Giovanni Dagli Orti; 139 © Roger Wood/CORBIS; 140a Byron Brett; 140c Photo Hirmer; 140b BM; 141a Richard Bryant; 141c PB; 141b Roger Wilson; 142 Andy Burnham; 143a © Dept. of Environment, Heritage & Local Government Photo Unit, Dublin; 143b Photo Courtesy USGS; 144a akg-images/Hilbich; 144c Catherine Lawrence & Claire Ivison; 144b RHPL; 145 © Francesco Venturi/CORBIS; 146a&bl Colin O'Connor; 146br Drazen Tomic, after Colin O'Connor; 147 Colin O'Connor; 148a&b Colin O'Connor; 149 RHPL; 150a Musée Cernuschi, Paris; 150b Polish Archaeological Mission to Palmyra; 151a Sally Nicholls; 151b © Patrick Ward/CORBIS; 152 Drents Museum; 153a WF; 153b © Cameron McPherson Smith; 154a&c British Archaeological Expedition to Kuwait; 154b © Mary Jelliffe/AA&A; 155 Sally Nicholls; 156a Photo Peter Howorth, courtesy of Santa Barbara Museum of Natural History; 156b John G. Ross; 157a&c © National Maritime Museum, London; 158a PB, after Seán McGrail; 158bl © Hulton-Deutsch Collection/CORBIS; 158br after H. P. Ray, *Monastery and Guild* (1986), fig. 4.1; 159a after J. Newcomer; 159b BM; 160 John Sherwood Illsley; 161a GL; 161b WF; 162 Metropolitan Museum of Art, Rogers Fund and Edward S. Harkness Gift, 1920; 163a National Museum of Denmark, Copenhagen; 163b © Gianni Dagli Orti/CORBIS; 164 Landesmuseum, Mainz. Photo Ursula Rudischer; 165a After J.-F. Champollion *Monuments de L'Egypte et de la Nubie*, 1835-45; 165r Staatliche Museen zu Berlin, Preußischer Kulturbesitz, Antikensammlung; 166l PB, after E. G. R. Taylor, *The Haven-Finding Art* (1971), fig. 5a; 166r Eckhard Slawik/Science Photo Library; 167a PB, after D. Lewis, *We the Navigators* (1972), fig. 14; 167b PB, after Seán McGrail; 168a&b GL; 169 Prof. John P. Oleson; 170–71 akg-images/Erich Lessing; 172 © Justin Kerr; 173bl PB; 173br © Paul A. Souders/CORBIS; 174a Scala; 174c Sally Nicholls; 175l Photo © RMN; 175b PB;

176a&b Peter Rowley-Conwy; 177l National Museum of Denmark, Copenhagen; 177ar&c PB; 177b BM; 178ar © James Mellaart, courtesy Çatalhöyük Research Project; 178bl Bibliothèque Nationale de France, Paris; 179 Jürgen Liepe; 180a Landesmuseum, Mainz; 180c PB; 180b Peter Clayton; 181a PB; 181c © The Trustees of the National Museums of Scotland; 181r Cultural Relics Publishing House, Beijing; 181b National Museum of Denmark, Copenhagen; 182l National Museum of the History of the Ukraine; 182b Griffith Institute, Ashmolean Museum, Oxford; 183l D.A.I., Athens; 183r Qin Terracotta Museum, Lintong, Shaanxi Province; 184al PB, after Dien, 1981/82, fig. 2; 184cl PB; 184ar BM; 184br Museum für Völkerkunde, Vienna; 185 © Gianni Dagli Orti/CORBIS; 186a akg-images/A. Lorenzini; 186b Scala; 187 akg-images; 188ar © Paul Almasy/CORBIS; 188bl akg-images; 189 Scala; 190a © Angelo Hornak/CORBIS; 190b © Chris Hellier/AA&A; 191a Graeme Peacock; 191b akg-images; 192a AA&A; 192b P. Newberry, *Beni Hasan* (1893); 193a akg-images/ Erich Lessing; 193b PB, after S. Grimbly, *Encyclopedia of the Ancient World* (2000), 240; 194a Sally Nicholls; 194b Roger Wilson; 195a PB, after E. W. Marsden, *Greek and Roman Artillery* (1969), fig. 1; 195c PB, after J. Alm, *European Crossbows, A Survey* (1994), fig. 44; 195b PB, after S. Turnbull, *Samurai Warfare* (1996), 12; 196a BM; 196b Photo Hirmer; 197a Index/Summerfield; 197b BM; 198a BM; 198b Morning Glory Publishers, Beijing; 199 Roger Wilson; 200 Jürgen Liepe; 201a akg-images/Erich Lessing; 201b akg-images; 202al Courtesy Boris Rankov; 202ar PB; 202b © Mike Andrews/AA&A; 203 akg-images; 204a Scala; 204b akg-images; 205 Scala; 206a P. Newberry, *Beni Hasan* (1893); 206b © Gianni Dagli Orti/CORBIS; 207a Peter Clayton; 207b The J. Paul Getty Museum, Malibu, California, Gift of Barbara and Lawrence Fleischman, h: 51 cm (20 $^1/_8$ in), diam: 42 cm (16 $^1/_2$ in); 208 BM; 209c © Danny Lehman/ CORBIS; 209b © Justin Kerr; 210cl Irving Finkel; 210b BM; 211a Brooklyn Museum of Art, Charles Edwin Wilbour Fund; 211c GL; 211b Cultural Relics Publishing House, Beijing; 212–13 Ministère de la culture et de la communication, Direction régionale des affaires culturelles de Rhône-Alpes, Service regional de l'archéologie; 214 SSPL; 215 Courtesy Francesco d'Errico, CNRS; 216a Picture with permission of Chris Henshilwood, African Heritage Research Institute, Cape Town, South Africa; 216b Photo by Hilde Jensen, Institut für Ur-und Frühgeschichte und Archäologie des Mittelalters, Eberhard-Karls-Universität, Tübingen; 217 Photo Thomas Stephan, copyright Ulmer Museum; 218a&b Ministère de la culture et de la communication, Direction régionale des affaires culturelles de Rhône-Alpes, Service regional de l'archéologie; 219 Jean Vertut; 220a Inštitut za arheologijo ZRC SAZU, Ljubljana. Photo Marko Zaplatil; 220b Institute of Cultural Relics & Archaeology of Henan Province, Zhengzhou, China; 221l University of Pennsylvania Museum of Archaeology and Anthropology, Philadelphia; 221b WF; 222a Scala; 222bl Kelsey Museum of Archaeology, University of Michigan; 222br National Museum of Vietnamese History, Hanoi; 223 Papyrologisch Instituut der Rijksuniversiteit Leiden; 224a Florida State Museum; 224b Instituto Mexiquense de Cultura: Museo de Antropologica e Historia del Estado de México, Toluca; 225ar © Justin Kerr; 225b BM; 226t Drawing by H. Breuil; 226b Ministère de la culture et de la communication, Direction régionale des affaires culturelles de Rhône-Alpes, Service regional de l'archéologie. Photo Jean Clottes; 227 BM; 228bl Musée du Louvre, Paris; 228br The Institute of Archaeology, CASS, Beijing; 229al Staatliche Sammlung Ägyptischer Kunst, Munich; 229c AA&A; 229br BM; 230a&b BM; 231al BM; 231ar PB, after R. Parkinson, *Cracking Codes* (1999), 84; 231b PB, after S. Singh, *The Code Book* (1999), fig. 2; 232 Sächsische Landesbibliothek, Dresden; 233a BM; 233b Institute of Nautical Archaeology; 234bl&br The British Library, London; 235ar Alexander Marshack; 235c Bibliothèque Nationale de France, Paris; 236a Landesamt für Denkmalpflege und Archäologie Sachsen-Anhalt, drawing by K. Schauer; 236b Landesamt für Denkmalpflege und Archäologie Sachsen-Anhalt. Photo Juraj Lipták; 237 © Ronald Sheridan/AA&A; 238a SSPL; 238b PB, after R. Gordon, *Journal of Mithraic Studies* 1(2) 1977; 239 Photo © RMN; 240a Mike Pitts; 240c, b PB, after A. Aveni, *Ancient Astronomers* (1993); 241a&b AA&A; 242a WF; 242b Heidi Grassley © Thames & Hudson Ltd; 243a AA&A; 243b Museo Egizio, Turin; 244 Cultural Relics Publishing House, Beijing; 245a SSPL; 245b The British Library, London; 246a Musei Capitolini, Rome; 246b Kunsthistorisches Museum, Vienna; 247ar BM; 247b Photo © RMN – Gérard Blot; 248al BM; 248c Eleanor Robson; 248ar after D. H. Fowler, *The Mathematics of Plato's Academy: A New Reconstruction* (1999), pl. 1; 249a after S. Cuomo, *Ancient Mathematics* (2001), fig. 1.4; 248c after M. Closs, in H. Selin, *Mathematics Across Cultures* (2000), 228; 249b SSPL; 250a&b BM; 251al&tr BM; 251b Cultural Relics Publishing House, Beijing; 252a,c&b BM; 253a BM; 253b Courtesy Museum of Fine Arts, Boston; 254al BM; 254ar Eleanor Robson; 254b National Palace Museum, Taiwan; 255a&b Staatliche Museen zu Berlin, Preußischer Kulturbesitz; 256a R. L. Moodie, *Paleopathology* (1923), fig. 43; 256b G. Elliot Smith, *The Most Ancient Splints*, BMJ (1908) 732–34; 257a Drazen

Tomic, after C. Singer & E.A. Underwood, *A Short History of Medicine* (1962), 46; 257b BM; 258a Archivi Alinari, Florence; 258b Romisch-Germanisches Zentralmuseum, Mainz; 259ar&c SSPL; 259b GL; 260a SSPL; 260b Staatliche Museen zu Berlin, Preußischer Kulturbesitz; 261sa SSPL; 261b Romisch-Germanisches Zentralmuseum, Mainz; 262a BM; 262b Photos: Ralph Jackson; 263a&b Photos: Ralph Jackson; 264l&r Joann Fletcher; 265 G. Elliot Smith, *The Royal Mummies*, 1901; 266a Joann Fletcher; 266 b W. R. Dawson, *Journal of Egyptian Archaeology* 13 (1927); 267a&b Joann Fletcher; 268–69 WF; 270 WF; 271l AA&A; 271r Metropolitan Museum of Art, New York; 272al Ashmolean Museum, Oxford; 272ar Joann Fletcher; 272b © Charles O'Rear/CORBIS; 273a&b Joann Fletcher; 274c Cultural Relics Publishing House, Beijing; 274b Joann Fletcher; 275a Petrie Museum, University College, London; 275b National Museum of Denmark, Copenhagen; 276l Scala; 276br Egyptian Museum, Cairo; 277a Ashmolean Museum, Oxford; 277b Egyptian Museum, Cairo; 278a Joann Fletcher; 278c&br BM; 278bl Museum für Völkerkunde, Vienna; 279a Musée de l'Homme, Paris; 279b BM; 280 University of Pennsylvania Museum of Archaeology and Anthropology, Philadelphia; 281a Museum of Deir ez-Zor, Syria; 281bl PB, after Jack Ogden; 281br Metropolitan Museum of Art, New York, Rogers Fund, 1908; 282a BM; 282c Jack Ogden; 282b Courtesy of Eskenazi Ltd; 283a&b BM; 284 Egyptian Museum, Cairo; 285a WF; 285b Musée du Louvre, Paris; 286l Hebei Provincial Museum, Shijiazhuang; 286ar Abdel Ghaffar Shedid; 287a WF; 287b Musée du Louvre, Paris; 288l BM; 288r Metropolitan Museum of Art, New York; 289a WF; 289b Massimo Borchi/Archivio White Star; 290a Harer Family Trust; 290b GL

Sources of quotations:

1 John Frere, Report to the Society of Antiquaries, London, regarding ancient stone implements and fossil animal bones found at Hoxne, England, 1799; 4 Grahame Clark, *Prehistoric Europe* (London, 1952); 5 Steven Mithen, *The Prehistory of the Mind* (London & New York, 1996), 170; 7 de Civrieux, cited by David M. Guss, *To Weave and Sing; Art, Symbol, and Narrative in the South American Rain Forest* (Berkeley, 1989), 103; 8 V. Gordon Childe, *Man Makes Himself* (London, 1956), 83–84; 9 Georgius Agricolo, *De re Metallica*, 1556, trans. H.C. Hoover & L. H. Hoover (London, 1912); 10 Homer, *Odyssey*, Book IX; 11 Pliny the Elder, *Natural History* XXXVI, 191–92; 12 From the Courtship of Inanna and Dumuzi, trans. D. Wolkstein and S. Kramer *Inanna. Queen of Heaven and Earth* (London, 1983); 13 Vitruvius, *Ten Books on Architecture*, Ingrid. D. Rowland & Thomas Noble Howe (Cambridge, 1999), 34; 14 M. Lichtheim, *Ancient Egyptian Literature* vol. II. The New Kingdom (Berkeley, 1976), 42; 15 Homer, *Odyssey,* Book XXIII; 16 Pliny the Elder, *Natural History* XXXVI, 200; 17 Frontinus, *On the Aqueducts of Rome* 1.16; 18 Marcus Aurelius, *Meditations* 8.24; 19 Homer, *Odyssey* XXI, 5–7 & 42–48, trans. Walter Shewring (Oxford, 1981); 20 Bruce D. Smith, *The Emergence of Agriculture* (New York, 1995); 22 Diodorus Siculus, I.35.3; 23 Antipater of Thessalonica, *Greek Anthology* 9.418; 26 Charles Darwin, *The Descent of Man* (London, 1871), 132; 27 Pliny the Elder, *Natural History* XIV, 28.137; 28 Apicius, *De re Coquinaria*, 1, 9; 29 trans. Michael D. & Sophie Coe; 30 Herodotus, *Histories*, 4. 74; 31 Thomas Drummond, 'The Canadian Snowshoe', *Transactions of the Royal Society of Canada* Series III, vol X, 1916, II, 305; 32 V. Gordon Childe, *Man Makes Himself* (London, 1936), 139; 34 Robert Louis Stevenson, *Travels with a Donkey* (London, 1878); 35 F. W. Robins, *The Story of the Bridge* (Birmingham, 1948); 37 James Hornell, *Water Transport* (Cambridge, 1946); 38 Basil Greenhill, *Archaeology of the Boat* (London, 1976); 40 Eric McKee, *Working Boats of Britain* (London, 1983); 41 John Masefield, *Sea Fever*; 42 Edward de Vere, Earl of Oxford, *The Labouring Man That Tills the Soil*; 43 William Blake, *Jerusalem*; 44 Richard Burton, *The Book of the Sword* (London, 1884); 46 Robert Bage, *Hermsprong* (Dublin, 1796); 47 Josephus, *The Jewish War*, V 6.3; 48 Homer, *Iliad* 20; 49 Pseudo-Xenophon, *The Constitution of the Athenians* 1.2; 52 Rudyard Kipling, *The Conundrum of the Workshops*; 53 Marius Schneider, 'Primitive Music' in E. Wellesz, *Ancient and Oriental Music* (Oxford, 1957); 54 H. G. Wells, *A Short History of the World* (London, 1922); 55 Whitfield Diffie, in R. Parkinson (ed.), *Cracking Codes: The Rosetta Stone and Decipherment* (London, 1999); 56 Rabindranath Tagore, *Fireflies*; 57 O. Neugebauer & R. Parker, *Egyptian Astronomical Texts III*, (London, 1969), 214–15; 59 *Panegyrics Latini* 9.20–21; 60 Aristophanes, *Clouds* 202–05, after A. H. Sommerstein, (Warminster, 1982); 61 Plato, *Republic* II, 371b; 62 Laws of Hammurabi, §108, trans. E. Robson; 63 R. Arnott, 'Healing and medicine in the Aegean Bronze Age', *Journal of the Royal Society of Medicine* 89 (1996), 265; 64 Celsus, *On medicine*, VII, Prooemium, 4; 65 Garcilaso de la Vega 1609, trans. H. V. Livermore, *Royal Commentaries of the Incas* (Austin, 1987); 66 Herodotus, *Histories*, Book V.6; 67 Nearchus, Fragment 11, 28, quoted in R. Lane Fox, *Alexander the Great* (London, 1973) 348; 68 Vannoccio Biringoccio, *Pirotechnia*; 69 J. Klein, in R.L. Zettler & L. Horne (eds), *Treasures from the Royal Tombs of Ur* (Philadelphia, 1998), 144.

Index